Faith in America

Faith in America

Changes, Challenges, New Directions

Volume 1
Organized Religion Today

EDITED BY CHARLES H. LIPPY

Praeger Perspectives

PRAEGER

Westport, Connecticut
London

Library of Congress Cataloging-in-Publication Data

Faith in America : changes, challenges, new directions / edited by Charles
H. Lippy.
    p. cm.
    Includes bibliographical references and index.
    ISBN 0-275-98605-5 (set : alk. paper) — ISBN 0-275-98606-3 (vol. 1 :
alk. paper) — ISBN 0-275-98607-1 (vol. 2 : alk. paper) — ISBN 0-275-
98608-X (vol. 3 : alk. paper)
    1. United States—Religion. I. Lippy, Charles H.
    BL2525.F33 2006
    200.973′090511—dc22   2006022880

British Library Cataloguing in Publication Data is available.

Library of Congress Catalog Card Number: 2006022880
ISBN: 0-275-98605-5 (set)
      0-275-98606-3 (vol. 1)
      0-275-98607-1 (vol. 2)
      0-275-98608-X (vol. 3)

First published in 2006

Praeger Publishers, 88 Post Road West, Westport, CT 06881
An imprint of Greenwood Publishing Group, Inc.
www.praeger.com

Printed in the United States of America

The paper used in this book complies with the
Permanent Paper Standard issued by the National
Information Standards Organization (Z39.48–1984).

10 9 8 7 6 5 4 3 2 1

Contents

Preface

The American religious landscape continues to baffle pundits. The land without a legally established church, analysts long suggested, would rapidly succumb to secularization and modernization. Fewer and fewer would identify with organized religion. Matters of faith and belief would have ever declining importance in public discourse. American men and women would increasingly regard religion as an anachronism.

All of that speculation proved wrong. Among the nations of the earth, the United States continues to nurture vibrant religious institutions; millions claim religious faith as vital to their own sense of well-being; politicians freely use religious language when talking about policy; matters of ethical import still stir controversy, often leading to court cases whose resolution frequently pleases no one.

If religious faith remains integral to America as a nation and to Americans as a people, that faith is not cut from a single cloth. The dynamics of religious life continue to change, bringing hope to some for an even greater influence of religion in common life and fear to others that should a single religious style gain too much influence, other perspectives will become seen as dangerous falsehood.

In 1976, *Newsweek* proclaimed the "year of the evangelical," marking the coming of age of one expression of Protestant Christianity in American life.[1] In December 2005, in a highly publicized court case, a judge overturned the policy of a local school board in Dover, Pennsylvania, that had required biology teachers to read a statement pronouncing evolution just theory and not a proven scientific fact and also to teach what proponents called "intelligent design," an understanding that detractors saw as injecting a particular theological approach into the curriculum.

The thirty years framed by those two incidents mark decades of ferment and sometimes heated discussion about the role of religion in American life. Three years before the "year of the evangelical," the U.S. Supreme

Court in *Roe v. Wade* had made abortion legal in the United States under particular sets of circumstances, sparking a debate over the meaning of life and theological controversies over when life itself began that continued into the years after the courts struck down the required teaching of intelligent design. Along the way, fresh controversy erupted over kindred issues such as euthanasia, stem cell research, and cloning. All those controversies had religious dimensions.

Meanwhile, mainline Protestant denominations bemoaned their declining memberships, even as they watched megachurches and unaffiliated congregations mushroom in size. If membership statistics remained relatively constant, there was in the decades since 1970 a shifting in terms of where folks actually became members and also a growing number who eschewed formal affiliation even if they declared themselves to be very spiritual, although not religious.

Other issues rocked the religious sector, from the fundamentalist and then Pentecostal resurgence that cascaded across American Protestantism to rancorous debates over whether gay, lesbian, or transgender persons should be welcomed into church membership, given religious blessing to unions on par with marriage, and offered opportunities to serve as clergy. Some continued to struggle with the influence of second-wave feminism; if more and more bodies ordained women to the professional ministry, the nation's two largest Christian groups, the Roman Catholic Church and the Southern Baptist Convention, remained adamant in their insistence that only men could serve in the ordained professional ministry.

Changes in immigration law in 1965 meant that the last decades of the twentieth century and the first decade of the twenty-first witnessed a dramatic growth in the number of Americans who identified themselves as Muslim, Buddhist, Hindu, or some variant thereof. As Harvard University professor Diana Eck put it, a Christian nation had become the world's most religiously diverse country.[2]

Add to this pluralistic mix a growing fascination with the Internet, a passion for nature and its spiritual resources, the horror of charges of pedophilia brought against Roman Catholic priests, debates over whether the wildly popular Harry Potter books and movies etched Satanic impulses into the minds of children, concern over the morality of stem cell research, an awareness that even dietary patterns have religious dimensions, and an array of other issues. It is clear that religion, however defined, and faith, however expressed, remain central features of American life, but features that bring a host of challenges.

The thirty-six essays that comprise the three volumes of *Faith in America: Changes, Challenges, New Directions* probe many of these currents in American religious life. The twelve in the first volume focus primarily on the transformations that have rocked organized religious life in the United States. Those in the second move broadly into areas of challenges that have come to religious practice, while the twelve essays in the third volume focus more on matters of debate and controversy. Together they suggest that faith in America is not only alive and well, but pushing in fresh directions to speak to changing circumstances and conditions of life.

General readers, scholars, and students will find in these essays summaries of the major trends in American religious life since the last half of the twentieth century. They will also find careful reflection and analysis on the changes and challenges that have come to religious institutions, on the array of new issues that have emerged on the religious scene, and on what the future seems to hold for that unfolding drama that is faith in America.

NOTES

1. Kenneth L. Woodward et al., "Born Again!" *Newsweek* 90 (October 25, 1976): 68–76.

2. Diana L. Eck, *A New Religious America: How a "Christian Country" Has Become the World's Most Religiously Diverse Nation* (San Francisco: HarperSanFrancisco, 2001).

Acknowledgments

When Praeger editor Suzanne Staszak-Silva first approached me about organizing these volumes, I knew at once that I could not undertake the task alone. After all, what stands out as a "must discuss" issue or topic to one interpreter of American religious life may seem to another to be peripheral at best. Hence one of my first moves was to invite a cluster of scholars to form an advisory board that would help identify the most pertinent topics for inclusion as well as scholars who might be poised to offer insightful appraisals of those topics. I am grateful to those fellow scholars who agreed to assist in this capacity: Philip Goff of Indiana University-Purdue University at Indianapolis, Marie Griffith of Princeton University, Paula Kane of the University of Pittsburgh, Anthony Pinn of Rice University, Amanda Porterfield of Florida State University, and Peter W. Williams of Miami University. Thank you.

Countless colleagues offered names of potential contributors, sometimes making an initial contact with them on behalf of the project before I had the opportunity to invite them to participate. Altogether, thirty-nine individuals shared their research, insight, and writing skills to bring these three volumes together. I owe each a great debt, although I am sure that there are a few who are looking forward with great delight to their appearance in print since publication will finally mean that I am no longer hounding them about an endnote reference, deadline, or seemingly awkwardly constructed prose.

Much of my work on these three books was completed during the fall semester of 2005, when I was fortunate to have been released from teaching responsibilities. For making that shift in teaching duties possible, I extend my thanks to William Harman, head of the department of philosophy and religion at the University of Tennessee, and to Herbert Burhenn, then dean of the university's College of Arts and Sciences and now acting university provost. I have benefited from the wise editorial counsel of

Suzanne Staszak-Silva and Lisa Pierce at Praeger; one cannot work on a project such as this without editorial support.

For more than forty years, the religious culture of the United States has consumed my intellectual interests. It is my hope that the thirty-six essays in these three volumes will stimulate your reflection on the multitudinous dimensions of religion in this most religious of nations.

CHAPTER 1

Growth and Decline in the Mainline

C. Kirk Hadaway and Penny Long Marler

T he dominant religious trend since the settlement of the United States has been growth and geographic expansion. Fueled by immigration, a high birth rate, and a large proportion of "unchurched" persons, reaping a bountiful religious harvest came relatively easy in the American context. For the main, religious denominations grew. Some grew faster than others, of course, but if growth is taken as a measure of denominational health and evangelistic success, then the churches of America were clearly healthy and successful.

Large-scale denominational decline therefore has been an aberration. When decline did occur, it did so as a result of severe conflict, schism, or, in a few instances, because of a denomination's becoming severely out-of-step with American culture. Following the American Revolution, the Anglican churches experienced precipitous decline as loyalist clergy left the country and churches were closed.[1] Growth only resumed in the nineteenth century when the church was able to become an American denomination, the Protestant Episcopal Church. The Civil War also caused severe drops in membership when many religious bodies divided along with the nation. Other, somewhat more recent, schisms occurred over theological or cultural issues: The "Christian" church movement early in the nineteenth century led to the disruption and decline of several denominations in the upper South and Midwest; and Presbyterians, Congregationalists, and Lutherans have split and lost members over theology and denominational mergers. By and large, when these declines occurred they were abrupt and the causes easily identified. And after large-scale losses, the affected denominations began to grow again from new starting points. When the initial crisis had passed, they had little reason to wonder about their long-term survival or to question their identity or viability.

The only true exception to the norm of continual, if briefly interruptible, growth was experienced by the Shakers, Unitarians, and Universalists—religious bodies that grew quite rapidly for decades before becoming out-of-step with American culture. In the case of the Shakers, the problem was one of procreation (or rather lack thereof) and insufficient converts when this novel faith lost its attractiveness. The rise of Unitarianism and Universalism between 1815 and 1820 also came in the form of a social movement that attracted numerous converts and provoked the defection of many churches from their former denominations. However, when the national interest in novel religious forms waned by the mid-nineteenth century, Unitarianism and Universalism began to decline.[2]

For the vast majority of religious bodies in America, growth continued unabated; the population grew through procreation and immigration, and a once largely unchurched population was slowly gathered in through the Great Awakenings and a near pervasive evangelical zeal among American churches. For much of American history, almost all Protestant denominations were evangelical, including those that are now called the mainline. Indeed, Methodism, now the numerically dominant mainline church, was the societal norm for an evangelical church from the late eighteenth century to the mid-twentieth.

The pattern of continual growth was finally broken in the mid-1960s when one after the other Protestant denominations collectively known as mainline began to experience losses in membership.[3] The Christian Church (Disciples of Christ) first declined in 1964; the United Church of Christ in 1966; the United Methodist Church in 1966; the constituent bodies of the Presbyterian Church (USA) in 1966; the constituent bodies of the Evangelical Lutheran Church in America in 1967; the Episcopal Church in 1968; and the Reformed Church in America in 1968. Early on, these losses were not severe and failed to attract much attention from denominational leaders or those who study American religion. Because many denominations do not publish statistics in a timely manner and aggregation in annual editions of the *Yearbook of American and Canadian Churches* delays public knowledge for another year after denominational publication, it takes more than a few years for a trend to become apparent.[4] Thus, the issue of mainline decline did not arise as a serious subject of concern until early in the 1970s, seven years after the decline first began. Dean Kelley's *Why Conservative Churches Are Growing* began the conversation (or argument) about mainline decline, and the first academic efforts to study the losses did not appear until 1978 as chapters in Dean Hoge and David Roozen's edited volume, *Understanding Church Growth and Decline.*[5]

In the years since Kelley and Hoge and Roozen wrote about mainline decline, these denominations continued to lose members, and debates about those losses have also continued. In this chapter we provide an overview of mainline decline, followed by an analysis of the decline within a larger context of religious and demographic trends.

THE MAINLINE PRIOR TO THE ERA OF DECLINE

The term "mainline Protestant" is used along with "mainstream Protestant" and "old-line Protestant" to categorize denominations that are affiliated with the National Council of Churches and have deep historic roots in and long-standing influence on American society.[6] In the mid-eighteenth century, mainstream denominations would have included only Congregationalists, Anglicans, and perhaps Presbyterians. However, after the American Revolution, religion spread westward in the form of popular evangelicalism, primarily benefiting the Methodists, Baptists, and Presbyterians.[7] During the second half of the nineteenth century and into the first decades of the twentieth century, Methodists, Christian Churches, and most Lutheran bodies lost much of their sectarian or immigrant flavor and, along with the Congregationalists and Presbyterians, formed the core of the "Protestant Establishment." These increasingly ecumenical and culturally centrist bodies epitomized Protestantism, as distinguished from Catholicism and Judaism. According to Martin Marty, "mainline religion had meant simply white Protestant until well into the twentieth century."[8]

However much the ecumenical "mainline" operated as a de facto standard for Protestantism in America, there was no true evangelical/mainline division until after the Fundamentalist-Modernist controversies of the 1920s and 1930s. According to Richard Quebedeaux, "it was that dispute which divided Protestantism in America into two hostile camps and resulted in a factionalism within the church from which it has never fully recovered."[9]

Both the cooperative mainline and noncooperative conservative Protestants continued to grow during the 1930s and 1940s, and all available evidence indicates that conservative Protestants, despite becoming more culturally marginal following the Scopes trial, were growing at a more rapid pace than the mainline. But since most mainline denominations were growing faster than the general population and were largely unconcerned about events in the conservative sector, there was no sense of envy or competition on the part of the mainline. This was an era in which the proportion of unchurched Americans was shrinking as churches—mainline and conservative—made evangelistic inroads and increased the overall percentage of Americans who were on the membership rolls of a local church.[10] "Total membership in all religious groups (except the Quakers, the Unitarians, and the Universalists) grew by leaps and bounds during the twentieth century as the general population increased threefold.... There were 42 million churchgoers by 1916, 55 million by 1926, and 72 million by 1942."[11]

In spite of the growth of Protestantism in America, there were signs that all was not completely well in the Protestant house. According to Sydney Ahlstrom, following the stock market crash of 1929, "unemployment and hunger proved inconducive to a revival of popular religion."[12] Furthermore, fertility rates that had dropped steadily since the 1800s were barely above replacement level from the late 1920s through the 1930s.[13] Like the mid-1970s, the 1930s saw a "birth dearth" that slowed membership growth in most mainline denominations and resulted in a few years of net loss for the Methodists and United Presbyterians.[14]

But the membership malaise of the 1930s did not last. The national mobilization for World War II ended the Great Depression, and birth rates increased thereafter, rising steadily during the early 1940s before jumping more dramatically in 1946 and 1947, the years usually designated as the beginning of the postwar "baby boom." Denominational growth rates soared, ushering in an era of pervasive growth for mainline and conservative churches. The growth of the 1950s came as a surprise according to most observers, and "mainline churches were equally unprepared for the shaky statistics of the early 1960s and for the stunning decline in membership, which gathered momentum as the decade ended."[15]

THE BASIC TRENDS IN MAINLINE GROWTH AND DECLINE: 1945–2003

Membership trends for the era of growth during the baby boom years and the decline that followed are best viewed graphically. Figure 1.1 shows the basic membership trends for United Methodists and six other mainline denominations. Methodists are graphed separately because they are so much larger than any of the other mainline bodies and would overwhelm a trend line in which they were included. The six aggregated mainline bodies include the Christian Church (Disciples of Christ), the Episcopal Church, the Evangelical Lutheran Church in America, the Presbyterian Church (USA), the Reformed Church in America, and the United Church of Christ. The American Baptist churches are also normally included as part of the Protestant mainline, but are excluded from our analysis here because of serious problems in their membership reporting.

As can be seen in Figure 1.1, the United Methodist Church (UMC) had around 9.1 million members in 1945, the year prior to the beginning of the baby boom. Methodist membership peaked in 1965 at 11.0 million members. In the next year membership declined by 0.15 percent, and every year thereafter the UMC lost members. The most severe year of loss was a decline of 1.7 percent in 1971. As of 2003, United Methodist membership stood at 8.2 million members, a figure that represents a decline of 0.8 percent from the previous year and a loss of 2.8 million members since 1965.

The six other mainline denominations in Figure 1.1 had an aggregate 11.4 million members in 1945, and as the steeper line on the graph indicates, they grew at a more rapid pace than did United Methodists during the early years of the postwar baby boom. The aggregate mainline peak was 1966 when these denominations totaled 17.2 million members. The following year they declined in membership by 0.2 percent. Declines accelerated thereafter, with a loss of 2.0 percent in 1973. Losses continue through the present. In 2003, aggregate mainline membership stood at 12.0 million members, representing a decline of 1.5 percent in 2003 and a loss of 5.2 million members since 1966.

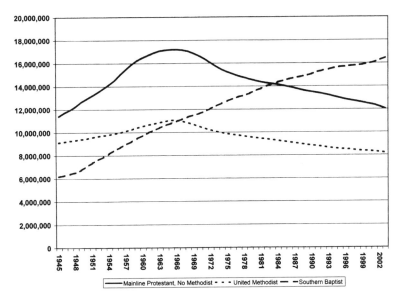

Figure 1.1. Mainline membership trends, 1945–2003.

Overall, these seven denominations (Methodists included) lost 8 million members from the mid-1960s to the present, or 28 percent of their total membership. Declines have been continuous for all of the seven denominations except for modest increases for the Episcopal Church in 1999 and the Evangelical Lutheran Church in America in 1982, 1990, 1991, and 1997. Thus far into the new millennium, no mainline denomination shows any sign of a return to consistent growth. Indeed, in the last few years, declines worsened in several religious bodies after showing signs of moderation. After growth in 1999 and tiny losses in 2000 and 2001, the Episcopal Church lost 8,000 members in 2002 and over 32,000 members in both 2003 and 2004. Similarly, the Evangelical Lutheran Church in America experienced rates of decline in 2002, 2003, and 2004 that were greater than any year since the early 1970s.

If the overall population of the United States began declining in the mid-1960s and all American denominations started to lose members at the same time, no explanation of mainline decline would be necessary. However, the U.S. population grew throughout the 1960s and continues to grow today; and among American denominational families it was only the mainline that began to decline. Almost all conservative denominations continued to grow, albeit at a slower pace.

The most simplistic explanation offered for decline is the status quo position of these groups. Mainline denominations are typically characterized as ecumenical, "liberal," and "weak." They lack the religious commitment, sense of moral rightness, and evangelical zeal of conservative denominations and are therefore at a strategic disadvantage in the American religious economy. This is the explanation used by Dean Kelley (1972) in *Why*

Conservative Churches Are Growing. In more recent years, the so-called "strictness" thesis has been elaborated by Laurence Iannaccone, Roger Finke, Rodney Stark, and other proponents of rational choice economic modeling.[16]

There is some face validity to the Dean Kelley/rational choice explanation: Polls show that members of mainline churches are somewhat less religiously active than their evangelical counterparts, mainline denominations start proportionately fewer churches, and mainline congregations put less emphasis on prayer and devotionalism than do congregations in conservative denominations.[17] However, these differences in religious actions did not suddenly appear in 1965, nor did the growth differential between mainline and conservative denominations. Conservative denominations were growing faster than mainline denominations throughout the post-World War II baby boom era. Furthermore, the growth rate of conservative denominations began to decline at the same time as that of the mainline. The difference was that conservative membership growth only slowed, whereas for mainline bodies the growth rate decreased to the point of actual membership loss by the mid-1960s.

Mainline denominations grew substantially in the 1940s and 1950s. In Figure 1.2 it can be seen that the United Methodist growth rate was relatively modest from the mid-1940s to 1964, before experiencing a slight downturn in 1965. The growth rate dropped greatly in 1966, to the point of minimal decline (−0.15 percent), before becoming a serious loss in 1967 (−0.65 percent), and reaching its worst level in 1971 (−1.66 percent).

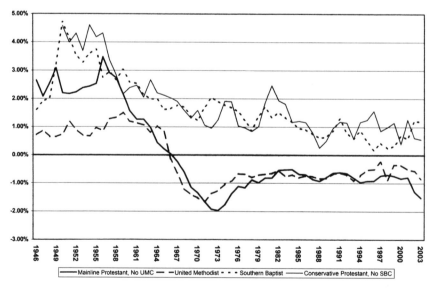

Figure 1.2. Yearly percentage change in denominational membership, 1946–2003.

Other mainline denominations grew much faster than the United Methodist Church on average. These bodies experienced growth exceeding 2 percent each year from 1946 to 1959. However, their aggregate growth rate dropped to 1.56 percent in 1960 and plunged in subsequent years, reaching +0.04 percent in 1966 and actual decline the year after (−0.23 percent). The decline reached its most severe levels in 1972 and 1973 when mainline denominations lost 1.93 percent and 1.97 percent of their members, respectively.

After the worst years of the early 1970s, mainline declines moderated, and as seen in Figure 1.2, the rate of decline essentially converged with the United Methodist trend line. Mainline declines fluctuated between −0.5 percent and −1.0 percent from the late 1970s through 2000.

The pattern for conservative denominations is similar to the mainline in some ways but clearly different in others. Figure 1.2 includes Southern Baptists on one line and seventeen other conservative bodies on another. Data are not available for all seventeen conservative groups prior to 1949, so that line begins in 1950. Conservative denominations were clearly growing much faster than mainline denominations in the 1950s. In 1950 the growth rate for Southern Baptist and other conservative groups was over 4.5 percent. After several years of extremely rapid growth, the rate of increase for Southern Baptists and other conservatives started to slow down. The drop was less precipitous than for the mainline, however, and during the mid-1970s conservative growth averaged between 1 and 2 percent each year. But unlike the mainline, the decline in the growth rate did not bottom out in the 1970s. Instead, the decline in the rate of growth continued, reaching its lowest point for conservative Protestants in 1988 and for Southern Baptists in 1996.

The primary similarity among all denominations in the chart is that decline in the growth rate began at nearly the same time. The main difference is that the decline for the conservatives was less severe and it continued for a longer period than for the mainline.

THE POSTWAR RELIGIOUS REVIVAL

The surge in church growth in the late 1940s and the 1950s is universally attributed to the postwar baby boom, suburbanization, and the pent-up demand for new churches and new church facilities among a population who valued the church as part of traditional nuclear family life. According to Milton Coalter, John Mulder, and Louis Weeks in their assessment of the Presbyterian Church during this period, "the expansion of membership in American Presbyterianism and mainstream Protestant denominations during the 1950s is largely the story of parents seeking out religious instruction for their children and church membership for themselves."[18] As people returned from military service they married and began to have children.

The year 1946 saw the highest number of marriages to date in the United States and the highest marriage rate ever recorded (before or since).[19] The second highest marriage rate was 1947. Dramatic increase in the birth rate reversed a century-long pattern of slow decline, and the rise was not only as a result of war returnees. The birth rate also rose among older age cohorts, greatly increasing the proportion of married-couple households with children in the home. "Births were bunched together in the 1950s," Dianne Crispell notes, because women "had children soon after marriage and spaced their children close together."[20] By 1960, almost half of all American households consisted of families with children under 18 years of age.[21]

Household homogeneity was compounded by the rise of the suburbs. Although suburbanization was not a new phenomenon, "the mass exodus of middle-class people from cities" in the 1950s created suburbs that were qualitatively different from earlier eras.[22] Millions of Americans in the same stage of the family life cycle now lived in close proximity to one another. A suburban culture was a byproduct.

Families with children were normative and pervasive, and part of normal family life was the church. Sydney Ahlstrom notes that "being a church member and speaking favorably of religion became a means of affirming the 'American way of life.'"[23] People flocked to the churches, and the denominations started new churches in the suburbs in order to reach people where they lived. New church development rates soared during the 1950s, and churches expanded facilities to accommodate families with children.[24] Ahlstrom reports that postwar church construction increased from $26 million to $409 million between 1945 and 1950, and continued to rise throughout the 1950s.[25] According to Robert Wuthnow, "the 1950s were the apex of a century and a half of church construction and membership drives."[26]

Growth in the 1950s, as noted by Coalter, Mulder, and Weeks, was not just a matter of enrolling the children of church members.[27] If this had been the case, mainline growth could not have exceeded that of the population. Since it did, the inescapable conclusion is that formerly unchurched persons joined churches along with their children and that the overall proportion of the unchurched declined during this time.[28] Data on baptisms support this conclusion: Even though child baptisms were extremely high, one-quarter of new Episcopal baptisms in 1950 were adults. From 1947 to 1952, the Presbyterian Church (USA) "received more on profession of faith and had more net gains than in the previous 20 years combined."[29] Other mainline denominations saw similar gains.[30] Throughout the 1950s, the birth rate remained high, and youth and young adults remained active in the many church-related activities provided for them.[31] As a result, it is likely that church affiliation in the United States reached its highest point ever in the mid-to-late 1950s.[32]

In summary, during the 1950s the U.S. population was growing rapidly because of the baby boom. Unprecedented numbers of churched and formerly unchurched nuclear families flocked to mainline and conservative Protestant churches. Denominations followed the population to the suburbs and expanded family-friendly programs and facilities. Going to the church "of your choice" was normative and the proportion of churched Americans increased.

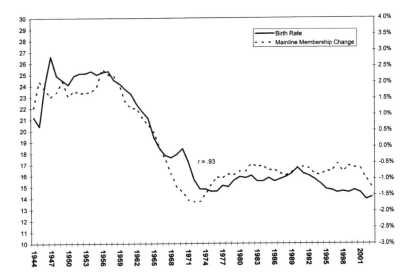

Figure 1.3. Raw U.S. birth rate and mainline membership change, 1944–2003.

Given that church growth of the 1950s is attributed largely to the baby boom, it is perhaps odd that the end of rapid growth in the 1960s is not typically attributed to the decline in the birth rate. However, if we superimpose a graph showing mainline membership change (all mainline bodies combined) onto a graph showing the raw birth rate, it can be seen that the trend line is very similar (see Figure 1.3).

There is a strong association between the mainline growth rate and the birth rate. In fact, the correlation between the data in these two graph lines is .93 and increases to .94 if the white birth rate is used. Squaring these correlations indicates that 88 percent of the variation in the rate of mainline membership change can be explained by reference to the white birth rate. So either the birth rate is driving membership trends among the mainline or some other variable is driving both trends.

INTERPRETING THE 1960s and 1970s

Although the churches were still growing, "during 1958 and 1959 ... discerning observers began talking about the postwar revival in the past tense (and) by 1960 this view was generally accepted."[33] Indeed, according to Margaret Bendroth, "by the late 1950s, even the most enthusiastic supporters of the Christian Faith and Life Program [a Presbyterian program] were forced to admit that it was foundering, largely because of indifferent and inconsistent support from parents."[34] Something changed in American society during the late 1950s and early 1960s that disproportionately affected the growth rates of mainline denominations, causing them not only to lose population share but also members, even as the overall population was growing.

The 1960s and 1970s were not like the 1950s. The familial conformity, conservatism, and traditionalism of the immediate postwar period gave way to the individualism, social experimentation, and anti-institutionalism of the 1960s and 1970s. This cultural sea-change, moreover, was not restricted to the United States. "It crossed international boundaries and profoundly affected (the postwar generation)" according to Wade Clark Roof, Jackson Carroll, and David Roozen.[35] Not only did values change among the general population (and particularly among youth) regarding sex and family, birth control, ideal family size, and civil liberties but denominational priorities also shifted. To a large extent more conservative groups were insulated by their social location in the South and among less well-educated segments of the U.S. population, but the mainline denominations were greatly affected.

According to Roozen, Carroll, and Roof, "During the 1960s and early 1970s the national denominational structures of mainline Protestantism gained a strong identity for universalizing notions of ecumenism and social justice, but at the cost of a weakened sense of personal spirituality, a weakened connection to the localism and voluntarism of their congregations, and significant decreases in membership."[36] These authors essentially blame mainline church decline on the directions that the denominations took following the 1950s. Other social observers make similar statements regarding the change in denominational priorities from education (including family programs) and evangelism to "discussions of racism, war, and sexual ethics."[37] In a twist on this thesis, Ahlstrom claims that the churches "muffed their chance" in the 1950s by sacrificing theological substance in favor of growth, leaving "both clergy and laity demoralized and confused" by the "harsh new social and spiritual realities of the 1960s."[38]

Dean Kelley's influential book, *Why Conservative Churches Are Growing,* also places the blame on mainline denominations, suggesting that it is in their nature to "diminish in number" while more conservative churches "will continue to increase."[39] In *American Mainline Religion,* Wade Clark Roof and William McKinney indicate that "for the most part, Kelley's interpretation holds" even though they find his interpretation of why the mainline stopped growing in the 1960s "unconvincing."[40] Essentially, Kelley makes a descriptive point that mainline churches are declining and conservative churches are growing. This point is obvious, and it does not explain why mainline churches stopped growing. But Kelley does make an analytic point as well, namely that liberal churches decline because they are weak and that conservative churches grow because they are strong. This point is less obvious, yet it too fails to be helpful because it cannot explain how the growth equation changed from the 1950s to the 1970s.

The descriptive side of the Kelley thesis, namely that conservative churches were growing and mainline churches were declining, led to the mistaken assumption of a conservative membership resurgence in the 1960s and 1970s. Wade Clark Roof and William McKinney suggest that a conservative resurgence occurred after the 1960s because "rigid and demanding beliefs, traditional values, certainty, absolutist moral teachings—all seemed to fill the needs of the times ... they offered a clear alternative to secular and diffusely religious points of view."[41] Martin Marty also seems to accept a resurgence explanation: "between 1965 and 1975 the new Evangelicals and many of the Fundamentalists experienced a new resurgence while the Mainline churches suffered setbacks."[42] Assumptions of conservative resurgence also support the more recent work of Rodney Stark, Roger Finke, and Laurence Iannaccone on strictness and denominational growth.[43] Statistically, however, there was no conservative resurgence during the 1960s and 1970s. Indeed, as Figure 1.2 shows, conservative denominations grew much more slowly during this period. There may have been resurgence in terms of conservative visibility but there certainly was no resurgence in terms of evangelical growth rates.

Even though the causes of mainline decline are not completely clear, the consequences of that decline are quite apparent. According to Roof and McKinney, "having made more accommodations to modernity than any other major religious tradition, liberal Protestantism shows many signs of tired blood: levels of orthodox belief are low, doubt and uncertainty in matters of faith common, knowledge of the Scriptures exceedingly low. A loss of morale and mission shows up in both its public demeanor and its corporate life."[44] This loss of morale is reflected in the following statement by a mainline church leader: "Our mainstream churches are not merely in decline; we who have been assigned responsibility to be leaders are frightened. We are huddled in dismay. We have a paralysis of mind and heart. We are dedicated to our tasks, but we have found that nothing we urge our people to do is curbing the stubborn decline of our membership, our ministry, and our cultural influence."[45] Clearly, certain changes were occurring in American society in the late 1950s and beyond that impacted the constituency of mainline churches. None of these changes helped the churches grow, and some of the reactions made by the mainline churches undoubtedly exacerbated declines.

BIRTH RATES AND MAINLINE AFFILIATION: EVIDENCE FROM SOCIAL SURVEYS

Although most explanations for mainline decline since the 1960s stressed what mainline denominations did (or failed to do) or some combination of denominational action/inaction and social change, more recent research emphasizes the "demographic imperative," suggesting that birth rates alone explain most of the decline in mainline constituency vis a vis the conservative Protestant sector.[46] According to Michael Hout, Andrew Greeley, and Melissa Wilde, "the shift of the Protestant population away from the mainline toward conservative denominations is overwhelmingly due to conservatives' higher fertility, which accounts for 70 percent of the change."[47] The remainder of the shift, they say, is the result of "the declining propensity of conservatives to convert to the mainline." So if these authors are correct, mainline Protestants have no need to wring their hands over their failure to keep pace with conservatives, other than perhaps that they became somewhat less attractive to potential converts from conservative denominations. The predominant force driving the membership trend is apparently the birth rate. Simply put, conservative Protestants have higher birth rates and mainline Protestants have lower birth rates, and even though neither denominational family has a pro- or anti-natal policy, birth rates largely determine their relative success.

The analysis by Hout and his associates helps explain a great deal about mainline trends, but it is not definitive. The study deals with affiliation (survey-based denominational identification) rather than membership, and it also does not adequately explain the rapid rise in mainline membership during the 1950s, the rapid downturn in membership during the 1970s, and the numerical extent of mainline decline. The vast majority of Americans have some kind of a religious identity, but not all of those who identify are on the membership rolls of a denomination. So, for example, the 2.0 percent of Americans who identified with the Episcopal Church in 2000 should have translated into 5.6 million members. However, only 2.3 million persons were actually members of the Episcopal Church in the United States of America, and other Episcopal/Anglican bodies accounted for not more than a hundred thousand or so additional Episcopalians. Thus, considerably less than half of Episcopal affiliates are actually members of Episcopal churches. The same situation exists for other denominations, and although there is some relationship between denominational affiliation and membership, the two are clearly not the same.

The second problem is that this demographic model suggests that the growth differential between mainline and conservative denominations was continuous and strong from 1900 through the late-1940s. Thereafter, the effect decreased somewhat and leveled off. As such, the model accurately predicts the long-term decline in the proportion of Americans with a mainline identity, but it does not explain the 1950s' upturn or the 1960s' downturn.

Finally, the magnitude of the decline in the birth rate among mainline Protestants is not sufficient to explain the magnitude of mainline loss, particularly in the 1970s. The correlation between the mainline birth rate and proportional mainline identity is strong, of course, but it may be a situation where "correlation does not necessarily mean causation." That is, broader social forces may be influencing both the birth rate and mainline decline. If birth rates were the sole determining factor, the same basic downward trend in membership would still be apparent, but it would not be as severe as the actual pattern observed from the late 1960s to the present.

Nevertheless, the analysis by Hout and his team has appropriately focused attention on two facts: Conservative Protestant religious bodies in the United States were growing faster than the mainline before, during, and after the "religious revival" of the 1950s, and more attention should be paid to changes in the potential mainline constituency (persons with a mainline identity) than to continuing differences in religiosity or irreligiosity of persons who affiliate with a mainline and conservative denomination. Mainline Protestants attend church less frequently than conservative Protestants. There has been no change, however, in the proportion of mainline Protestants who say they attend church every week, at least from the early 1970s to 2002. There also has been no rise in the rate of worship attendance among conservatives. By these measures of religious involvement, mainline Protestants are not attending church less and conservative Protestants are not attending church more. Rather, what has changed is the proportion of the population who claim a mainline Protestant identity and the proportion of those who say they were reared mainline Protestant. Both proportions declined nine percentage points from the early 1970s to 2002. It is also important to note that the proportion of conservative Protestants has not increased in absolute terms among the general population of the United States. Nevertheless, looking only at Protestants, the conservative proportion has increased relative to the mainline.

Switching from a mainline to a conservative Protestant identity is and has been a minor phenomenon in American religion, despite anecdotal stories about sons or daughters of mainline parents who find Jesus in a dramatic way in conservative churches. Historically, conservative to mainline switching has been much more prevalent than mainline to conservative switching, but in recent decades conservative to mainline switching has declined. The predominant changes in mainline religious identity are decreasing rates of mainline affiliation and a more recent tendency (from the late 1980s to the present) for mainline persons to switch out of religion altogether, thus decreasing the retention rate of the mainline from 74 percent in the mid-1980s to 67 percent from the late 1990s through 2002. And the younger the age cohort, the more likely is a person reared in the mainline to switch out of religion altogether.

In addition, a small part of the explanation for the reduction in mainline identification is "selective remembering" on the part of persons reared in the mainline. Persons in the oldest age cohort (persons born prior to 1920) in the aggregated polls used in the Hout study are more likely to say they are mainline and were reared mainline in recent surveys than they were in surveys administered during the 1970s. Conversely, the cohorts born 1934–1945 and 1946–1959 are slightly less likely to say they were reared in mainline denominations today than they were in the mid-1970s. Some reinterpretation of one's childhood experience has occurred among the World War II generation and older baby boomers, thus decreasing the proportion of more recent age cohorts who say they were reared in the mainline.

In summary, survey data show that there has been a rather large decrease in the proportion of persons who currently claim a mainline identity and in the proportion of persons who say they were reared in a mainline denomination. Part of that decrease is a result of recent declines in persons switching into the mainline. Another part has been increasing percentages switching to no religion (particularly among younger cohorts). Still another part has been selective remembering on the part of more recent age cohorts. However, the most important trend has been that fewer and fewer persons in each successive age cohort were reared in a mainline denomination. This can be explained by lower mainline birth rates and, perhaps, by a decreased emphasis on (or the diminished effectiveness of) mainline Protestant acculturation.

BIRTH RATES AND MAINLINE MEMBERSHIP: EVIDENCE FROM DENOMINATIONAL RECORDS

Denominational identification is not the same thing as membership or participation. Even though it is clear that conservative growth generally exceeded mainline growth throughout the twentieth century, birth rate data and rates of denominational identification cannot explain the religious revival of the 1950s or the actual declines in membership that began in the 1960s and accelerated during the 1970s to the present.

The demographic model noted above predicted continuous declines in mainline affiliation from the late 1940s through the 1950s based on birth rate differentials between mainline and conservative affiliates. However, the actual pattern was not continuous. The decline in mainline identification relative to conservative denominations actually stabilized during this period.[48]

Denominational membership (rather than affiliation) statistics during the late 1940s and the 1950s reveal an even more dramatic departure from previous trends. Dean Hoge, Benton Johnson, and Donald Luidens show that the Presbyterian Church (USA) was growing slower than the general population from 1924 to 1935.[49] From 1935 to 1945 the Presbyterian Church (USA) grew at about the same rate as the general population, maintaining the same percentage (2.0 percent of the U.S. population was counted as members). Thereafter, until around 1960, Presbyterian growth greatly exceeded that of the national population. The reason for this rise was that the Presbyterian infant baptism rate was much higher than the national birth rate from 1949 to 1961. From 1953 to 1956 the Presbyterian infant baptism rate was over 40 percent higher than the birth rate for white Americans. The baptism rate then declined steadily for the next decade and a half before reaching the point in 1970 where the infant baptism rate for Presbyterians was lower than the birth rate for white Americans. The year 1955 marked when the infant baptism rate exceeded the birth rate by the greatest margin (45.8 percent higher), and it also was the year that the number of adult baptisms (51,840) was highest.[50]

The Presbyterian Church grew slower than the national population from 1924 to 1935, and slightly faster than the national population from 1945 to 1950, but greatly exceeded the growth of the national population from 1950 to 1960 (+36 percent vs. +18 percent). Yet from 1960 to 1970 the Presbyterian Church actually lost 5 percent of its membership, although the population continued to grow at 13 percent for the decade. Trends for the Episcopal Church and other mainline denominations are essentially the same: slower growth than the population before the baby boom, growth faster than the population during the late 1940s and throughout the 1950s, and then slower growth during the early 1960s, followed by actual declines in membership in the mid-1960s, with declines accelerating in the early 1970s.

Why the mainline fared better than would be expected, given population trends (including the birth rate) during the 1940s and 1950s, has been considered above. So the question is, "Why did the mainline fare so much worse than would be expected given population trends in the 1960s and beyond?"

The key to understanding what happened to the mainline during the 1950s and beyond is found among the younger age cohorts. Survey data on church participation show that there was no generation gap during the 1950s.[51] Young adults (21–30), median adults (31–55), and older adults (over 55) attended church at nearly the same rate in the mid-1950s. Thereafter, from the mid-1960s to the present, a gap appeared whereby the attendance rate for young adults was lower than for any other age group and was highest for older adults, with median adults in the middle. What this meant in the 1950s was that young parents, who were unusually fertile during this decade, were more likely to be found in church along with their large numbers of offspring. After the 1950s, attendance among young adults dropped and these same young adults began having fewer children. The baptism rate declined greatly as a result, and denominational death rates began to rise as the average age of membership increased.

Survey data, even though employing affiliation rather than membership, also show substantial age-related change. Using combined national polls from the National Opinion Research Center, by the mid-1970s the proportion of active (attending church once a week or more) mainline Protestants age 18–32 was already lower than for moderate and conservative Protestants, and the percentage of active mainline Protestants age 66+ was higher than for other Protestant groups. Yet from the mid-1970s to 2002, the proportion of younger active affiliates dropped an additional 8 percentage points and the proportion of elderly active affiliates rose a further 14 percentage points.[52]

The only available time series data dealing with age for actual church participants are from the United Church of Christ (UCC), a liberal mainline denomination. The first study was conducted in the mid-1970s and included surveys from nearly 200,000 worshippers attending services in over 2,000 UCC churches. The second study, conducted in the spring of 2002 included 4,102 worshippers in a random national sample of 227 UCC congregations. In both cases, survey forms were distributed to all worshippers age 15+ in the participating congregation at all worship services. As was seen in the survey data, a disparity between the church population and the general population already existed by the mid-1970s. In the UCC, the proportion of attendees age 15 to 34 was only 24 percent, as compared to 45 percent of the national population. On the other end of the age spectrum, 23 percent of UCC attendees were age 65 or older, as compared to 14 percent in the general population. Commenting on this situation, William McKinney concludes, "the children of the baby boom represent a lost generation for the United Church of Christ ... our membership is aging and is producing fewer children than in earlier generations."[53]

As dire as the situation was in the mid-1970s, it was much worse by 2002. Attendees age 15 to 34 declined from 24 percent in the mid-1970s to only 10 percent in 2002 and attendees age 65 or older grew from 23 percent in the mid-1970s to 43 percent of all UCC attendees in 2002. The large age disparity between UCC attendees age 15–34 and the U.S. population widened slightly from 21 percentage points to 25 percentage points between the mid-1970s and 2002, whereas the disparity between UCC attendees age 65+ and the U.S. population grew enormously, increasing from 9 percentage points to over 27 percentage points.

There are, unfortunately, no similar studies of attendees in the 1950s or 1960s. However, we know that from the mid-1960s to the mid-1970s the proportion of UCC members with children under 18 in the home dropped from 66 percent to only 32 percent—a precipitous decline.[54]

Persons born during the baby boom years, which should have composed the largest share of mainline members in the 1970s, were in fact a minority compared to older generations even at that time. Many dropped out and did not return to the church, although most probably maintained a church identity. Furthermore, whether they returned to the church or not, they had fewer children on average than did their parents. Since older generations remained in the church, the consequence was a steady increase in the proportion of elderly church participants, from the 1970s through the present. In the 2002 UCC sample, 43 percent of active attendees were retirement age or older. In national surveys dealing with active mainline affiliates, the percentage of elderly mainline affiliates is also quite high: 40 percent. Over half (57 percent) of mainline churches reported that "many or most" of their active members are age 60 or older, as compared to 28 percent of conservative churches.[55] With fewer members in child-bearing years and a high rate of disaffiliation among the children of the mainline, the membership problems have continued to worsen, generation by generation since the 1950s.

BIRTH RATES VERSUS OTHER FACTORS

The large correlation between the birth rate and mainline membership change results from the fact that when the birth rate was high, membership growth was also very high. Conversely, when the birth rate dropped, membership growth turned into decline. However, the relationship could not have been completely causal, in that all of the growth was caused by the addition of x number of children being born to mainline families and decline by not enough births to offset deaths among mainline members. Rather, membership growth greatly exceeded what would be expected by the increase in the birth rate, and decline greatly exceeded what would be expected by the decrease in the birth rate. Still, the correlation was very strong because the rates co-varied. So although an explanation for mainline growth in the 1950s and decline must include the birth rate, the story is not just the birth rate but also social and cultural forces that influenced the birth rate and patterns of mainline church involvement.

In the 1950s the birth rate rose to a very high level. Mainline membership would have grown during this period even without additions from persons who were previously uninvolved. However, the same cultural trends that drove the rise in the birth rate also "drove" people to church. That is, the nuclear family ideal led to large numbers of births and the meshing of the church with that ideal led to more families attending church, even among the previously unchurched. The churches responded to the growth by building new suburban churches and with family-oriented programming, actions that helped the churches grow even more.

As the children of the early baby boom began to approach their teen years and as household structure began to shift from the 1950s nuclear family norm, it became more difficult for churches to hold onto the families that they had attracted and involved in the 1940s and 1950s. Not only did their 1950s constituency age and change in household structure, but no commensurately large and fertile nuclear family cohort replaced them. From 1960 to 1990, the proportion of U.S. households composed of married couples with children declined precipitously from 45.6 percent to 26.3 percent. Divorce rates rose; marriage rates declined; age at first marriage increased; and women had fewer children and went to work.[56] According to Carothers, "By 1975 the typical family of the 1950s sitcom, with two parents, two children, and a nonworking mother, accounted for only 7 percent of all households."[57] Denominations increasingly competed over (and waxed nostalgic for) a shrinking proportion of American households.[58]

By 1960 the birth rate was already beginning to decline, although greater drops caused by the national legalization of "the pill" were still several years away. Nevertheless, the climate for the family and the church was beginning to change. As suburbs aged, they stopped growing and became less homogeneous. White churches in those suburbs began having growth problems that were exacerbated in many cities by white flight. The communal joining ethic of the 1950s that supported church involvement was displaced by a more individualistic ethic that was less supportive of church involvement.[59] Indeed, the church was actually attacked as being part of the "system" that impeded necessary social changes in society.[60] The emergence of the new ethic, along with institutional suspicion, was associated with age, education, and region. Youth and young adults in mainline denominations were most greatly affected. Levels of education in the mainline were higher and these denominations are disproportionately concentrated in regions outside the South.

Just as the mainline denominations in the 1950s responded to societal changes by providing new churches and family-oriented programming, the mainline denominations in the 1960s and 1970s responded to societal changes by questioning all that they had done in the 1950s. Books decried the "suburban captivity of the church," and new church development virtually stopped. Justice concerns displaced Christian education and family programming. Adult Christian education was virtually eliminated in many mainline churches, and church school enrollment for children declined faster than overall membership. Meanwhile, conservative denominations either tried to pretend that nothing different was happening in the 1960s and 1970s or attacked the changes that were coming their way, interpreting social change through a premillennial lens that quickened evangelistic zeal and/or capitalizing on white flight through continued suburban church development. So, for instance, even though conservative denominations saw new church development rates drop greatly in the 1960s, their reaction in the 1970s and 1980s was to gear up new church development until new church plants nearly equaled the production of the 1950s.[61]

The 1980s and 1990s saw birth rates rise somewhat, and the social questioning of the 1960s and 1970s was replaced by acquisitiveness and an emphasis on therapeutic self-expression. The culture remains quite individualistic but not directly antagonistic toward the church. In the case of the Episcopal Church and Unitarian Universalist Association, the spiritual seeking of the 1990s did coincide with numerical growth for a number of years. For the rest of the mainline, however, the severe declines of the 1970s moderated in the 1980s and 1990s, but decline continued nonetheless. They are still plagued by problems associated with increasing age, low rates of birth (and child baptisms), and low rates of retention.

In the early 1990s, Penny L. Marler and C. Kirk Hadaway conducted a national study of American Protestants who identified with a mainline or conservative denomination but who no longer belonged to a church and/ or attended regularly. This research confirmed the importance of religious socialization in maintaining church involvement. Mainline "unchurched" Protestants were significantly less likely than their churched counterparts to report that they said grace at home as a child or attended youth programs or church camps. Mainline unchurched respondents were also much more likely to report that their fathers never attended church when they were growing up and much less likely to report that their mothers attended regularly. Although unchurched mainline Protestants were less likely than the churched to hold traditional views of God and the Bible, both churched and unchurched mainline respondents were considerably less orthodox than conservative Protestants.[62] Further, unchurched mainline respondents tended to report lower levels of church involvement among their own children than they themselves experienced.[63] Indeed, what seems to account for lowered retention among mainline Protestants is childhood religious socialization rather than conservative or liberal theology per se. If this is the case, then, an observed trend for lower levels of church involvement and identification among successive generational cohorts is not surprising.

Furthermore, all mainline denominations remain embroiled in controversies and conflicts over social and sexual issues that alienate older and more conservative members, consume a disproportionate amount of time and energy, and lead to the withdrawal of many entire congregations. So the membership problems that would be present anyway, given the demographics and retention trajectory of mainline denominations, are worsened by the loss of disaffected churches and disaffected members. From a structural standpoint, mainline denominations seem to lack the creative energy, necessary resources, and/or the simple will to engage in the kinds of new church development, evangelistic outreach, or Christian formation and education that would be required to slow or even stop the membership decline.

MOVING INTO THE TWENTY-FIRST CENTURY

In the late 1940s and throughout the 1950s mainline denominations grew much faster than the general population. By the mid-1960s mainline denominations were in decline, even as the population continued to grow. Conservative evangelical denominations did not experience resurgent membership growth during this latter period, but still managed to grow. Given slower rates of mainline growth prior to the postwar revival, the 1950s represent an aberration in a longer-term trend, and to a certain extent, the declines of the 1960s and 1970s represent a return to normalcy as members who joined the church in the familial 1950s drifted away once that era had passed. This does not, however, account for the accelerated pace of that decline.

As we have shown, mainline decline after the 1950s can be explained by two primary factors: one, a differentially low birth rate; and two, a differentially poor record of retention (particularly among younger age cohorts). Both are linked to social and cultural changes which directly affect the birth rate and religious socialization and especially impact mainline constituencies. Many of these changes reflected new opportunities for women through the reproductive and equal opportunity revolutions of the 1960s, and all denominations were negatively affected.[64] Conservative Protestants witnessed slower growth in the decades that followed while mainline Protestants realized actual membership loss.

Nevertheless, equal rights for women and endangered "family values" did become effective wedge issues in the conservative political revolution of the 1970s and 1980s. As a result, conservative Protestants gained a measure of social and political clout as well as organizational strength through the political coalitions and parachurch networks of the "religious right." The response of mainline Protestants was more ambivalent: Although some denominational leaders and younger, well-educated laity openly embraced these changes, the majority took a more tempered approach for fear of alienating older, more traditionalistic constituencies. What became a catalyst for growth among some conservatives was an occasion for indecision and inaction among mainline Protestants. In his recent work, *The Transformation of American Religion*, Alan Wolfe concludes that the "culture of no offense" that continues to operate in mainline churches reflects a desire to "hold on to those declining numbers of members they have" rather than to attract new members.[65]

Interpretations of mainline growth and decline that emphasize values or theology confuse correlation and causation. Both mainline and conservative Protestant denominations grew in the 1950s, not because the mainline became more conservative, but because both groups capitalized on the baby boom and because the mainline attracted new adult members. It is important to note that conservative Protestant groups were, in fact, growing much faster than the mainline prior to the 1950s, but during that decade mainline denominations nearly equaled them. Afterwards, mainline Protestant denominations returned to their pre-1950s levels before dropping into uncharted territory: unabated decline. Birth rates fell for mainline Protestants and conservatives, but remained higher for conservatives. Because they failed to retain so many of the children born during the baby boom, the mainline effectively lost the children of the boomers. The net result was ever-increasing average age and ever-decreasing numbers of children to pass on the tradition. The issue of retention is more likely related to a decline in religious socialization or a weakening of mainline acculturation than to the particular theological content of their tradition.

Declining birth rates are affected by a number of factors including reproductive freedom and choice, the increased availability of and access to higher education, new opportunities for professional careers among women as well as men, improved daycare and more flexible maternity and paternity workplace policies, and heightened lifestyle expectations accompanied by realistic concerns about economic futures. As in other developed nations, the fortunes of organized religion are largely tied to the birth rate, and the birth rate, in turn, is related to similar socioeconomic advances.[66] Denominational retention, on the other hand, is primarily related to the strength and effectiveness of socialization processes in the family and in the parent organization.

If doctrine and practice are valued and shared, a religious denomination is more likely to grow through new adult recruits, the conversion or confirmation of children, or both. Indeed, during the 1950s mainline denominations did both and they grew disproportionately. From the 1960s onward, they experienced increasing difficulty with both and they declined precipitously. Their values and the extent to which they were supported by the larger culture helped at some points (in the 1950s) and were problematic at others (in the 1960s). Moreover, what mainline denominations did made a positive difference at one time (in the 1950s) and became a decided problem at another point (in the 1960s and 1970s).

In the end, the best thesis for explaining church growth and decline is actually an ancient one: Strong churches "train children in the right way, and when old, they will not stray" (Proverbs 22:6, NRSV). And growth is accelerated if birth rates and/or adult converts exceed replacement levels.

NOTES

1. See Winthrop S. Hudson, *American Protestantism* (Chicago: University of Chicago Press, 1961).

2. Ibid.

3. Even though mainline denominations were growing prior to the mid-1960s, they were still losing "market share" to more conservative religious bodies,

owing to a more rapid growth rate among the latter. See Roger Finke and Rodney Stark, *The Churching of America, 1776–1990* (New Brunswick, NJ: Rutgers University Press, 1992).

4. See Constant H. Jacquet, Jr., ed., *Yearbook of American and Canadian Churches* (Nashville, TN: Abingdon, 1991), as well as other yearly editions of the *Yearbook*.

5. Dean Kelley, *Why Conservative Churches Are Growing* (San Francisco: Harper and Row, 1972); Dean Hoge and David Roozen, eds., *Understanding Church Growth and Decline* (New York: Pilgrim, 1978).

6. J. Edward Carothers, *The Paralysis of Mainline Protestant Leadership* (Nashville, TN: Abingdon, 1990), 11, 14; Milton J. Coalter, John M. Mulder, and Louis B. Weeks, *Vital Signs: The Promise of Mainstream Protestantism* (Grand Rapids, MI: Eerdmans, 1996), xii.

7. Hudson, 97.

8. Martin Marty, *A Nation of Behavers* (Chicago: University of Chicago Press, 1976), 53.

9. Richard Quebedeaux, *The Young Evangelicals* (New York: Harper and Row, 1974), 5.

10. See Finke and Stark and also Phillip E. Hammond, *The Dynamics of Religious Organizations: The Extravision of the Sacred and Other Essays* (New York: Oxford University Press, 2000).

11. Barry A. Kosmin and Seymour P. Lachman, *One Nation Under God: Religion in Contemporary American Society* (New York: Harmony Books, 1993), 46.

12. Sydney Ahlstrom, *A Religious History of the American People*, Vol. 2. (Garden City, NY: Doubleday/Image, 1975), 445.

13. U.S. Bureau of the Census, Historical Statistics of the United States, *Colonial Times to 1970, Bicentennial Edition, Part 2* (Washington, DC: U.S. Government Printing Office, 1975), 49; Diane Crispell, "Myths of the 1950s," *American Demographics* 14, 8 (1992): 43.

14. General Assembly Missions Council, *Membership Trends in the United Presbyterian Church in the U.S.A.* (New York: General Assembly Missions Council, United Presbyterian Church, U.S.A., 1976), 11.

15. Carl Dudley, *Where Have All Our People Gone?: New Choices for Old Churches* (New York: Pilgrim,1979), 4.

16. See Kelley; Laurence Iannaccone, "A Formal Model of Church and Sect," *American Journal of Sociology* 94 (1988): S241–S268; Finke and Stark; Steven Warner, "Work in Progress Toward a New Paradigm for the Scientific Study of Religion in the United States," *American Journal of Sociology* 98 (1993): 1044–93; and Laurence Iannaccone, Daniel V.A. Olson and Rodney Stark, "Religious Resources and Church Growth," *Social Forces* 74 (1995): 705–31.

17. Penny L. Marler and C. Kirk Hadaway, "New Church Development and Denominational Growth (1950–1988): Symptom or Cause?" in *Church and Denominational Growth*, ed. David A. Roozen and C. Kirk Hadaway (Nashville, TN: Abingdon, 1993), 47–86; Data on religious activity are from the NORC General Social Survey: James A. Davis, Tom W. Smith, and Peter V. Marsden. *General Social Survey, 1972–2002: [Computer file]. 2nd ICPSR version.* (Chicago, IL: National Opinion Research Center [producer], 2003; Storrs, CT: Roper Center for Public Opinion Research, University of Connecticut/Ann Arbor, MI: Inter-university Consortium for Political and Social Research [distributors], 2003). Data on prayer emphasis and devotionalism are from the 2000 Faith Communities Today Survey; see C. Kirk Hadaway, *A Report on Episcopal Churches in the United States* (New York: Domestic and Foreign Missionary Society, 2002), 43.

18. Milton J. Coalter, John M. Mulder, and Louis B. Weeks, *The Re-Forming Tradition: Presbyterians and Mainline Protestantism* (Louisville, KY: Westminster/John Knox, 1992), 73.

19. See Annie Gottlieb, *Do You Believe in Magic?: The Second Coming of the Sixties Generation* (New York: Times Books, 1993), 23, and U.S. Bureau of the Census, 1975, 64.

20. Crispell, 41.

21. Penny Long Marler, "Lost in the Fifties: The Changing Family and the Nostalgic Church," in *Work, Family and Faith: New Patterns Among Old Institutions*, ed. Nancy Ammerman and Wade Clark Roof (New Brunswick, NJ: Rutgers University Press, 1993), 23–60.

22. Ibid., 42.

23. Ahlstrom, 447.

24. Marler and Hadaway, 50.

25. Ahlstrom, 448.

26. Robert Wuthnow, *After Heaven: Spirituality in America Since the 1950s* (Berkeley: University of California Press, 1998), 31.

27. See Coalter, Mulder, and Weeks.

28. Margaret L. Bendroth, *Growing Up Protestant: Parents, Children and Mainline Churches* (New Brunswick, NJ: Rutgers University Press, 2002), 99.

29. Milton J. Coalter, "Presbyterian Evangelism: A Case of Parallel Allegiances Diverging," in *The Diversity of Discipleship: Presbyterians and Twentieth Century Christian Witness*, ed. Milton J. Coalter, John M. Mulder, and Louis B. Weeks (Louisville, KY: Westminster/John Knox Press, 1991), 43.

30. Ruth T. Doyle and Sheila Kelley, "Comparison of Trends in Ten Denominations, 1950–1975," in Hoge and Roozen, eds., 151.

31. Jackson W. Carroll, "Understanding Church Growth and Decline," *Theology Today* 35 (April 1978): 74.

32. Wuthnow, 30; Bendroth, 99.

33. Ahlstrom, 461.

34. Bendroth, 115.

35. Wade Clark Roof, Jackson W. Carroll, and David Roozen, "Conclusion: The Post-War Generation—Carriers of a New Spirituality," in *The Post-War Generation and Establishment Religion: Cross-Cultural Perspectives*, ed. Wade Clark Roof, Jackson W. Carroll, and David Roozen (Boulder, CO: Westview Press, 1995), 244.

36. David A. Roozen, Jackson W. Carroll, and Wade Clark Roof, "Fifty Years of Religious Change in the United States," in Roof, Carroll, and Roozen, eds., 70.

37. Bendroth, 115–16.

38. Ahlstrom, 460.

39. See Kelley, *Why Conservative Churches Are Growing.*

40. Wade Clark Roof and William McKinney, *American Mainline Religion: Its Changing Shape and Future* (New Brunswick, NJ: Rutgers University Press, 1987), 20.

41. Wade Clark Roof and William McKinney, "Denominational America and the New Religious Pluralism," *Annals of the American Academy of Political and Social Sciences* 480 (1985): 23, 30.

42. Marty, 92.

43. See Finke and Stark; Laurence Iannaccone, "Why Strict Churches are Strong," *American Journal of Sociology* 99 (1994): 1180–1211; and Iannaccone, Olson, and Stark.

44. Roof and McKinney, *American Mainline Religion*, 86.

45. Carothers, 11.

46. Michael Hout, Andrew Greeley, and Melissa J. Wilde, "The Demographic Imperative in Religious Change in the United States," *American Journal of Sociology* 107, 2 (2001): 468–500; Michael Hout, Andrew Greeley, and Melissa J. Wilde, "Birth Dearth," *Christian Century* 122, 20 (2005): 24–27.

47. Hout, Greeley, and Wilde, "Birth Dearth," 25.

48. Ibid, 27.

49. Dean R. Hoge, Benton Johnson, and Donald Luidens, *Vanishing Boundaries: The Religion of Mainline Protestant Baby Boomers* (Louisville, KY: Westminster/John Knox, 1994), 5.

50. General Assembly Missions Council, 99, 103.

51. David A. Roozen, *Church Membership and Participation: Trends, Determinants, and Implications for Policy and Planning* (Hartford, CT: Hartford Seminary Foundation, 1978), 26; Warren E. Miller and the National Election Studies, *American National Election Studies Cumulative Data File, 1952–1992 [Computer file], 6th release* (Ann Arbor, MI: University of Michigan, Center for Political Studies [producer], 1994; Ann Arbor, MI: Inter-University Consortium for Political and Social Research [distributor], 1991).

52. See Davis, Smith, and Marsden.

53. William McKinney, *Population Changes and the Growth and Decline of the United Church of Christ* (New York: United Church Board for Homeland Ministries, 1982), 30.

54. Ibid.

55. Hadaway, 16.

56. Marler, 28–31.

57. Carothers, 121.

58. Marler, 34–40.

59. Robert Putnam catalogues rather dramatic postwar membership decline in many "secondary associations," that is, in social organizations that generate "dense networks of civic engagement" and that "broaden the participants' sense of self, developing the 'I' into the 'we.'" Such groups include labor unions, PTAs, the League of Women Voters, the Red Cross, the Jaycees, the Boy Scouts, and bowling leagues. Although most polls do show a modest decline in rates of church membership over the same period, the self-reports of all mainline denominations in the United States for the last thirty years reveal more serious losses. Robert Putnam, "Bowling Alone: America's Declining Social Capital," *Journal of Democracy* 6 (1995): 65–78.

60. Jeffrey Hadden, *The Gathering Storm in the Churches* (Garden City, NY: Doubleday, 1969).

61. Marler and Hadaway, 50.

62. Penny Long Marler and C. Kirk Hadaway, "Methodists on the Margins: 'Self-Authoring' Religious Identity," in *Connectionalism: Ecclesiology, Mission and Identity*, ed. Russell E. Richey, Dennis M. Campbell, and William B. Lawrence (Nashville, TN: Abingdon, 1997), 289–316.

63. Penny Long Marler and C. Kirk Hadaway, "Toward a Typology of Protestant Marginal Members," *Review of Religious Research* 35 (1993): 53–73.

64. Penny Long Marler, "Religious Change in the West: Watch the Women," *Women and Religion in the West: Challenging Secularization*, ed. Kristen Auene (London: Ashgate, forthcoming).

65. Alan Wolfe, *The Transformation of American Religion: How We Actually Live Our Faith* (New York: Free Press, 2003), 87.

66. Marler, "Religious Change."

SUGGESTIONS FOR FURTHER READING

Hoge, Dean, Benton Johnson, and Donald Luidens. *Vanishing Boundaries: The Religion of Mainline Protestant Baby Boomers.* Louisville, KY: Westminster/ John Knox, 1990.

Hout, Michael, Andrew Greeley, and Melissa Wilde. "The Demographic Imperative in Religious Change in the United States." *American Journal of Sociology* 107, 2 (2001): 468–500.

Roozen, David, and C. Kirk Hadaway. *Church and Denominational Growth.* Nashville, TN: Abindgon, 1993.

CHAPTER 2

Post–Vatican II Catholicism: A New Church for a New Day?

Chester Gillis

The Second Vatican Council (1962–1965) sent shockwaves of change to every corner of the Roman Catholic Church. Announced unexpectedly by Pope John XXIII after being in office for only a few months, the idea of a universal council met with approval and anticipation by some bishops and cardinals and with hesitation and resistance by others in the hierarchy. John XXIII made it clear that he wanted a council that would address pastoral rather than doctrinal issues in the church. He believed that the time had come to update the church and to open it to the modern world. Many bishops and cardinals believed that it was more than time for the church to consider new ways to make its message and presence relevant, and they rejoiced at the prospects of a council that would consider practices and dispositions ranging from liturgy to the church's relations with other Christians and other religions.

However, there were also those who thought that the church need not and should not change since change might signal discontinuity, resulting in an erosion of tradition. Encouraged by John XXIII's leadership and vision, the universal church met in council to set a course for the church in the latter half of the twentieth century and beyond. During the course of four sessions in which bishops, archbishops, and cardinals met in Rome, along with their theological advisors, under the direction of the pope, the council produced sixteen documents that addressed the church's relationship with the contemporary world. The effects of this council are still being felt today and will likely continue to shape the church for much of the twenty-first century.

The very title of this chapter, "Post–Vatican II Catholicism," suggests that "pre–Vatican II Catholicism" differed from what the church has experienced since 1965. And differ it did. The church had not convened a council since Vatican I (1869–1870) and that council dealt with dogma more than pastoral practice. Vatican II made changes in church practices that immediately and directly affected ordinary Catholics, the most obvious of which involved the celebration of the mass. For centuries the church celebrated the mass in Latin with the priest's back to the congregation. Vatican II's document on the liturgy changed the language of the mass to the vernacular, instructed that the altar be turned around so that the priest-celebrant could face the people, permitted contemporary forms of music, and invited the laity to participate in the liturgy by responding in English (in the United States) to prayers and to be lectors as well as, eventually, Eucharistic ministers. Lay participation in the liturgy proved to be only one manifestation of increased lay involvement in the church. Parishes created councils that advised pastors on various policies including finances, governance, and worship. Responding to their own vocation given in baptism, the laity emerged from the shadows to take on leadership roles and to participate at almost all levels of church life.

In the Roman Catholic Church in America, the period immediately following Vatican II brimmed with hope and promise but proved to have some serious difficulties as well. Chronologically, it coincided with the tumult that characterized the 1960s in America. The sexual revolution, the Vietnam conflict, rock music, recreational drugs, more permissive media, distrust of government and authority, widespread access to higher education, the rise of a consumer culture, the cold war, increased personal freedom, and more, all contributed to a unique era in American history. The church's opening up to the world meant that a tide of change would sweep through the church as it did society and culture.

The effects of Vatican II have not completely subsided as it continues either to inspire or to worry various church observers. Some think that it was simply too much too fast. Others believe that it did not go far enough to change the culture of the church. Some argue that the church needs a new council to revise and extend the reforms of Vatican II. Others hold that the church continues to absorb the changes instituted by that council and that further revisions would not be prudent until all of the changes inaugurated by Vatican II have had a chance to settle. Others would like to repeal some, if not all, of the changes instituted by the council, preferring to return to what they believe to have been the stability and security of the pre–Vatican II church. Within days of his election as pope, Benedict XVI reassured Vatican officials and the faithful that he would continue to carry out the reforms initiated by Vatican II.

In Benedict's first homily after being elected (April 20, 2005), addressed to the cardinals who elected him pope, he stated:

> Thus, as I prepare myself for the service that is proper to the Successor of Peter, I also wish to confirm my determination to continue to put the Second Vatican Council into practice, following in the footsteps of my predecessors and in faithful continuity with the 2,000-year tradition of the Church. This very year marks the 40th anniversary of the conclusion of the Council (8 December 1965). As the years have passed, the Conciliar Documents

have lost none of their timeliness; indeed, their teachings are proving particularly relevant to the new situation of the Church and the current globalized society.[1]

Some interpreted Benedict's words as a genuine commitment to the vision of Vatican II. Others interpreted them as a way to preempt those who might call for a Vatican III. In either case, the shadow of Vatican II continues to loom large over the current horizon of the church. The council touched so many areas of church life and practice with documents concerning the church, revelation, religious freedom, ecumenism, non-Christian religions, the Eastern Rite, relations with Jews, missions, education, religious liberty, bishops, laity, liturgy, religious life, priestly training, and communications that little was left untouched.

STATISTICALLY SPEAKING

So what does the post–Vatican II church in America look like? Statistics tell part of the story but, as sociologists know, statistics require interpretation. In 1965, at the end of Vatican II, American Catholics numbered 45 million. In 2005, they numbered 65 million. Much of the recent growth in the Catholic population comes from the immigrant Hispanic community.[2] In 1965, approximately two-thirds of American Catholics attended church weekly. In 2005, that percentage has declined to one-third, with older (pre–Vatican II) Catholics attending more regularly than younger (post–Vatican II) Catholics. In 1965, there were no permanent deacons (since the rite had not yet been reinstituted after centuries of inactivity). In 2005, there are more than 14,000 permanent deacons. In 1965, there were about 550 American parishes without a resident priest. By 2005, that number has risen to more than 3,000, and in many cases multiple parishes are served by one priest. In 1965, America had 58,000 priests. In 2005, America has 42,000. In 1965, 180,000 sisters served the church, while in 2005 there are fewer than 78,000. In 1965, America had 12,000 brothers; it now has 5,000. Today's average age of 70 for sisters and 62 for priests tells even more of the story. Fewer professed sisters and ordained priests, and an average age above or near retirement, signal difficulties for the church at large as well as for religious orders and dioceses. Seminaries operate below capacity and many orders of religious women have only a handful of postulants in formation. Some orders of nuns will survive because they have novices on other continents, such as Africa and India. However, some orders will simply die because they have no replacements for their aging sisters.

The church, of course, should not be exclusively identified with clergy, nuns, and brothers. Nevertheless, these key positions of leadership play an important role in the daily running of the institution. Many of the functions previously carried out exclusively by priests, sisters, and brothers—for example, teaching, ministering to the sick and the poor, supervising youth groups, overseeing parish organizations, and the like—have been assumed by laity, which both engages the laity in responsible work and frees priests for sacramental ministry and sisters and brothers for specialized roles. However, a church that relies too heavily on lay leadership and participation can overly tax volunteers (and professionals) and can risk marginalizing priests, sisters, and brothers.

The laity, often with clerical assistance, has created a number of post–Vatican II organizations. Some of these supported a more democratic or liberal approach to church life, for example, Dignity (for gay and lesbian Catholics), Corpus (for resigned priests), Women's Ordination Conference, Call to Action (a lay group advocating further change), and Voice of the Faithful (founded in response to the sexual abuse crisis). Traditional or conservative groups include the following: Catholics United for Faith, Opus Dei, Women for Family and Faith, and the Fellowship of Catholic Scholars.

JOHN PAUL II'S LENGTHY PAPACY

The papacy of John Paul II closely rivals Vatican II in importance because his reign was so active and so long—almost twenty-seven years— the third longest in history. Elected in October 1978 at the age of fifty-eight, the first non-Italian pope since the sixteenth century, John Paul followed the brief (thirty-three days) papacy of John Paul I and the immediate post–Vatican II papacy of Paul VI, a pope who saw the Second Vatican Council to its conclusion and guided the church through many changes, some of which he disliked but permitted. Paul VI, a career diplomat, made a commitment to implement the changes inaugurated by Vatican II, but personally lacked the charismatic personality of the pope from Poland. John Paul II took to his role immediately and charmed the crowds with his first public words as pope when, from the balcony of the Vatican where he was first introduced with his chosen papal name, the Polish pope spoke in fluent Italian catching and correcting himself when he said he would "speak in your, I mean, our language." An actor in his youth, he possessed a stage presence unparalleled in recent papal history.

John Paul II brought the papacy to the world. He made more than one hundred foreign trips, each time greeted by world leaders, politicians, cardinals, bishops, priests, brothers and sisters, and, most important, enthusiastic crowds of laity who often waited hours just to get a glimpse of the pontiff. He presided over Eucharistic liturgies in celebrated American venues usually reserved for sporting events and rock concerts: Yankee Stadium in New York; Grant Park in Chicago; Camden Yards in Baltimore. And he filled them. His charisma was so palpable that one easily got the sense that he enjoyed being pope. He also had very definite ideas about what direction the church should take. Clearly, he thought that the reforms instituted by Vatican II had in some cases gone too far, too fast.

During the course of his long papacy, John Paul II reigned in experimentation and momentum for change that had swept the church in the decade immediately following the council. He preferred traditional forms of spirituality. Thus, for example, he empowered the conservative movement Opus Dei by favoring it with the unusual status of a personal prelature to the pope, allowing it to circumvent the usual authority structures under bishops and report directly to him. Thus, it could operate its own seminaries and ordain priests. In Latin America, he opposed those who advocated liberation theology and appointed bishops who aligned themselves exclusively with his thinking. He confronted American society, claiming that it (along with other Western societies) promoted a culture of death because of its legalization of abortion and capital punishment, efforts to enact laws permitting physician-assisted suicide, and stem-cell research. He opposed same-sex marriage, as well as partner benefits and rights, arguing that they were both unnatural and undermined the family. At the same time, he championed human rights around the world, spoke on behalf of the poor, and, in most cases, opposed war and capital punishment.

John Paul II also displayed a deep spirituality that provided an example of holiness for ordinary Catholics to follow. Even those who disagreed with some of his policies admired his piety. Equally comfortable with small groups and with huge throngs, he invited bishops, clergy, and laity to pray with him as he celebrated daily Eucharist in his private chapel at the Vatican. Thus, the world knew him as a man of action and contemplation.

John Paul II's style for governing the church could not be characterized by a single phrase. He did not micromanage the Vatican, preferring that Vatican congregations attend to the daily business of the church. At the same time, he set the tone and agenda for the direction of the church and saw to it that his vision was implemented at all levels of church life. In the early years of his papacy, he listened to bishops' concerns and tried to understand geographical and cultural differences in the church. In his later years, unity mattered more than particularism, and he steadfastly upheld a universalism that originated in Rome. The conservative direction of John Paul II's papacy was echoed in a neoconservative movement in American politics and within certain quarters of the church. The growth in numbers and strength of evangelical Protestants in America and their political and social influence during the administration of George W. Bush engendered hope in conservative Catholics that together with evangelicals they could wrest back the social mores of the nation. With a Christian conservative in the White House, they began targeting the judicial and legislative branches in the hope that they could reverse what they perceived to be decades of permissive moral and social laws and judicial rulings.

The political reach of the church extends far beyond the Vatican. Even a cursory examination of political activity in the United States reveals that the church, particularly through its bishops, weighs in on numerous social and political issues. It often assumes the role of moral guardian in American society. Making rules and pronouncements designed to bind Catholics, the church also attempts to influence the larger culture by providing moral norms and guidelines, for example, in its marshaling of a well-organized and funded pro-life effort. In practice, some Catholics ignore some of the norms proposed, and some non-Catholics resent the church for "meddling" in political policy and personal life as it attempts to set the moral compass for American society. But moral concerns represent a central element of the church's mission and teaching.

Illustrative of John Paul's concern that religion have a place in public discourse is the pope's charge to the Honorable Lindy Boggs as Ambassador to the Holy See on December 16, 1997:

> It would truly be a sad thing if the religious and moral convictions upon which the American experiment was founded could now somehow be considered a danger to free society, such that those who would bring these convictions to bear upon your nation's public life would be denied a voice in debating and resolving issues of public policy. The original separation of church and state in the United States was certainly not an effort to ban all religious conviction from the public sphere, a kind of banishment of God from civil society.[3]

No moral issue has divided the Roman Catholic Church in America as much as the controversy about abortion. Even characterizing it as a moral issue is a signal that it should be considered an ethical-moral-religious concern rather than a "social" or "personal" issue, as many political analysts describe it. On this issue the bishops line up staunchly behind the Vatican. Abortion is, at the same time, an intensely private matter and a widely debated public issue. Over this ethical conundrum, private morality and public morality collide in a battle that has divided the nation as well as affected the church. The institutional church, via the hierarchy and the offices of the United States Catholic Conference, attempts to influence public policy; the church joins its protest with the protests of evangelical Christians in an alliance that some call unholy, and individual bishops and priests have made it the focal point of their ministry. The stances on abortion are as divisive as they are decisive. Reacting to the 1973 Supreme Court ruling in *Roe vs. Wade* that legalized abortion, the American bishops issued a "Pastoral Plan for Pro-Life Activities" in 1975 in order to coordinate Catholic efforts to counter the court decision. In 1995, in his encyclical *Evangelium Vitae*, John Paul II stated that the church's teaching on abortion

> is unchanged and unchangeable.... This doctrine is based upon the natural law and upon the written word of God, is transmitted by the Church's Tradition and taught by the ordinary and universal Magisterium. No circumstance, no purpose, no law whatsoever can ever make licit an act which is intrinsically illicit, since it is contrary to the law of God which is written in every human heart, knowable by reason itself, and proclaimed by the Church.[4]

At the pope's summer residence, Castel Gandolfo, Italy, John Paul addressed George W. Bush on July 23, 2001, about the right to life, including a warning about stem-cell research:

> Another area in which political and moral choices have the gravest consequences for the future of civilization concerns the most fundamental of human rights, the right to life itself. Experience is already showing how a tragic coarsening of consciences accompanies the assault on innocent human life in the womb, leading to accommodation and acquiescence in the face of other related evils such as euthanasia, infanticide and, most recently,

proposals for the creation for research purposes of human embryos, destined to destruction in the process.... America can show the world the path to a truly humane future in which man remains the master, not the product, of his technology.[5]

During the presidential election of 2004 some members of the church hierarchy injected themselves into the political process. John Kerry, the Catholic Democratic candidate for president, came under severe criticism for his support for pro-choice legislation. Like some other politicians before him (for example, New York Governor Mario Cuomo and vice-presidential candidate Geraldine Ferraro), Kerry personally opposed abortion as a Catholic but believed as an elected official that he had an obligation to uphold the law of the land. Hoping to dissuade Catholics from voting for him, some bishops openly condemned Kerry.

One example of such action drew both praise and condemnation. On May 1, 2004, in anticipation of the November national elections, Bishop Michael Sheridan of the Diocese of Colorado Springs wrote a pastoral letter to his diocese, "On the Duties of Catholic Politicians and Voters." The letter stated:

> When Catholics are elected to public office or when Catholics go to the polls to vote, they take their consciences with them.... Anyone who professes the Catholic faith with his lips while at the same time publicly supporting legislation or candidates that defy God's law makes a mockery of that faith and belies his identity as a Catholic.
>   There must be no confusion in these matters. Any Catholic politicians who advocate for abortion, for illicit stem cell research or for any form of euthanasia *ipso facto* place themselves outside full communion with the Church and so jeopardize their salvation. Any Catholics who vote for candidates who stand for abortion, illicit stem cell research or euthanasia suffer the same fateful consequences. It is for this reason that these Catholics, whether candidates for office or those who would vote for them, may not receive Holy Communion until they have recanted their positions and been reconciled with God and the Church in the Sacrament of Penance.[6]

Some bishops agreed with him, but the majority resisted about instructing Catholics how to vote and about denying communion to politicians. In response to such initiatives by individual bishops, the United States Catholic Conference of Bishops appointed a task force chaired by Cardinal Theodore McCarrick of Washington, D.C., to study the matter. The committee, after consultation with the Vatican, produced an interim report in June 2004. The document encouraged all Catholics to examine their conscience before receiving the Eucharist. With regard to politicians and bishops it states:

> Given the wide range of circumstances involved in arriving at a prudential judgment on a matter of this seriousness, we recognize that such decisions rest with the individual bishop in accord with the established canonical and pastoral principles. Bishops can legitimately make different judgments on the

most prudent course of pastoral action. Nevertheless, we all share an unequivocal commitment to protect human life and dignity and to preach the Gospel in difficult times.[7]

Thus, the document did not interfere with the right of individual bishops to govern their dioceses. At the same time, not wanting the Eucharist to be an instrument of politics, the document recognized that "[t]he polarizing tendencies of election-year politics can lead to circumstances in which Catholic teaching and sacramental practice can be misused for political ends." The bishops walked a tightrope that balanced the church's moral position against the separation of church and state.

AMERICAN BISHOPS

Bishops, appointed by the pope, know what the Vatican expects of them, namely, leadership and loyalty. Sometimes they find it difficult to exhibit both qualities simultaneously. If they listen to their constituency of American Catholics, they recognize both faithfulness to the core beliefs and dissent from some teachings, particularly those dealing with procreation and sexual ethics. If they enforce Vatican rules, they risk alienating their own Catholics; if they ignore Vatican rules, they risk their appointments. In recent years, the Vatican has been vigilant about appointing bishops who are steadfast loyalists whom Rome can count on to "keep the faith."

In the 1980s, the American bishops addressed a number of sensitive public policy issues. In doing so, they appealed both to the ecclesial community and to the civil community, using arguments constructed from the scriptures and from natural law. By grounding their documents in the Bible, they appealed to revelation that underpins all Christian theology. By employing a natural-law argument, they were being consistent with Catholic theology that has relied on natural-law reasoning since at least the time of Thomas Aquinas. Using natural law, they attempted to influence public opinion and government policy by explicitly using a philosophical argument that did not require that the public (and public officials) share the faith disposition of the bishops. The pastoral letters ("The Challenge of Peace," 1983, and "Economic Justice for All," 1986) addressed all Americans, not simply Catholics, and were not only bold in content but were also the product of an extraordinarily consultative process.

The impetus for the pastorals came from Vatican II and particularly from the *Pastoral Constitution on the Church in the Modern World*, which encouraged the bishops to read the "signs of the times" and to respond to them in ways consistent with the gospel. In the area of war and peace, the bishops' reading of the times indicated the need for a quest for peace, emphasized the unique destructive powers of nuclear weapons, and underlined the need to curb the escalating arms race. The peace pastoral attempted to analyze the moral issues involved in nuclear warfare and to suggest ways to peace. The church has traditionally defended a just-war theory which allows for warfare under certain conditions. Nuclear war, the pastoral argued, no longer fit under this rubric since nuclear weaponry cannot compare with conventional weapons. Nuclear weapons are capable of destroying entire countries in a matter of minutes, and they readily violate all principles of proportionality. It is virtually impossible to contain their destructive effect to exclusively military targets. Thus, "a limited nuclear war" seems an oxymoron. War, in any form, is no longer morally viable in the modern world, according to the bishops. Citing one of Pope John Paul II's homilies, the document asserts the following: "Today, the scale and the horror of modern warfare—whether nuclear or not—makes it totally unacceptable as a means of settling differences between nations. War should belong to the tragic past, to history; it should find no place on humanity's agenda for the future."[8]

To some lay people, this sounded like a utopian dream. To others, it was the only stance possible in an unstable world in which the weaker nations were likely to suffer at the hands of the powerful. The document is careful to distinguish those who are Christian (and Catholic) from those who "do not share the same vision of faith," although the document is ultimately intended for everyone regardless of religious commitment. For Catholics, it is an internal authoritative voice; for other Christians, it is a plea for peace based on Christian scripture; for non-Christian America, it is an appeal to rationality and sanity in a time when all sense of reason could evaporate in the heat of nuclear conflict.

The committee charged with writing the draft of "The Challenge of Peace" included five bishops headed by Cardinal Joseph Bernardin of Chicago. One of the committee members, Cardinal John O'Connor, held the rank of admiral in the Navy and had served as the bishop for U.S. armed forces. Prior to this document, most church statements were the exclusive product of bishops and perhaps theologians. The committee overseeing this pastoral invited comment from a wide range of constituents who reacted to the drafts, including scientists, government officials, the military, politicians, and ordinary Catholics and non-Catholics. The discussions were open and frank. People within and without the church debated the content. Such collaboration was unprecedented. The entire process took thirty months and required the scrutiny of hundreds of potential amendments.

The road to passage was not always a smooth one, however. Some Catholics who were more hawkish disagreed vehemently with the document's position that first-strike nuclear war cannot be justified under any conditions. In general, conservatives inside and outside the church disagreed with the bishops. Those with a more liberal bent agreed with the document, and those within the church were heartened by the support for the document in circles outside the church. Both sides were surprised and encouraged by the consultative process by which the document was conceived.

Despite the widespread consultation in the creation of the pastoral, and the accompanying publicity it received, many Catholics either ignored it or were unwilling to invest themselves in a quest for peace partly because in the 1980s, as American church historian David O'Brien pointed out: "Episcopal and papal authority is weaker, the church has become more voluntary, and few Catholics are familiar with church teaching on social justice and world peace, even fewer with the natural-law tradition on which so many of these teachings are based."[9]

The second major pastoral letter by the American bishops in the 1980s, drafted under the leadership of Archbishop Rembert Weakland of Milwaukee, dealt with the moral questions underlying the American economy. This was an area which appeared to some as beyond not only the competency but the authority of the bishops. After all, bishops are meant to be shepherds and administrators, not economists. The *Los Angeles Times* reported "that the letter will make the anti-nuclear statement seem like a 'Sunday-school picnic' by comparison."[10] But the bishops thought that it was time to address economic structures that favor the wealthy, spend more on weapons than welfare, foster a permanent underclass, and distribute economic advantage unevenly. The pastoral "calls for the establishment of a floor of material well-being on which all can stand" and "calls into question extreme inequalities of income and consumption when so many lack basic necessities."

The pastoral "Economic Justice for All: Catholic Social Teachings and the U.S. Economy" dealt with a wide range of economic issues, principal among them being employment, poverty, food and agriculture, and the U.S. role in a global economy.[11] It was published at a time of high unemployment and accompanying hardships. The bishops argued that individuals have a right to work, and that every effort should be made to provide jobs in both government and the private sector. While the pastoral acknowledges that some of the reasons for unemployment—such as population growth and women increasingly entering the work force—are beyond the control of the government or private industry, it is critical of policies such as overseas manufacturing because of lower labor costs, increased defense spending on high-tech weaponry, and lack of job training programs for the unskilled or underskilled worker. The bishops deplored the fact that one in seven Americans now lives below the poverty line in one of the wealthiest countries on earth. This is particularly reprehensible since many of these are children. They also called for an overhaul of the welfare system, not to diminish the assistance given but to improve it. Theologically, the pastoral favored a preferential option for the poor, a tenet that is biblically grounded, found in Vatican II documents, and stressed in many contemporary liberation theologies.

The American bishops built on an established tradition. They spoke on similar topics in the past (on unemployment in 1930, on the social order in 1940, and the economy as recently as 1970). However, this was the first time that the bishops, as a body, addressed American society as a whole on this topic and received a spirited public reaction. This prophetic action (in the sense of biblical prophets who brought God's message to the attention of a sometimes reluctant people) reflected the fact that American Catholics and their episcopal leaders no longer thought it incumbent on them to support American public policy at all costs. The Catholic community in America was no longer an exclusively immigrant one seeking confirmation of its patriotism. It had toed the mark long enough to gain respectability and had risen above the suspicion that it was beholden to a foreign power in Rome. These pastorals symbolically represent an American Catholic community come of age.

The pastoral on the economy was directed at the American people, Catholic and non-Catholic alike. But it addressed issues of economic justice that affect people all over the world. The economy must serve all people, including the poor. The objectives are noble, as noted in the pastoral: "[S]ociety has a moral obligation to take the necessary steps to ensure that no one among us is hungry, homeless, unemployed, or otherwise denied what is necessary to live with dignity." Some critics of the economic pastoral challenged the church to live by its own words. Joseph A. Pichler, president and chief operating officer of Dillon Companies, wrote the following:

> The Church must witness its commitment to self-determination and voluntarism through its own actions as employer, educator, and minister. Church-related institutions must be a sign to all of managerial behavior that respects the dignity of work and of workers. This entails multiple obligations to: avoid all forms of discrimination based upon race, sex, and other arbitrary dimensions; provide employees with full information regarding their performance and status; recognize the right to collective bargaining; limit restraint placed upon employees to those which are necessary for the effective performance of duties; hear and accommodate the personal needs of employees insofar as they are consistent with the task at hand; and avoid actions that would foreclose the freedom of others to seek self-improvement.[12]

Economists took exception not to the objectives of the pastoral but to the methods it proposed to achieve those objectives. Some argued that the bishops were naive or misdirected in their proposals to achieve admirable objectives. For example, the Nobel Prize winning economist Milton Friedman argued that the means proposed in the pastoral would result in effects diametrically opposed to those the bishops desired.[13] Adhering to the tenets of the pastoral would create more unemployment and weaken the economy. The bishops wanted to invest the government with greater authority over economic matters; Friedman saw little hope that the government could correct what it was largely responsible for creating. He wanted to empower the free-market private sector, not the government. Walter Block, senior economist at the Fraser Institute and director of its Centre for the Study of Economics and Religion, was troubled by the bishops' "lack of comprehension of the free marketplace."[14] Carl Christ, an economist at Johns Hopkins University, commented: "Admirable though the aims of the pastoral letter are, they are sometimes [perhaps deliberately] stated in imprecise terms and hence give little quantitative guidance."[15] Clearly, some among the professional ranks of economists thought that the bishops ventured beyond their area of expertise in writing such a document.

While it may have been true that the bishops were beyond their competency as far as economic theory was concerned, they had not exceeded their moral authority. The gospel is clear in its call for justice and its mandate to care for the poor. In lobbying the American people in such a direct and public manner, the bishops were fulfilling their role as prophetic voices. The details of the letter may be subject to legitimate debate and criticism, but the rationale for such a document is unquestionable in Catholic theology.

THE SADDEST CHAPTER IN THE CHURCH'S HISTORY

Although another chapter in this volume will address in detail the sexual abuse crisis in the church, it is important to note it here since, clearly, it comprises a significant chapter in the church's post–Vatican II history. No one knows for certain exactly when sexual abuse by priests began, but everyone knows that it came to light in the 1990s. The abuse had been going on for decades, and the cover-up by bishops, equally as long. As a result of this scandal the Roman Catholic Church in America suffered the most painful, disturbing, and publicly embarrassing chapter in its history. Among the most notorious of cases were those of John Geoghan and Joseph Shanley, in Boston; Rudy Kos, in Dallas; James Porter, in Fall River; and Gilbert Gauthier, in Lafayette. But the abuse touched virtually every diocese in America to some degree. Many of the cases exhibited similar characteristics: an abuser who was himself abused by a priest, multiple victims over many years, negligent supervision, unsuccessful therapy, legal wrangling, the press's role in exposing the case, prison sentences, dismissal from active ministry or from the priesthood itself, and lawsuits against dioceses with sometimes devastating financial consequences. While no two cases are identical, most exemplify the complexity, the idiocy, and the tragedy of clerical sexual abuse and the institutional church's mishandling of cases.

Unchecked power of the clergy also contributed to the sexual abuse crisis. Because parishioners revere the role of priest, too many victims were intimidated, as well as abused, preventing them from coming forward. To make matters worse, instead of acting in a pastorally sensitive manner, some bishops relied mostly upon lawyers for advice when dealing with victims, further exacerbating their pain and disenfranchisement. So both clergy and bishops abused their power by acting in authoritarian ways. In an attempt to protect themselves and the institution, Rome and the bishops tried to neutralize the sexual abuse crisis through a series of mechanisms that deflected admission of and responsibility for their malfeasance.

Many observers believed that John Paul II, by this time visibly affected by the effects of Parkinson's disease, did not react quickly enough to the crisis in the American church. The slow reaction from Rome may have been a result of the pope's illness, but it also may have been caused by Rome's underestimation of the widespread nature of the abuse, its belief that the scandal was created by a hostile press or that self-absorbed Americans had exaggerated conditions in their church. Whatever the reasons for not acting swiftly, the growing cry from Boston Catholics (and others) for the resignation of Cardinal Bernard Law, a close confidant of the pope, brought the crisis to papal attention. Cardinal Law met with the pope and offered his resignation, but the pope declined to accept it, preferring that the cardinal remain in office so that he could address and correct the problems in his archdiocese. However, Boston Catholics and a number of the priests from the Archdiocese of Boston completely lost confidence in Cardinal Law to the degree that it became difficult for him to appear in public without protests. Finally, he and the pope recognized that his leadership was no longer viable, prompting the pope to accept Cardinal Law's resignation on December 13, 2002. In July 2003, his successor, Bishop Sean O'Malley, a Franciscan with a record for cleaning up abuse scandals in the Dioceses of Fall River, Massachusetts, and Palm Beach, Florida, became archbishop of Boston. He met with abuse victims, sold diocesan property, and settled outstanding lawsuits. But the damage had been done, and the Archdiocese of Boston suffered financially and morally as the abuse crisis took its toll, eroding the morale of priests and the trust of the laity.

Boston may have been the eye of media attention, but it was hardly the only place to be devastated by the abuse. Three dioceses (Portland, Oregon; Tucson, Arizona; and Spokane, Washington) filed for bankruptcy. Almost every diocese in the nation faced charges of sexual abuse by priests and paid hundreds of millions of dollars in claims. Bishop Tod Brown of the Diocese of Orange, California, made the largest payout ($120 million), believing that victims deserved an apology from the church that had wronged them and just compensation without a protracted legal battle that served neither the victims nor the church well. Cardinal Roger Mahoney of Los Angeles, facing more than 500 allegations, employed numerous legal maneuvers to protect the church's privileged internal communications.

The American bishops, under the leadership of the U.S. Conference of Bishops' Wilton Gregory, were forced to do a great deal of soul-searching, damage control, and apologizing. They devoted their annual meetings in Washington in November 2002 and in Dallas in June 2003 to the crisis, creating detailed policies for dioceses to follow. The bishops established a distinguished panel to oversee the church's compliance with sexual abuse policies. Bishop Gregory appointed former Oklahoma Governor Frank Keating to head the oversight commission. Keating angered many bishops when he openly criticized them for covering up their negligence. The backlash among bishops to Keating's style of leadership led to his stepping down.

The consequences of the abuse scandal defy summarization. It will take years, if not decades, for the church to recover. Horrified, the laity lost trust in the church as an institution, in individual priests and the priesthood, and in the bishops whom they blamed for lack of oversight and action. Priests lost the respect of their people, had to endure harsh (and in some cases unfair) criticism, and suffered a sharp decline in morale. Bishops became the targets of anger from laity and priests, the wider public, and the press. Tragically, the situation resembled Shakespeare's *Romeo and Juliet* in which "all are punished."

RESPECTING BUT NOT ALWAYS FOLLOWING
THE CHURCH

In the post–Vatican II era, American Catholics continued to profess that they love their church, but they heed its teachings selectively. For numerous reasons they think and act independently. Much has to do with American society and culture, to which Catholics contribute and by which they are affected. Americans are democratic; Catholicism is not. Americans often follow—or even set—trends. Seldom has the church been accused of being trendy. Americans live in a pluralistic society that values tolerance for many views and practices, whereas the church holds moral and dogmatic positions that do not abide tolerance in its beliefs or practices. Americans live in an affluent, developed, and materialistic country. The church promulgates the gospel mandate to identify with the poor. Americans prize their independence. The church "takes care of" its children. Often, Americans are asked to compete and win at work. The church asks them to form a community of forgiveness and compassion. Americans demand reasonable answers to difficult questions from their political leaders. The church asks them to accept some things on faith alone or on the sole basis of the authority vested in the church.

Several observers of the church have opined that this distancing from Vatican control had its origins in the reaction to Paul VI's 1969 encyclical *Humanae Vitae*, prohibiting, under pain of sin, Catholics from practicing artificial birth control. Catholics might like or dislike liturgical changes, the reintroduction of the permanent diaconate, and contemporary musical instruments instead of the classical organ, and they might or might not be aware of the nuances of theological disputes, but none of these struck at the core of family and economic life the way that banning artificial birth control did. It did not help when American Catholics (and others, worldwide) learned that Paul VI had issued his encyclical against the advice of a committee he had established to study the issue. Not permitting Catholics to limit the size of their families by the use of readily available and safe artificial birth control in an economy that required ever increasing resources to feed, clothe, and educate a child, loosed the ties that bind for the vast majority of the faithful. They refused to be faithful on this issue. Instead, they ignored the teaching against artificial birth control yet continued to practice the faith. Many went through heart-wrenching pangs of conscience, not wanting to disobey their church but at the same time not willing to have more children whom they could not afford to raise with sufficient opportunities to succeed in the world. Some tried the church-approved natural family planning method but found it cumbersome and sometimes unreliable. Some still favor this method, but they represent a small minority of American Catholics.

Whether or not the birth control teaching was the watershed event that signaled profound disagreement with their church, since that time many American Catholics (on a number of issues, a majority) have elected to think and act contrary to numerous church teachings. Thus, they procure abortions at about the same rate as other Americans; they believe that divorced and remarried Catholics should be permitted to receive the Eucharist without going through the legal complexities of what many perceive to be an intrusive process; they favor ordaining women as priests; they are tolerant of same-sex relationships; and they favor capital punishment for the worst criminals. In other words, they remain Catholic but they do not practice their Catholicism on Rome's terms.

CURRENT ISSUES AND CHALLENGES

At the beginning of the twenty-first century, the Roman Catholic Church in America faces a number of challenges. The greatest of these is the quest for an adequate number of clergy. Not confined to the United States, this problem became part of the focus of the October 2005 international synod on the Eucharist convened by Benedict XVI in Rome, in which 256 bishops from 118 countries participated. During the course of the synod, bishops discussed the shortage of priests in various parts of the world. While the shortage has caused concern in the United States, it is not nearly as acute as in some other countries. For example, Bishop Lorenzo Voltolini Esti of Honduras reported that his diocese has only one priest for every 16,000 Catholics.[16] The shortage leads to spiritual and sacramental concerns. The gift of the Eucharist remains central to Catholic spiritual life. In order to have the Eucharist, the church needs priests who celebrate mass and consecrate the Eucharistic bread and wine for Catholics to receive—no priests, no Eucharist. The synod discussed the critical shortage of priests with some bishops, suggesting that the church reexamine whether the policy requiring priests to remain celibate discourages vocations and contributes to the shortage. However, in the end, the synod, under the direction of Benedict XVI, reaffirmed the celibacy requirement and recommended that the church redouble its recruitment efforts to fill the clerical ranks. Such a tactic would suggest that the vocations shortage may only be a temporary condition and that, guided by prayer and focused recruitment efforts, the ranks of the priesthood will swell again. Of course, only time will tell whether this strategy succeeds. However, if it does not bring men in far greater numbers into the priesthood, the church faces an increased hardship for priests who already show signs of overwork, and the Eucharist in the context of the liturgy will be less available to Catholics.

A second issue is the changing face of the American church, with Latino/Latina and Asian American Catholic populations increasing in number who require services in their native languages. Increasingly, in many regions in America, priests must be bilingual to serve their parishioners. In Southern California, for example, the church requires virtually all priests to speak Spanish as well as English. Estimates of the percentage of Hispanic Catholics in the United States vary, but no one disputes that this population is growing faster than the traditional Anglo population.[17] According to U.S. census figures, from 1990 to 2003 the Hispanic population grew at a rate of 78 percent (from 22.3 million to 39.9 million), while the non-Hispanic population grew at a rate of 11 percent (from 226.4 million to 250.9 million). While Hispanic Americans traditionally have been Catholic, that affiliation can no longer be guaranteed, as a sizable portion elect to join either mainline Protestant churches, or, more commonly, evangelical churches. To what degree Hispanic Catholics desire and are able to assimilate into American Catholic patterns remains to be seen. Some Hispanic Catholics want the church to appropriate the Latino language and habits; others prefer to learn the language and customs of the established community.

The role of women in the church presents a third challenge for Catholicism in America. This issue perhaps stirs more passion in America than in some other countries where the roles and rights of women are not as prominent. However, in the United States, where women have been voting for nearly a century, where they serve prominently in national political office, the military, the academy, and the corporate world, to name a few of the roles they have regularly assumed, precluding service in the diaconate and priesthood continues to concern a significant portion of Catholics, both men and women. John Paul II spoke forcefully and quite definitively on theological grounds about the ineligibility of women to serve in these capacities, but the issue remains a concern, increasingly so as the priest shortage worsens.

However, despite these and other challenges, American Catholics remain faithful to the central beliefs of the church. In the first half of the nineteenth century, Alexis de Tocqueville wrote in *Democracy in America*: "The [people] of our days are naturally little disposed to believe; but as soon as they have any religion, they immediately find in themselves a latent instinct that urges them unconsciously towards Catholicism. Many of the doctrines and practices of the Roman Catholic Church astonish them, but they feel a secret admiration for its discipline, and its great unity attracts them."[18] Not only has its unity attracted them, it has maintained their interest. American Catholics seem to like the universal character of the church while at the same time objecting to certain practices and beliefs that underlie this unity. Most do not envy their Protestant brothers and sisters, and they do not wish to emulate the divisions that Protestant Christianity displays. Besides, declaring independence from Rome would not resolve all of the issues that differentiate American Catholics from each other. There would still be those who favor and those who oppose women priests and noncelibate clergy, and those who prefer local autonomy as opposed to universal compliance and more rules as opposed to fewer rules.

The combination of Vatican II and the cultural revolution in the 1960s in America left Catholics reeling. Perhaps the American canonist James Provost is correct when he reflects that it will take a long time for the church to absorb Vatican II in its entirety. But his prediction that "[w]e must anticipate a period—perhaps a century or two—of unsettled times"[19] is not very comforting to Americans who are accustomed to change but fear anarchy. Nevertheless, it may take much longer than forty years for the church to implement Vatican II wisely. Or, since the world evolves so quickly, it may require a Vatican council every fifty years simply for the church to keep up with cultural and social change.

But while one can confidently predict what the hierarchy of the church will look like in the national and international arena in the near future, the local leadership, particularly at the level of the parish, is changing rapidly. Pastoral ministry no longer equals clerical ministry. The male and female lay professional presence has changed the face of institutional Catholicism. To some degree, lay women replace the sisters who toiled before them in various ministries—sisters whose numbers have shrunk so that even a consolidation of orders (an unlikely event) or a narrower focus of ministry will not result in a presence and influence that even approach that of forty years ago.

Of course, the laity who take up the mantle of professionally caring for the church, are themselves of all different stripes—some more doctrinally rigid, some wishing to revive the subculture of a previous era, some maneuvering for the day when they can operate without clerical "interference," some eschewing all politics in the church, all wondering what the future will bring and praying that the Holy Spirit will lead them in the right direction. Increasingly, the laity is taking responsibility within the church. In 1950, 17,000 lay people worked full-time for the church; by 2005, that number grew to 180,000. Lay influence grows daily, and it is bound to have a long-term impact.

American Catholics are diverse in their beliefs, practices, and levels of affiliation, loyalty, and identification with the church. As journalist Paul Wilkes accurately observed: "Indeed, there is more room in Catholicism than a person might imagine. From Bible-quoting fundamentalist Catholics to Catholics who have found a spirituality rooted in Buddhist meditation, from Catholics who celebrate the mass in an uproarious charismatic celebration to those who prefer the quiet dignity of a Tridentine mass, the church is broad enough for all."[20]

In many ways diversity serves the church well. And there is no sign that a homogenous community is on the horizon. The followers of Jesus in the Roman Catholic Church reflect the ways in which he himself served. The director of a soup kitchen is doing Jesus's work of feeding the hungry. The hospice volunteer or nurse is comforting the dying as Jesus would have them do. The university theologian follows Jesus's example as a teacher. The protester against capital punishment or abortion emulates Jesus's cries against injustice and immorality. The inspiring preacher brings Jesus's parables and narratives to life for a new generation. The religious education teacher suffers the little children to come unto her as Jesus instructed his disciples to allow him to do. The retreat director uncovers a path to God as Jesus did for those willing to listen to him. The liturgical scripture reader proclaims the Word of the Lord. The finance committee chairperson ensures that the resources to do Jesus's work are sufficient to the task. The parish social life committee members help to create a community that knows each other by name instead of a group of anonymous churchgoers. The youth minister nurtures tomorrow's leaders with respect for their presence in the church today. The pastor spends himself so that others may know the gospel and encounter the living God. The rich talents of many in this diverse community enable the church to serve a wide variety of needs and will enable it to continue to flourish in the twenty-first century.

NOTES

1. http://www.vatican.va/holy_father/benedict_xvi/messages/pont-messages/2005/documents/hf_ben-xvi_mes_20050420_missa-pro-ecclesia_en.html, accessed October 15, 2005.

2. An accurate account of the Catholic Hispanic population is notoriously difficult to acquire. See Paul Perl, Jennifer Z. Greeley, and Mark M. Gray, "How Many Hispanics Are Catholic? A Review of Survey Data and Methodology" (2004), The Center for Applied Research in the Apostolate, http://cara.georgetown.edu/Hispanic%Catholics.pdf, accessed September 2, 2005. First-generation Hispanics tend to be Catholic in greater number (nearly 90 percent) than subsequent generations, with third-generation Hispanics' identification with Catholicism being as low as 62 percent in some surveys.

3. http://www.vatican.va/holy_fatter/john_paul_ii/speeches/1997/december/docments/hf_jp-ii_spe_19971216_ambassadoe-usa_en.html, accessed August 8, 2005.

4. http://www.vatican.va/edpcs/ENG0141/INDEX.HTM, accessed June 4, 2005.

5. http://www.vatican.va/holy_father/john_paul_ii/speeches/2001/documents/hf_jp-ii_spe_20010723_president-bush_en.html, accessed November 16, 2005.

6. http://www.diocs.org/CPC/Corner/pastoralletters_view.cfm?year=2004&month=May, accessed June 6, 2005.

7. http://www.usccb.org/bishops/catholicsinpoliticallife.shtml, accessed July 2, 2005.

8. *The Challenge of Peace: God's Promise and Our Response* (Washington, DC: United States Catholic Conference, 1983), par. 219.

9. David J. O'Brien, "American Catholics and American Society," in Philip J. Murnion, ed., *Catholics and Nuclear War: A Commentary on the Challenge of Peace, the U.S. Catholic Bishops' Pastoral Letter on War and Peace* (New York: Crossroad, 1983), 26.

10. Quoted in John W. Houck and Oliver T. Williams, eds., *Catholic Social Teaching and the U.S. Economy: Working Papers for a Bishops' Pastoral* (Washington, DC: University Press of America. 1984), 4.

11. See Douglas Rasmussen and James Sterba, *The Catholic Bishops and the Economy: A Debate* (New Brunswick, NJ: Transaction Books, 1987); Walter Block, *The U.S. Bishops and Their Critics: An Economic and Ethical Perspective* (Vancouver, BC: Fraser Institute, 1986); and Houck and Williams.

12. Joseph A. Pichler, "Capitalism and Employment: A Policy Perspective," in Houck and Williams, eds., 67. For a study of the church's relationship to unions within its own organizations, including schools, hospitals, and other church agencies, see Patrick J. Sullivan, *U.S. Catholic Institutions and Labor Unions, 1960–1980* (Lanham, MD: University Press of America, 1985).

13. Milton Friedman, "Good Ends, Bad Means," in *The Catholic Challenge to the American Economy*, ed. Thomas M. Gannon (New York: Macmillan, 1987), 99–106.

14. Block, 11.

15. Carl Christ, "Unemployment and Macroeconomics," in Gannon, ed., 117.

16. See Ina Fisher, "Uninvited Guest Turns Up at a Catholic Synod: Issue of Married Priests," *New York Times*, October 7, 2005.

17. See Perl, Greeley, and Gray.

18. Alexis de Tocqueville, *Democracy in America*, vol. 2, book 1, chap. 6 (New York: Vintage, 1945), 30.

19. James Provost, "The Church in a Post-Council Era of Transition," *Origins* 26, 42 (April 10, 1997): 691–95.

20. Paul Wilkes, *The Good Enough Catholic: A Guide for the Perplexed* (New York: Ballentine, 1996), xx.

SUGGESTIONS FOR FURTHER READING

Froehle, Bryan T., and Mary L. Gautier. *Catholicism USA: A Portrait of the Catholic Church in the United States.* Maryknoll, NY: Orbis, 2000.

Gillis, Chester, ed. *The Political Papacy: John Paul II, Benedict XVI, and Their Influence.* Boulder, CO: Paradigm Press, 2006.

Gillis, Chester. *Roman Catholicism in America.* New York: Columbia University Press, 1999.

Steinfels, Peter. *A People Adrift: The Crisis of the Roman Catholic Church in America.* New York: Simon & Schuster, 2003.

CHAPTER 3

Roman Catholicism after the Sex Scandals

Paul Lakeland

T he scandal of clerical sex abuse of minors that broke upon the Catholic church at the beginning of 2002 was the result of events that had been taking place for at least three previous decades, perhaps much longer. In their different ways, the press, the legal profession, Catholic lay persons, and the American public were informed about and became involved in unprecedented fashion in the inner working of the clerical establishment. For Catholics themselves, the scandal of sex abuse led to a new awareness of deeply dysfunctional elements in the church. The result has been a crisis in the church, perhaps the most significant crisis ever to hit the American Catholic church, and arguably the biggest crisis for Catholics around the world since the days of the Protestant Reformation. This crisis continues today, as church leaders, theologians, and ordinary Catholics try to come to terms with its implications for ecclesial structures, for patterns of ministry, and even for the continued long-term viability of the church itself as a major Christian denomination in American life. In order to explain a phenomenon of this magnitude, it will be necessary to go back a little into the recent past to uncover the proximate origins of the scandal, to recount the major events of the year in which the scandal first came to public awareness, to examine what the church has done and tried to do to address the scandal, and to probe some of the major implications for American Catholics.

BACKGROUND TO THE SCANDAL

It is impossible to determine when clerical sex abuse of minors became a problem in the Catholic church. There are two principal factors that make such a determination difficult, both stemming from the inevitably secretive nature of abusive behavior. The first is that there are no records, obviously, beyond criminal records or diocesan files and these do not stretch back very far. The information that has come to light from so many victims and their families over the past few years of its nature only goes back at most to the 1950s and usually only to the 1960s and 1970s. Many of the accused clergy are dead or old, as are many of the oldest of the abused. Memory cannot carry us much further back than fifty years ago. We can, in consequence, only speculate about the incidence of sexual abuse before the middle of the twentieth century.

The second complicating factor is the changing character both of the perception of what constitutes sexual abuse and of the attitudes of Catholic lay people to their rights and responsibilities when incidences of abusive behavior come to their knowledge. Although rape is always rape, what were objectively less serious offences in past decades were often dismissed as inappropriate but harmless. And although abuse is always abuse, in days gone by, the typical Catholic awe of the clergy meant that ordinary lay persons were unwilling, even fearful, to bring abuse to the attention of the ecclesiastical establishment, still less before the legal system. So, moving the clergy on, buying silence, or using victims' shame to encourage silence were more commonly the ways in which the more egregious forms of abuse were handled, and supposedly minor offences of touching, fondling, and so on were not taken seriously, perhaps not even reported at all. Shame, in particular, may have meant that many instances of more serious forms of abuse also went unreported, and that failure to report contributes to the difficulty of estimating the length and the scope of the problem.

It is therefore entirely possible to argue reasonably plausibly that human nature doesn't change and that we can extrapolate from what we know about the second half of the twentieth century to conclude that this kind of abusive behavior is something we have had as long as the Catholic clergy and Catholic youth have been thrown together—in other words, always. But it is equally possible to construct a view that links the incidences of sexual abuse that have recently come to light to specific cultural forces or trends in the world of the very recent past and so to argue that before these trends came to light, abuse was probably much less of a problem. The first argument could obviously be used by those wishing to pin abuse to clerical celibacy, the second by those who want to explain it as a product of twentieth-century sexual permissiveness. Neither has much hope of ever making the case because the facts of the matter are largely hidden.

One of the most important factors in explaining so much about the sex abuse scandal is the privileged and unusual position of Catholic priests in the lives of working-class Catholics in the mid-twentieth century. As is well-known, the mid-century was the high point of Catholic expansion in America. All across the country, but most especially in the Northeast and in the major cities of the industrial Midwest, Catholic parishes and schools flourished, staffed by a plentiful supply of priests and religious sisters. Each parish provided for its members an entire framework for both religious and social life. A typical urban Catholic in 1950 identified the part of the city she or he lived in by naming the parish, not the neighborhood or even suburb. Dances, sports leagues, youth clubs, men's and women's charitable organizations, educational opportunities, devotional groups of all kinds—all proliferated at the parochial level. In consequence, a Catholic need never and frequently never did step outside the structures of the church for much other than secular employment. The church provided everything else, and the good Catholic participated. In some ways this culture reflected patterns from the old Catholic world in Europe, although in others it was a brilliant re-creation of that world for the express purpose of maintaining Catholic life in what was, or seemed to be, so obviously a Protestant society.

In the culture that dominated Catholicism really until the Second Vatican Council (1962–1965), the priest was king, or, more accurately, the pastor was king.[1] Every urban parish was run by a pastor who had been appointed by the bishop but who, once appointed, ruled (and that is the correct word) with little or no reference to higher authority. He would have a staff of one or two or more assistant priests and a convent of nuns who took principal responsibility for the education of children in the parochial school, for the maintenance of a clean church, and undoubtedly for many valuable pastoral services to the women of the parish, though in an entirely informal capacity. But the pastor was in charge of everything. Nothing happened in the parish that he was not at least nominally leading. From preaching at the High Mass late on a Sunday morning to counting the money taken in the collection baskets, from decisions about the conduct of the school to decisions about where to get a deal on repaving the playground or the parking lot, he was at the center of everything. Whether personally generous or mean-spirited, intelligent or ignorant, devout or cynical, he was a true prince-bishop in miniature.

One of the little team of assistant priests would typically be a newly minted clergyman, fresh from the seminary. Ordained at twenty-three, he might have been in minor and major seminary since the age of fourteen. As low priest on the totem pole in the parish, he was very much an apprentice, though often thrown in at the deep end to sink or swim. He in all probability knew very little about the challenges that pastoral responsibilities might bring to him, but doubtless he was ready to learn. Unlike today, he might expect quite a long term as an assistant with no final assurance that he would become pastor one day of his own parish and its people. In those days of plentiful clergy, the less talented among them—however talent was measured—might expect to serve thirty or more years in the role of assistant at a series of parishes around the diocese and might never attain the coveted role of pastor. He could also reliably expect that his special responsibilities in the parish would be those the others did not especially covet. He was young, so he could be in charge of the youth group or the Boy Scouts. He was full of energy, so he could get up in the middle of the night to attend a sick bed. He was young, so he could teach catechism in the parochial school. He was junior, so he could have the least well-attended mass at the least desirable time on Sunday. Since in those days Catholics were required to fast from midnight on the day

before receiving Holy Communion, he might expect more than his fair
share of the late masses, while the pastor tucked into eggs and bacon in
the rectory, served by the housekeeper.[2]

However easy it might be to caricature this clerical world, now largely a
thing of the past, there is no doubt that it made for a very stable world in
which the clergy were highly respected, perhaps the most highly respected,
members of the Catholic community. While this respect was largely, no
doubt, well-deserved and led to all kinds of desirable outcomes for the
Catholic laity, the absolute trust that the laity placed in their priests had its
potential shadow side. Trust was essential if you were going to confess
your darkest secrets or your most shameful little peccadilloes to someone
who sat on the other side of the screen in the confessional but who
undoubtedly knew who you were. But such a level of trust could and
would sometimes turn out to be devastating when the priest was untrust-
worthy. The very possibility of sex abuse on the scale and of the kind that
has been uncovered in the church between 1950 and 1990 depended on
exactly the level of trust that was necessary for the efficient functioning of
the clergy/laity relationship in the Catholic church.

Subsequent investigations have shown that in this world as I have
described it, 3 or 4 percent of the clergy were occasionally, if not frequently, engaged in the sexual abuse of children under their charge.[3]
Some of this happened in boarding schools or orphanages, but most commonly it occurred somehow in rectories and in the children's homes, on
parish property or in motel rooms on trips with Father. Some of it began
as little more than a hug or a kiss, but mostly it did not stop there. Fondling led sometimes to mutual masturbation, oral sex, viewing of porno-
graphic images, and even rape. Almost all of it was accompanied by
injunctions to silence. Here the power of the priest was at its greatest, not
only abusing the child but also doing it in the context of a relationship of
trust that enabled the offender to manipulate the victim into terrified or
shamed silence. Many of the victims were pre-pubescent children. Some of
the victims were female. But the clear majority of the victims were adoles-
cent boys. Some were abused once, some multiple times. Some abusers
did so only once; others were serial predators of the worst kind. All of this
behavior was entirely reprehensible, but no doubt some of it was objectively more serious, some less so. And the power of the priesthood was
employed to ends that made a mockery of the church itself and irreversibly
damaged the lives of so many children.

How did all this happen? Didn't people know what was going on?
Didn't abused children at least sometimes inform their parents of what
had happened? The evidence uncovered in the last few years suggests that
the answers here are "yes, people did sometimes know" and "yes, children
sometimes did speak out." But also, no one did enough, no one spoke
out enough, no one took any of this with the seriousness that the situation justified. Shame not only kept children quiet much of the time, but
also made parents reluctant to approach the pastor or, still worse, the
bishop. Expediency and "fear of scandal" often made pastors and particularly bishops act to hide the problem by reassigning offending priests to

other parishes where, all too frequently, they became repeat offenders and were reassigned once again. Some were shipped off for treatment, quickly rehabilitated or "cured" and returned to work. Doubtless, people generally were not as aware thirty or forty years ago of the lasting effects of even mild sexual abuse on minors, but it is hard to see that as much of an excuse for the practice of enabling abusers that is the only way one can describe the worst examples of episcopal mismanagement.

THE YEAR THE SCANDAL BROKE: 2002[4]

One evening in January 2002, twenty-five people met at St. John the Evangelist Church in Wellesley, Massachusetts, to consider the breaking stories of sex abuse whose epicenter seemed to be the Archdiocese of Boston. The organization they formed that day, Voice of the Faithful (VOTF),[5] drew more than 4,000 people to its first convention in July that same year, and about one year later could claim some 25,000 members across the Catholic world. The rapid growth of the young movement, certainly unparalleled in the Catholic church and notable in any context, testified to the deep well of anger and hurt that lay people had come to feel about the often shameful treatment of the victims of abuse and the usually tepid response, at best, of bishops called on to address the whole range of problems which the sex abuse scandal was bringing out into the open.

The scale of the sex abuse problem among Catholic clergy began to filter into the consciousness of the lay faithful, at least in the Northeast, as early as 1992 when the notorious ex-priest and serial predator James Porter was sentenced to 18–20 years on the 41 counts to which he pleaded guilty in New Bedford, Massachusetts. Over a six-year period he had raped, sodomized, or otherwise abused countless children, male and female. While the offences took place in the neighboring diocese of Fall River, in response to heightened concerns the Archdiocese of Boston developed a dramatically revised pastoral plan the following year to deal with accusations of abuse. It included adding two lay people to the review board, and the victims were to be offered psychological and spiritual counseling. A priest and a nun were named as individuals to whom victims could turn to initiate the process of bringing a complaint before the diocesan tribunal, a step that occasioned some criticism of Cardinal Bernard Law for keeping at least the early stages of any process entirely within ecclesiastical circles. But nevertheless there was some agreement that the procedure was a great improvement on what had preceded it.

Even before the 1990s, the American bishops had been aware of the problem of sex abuse among clergy and church workers. From 1982 onwards, especially after the well-publicized case of Fr. Gilbert Gauthe in Louisiana, the United States Catholic Conference (USCC) had begun to consider legal and pastoral issues connected to sex abuse accusations. In 1985 two priests, Michael Peterson, president of the St. Luke Institute, and Thomas Doyle, canon lawyer on the staff of the Apostolic Nunciature, submitted a lengthy report written on their own initiative, titled *The*

*Problem of Sexual Molestation by Roman Catholic Clergy: Meeting the Prob-
lem in a Comprehensive and Responsible Manner.*[6] This document essentially laid out what would happen to the reputation of the church if
serious steps were not taken to address the problem. Although it is probably accurate to say that the report was not given the attention it
deserved, some steps were taken and the so-called "Five Principles"
became the cornerstone of the Conference's policies. These principles
addressed victims' rights (and those of the accused) and spoke to a new
concern for the scope and seriousness of the problem. They were the basis
for the 1993 restructuring in the Archdiocese of Boston. But neither they
nor the many other discussions and debates that the Catholic bishops had
over the remainder of the decade seem to have communicated much of
a sense of urgency. The sex abuse problems remained the ticking time-
bomb to which the Peterson-Doyle report had tried to alert the bishops
in 1985.

In January 2002 the people of Boston were sufficiently alarmed by the
growing awareness of the problem of sex abuse that VOTF took off. The
genesis of the organization and its continued identity to this day are
closely tied to the problem of sex abuse. Its well-publicized "pillars"
include support for victims, support for priests of integrity, and "structural
change" in the church, by which it means attention to structures of communication and an end to the culture of clericalism which it identifies as a
primary enabler of abusing clergy. Although there are many sympathizers
among the clergy, the organization is almost entirely lay, led mostly by
the "ordinary faithful" of Catholic parishes, with a sprinkling of management professors and other academics from Boston area schools. It includes
no bishops among its members and has very few if any academic theologians in its leadership ranks. Despite occasional charges of being a front
organization for disaffected liberals with more radical agendas to do with
an end to clerical celibacy or even priestly ordination for women, VOTF
has kept its head and its dignity as a truly grass-roots cleansing operation.
Its ranks include a wide variety of Catholics from every perspective in the
church except the far right. What united them in the first place and keeps
them together today is their concern for a church where sex abuse will be
much less likely than it was in the past, and where ecclesial patterns of
control do not place the needs of victims in the lowest place on the list of
priorities.

On January 10, 2002, the *Boston Globe* reported Cardinal Law's
apology for the 1984 reassignment of Fr. John Geoghan to a diocesan parish. Geoghan's was one of the most well-publicized cases of a serial predator. He, it turned out, had been moved frequently, often after relatively
brief periods. Accusations of abuse followed him from parish to parish,
from his earliest days as a young priest even into his days of retirement.
But in January 2002, for all the horror at Geoghan's behavior and the
harm he caused, the spotlight was turned more on the role the church
had played in ignoring and even facilitating Geoghan's career of abuse.
The attorney for all 118 victims bringing suit against Geoghan remarked
that he had been dealing with the case since 1994, and Cardinal Law

should surely have known before January 2002 that something was wrong. Law issued a handsome apology, saying that "in retrospect" he regretted decisions made earlier, though at the time he had thought they were the right decisions. He announced a further tightening of rules in the archdiocese, and he added that to his knowledge at this time, there was no priest active in the archdiocese who was "guilty of sexually abusing a minor." This last remark was going to come back to haunt him, as throughout the months to come the *Globe* revealed story after story of priest after priest. Either Law was lying, people came to think, or he was asleep on the job. In either case, the Catholics of the archdiocese thought in increasingly large numbers that he had to go. By the end of that turbulent year, in December, Pope John Paul II accepted his resignation. He retired to the obscurity of a convent in Maryland, only to be appointed in 2004 to a prestigious but largely honorary position in Rome.

The story of the sex abuse scandal went on beyond 2002 and continues today. It is well-documented, most especially in the incomparable Web archive of the *Boston Globe*, "Spotlight Investigation: Abuse in the Catholic Church." But in that single year most of the issues emerged, most of the implications began to filter through to various sectors of the church. Lay people were outraged. The American bishops met in a crisis session in Dallas in July, producing their Charter for the Protection of Young People and establishing a National Lay Commission. The Vatican responded by summoning the American cardinals to Rome for a meeting with the pope and other senior leaders. Various Vatican representatives, official and unofficial, spoke of how overblown was the American response to the scandal. Books began to appear, analyzing the events and their implications. Awareness of the problems became much more widespread as victims came forward across the country and diocese after diocese entered into negotiations with victims and their attorneys, often resulting in huge financial settlements. These brought their own set of problems, as bishops wondered how to pay them and ordinary Catholics began to rein in their generosity to dioceses, feeling that their financial support should not be used to pay for a scandal that was of the clergy's own making. But was it, in fact, as simple as that? Could the scandal be explained simply in terms of abusing priests and bishops who were blind to the scope and the nature of their crimes?

THE UNDERLYING ISSUES

The short and even slick response to the questions at the end of the previous paragraph is to say that while the scandal was mostly of clerical making and episcopal enabling, the crisis that emerged went much further and continues to reverberate deep within the foundations of Catholic polity. There is much truth in this assessment. Certainly, the scandal of sex abuse, horrible and tragic as it has been, is but the "presenting problem" for a whole set of deeper issues that speaks to central features of the life of the Catholic church. Sex abuse did not just "happen." Of course, it happens, and the incidence of sex abuse on the part of Catholic clergy is below that in the male population of America as a whole. Four percent is not a large figure, but it is a significant number of people when we remember that these are the ones in whom the church placed the most trust. Attention almost inevitably shifts, then, from the actual abuse and the abusers to an effort to determine which structures failed. After all, the second most important task, after concern for the victims themselves, is to prevent further instances of abuse.

One of the striking features of the response to the scandals was the way in which the outrage cut across the usual ideological differences among Catholics. Representatives of both right and left were outraged, not only at the abuse (who wouldn't be?) but more particularly at the terrible mishandling of the problems evidenced by the American bishops as a whole. Authors as various as Garry Wills on the left and George Weigel on the right took the episcopacy to task for lack of spiritual leadership and the absence of effective management.[7] True, they did not always agree about where exactly the bishops had failed, still less about the remedies, but they were of one mind that much of the responsibility for the crisis lay with American church leaders.

So the first underlying issue to address is that of the American episcopacy. The majority of cases of abuse uncovered thus far are clustered in the 1960s and 1970s, with a serious falling-off in numbers after about 1985. The bishops who presided over the church while the sex abuse was apparently most rampant were not those who today are accused of inadequate responses to the problems. The earlier generation of bishops was doubtless one of men who were variously holy and variously competent. But they lived in an age when the general public was not attuned to the extent of sex abuse in the population at large and not inclined to understand it to be as serious for either the victims or the perpetrators as we know it to be today. Like the people as a whole, the bishops were not sufficiently aware of the crime of sex abuse and did not take it all that seriously when it was uncovered. Covering up the problem by moving the priest was common. Ignoring the plight of the victim was almost universal. Blaming the victim was not a rare event.

Moreover, the bishops of thirty or forty years ago were even more unanswerable for their practices than they are today. Oversight committees within dioceses were largely unknown and the press was far, far more deferential than it is today. Perhaps most significantly, the role of lay people has changed considerably, if not quite as much as some would like to see, and certainly rather more than many bishops are comfortable with. If deference and lack of self-confidence marked the average Catholic of the mid-twentieth century, the more educated lay people of today are far more likely to be ready to ask awkward questions and expect accountability, even from their leaders in the faith. A more professional laity is so accustomed to professional standards of conduct in public and working life, and not unreasonably expects at least the same high standards among church personnel.

If today's bishops can be accused of anything, it is surely of having buried their heads in the sand and hoped that the problem would go away.

The Web site of the American Conference of Catholic Bishops details the many initiatives that the episcopacy took in the twenty or so years before the scandal hit.[8] No bishop could claim that he was unaware of the potential dangers to the church from adverse publicity, nor could he say that there was no advice available over what steps to take to reduce the incidence of sex abuse and guard against charges of inattention or incompetence. Incredibly, none of them seems to have been proactive in removing offending clergy. Only when such decisions became unavoidable were steps taken. Often, concern for the good name of the accused was judged more important than attending to the needs of victims. Above all, the bishops seem largely to have employed one criterion for dealing with sex abuse: What can we do to avoid scandal? The almost universal answer seems to have been to try to hide the problem. A prudent leader ought to be expected to see that doing this is only postponing the problem, not addressing it, and that the end result of such conduct is that the scandal, when it eventually breaks, is all the worse. By that standard there were no prudent members of the American Catholic episcopacy.

Why did the bishops fail to deal forcefully and intelligently with a problem of such magnitude with potentially disastrous consequences for the public credibility of the church and for the continued allegiance of many of the lay faithful? The bishops are not bad men, nor for the most part are they lazy or cynical or ignorant. Yet character is surely where we have to turn for our answers. It seems as if leadership was and is in short supply in the ranks of the American episcopate. There are certainly a number of bishops who manage their own dioceses forcefully and with integrity, but the demands of national leadership seem to escape most of them. In 2002, the "year of the scandal," the only real heroes among the episcopate nationally seem to have been Bishop Wilton Gregory, at that time bishop of the diocese of Belleville, Illinois, and president of the U.S. Bishops' Conference, and Cardinal Theodore Edgar McCarrick, archbishop of Washington, D.C. The rest were either quiet or in virtual hiding. Cardinal Law was in full retreat from the press and the public eye, and other major figures like Cardinal Edward Egan in New York and Cardinal Roger Mahony in Los Angeles had enough problems of their own to contend with.

Two factors help explain the poor performance of the bishops. The first, which goes to the issue of character and lack of leadership, has to do with the process by which bishops are selected. While in principle the complicated system is set up as a meritocracy in which talented priests are placed on a list of potential bishops from which junior appointments are made and more senior appointments come through considered reflection on the part of the American cardinals and at least some of the archbishops, in effect the choices are made by very few people. One or two American cardinals who have particular political influence can all but dictate which names go forward (Cardinal Bernard Law was a particularly notorious example) to the Papal Nuncio, the Vatican representative to the United States. The Nuncio may himself be influential, too, but the short list of names is then transferred to Rome where the Congregation for Bishops scrutinizes it and it eventually makes it to the desk of the pope, who can accept the advice offered by any or all of the above, or who can, indeed, appoint anyone he wishes. The conclusion then has to be that the particular composition of the American episcopate is a direct reflection of Vatican intentions, especially during a very long papacy. If they are not good leaders, then that is because they were chosen as part of a deliberate policy to appoint people who, whatever their other virtues, were unlikely to act forcefully unless they were responding to direct Vatican intervention. So, strong statements on abortion or challenges to "secularism and relativism" might be forthcoming, while anticipatory judgment and proactive engagement with matters that might bring public scrutiny upon church personnel would be quite another.

The second explanation for the weakness of the bishops is connected to the first, namely, the structure of the U.S. Conference of Catholic Bishops and the character of their corporate self-understanding. Just as the Vatican during the pontificate of John Paul II has created an American episcopate of weak leaders, whether by accident or design, so it has also undermined the authority of the national bishops' conference. The logic of this perhaps puzzling strategy is not difficult to see. The papacy of John Paul II was a time of re-centralization of authority and leadership. No one could doubt that the pope himself was a strong leader, and unlike his predecessor Paul VI (1963–1978), he sought to re-impose a strong papacy. One of the steps that had to be taken if he was to be successful was to undercut the "collegiality" of the bishops, an idea that the Second Vatican Council had strongly supported, perhaps as a counterweight to the exclusive attention paid to the authority of the pope in the documents of the First Vatican Council a century earlier. Of course, appointing bishops with poor leadership skills was in itself one way of undercutting the authority of the national conference, but they were also directly challenged by a series of statements from Joseph Ratzinger, then Prefect of the Sacred Congregation of the Faith (and now Pope Benedict XVI). To some degree, these steps were motivated by Vatican unhappiness with two major statements of the U.S. bishops on the nuclear arms race (1984) and on the U.S. economy (1986). Not only had both documents been prepared through an extensive process of consultation with the whole church, but their conclusions directly challenged American policy in ways that led conservative American Catholics to criticize the bishops openly and, of course, to complain to the Vatican.

Attention to the bishops in its turn brought scrutiny upon what may eventually turn out to have been the biggest contributory factor to the incidence of sexual abuse and the practice of covering it up, namely, the pathological element in clerical culture that goes by the name of "clericalism." Anyone who knows anything about Catholicism is aware that there is a cultic and cultural divide between clergy and laity like no other Christian denomination. Even the Orthodox church includes many married clergy within its ranks. Though there have been minor modifications in ministries to allow for permanent married deacons and a very small number of convert clergy from other denominations who wish to serve as priests but are married, the overwhelming majority of Catholic clergy make a promise to live a celibate life. Their lifestyles even today are thus different in so many ways from those of lay Catholics. Although the gap between them and the laity may have changed considerably since Vatican II, they live within their careers so to speak: They live either in a small group of celibates or, more commonly these days, they live alone, and they exist without the usual structures of accountability that family or domestic life imposes upon lay people.

Clerical culture becomes clericalism when the distinctive lifestyle of the few reflects a structure in which all voice, power, and decision making in the church is the private preserve of that clerical culture, and it acts as a closed society within the larger community. This is, of course, exactly the situation in the Roman Catholic Church. No lay person, male or female, has any formal decision-making authority in the church. No lay person, male or female, has any formal role in determining teaching on doctrinal or ethical issues. These are the facts, though it is equally true that many lay people are more experienced and effective leaders than at least some clergy, and many lay people are much better trained in theology and Christian ethics than are most clergy. Clericalism, then, refers to the de facto situation of a privileged elite who make all decisions and hold all positions of major responsibility in the institution. It is a particularly appropriate word to express the sense that this closed society is intent upon maintaining its own position, whether for good reasons or bad.[9]

One of the principal characteristics of tightly knit groups is that in moments of crisis they close ranks and act to protect themselves and their power within the particular system. This seems to be exactly what has happened in clericalism's response to the scandal of sex abuse. It is this which explains the unwillingness to face the potential enormity of the crisis. It is this which allowed the bishops to bring upon themselves a much bigger scandal than would have occurred had they acted earlier and more decisively to put their own house in order. It is this which accounts for their long-standing inclination to care more for the good name of the accused priest than for the mental health and spiritual equilibrium of the victim. And although things today are certainly an improvement upon what they were even in 2000, this also explains the continued sluggish response of at least some bishops to the new structures developed by the Bishops' Conference in Dallas in 2002 to help deal with the scandal. Above all, it explains the continuing reluctance of many bishops to pay due attention to the national oversight body which they themselves established. Is it entirely accidental many bishops do not take seriously a body overwhelmingly composed of lay people?

THE CONSEQUENCES FOR THE CHURCH TODAY

A crisis of such proportions has inevitably had major consequences for the American Catholic church. However, as the cliche puts it, every crisis is an opportunity, and it would be a mistake to imagine that it is all bad news. There are also some promising developments for the prevention of further scandal, for theology, and for the structures of the church. Never-theless, the jury is still out, and will be out for some time to come, on whether or not the enduring consequences of the crisis will be more on the debit or the credit side of the equation. Good news or bad, however, it seems inevitable that the church will be dramatically changed.

The unfortunate consequences of the scandal of sex abuse and the at-tendant crisis of leadership are mostly easy to see, large in their implica-tions, and demoralizing to large sectors of the church. Trust in the clergy on the part of the lay faithful has been damaged, perhaps irreversibly. While this has not for the most part harmed attitudes to a particular pas-tor, the clergy as a whole are no longer a class of people deemed automati-cally trustworthy. Suspicion of the clergy is even stronger among people outside the Catholic church. The perception of moral failing and lack of spiritual leadership among the bishops in particular has led the lay faithful and even the American public to diminished respect for the ethical posi-tions taken by the church, even when these have nothing at all to do with sex abuse. Prominent Catholic lay leaders like Justice Antonin Scalia can say publicly that the moral authority of the Catholic church is compro-mised. Nationally, an important voice in our cultural debates has become harder to hear.

Within the church, religious practice has become harder not easier, and significant numbers of people have left the Catholic church or stopped practicing. Others have stopped contributing financially, especially to bish-ops' appeals, even though that has meant that many worthy charitable organizations that depend on church largesse have been severely handi-capped. Several dioceses have been forced to declare bankruptcy in the face of huge legal settlements for victims, and more will follow. Lay people have been placed in important positions in the house-cleaning that the church has been engaged in since 2002, and then their actions and con-clusions have been second-guessed by bishops not accustomed to taking orders from anyone outside the hierarchical chain of command.

To these indubitable effects, some would add that the new regulations and so-called "zero tolerance" policy have led to some priests being unjustly removed from their ministries because of one minor infraction committed many years ago. Others point to the fact that while many priests have been suspended and a few laicized as a result of the scandal, no bishop has yet lost his job because of mismanagement or poor leader-ship, though one or two have themselves been removed because of credi-ble accusations of sexual impropriety. Efforts to bring an end to the scandal have led to the scapegoating of gay clergy, while almost no atten-tion has been paid to the possible relationship between the clerical lifestyle and the incidence of emotional and sexual immaturity among ministers. Overall, it seems fair to say, this is not an easy time to be a Catholic, par-ticularly not a Catholic priest or bishop. Many more liberal Catholics see this, however, as a chance to make broad and sweeping changes in church structures. And many more conservative Catholics suggest, in contrast, that holding fast to traditional patterns will be the best way to address the sex abuse scandals and, not incidentally, to begin to build a church for the future which, purged of liberals, will be smaller but more faithful and therefore more effective.

Probably the single most promising outcome of the crisis in the church is the crisis itself. That is to say, beyond the horrors of sex abuse and the redress of victims' grievances, the crisis of leadership has occasioned a debate of major proportions about the future directions in which the church might go and the structural changes that might be necessary to get there. At the heart of the conversation is the question of the relationship between the roles of lay people and clergy. Although Catholics as a whole tend either to throw up their hands in defeat and walk away from the church or, more commonly, to focus down upon their own parish and the Sunday worship, a significant minority of Catholics have been empowered and emboldened by what they see as the inadequacy of ecclesial responses to the crisis. Before the crisis, issues of clerical celibacy or the clerical lifestyle, of the relationship between lay and ordained ministry, of the place of women in the church, were not raised much in any serious manner outside the ranks of liberal theologians. Today, these questions—and a range of answers to them—have become common subjects of debate among more active Catholics. While there is no clear consensus on all or any of these questions, there is definitely a new sense that change can and perhaps should occur in a body whose faithful have tended in the past to see it in more monolithic terms. A liberal theologian might argue for new attention to the baptismal priesthood or the female diaconate on historical or theological grounds, but there is more impetus to change when the same issues and more come from grassroots Catholics moved simply by the all-too-evident failure of the old clerical system.

The degree to which one approves of the developing inclination of sectors of the laity to insert themselves into processes and issues which Catholics have traditionally left to the clergy is affected by the individual's theological and perhaps social conservatism. Some on the right of the church are looking for a smaller, more "faithful" church to emerge in the wake of the crisis. To them, the louder voices of the laity represent the clamor of social liberals who are attempting to capitalize on the crisis to further their own agendas. Faithfulness to the gospel, faithfulness to ecclesial discipline, faithfulness to prayer are all advocated by more conservative Catholics, especially bishops, as the way to return to the supposed greater faithfulness of some previous age. There is powerful support for this view in the higher ranks of church leaders, a view in which a negative assessment of the upheavals of the 1960s and a conspiracy theory about liberals kidnapping Vatican II are blended into a particularly Catholic version of the culture wars.

The confrontation between more liberal and more conservative evaluations of the cultural roots of the sex abuse scandal has become by degrees a debate about the future shape of the church. In the end, the disputes between those on the right and on the left are not about the importance of prayer, the virtue of celibacy, or the teaching authority of the bishops. They are about determining how an adult laity can and should function in a church whose polity was crafted in an age that no longer exists.[10]

Despite the imperfections and abject failures that sometimes afflict the American political experiment, Americans expect true democracy and the rewards of living in an open society. American Catholics are no less American than those of other faiths, and they share these yearnings. What is new, perhaps, is that they are increasingly unwilling to exempt their church from the need to promote participation and a share in decision making that is the hallmark of democratic societies. Catholicism has always taken some of its governance structures from the prevailing secular polities. Always, that is, until democracy emerged in the aftermath of the French and American revolutions. For some reason, the church that adopted the patterns of imperial Rome and of absolutist monarchies has found it so far impossible to adapt to the democratic imperatives of liberty, equality, and fraternity.

The ordained ministry, especially the priesthood, is turning out to be the battleground on which most of the issues of governance and participation are being fought out. Here a whole lot of concerns come together: the question of celibacy, the adequacy of seminary formation, the exclusion of women from ordained ministry, clerical culture and the clerical lifestyle, the issue of candidates for the priesthood who are gay but committed to celibacy, the legitimate roles of the laity in the rituals of public worship, processes for the selection of pastors and bishops, and the desirable extent of lay responsibility for decision making at the parish level, especially but not exclusively in financial matters.

One of the major reasons that relations between clergy and laity are open for reconsideration at this time is that the role of the priest in Catholicism has changed greatly in recent years, not only or even primarily because of the scandal of sexual abuse. Although there remain large numbers of clergy who continue to hold to a broadly autocratic vision of the ordained ministry and although some of the younger, so-called "John Paul II priests" may be clinging to this particular perception, in effect most clergy try these days to adopt a collaborative and communal approach to the day-to-day running of parishes. Typically, Catholic parishes employ significant numbers of lay staff, some of them doing work that in an earlier generation would have been the preserve of priests or religious sisters, others engaged in more practical and less obviously "ministerial" roles. To some degree this changed role of the priest has been forced upon the clergy by the decline in their numbers. They are fewer and, on average, older, and consequently they cannot shoulder alone the work of a large parish, but must turn to laity for help. To some extent it is also recognition of the changed status of the Catholic laity. Sociologically, Catholic lay people are far better educated than they were a couple of generations ago, and one can no longer assume that the priest is the most learned member of the community, not even in theological matters. Theologically, the Second Vatican Council taught the need to recognize the rights and responsibilities of the lay members of the church to speak out for the good of the church and to engage constructively in its mission.

Although there are hopeful signs in a more communitarian approach to parish ministry, the theology of ordained ministry in Catholicism continues to impede real change in lay/clergy relationships. The realignment in ministry that is sorely needed in the church is handicapped by an excessive focus on ordination and by a theology of orders that stresses substantial or ontological change. Moreover, any serious attention to those theological concerns is almost precluded by the institutional insistence on the norm of priestly celibacy and the exclusion of women from the ranks of the ordained. Addressing the theological issues involved in ministry would be a whole lot easier if it were not necessary to assume that the ordained person is a celibate man, since that very condition reinforces the inclination to think of the ordained as somehow fundamentally different from the nonordained.

The "turn to the laity" that was one of Vatican II's enduring legacies has its source in the rediscovery of the baptismal priesthood.[11] It is a striking fact that Catholics in general would never think of their status as priestly, even as an afterthought, though Catholic theology is united in its recognition that baptism confers a priestly status on each individual Christian. Vatican II reaffirmed this sometimes forgotten piece of Catholic doctrine, though it was careful to clarify that ministerial priesthood differs in kind and not only in degree from that acquired through baptism. It is the priestly character of the baptized, of course, that gives the specifically theological impetus to the growth of lay ministry and the general sense that all the baptized possess a mission beyond that of merely obeying the pastors, which was what the First Vatican Council (1870) had indicated was their sole role.

As the Catholic church faces the future, one can only imagine an intensification of the problems that exist in the church of today, since institutional authority seems to be so firmly on the side of maintaining the ecclesiastical status quo. In October 2005 the Rome Synod of Bishops deliberated over the place of the Eucharist in Catholic life and piety and concluded the two-week-long session by delivering fifty points for consideration to Pope Benedict XVI, which he was to use to help him craft an encyclical letter on this theme over the months that followed. The words of the bishops do not inspire confidence in those who would like to see change, though they doubtless confirm more conservative Catholics in their sincere commitment to the tried and trusted ways.

In particular, the bishops drew back from two issues on which there had been speculation that they might wish to encourage change. They heard several bishops urge consideration of the possibility of a relaxation of the law of celibacy so that certain *viri probati* (mature men of virtue) might be advanced to ordination to the priesthood. But they rejected this suggestion and forcefully reaffirmed their belief in the central importance of celibacy for the priesthood in the Roman Catholic Church. Second, they gave more serious attention to the difficult position that divorced and remarried Catholics find themselves in when they attend worship. Technically, such Catholics may not receive the Eucharist. The pastoral concern of the bishops for this large group of people led them to think about a change in the law, presumably hearing the common argument that since the Eucharist, as the other sacraments, is a God-given aid to salvation, it should be available to those whose lives are more difficult, not just to those whom fortune has placed in a less stressful situation. Again, however, they stepped back from any change, only affirming their wish that the divorced and remarried should be made welcome at church, and offering the rather unrealistic solution that if they were able to live in their canonically irregular marriages—to use the time-honored phrase—"as brothers and sisters," then they might be able to receive the Eucharist.

The Rome Synod on the Eucharist is a suitable place to draw this discussion of the state of Catholicism after the sex abuse crisis to a close, since it provides a clear instance of the division among Catholics over major issues in the church today. All Catholics would agree that the Eucharist is absolutely central to what it means to be church, and most if not all would concur that the growing shortage of priests, relative to the numbers of Catholics, makes access to the Eucharist more rather than less difficult. The bishops themselves recognized this fact, and the one among their number who is reported to have said at an early session of the synod that the Eucharist is not a right but a privilege can be assumed to be a minority voice, if not a lone voice. However, their deliberations and conclusions would suggest that the bishops believe that access to the Eucharist is not so important that it should be allowed to override the long-established practice of a celibate clergy or the exclusion of the divorced and remarried from the sacrament.

Gazing into a crystal ball, one can only say that if the leadership of the church is not willing to be more constructive in its approach to major problems, and more welcoming of a concerned and intelligent progressive sector of the laity, then the future of Roman Catholicism is going to be very different from the past that more traditional Catholics might long for. As the shortage of priests becomes critical around the world—and we should not forget that most Catholics live in parts of the world south of the Equator—there will be defections in larger numbers. In Africa it may be to Islam, in Latin America it will certainly be to evangelical Protestantism, and in the North it will almost certainly mean a slow drift into the postmodern relativism, materialism, and hedonism that Benedict XVI has set his papacy to reverse. In North America the priests will continue to age, and while lay ministry will supply for their lack of energy, the problem can only become more acute. In sum, by stages and over a couple of decades, it seems likely that the resistance to change now can only bring closer an eventual crisis. In the face of crisis, changes will probably begin to happen, and patterns of ministry will be adapted to allow for ordained ministers who are perhaps not necessarily either celibate or male. Of course, the need for change is better addressed at times when the problems have not become critical, but the practice of institutional governance, whether secular or religious, is usually to postpone difficult decisions until the casualties are inevitably larger, and even until it is just plain too late. Those who are committed to a lively future for the Catholic church have to hope that this will not be its fate.

NOTES

1. For those who have no sense at all of the world I am describing, there is no better source for a picture of it, and of the attendant clerical culture than the incomparable stories of J.F. Powers. Read freely within *The Stories of J.F. Powers* (New York: New York Review Books, 2000).

2. A very accessible and entertaining source for the lives of young Catholics and their entry into priesthood and religious life during the years at which the sex abuse scandal was brewing is Peter Manseau's engaging biography of his parents, *Vows: The Story of a Priest, a Nun, and Their Son* (New York: Free Press, 2005).

3. Richard Sipe was writing about these problems before the full extent of the scandal became apparent to the American public. See his *Sex, Priests and Power* (New York: Brunner/Mazel, 1995).

4. While there are quite a few books on the unfolding crisis, the best place to go to get a sense of the drama is to the Web site of the *Boston Globe*, where you can explore the archives of the paper's unparalleled coverage of the scandal of sex abuse. See http://www.boston.com/globe/spotlight/abuse or *Betrayal: The Crisis in the Catholic Church*, by the Investigative Staff of the Boston Globe (Boston: Little, Brown, 2002).

5. Voice of the Faithful continues to be a major progressive influence in the American church. It can be explored at www.votf.org.

6. This document is available on the Web at http://altarboys.tripod.com/moutonreport/Mouton_Reportx.html.

7. Garry Wills, *Papal Sin: Structures of Deceit* (Garden City, NY: Doubleday Image, 2001); and George Weigel, *The Courage to Be Catholic: Crisis, Reform and the Future of the Church* (New York: Basic Books, 2002).

8. The Web site for the U.S. Conference of Catholic Bishops is http://www.usccb.org/index.shtml.

9. For clericalism and its ill effects on the church see Donald Cozzens, *Sacred Silence: Denial and the Crisis in the Church* (Collegeville, MN: Liturgical, 2004).

10. See on this topic Paul Lakeland, *The Liberation of the Laity: In Search of an Accountable Church* (New York: Continuum, 2003).

11. A very helpful discussion of the emerging theology of orders can be found in *Ordering the Baptismal Priesthood: Theologies of Lay and Ordained Ministry*, ed. Susan K. Wood (Collegeville, MN: Liturgical, 2003).

SUGGESTIONS FOR FURTHER READING

Lakeland, Paul. *The Liberation of the Laity: In Search of an Accountable Church.* New York: Continuum, 2003.

Oakley, Francis, and Bruce Russett, eds. *Governance, Accountability, and the Future of the Catholic Church.* New York: Continuum, 2004.

Pope, Stephen J., ed. *Common Calling: The Laity and Governance of the Catholic Church.* Washington, DC: Georgetown University Press, 2004.

Steinfels, Peter. *A People Adrift: The Crisis of the Roman Catholic Church in America.* New York: Simon and Schuster, 2003.

CHAPTER 4

The Spirit of the Law: Spirituality in American Judaism

Sarah Imhoff

The first Jewish immigrants to colonial America functioned without a rabbi. So did their children. For almost 200 years, American Jews were without ordained leadership but managed to live, work, and practice Judaism. Since these pioneers, each successive generation of American Jews has juggled the desire to adhere to tradition and the need to cope creatively with new demands of its environment. By the middle of the nineteenth century, they turned their attention to worries about "decorum" and functioning in Christian society. Sparked in part by a wave of new Jewish immigrants, these concerns forced established and immigrant communities to negotiate ways to be American, even when it meant the appropriation of some outwardly Protestant forms of worship and education such as organs and unison prayer in synagogues. The early twentieth century marked another surge of immigrants and the rise of anti-Semitism, which forced Jews to craft an explanation for simultaneous sameness and difference from other Americans. A 1950s mile-wide, inch-deep "revival" swept religious communities with the spirit of universalism, interfaith involvement, and institution-building. But the mood of the 1950s faded in both Christian and Jewish communities, the Six Day War in Israel broke out, and once again American Jews turned their focus to what was distinctive about Judaism and Jewish people. Then in a development that historian Jonathan Sarna characterizes as a "turn inward,"[1] in the 1970s, American Judaism began to shift its focus from universalism and world Jewry to the cultivation of community and the individual soul.

In 1967, Shlomo Carlebach, sometimes called "the Singing Rabbi" or "the Dancing Rabbi," founded the House of Love and Prayer for Jewish hippies in search of something more. Another charismatic leader known as Reb Zalman agreed with the mystics of tradition and proclaimed: "[Y]ou can experience the Infinite right now."[2] Small Jewish study groups unaffiliated with any synagogue, called *havurot*, listened to Reb Zalman and began to add a serious spiritual dimension to their study. These were just a few of the harbingers of the changing tide of American Judaism. Bubbling to the surface in the late twentieth century, spirituality among American Jews is coming to a full boil in the beginning of the twenty-first.

The most commonly observed trend in turn-of-the-millennium American Judaism is a greater degree of observance across the Jewish spectrum, what some characterize as a general shift to the right. Orthodoxy—the most traditional of the four major movements—has attracted a significant number of young new adherents, the middle-way Conservative movement has seen a new emphasis on performance of commandments, and many of the liberal Reform Jews have re-embraced practices once discarded under the labels "indecorous" or "Oriental." Even sectarian groups like Chabad Lubavitch continue to draw new members. But this widespread return to ritual is not a stand-alone phenomenon: Contained within these outward forms, although less obvious to the observer and less frequently commented upon, is the rise of Jewish spirituality. Given these trends, this chapter will organize the story of contemporary American Judaism around the idea of spirituality. Unfortunately, as any story, this one comes at the expense of others; important topics such as American-Israeli relations, Holocaust issues, and *halakah* or Jewish law—any of which arguably could have played the starring role—are the supporting cast here.

Religion in the United States, historians have long noted, is voluntary. For American Jews, this "spiritual marketplace"[3] means the choice of one particular movement—Orthodox, Conservative, Reconstruction, or Reform—or none at all. When some American Jews wanted more spirituality but found synagogues incongruous with their religious needs, they had many avenues for cultivating this newly popular aspect of their religious lives. Beginning in the late 1970s, some American Jews began to form extra-denominational groups whose main draw was "spirituality." By the mid-1990s, mainline synagogues were responding to the persistence of these movements and the popular quest for spirituality by mirroring many of the ideas, values, and practices from these movements.

WHAT IS SPIRITUALITY WITHIN JUDAISM?

Is spirituality only "a catchword for whatever one finds lacking in contemporary Judaism"?[4] Because of spirituality's current popularity and association with American (dominantly Christian) culture rather than specifically Jewish culture, some leaders are wary of continued calls for more personal religious experience in the synagogue. Are these genuine expressions of desire for a deeper Judaism, they wonder, or are they simply a request for some pleasant music, less structure, and a generally feel-good religion at the expense of truly Jewish content? Others suggest that any expression of interest in Judaism is worth serious consideration if it might draw more Jews back into the pews. Although some individuals may be after a warm and fuzzy, content-free worship, it seems that many American Jews interested in spirituality are in fact looking for a greater connection to Judaism and tradition.

These two opposing views of the clamor for more spirituality highlight a more fundamental question: What is spirituality in Judaism? The Hebrew word for "spirituality," *ruhaniut* (literally spirit-ness, from the root meaning spirit or wind), is a modern addition. The ancient and medieval Jewish thinkers did not employ such a category because, in their minds, spirituality was part and parcel of practice. Each action and commandment was to be accompanied by *kavvanah*, or proper intention, which they understood as aligning one's mind or soul with God's will. Most forms of Kabbalah, Jewish mysticism dating back to the Middle Ages, give *exclusively* spiritual reasons for the performance of the commandments. The Hasidic movement later picked up on this ideology: It began as a populist reinterpretation of Judaism that valued the performance of the commandments as fundamentally an act of spiritual devotion. Thus, despite a long history of spiritual practices and ritual imbued with divine content, it was not until the popularity of spirituality as its own category in American culture that there was a widespread consideration of a separate role of "spirituality" within Judaism.

Even the casual observer can immediately identify some Jewish practices as spiritual, however the term is defined. Prayer, perhaps the most apparent spiritual exercise, has enjoyed a long history both personally in the home and communally in the synagogue. (In fact, the Hebrew word for a synagogue service, *teffilah*, is the same word for prayer.) Another clearly spiritual exercise, personal reflection, is encouraged year-round, and especially so at the fall holidays of Yom Kippur and Rosh Hashanah. The most popular rituals among less observant Jews are those that are less frequent, like yearly holidays and life-cycle events. Although many researchers have noted the community and family aspects of these rituals,[5] most of these practices also foster an inner sense of awe, wonder, and connection to God and tradition. For example, when a bar or bat mitzvah reads a portion of the Torah or a woman lights Sabbath candles, the spiritual atmosphere is undeniable. But few would suggest that eating latkes, even though it is a popular ritual, constitutes a personal religious experience. So without a clear consensus on its value, must we be content to think of spirituality in the way that Supreme Court Justice Potter Stewart said of pornography: I cannot define it, "but I know it when I see it"?

One need only ask an average religious person in order to be convinced that there is something more to spirituality than simply semantics or observers' opinions; in fact, the experiences of individual Jews themselves afford a useful foundation for defining spirituality. More often than not, these experiences are tied to the performance of a ritual or physical presence at a historic site, such as Auschwitz or Jerusalem. Despite her terror at her first call to read the Torah in a women's prayer group, one Orthodox woman explained: "As I uttered the blessing, however, I felt myself moving through time and space."[6] She used unquestionably spiritual language to describe her performance of this ritual, employing words of profound connection with tradition to describe her sensation. Another Orthodox woman wears the conventionally male garments because of the religious feelings they evoke. She said that the recitation of the traditional blessing "as I bind *tefillin* [phylacteries] on my arm, the awareness of being enveloped in a *tallit* [prayer shawl] evokes very powerful feelings in me."[7] As one scholar paraphrased Jewish philosopher Franz Rosensweig: "[to] the pious Jew, the mitzvot are hardly laws but are a rhapsodic occasion to behold God's Presence."[8]

Many first-time visitors to Israel also describe a unique feeling of connection to God, history, and the Jewish people. In a 2000 sociological study, participants described their visits to Israel as "the most powerful pro-Jewish experiences that I had" and "overwhelming." Those who could articulate the source of their sense of awe traced it to physical ties with tradition and history. One unobservant respondent said: "One has to confront the fact that you have a wall or something and you see this piece of rock that people have been praying at, you know, for so long, and you have to confront a sort of mysticism. That actually holds some appeal for me."[9] Only a minority of American Jews has visited Israel, but those who have frequently describe their experience in spiritual terms.

Although some Jews are inclined to agree with the classical definition of spirituality as "the opposite of 'corporeality' or 'materiality,' "[10] these examples illustrate that for American Jews, the physical inspires the spiritual. Contra many Christian worldviews, the body and soul are not a dichotomy, not even two sides of one coin. The two are fundamentally interconnected: A twenty-first-century American woman, just like a sixteenth-century European male kabbalist, experiences a profoundly emotional connection to the divine when performing a commandment. These experiences were certainly not the same—in fact, likely quite dissimilar—but both illustrate the bond between body and soul, action and spirituality. Modern Jewish notions of spirituality, then, are not so far from traditional interpretations.

Despite an emphasis on personal experience, the spiritual is not individual at the expense of being communal. In *Spiritual Judaism*, David Ariel defines spirituality as "a highly personal outlook about what is sacred to us."[11] But most Jews develop this "personal outlook" with and through community. Although this is also true of many religions, community and peoplehood are fundamental values of Judaism. Reflecting on chanting her Torah portion on her bat mitzvah while surrounded by her community of observant women, one woman said simply: "This wonderful experience made me feel close to God."[12] She had practiced chanting this portion many times by herself, but participation within her religious community was the source of her spiritual experience of intimacy with God. Modern Jewish spirituality, then, is steeped in people as well as values, the body as well as the soul, and the past as well as the present; it is a sense of awe, wonder, and profound respect for a greater good that one continually develops through interaction with tradition, ritual, and community.

AMERICAN JUDAISM'S SPIRITUAL JOURNEY

According to a 2005 *Newsweek* poll, Jews were no different from most other Americans in their quest for spirituality: "Americans are looking for personal, ecstatic experiences of God, and, according to our poll, they don't much care what the neighbors are doing."[13] In addition to some distinctively Jewish factors, this American trend of rising personal religiosity crosses religious lines, which indicates additional cultural factors not limited to a specific religion.

Jewish spirituality in American culture existed before the 1970s, but it was neither common nor institutional. For instance, in 1946 Rabbi Joshua Loth Liebman published *Peace of Mind*, a book exploring social justice that touched on Jewish spirituality. But Liebman argued for spirituality only through the lens of psychology: He claimed that if one were to grow spiritually, she must first be psychologically mature. Few commented on Jewish spirituality, and when they did, it was only a tangential interest because of its relevance to social justice, psychology, or Israel.

If the 1950s were about affiliation, joining, and universalism for American Judaism, then the 1960s and early 1970s were about world Jewry, the Holocaust, and Israel. When the Six Day War in 1967 raised American consciousness of Israel among individual Jews and institutions, Israel surged to the front page of American Jewish concerns; it became a focal point for fund-raising and education. But as the 1970s wore on, the political and social problems of Israel incited critique and marked the end of the honeymoon. Since 1977, when Israel elected a right-wing government, sociologist Steven Cohen explains, several political events have caused "considerable discomfort" for American Jews: hard-line policies toward the West Bank, Israeli instigation of the war with Lebanon, the election of racist Knesset member Meir Kahane, violent religious-secular conflicts in Israel, and the tough military responses to the Intifada.[14] As these events transpired, a slow but steady decrease in pro-Israel philanthropy[15] was accompanied by a drop in interest and participation among individual Jews. Cohen stated frankly: "Since the mid-1970s, ... Israel no longer excites the passions of the top (or even middle) rung of Jewish volunteer leadership."[16] The declining feeling of attachment is a result of actions and policies indicative of Israel as a modern political entity capable of wrongdoing in the eyes of American Jewry. As Chaim Waxman suggests, the change was less a weakening and more a transformation in nature: Americans saw Israel less through the lens of political and religious Zionism and more as modern society with sovereign Jews.[17] As simply another modern, democratic country—albeit one with many Jews—rather than a symbol of the fulfillment of religious goals and prophecies, Israel no longer captivated American Jews as it once had. At worst, as it lost its salvific status, it contributed to disillusionment with modern culture and politics.

Although the Holocaust remains an identifying marker of Jewish cultural identity, over time, like Israel, it has become less a part of institutional Jewish life. In 1992, sociologist Arnold Eisen noted: "Proximity to the Holocaust and to the founding of the State of Israel has stimulated Jewish energies for more than 40 years. There are already signs that the influence of these forces is on the wane."[18] With greater incorporation into general American consciousness, the Holocaust has become less distinctly Jewish. The opening of the United States Holocaust Memorial

Museum in Washington, D.C., and the addition of Holocaust studies to required public school curricula have increased non-Jewish interest while lightening the obligation of synagogues and Jewish schools to provide comprehensive instruction to all. Increased emphasis in American culture has thus made knowledge and history of the Holocaust less and less a marker of Jewishness and involvement in Jewish community. As the 1970s closed, interest in international issues of the Holocaust and Israel thus slowly took a backseat to new concerns.

One of these new concerns was the effect of feminism. As women took more leadership roles in the Jewish community and became more visible in the synagogue, traditionally "feminine" qualities also gained more attention. Historically, women in Judaism, as well as in many other religions, have frequently been lauded as "more spiritual" than men, a characterization that has continued into the present. Anthropologist Susan Starr Sered found this sentiment expressed by men and women alike in her study of traditional Jewish women in Jerusalem: "the traditional female religious sphere may sometimes acquire new significance or prestige as women come to be seen as guardians of old ways, as experts in traditional religion. In a number of interviews, children of women I studied made comments such as, 'my mother is closer to God than I am,' 'the way my mother does it [religion] is better, but I myself am not strong enough to do it like she does.' "[19] Generally, women are perceived as possessing heightened spiritual qualities, and therefore, an expanding women's role will result in increasing attention to spirituality.

By the close of the 1970s, American culture had begun to move away from its former days of experiment, rebellion, and revolution. Individuals worried about themselves, and sweeping love-of-everyone faded. American Jews, too, began to turn their emphasis from world Jewry to themselves. Synagogue membership that had failed to rebound after the decrease of the early 1960s, dramatically increasing intermarriage rates, low birth rates, assimilation, and feminism—all on the home front—occupied the thoughts of those concerned about American Jewry.

In retrospect, the 1980s were a time of personal questions. Less kindly, it was a decade of self-interest and self-indulgence, of yuppies and unemployment. Like American culture at large, American Jews as individuals and families concentrated on themselves and thereby created a more personally defined and practiced form of Jewishness. In 1992, one scholar explained this development:

> In short, there appears to be a decline in associational Jewishness, as expressed in denominational identification, and a corresponding increase in what Thomas Luckmann might have called invisible Jewishness: a privatized sense of longing, belonging, and meaning that is more psychological than communal, more felt than articulated. Such invisible religion, as Luckmann called it, draws from the same wellspring of collective symbols and memories as institutionalized religion. But it refuses to be constrained by the boundaries and social controls of the formal institutions (synagogues, Jewish organizations, schools).[20]

Prior to the late 1980s, scholars studied these "formal institutions" almost exclusively when they wanted to know about American Judaism. In the 1991 *Jewish Identity in America*, the editors presented a comprehensive review of the studies of American Jews in the preceding twenty years. Not one study asked questions or drew conclusions concerning spirituality; the closest was a survey question asking for the frequency of prayer.[21] The scholars measured the number of American Jews, attendance, revenue, membership, intermarriage rate, and even ritual performance. But few seemed to notice the role of spirituality, which had begun to grow.

In 1982, American religious historian Martin Marty suggested that in the United States, "rather than being contained within formal institutions, religion has unmistakably and increasingly diffused throughout culture, and has assumed highly particularized forms in the private lives of citizens."[22] Although the trend encompasses both Christian and Jewish communities, this growth of private spirituality may be less noticeable within Jewish communities because of the forms it takes. Today many Christians voraciously devour devotional and spiritual media like the *Left Behind* series, *The Passion of the Christ* movie, and contemporary Christian music, but Jews turning to spirituality tend to approach it through less publicly visible modes of study and meditation. Since much of the spiritual growth among Jews has taken place outside of formal institutions and mass media, it took years for scholars and rabbis to understand its significance.

But by the 1990s, the popularly perceived spiritual lack in American Jewish institutions was undeniable, and many who noticed were instant critics. When recession of both American economic and rational frameworks hit, Jews who turned to the synagogue looking for something other than community and study—something more like personal growth or affirmation of God—had to look hard. Author David Ariel said, "Many of us still do not feel at home in our synagogues. We see Jewish institutions, especially synagogues and temples, as too preoccupied with institutional rather than spiritual concerns."[23] American Jews went looking for personal religious experience but found only scripted services and business concerns. Scholar of modern Judaism Deborah Lipstadt said of institutional Judaism in 1992, "There is no genuinely spiritual aspect present."[24] Arthur Green lamented the plight of Jewish baby boomers and their children; they had missed the truly spiritual aspect of the synagogue:

> [They] know little of the real act of prayer, and their mostly negative associations, either with traditionalist rapid mumbling or with the formalism of the large liberal synagogue, will continue to serve as roadblocks. Only rabbis with smaller congregations and groups of Jews in informal *havurot* will be able to make accessible to Jews outside Orthodoxy a sense that prayer, including liturgy, needs to be the most spontaneous and least routinized of human activities. The popularity of such leaders and groups will be great, and not just among the young.[25]

Only the cultivation of personal spirituality could draw Jews back to Judaism, he claimed. Critics, however, were not wholly pessimistic about the future of the synagogue. Even Lipstadt, a strong voice of discontent, insisted that it was possible "to enhance the spiritual aspects of American Jewish life and to strengthen the realm of private or personal Jewish activities."[26]

For Ariel the necessity was "to turn our synagogues into places of the heart once again."[27] Like American Jews of the past, these analysts saw the opportunity to hold on to tradition while creatively instituting change to fit the needs of practitioners.

When American Jews themselves—individuals, rabbis, and scholars—describe the root causes of their growing need for personal religiosity, they use different vocabulary to describe the growing importance of spirituality in individual lives and society, but many of them point to similar themes of disillusionment, vacuous culture, and the falsity of the American dream. In 1992, Jack Wertheimer cited "the failure of modern culture, especially the United States, to provide a coherent identity and communal anchor"[28] as the cause of a desperate search for a new feeling of religiosity. The immense diversity, change, and disagreement left individuals wondering where they fit in and feeling lost. Because tradition and peoplehood are fundamental Jewish principles, unstable American identity and community were certain to take a toll on the confidence Jews placed in American value systems. Ariel also held modernity ultimately responsible for the spiritual void: "The price of admission into the non-Jewish world has been the surrender of our spiritual integrity as Jews."[29] The problem is not Judaism, but, rather, the choice of Jews to enter into the fundamentally flawed matrix of modernity. Modern Jews had wrestled with assimilation and tradition, chose to creatively engage modernity, and were eventually let down by the once-hidden holes in modernity.

One Reform rabbi explained the new turn towards the spiritual in more traditionally religious language: "We have wanted our inner needs fulfilled, for we often feel empty inside, even though we seem to be full and satisfied on the outside. The physical home of the American dream has not filled the spiritual home of the Jewish dream. So many of us, along with our congregants, search. They and we may call it God. Yes, God is making a comeback because we seek and long for the spiritual side of ourselves."[30] As a career pulpit rabbi, he uses God-language similar to that of his congregants to describe the quest for spirituality, but his diagnosis of the problem is consistent with both more observant and secular explanations.

With the dawn of the twenty-first century, most Jews continue to put explanations in a national perspective. Even many Jews who do not label themselves "religious" recognize the need for spirituality and label society's unkept promises as causes. They are more likely to use economic and pursuit-of-happiness terms to describe these failings, and like less observant, liberal Jews, they are less likely to blame modernity itself but rather specific cultures and media. A self-proclaimed "secular Jew," one who does not believe in God but retains Jewish values and interest in Jewish social and political causes, explained: "despite the affluence, the last thirty years have been years of disillusionment and frustration for many young people. Urbanization, anonymity, mobility, unemployment, and family breakdown have taken their toll. People are no longer sure that ordinary power is available to guarantee their happiness."[31] Even secular people, he insists, have begun to search for something other than "ordinary power." Whether it be through yoga classes, meditation, or dedication to a cause such as environmental conservation, people need an anchor. Even if this anchor is not a traditional God, they need an organizing structure to their lives, and so they may begin a spiritual quest for a higher power.

Another spokesman for secular Judaism explains the societal ills that plague modern Americans, leaving them with an empty feeling. "These main developments have made secular people, Jews and non-Jews alike, feel a need for a spiritual dimension to their lives: the break-up of communities, a cultural diet composed entirely of mass entertainment, and schools that have replaced cultural education with vocational training."[32] He places the blame squarely on the media and on the lack of substantial culture. Without a coherent sense of culture to help them create personal or communal meaning, they desperately search for something else to fill the void. Since culture and media are the systems that have failed them, they eventually look for fulfillment outside those systems.

Although the general consensus has been to describe a particularly American cause for spiritual emptiness, some scholars, like Arthur Green, changed the setting to one of global fear. In his 1992 prediction, he boldly asserted that the postmodern world and its technology have placed a heavy burden on the soul:

> The individual confrontation with mortality is heightened in our day by a collective sense of potential danger, making this an age in which the role of prayer is increased rather than diminished.... For all the continued growth of human knowledge in biomedical and other scientific areas, the sense that the keys to both life and death lie in hands that reach beyond human understanding or control has not been lost. Now as the greatest of human fears shifts from that of nuclear holocaust to that of ecological devastation (a shift that has taken place before our eyes), the sense of divine involvement in the fate of the world will grow.[33]

Because of human technological developments and mismanagement of resources, the human race is threatening its own long-term existence. With human mortality on display at every turn—the media, news, politics, healthcare—world citizens are forced either to contemplate their worldviews or live in a constant state of denial. Green has replaced the failure of the American dream with the failure of humankind: Technology and usage of resources that once seemed the promise of the future have turned out to be empty. People cannot derive positive meaning from these systems that threaten destruction, so they turn to a different version of the greater good.

Modernity brought not only anxieties but also unrestricted inclusion in society. Therefore especially in the United States, many are concerned that Jews will lose their distinctiveness. No longer forcibly ghettoized and branded "Jew," individuals can choose to cease practicing, even self-identifying, as Jews. The American suburbanization of the 1950s exacerbated this problem; no longer were the majority of Jews in urban, tight-knit Jewish communities. They were spread out, living in neighborhoods with few other Jews and no synagogues. If and when they decided to build a synagogue, they found that affiliation with one movement was their choice. Again, creatively negotiating with tradition and new life circumstances, American Jews found themselves making choices about how (and whether) to be Jewish. In the 1950s, the general American milieu of joining, belonging, and institution-building convinced many of these suburban Jews to remain within Judaism. But faced with similar choices of continuing to affiliate in an age of disillusionment and individuality, the Jews of the twenty-first century could choose to discard a Judaism that they find unfulfilling in favor of another religion or a secular life.

THE GROWTH OF SPIRITUALITY IN AMERICAN JUDAISM

A fear of defection from institutional Judaism over lack of spiritual content is not an unfounded one. Across the American Jewish spectrum, from secular humanists to Chabad Jews, a renewed interest in spirituality has blossomed over the last decades. This distinctly modern spiritual quest(ion) has been put most eloquently by Jewish thinker Paul Mendes-Flohr: How can we "retrieve the Jewish past and an innocent faith without forfeiting knowledge?"[34] Modern Jews struggle to hold on to tradition and the history of a people while still interacting with modern science, technology, and history.

Some solve this question by placing spirituality at the heart of their Judaism, understanding tradition and faith are through the heart and community, not through law. The Jewish Renewal movement, the legacy of Rabbi Zalman Schachter (or Reb Zalman), insists on an intellectual dimension of spirituality, not blind faith; it calls for experience and personal validation of its precepts. Michael Lerner explains the concept of transcendence in Jewish Renewal as "a spiritual reality—the ability to recognize God in one another."[35] Jewish Renewal retains the values of both tradition and community, but it discards the need for absolute belief and practice consistent with a legislative Judaism. The movement has its foundation in the thought of Reb Zalman, an Orthodox Jew and Holocaust survivor who immigrated to the United States. A seeker himself, Reb Zalman became a teacher of seekers. He sought to learn about other systems of belief—from Buddhism to Native American religions, all without leaving Judaism—and taught students young and old how to rediscover the joy and spirituality within Judaism.

Jewish Renewal also builds on the thought of philosopher Martin Buber who believed that "the ultimate ground of Judaism as an enduring and existentially meaningful community of faith" is "an inner, spiritual process."[36] This formulation does not negate tradition or text; instead it places them as valuable because they are means to nurture one's relationship with God and humans. Jewish spirituality needs Sabbath observance, Jewish holidays, and revision—not rejection—of traditional prayer books. In fact, Lerner claims that the movement has reclaimed the original message of Judaism, which was "repressed and abandoned"[37] over the generations. Jewish Renewal is therefore sensitive to environmental, social, and gender issues; it strives to

improve the world and nurture its adherents. Lerner and Ariel both emphasize tradition; Ariel calls the modern quest "the same journey that our
ancestors took as they set out into the uncharted waters of their day,"[38]
while Lerner concludes: "we stand on the shoulders of a hundred generations."[39] Despite a desire to create a Jewish perspective different from those
of existing institutions, supporters of Jewish Renewal continue to value tradition highly.

Many others consciously began something new; they chose to create
their own Jewish practice and balance innocent faith and knowledge for
themselves. One group of young, educated Jews dissatisfied with both
Jewish institutions and obsessive material culture formed the first small
study group—*havurah*—called Havurat Shalom in 1967. They shunned
strict hierarchies, welcomed women, dressed casually, exchanged ideas
freely, sang and prayed together, and tried to forge a way to be Jewish that
would resonate with their ideologies and emotions. As Reb Zalman, a
founding member and continuing inspiration for other *havurot*, explained:
"Our concern was to create a group that could function democratically as
a 'family of friends,' who shared the goal of spiritual growth.... We imagined a setting in which the inner experience of our souls' search for God
could take place with group support."[40] The idea was catchy: All over the
country, young people began to meet in small groups, sit in circles, study
Torah, and pray by candlelight.

Although at first they were not consciously feminist, many progressive
women joined and became organizers. Judith Plaskow explained the close
relationship between feminism and the *havurah* ideologies of personal development through community and human relationship with God: "Certainly,
it is no accident that *havurot* have provided a first prayer home for many
feminist Jews, at the same time that they have created an intimate space
for the experience of God's immanence."[41] These *havurot* brought some
women back into Judaism; for others, they provided a more comfortable
home within the tradition. But in general they increased the involvement
and affirmation of women as well as traditionally female modes of worship
emphasizing spirituality.

In 1973, the *havurah* movement went public: Several members com-
piled the *Jewish Catalog*, a do-it-yourself guide to Judaism. Its witty
explanations, amusing illustrations, and inclusive tone charmed Jews across
the country. Second to the Bible, it is the best-selling book ever published by the Jewish Publication Society. It seemed that American Jews
were searching for their own personal ways to be Jewish; if they did not
find enough support for personal religiosity within their synagogues, they
found other resources and other people like them.

Havurot did not vanish with many other seeking groups of the 1970s,
and some found this resilience surprising. In 1992, one rabbi was struck by
"the resurgence of [American Jews'] sense of religious and spiritual connection with some aspects of Jewish tradition—as understood by such teachers
as Martin Buber, Abraham Joshua Heschel, and Mordecai Kaplan [three
thinkers frequently cited as precursors to today's spirituality]; as influenced
by feminism; and as practiced in *havurot* and other networks of Jewish

renewal."[42] Although these groups marked a rise in interest in personal religiosity, they also revalued former institutional priorities through the lens of spirituality. As the emphasis on social justice decreased in institutions during the 1980s, it found new life through the *havurah* small-group model. Several liberal thinkers put their hope for the future of Jewish social justice in the hands and ideals of these very same people and movements. Another American Jewish scholar defines the ideal social justice for today's American Judaism in spiritual terms: "I suggest that our challenge today in creating a socially just world ... is to continue our pursuit of the Light of God and ultimately to bring it into the universe."[43] Here social justice is primarily an exercise in inner religiosity. Arnold Eisen, in his prescription for an improving Jewish future, first calls for using *havurah*-style spirituality as a basis for increasing other aspects of Jewish communal life: "At a minimum, we can further reanimate our synagogues with *havurot* meant for life-cycle celebrations and Sabbath study, building outward from religious commitments to political action, ecological concern, and so on.... Every effort that serves Jewish bodies is an opportunity to serve Jewish spirits as well."[44] *Havurot*, while still small, have proved to be not only more than a passing fad, but also a model for revaluing and revitalizing institutional values.

Out of similar ideologies to the *havurah* movement came a Jewish retreat center, Elat Chayyim, in 1992. One of its founders explains its role as a place where American Jews "can be exposed to a contemporary version of Jewish life that emphasizes on the focus of oneness of God on all things"[45] through exposure to the Ba'al Shem Tov, an eighteenth-century mystic and primary inspiration of Reb Zalman. As the first major institution focused on Jewish spirituality, it served as a sort of pilot program in the field. Teaching and learning outside of a particular movement (drawing members from all four movements and unaffiliated Jews) was nothing new in the United States; nondenominational Jewish community centers had been doing it for years. But an institution organizing the teaching and practice of a kind of contemporary Jewish mysticism was unprecedented.

The success of Elat Chayyim demonstrated the demand for spiritual resources outside of denominational lines. Rabbi Jeff Roth explained: "At the time we started, there was no serious exploration of spirituality, no organized way of accessing Jewish mystical practices." Jews who were curious about exploring their spirituality through Judaism were forced to find an individual rabbi who was knowledgeable in the right texts and teachings and willing to help with a spiritual journey. Even interested rabbis had scant resources for exploring their own spiritual development, let alone the development of their members. When Elat Chayyim first opened its doors, Roth recounts, "teachers and students both gravitated toward us."[46]

The moderate growth of Elat Chayyim also points to an increase in Jewish meditation. Some types are very much in the public eye: Popular culture (figures such as singers Madonna and Britney Spears) and the Internet promote Kabbalah, and new books fly off bookstore shelves. But religiously serious Jews like those who study at Elat Chayyim, interested in more than a twenty-minute do-it-yourself enlightenment, have also shown increased interest. In 1996, Mark Verman, the author of *The Histories and Varieties of Jewish Meditation,* was finally able to sell his manuscript after fifteen years of attempts. Suddenly, it seemed to some (including publishers), Jews were interested in meditation. But like Jewish Renewal supporters, those who practice meditation deny they are doing something new. With chapter titles like "Ancient Roots of Jewish Meditation" and continued comparisons of modern meditating Jews to medieval mystics,[47] Verman insists that meditation is nothing innovative; to the contrary, it connects the practitioner to tradition.

Other noninstitutionalized Jewish movements perceived the cultural and personal need for spirituality and then incorporated spirituality into their already-existing ideologies. In the case of Jewish secular humanism, even in the absence of God, spirituality has become a critical piece of the philosophical puzzle. Proponents of this philosophy point to the decline of religion as the very cause of a cultural increase in spirituality. Sherwin Wine, an ordained rabbi and yet a self-proclaimed secular humanist, explains: "As faith in religion and political ideology crumbles, the desire strengthens for a spiritual dimension to life."[48] The absence of religion in a human life would accentuate "the obvious human *need* for spirituality."[49] As people rationally move away from superstitious and mythological religion, the need to nurture their souls becomes more and more apparent. Wine explains that the Jewish secular humanism's "new spirituality" includes "transcendence," a word already loaded with religious meaning, that is characterized by the feelings of "awe, wonder, and empowerment" and the distinct impression of "being part of something greater and more powerful than oneself."[50] Education, study of text and art, and above all, communion with people and nature replace "God" as the crucial venues to experience and cultivate this spirituality. Even to those who deny the traditional God, many Jews across the spectrum of belief and practice have come to emphasize elements of the human spirit.

Some individuals in search of spiritual answers turned to the other end of the spectrum on their quest for deeper religious experience. For example, Ba'alei Tshuva (BTs for short) are Jews who turn to strict Orthodoxy; their answer to the question of modernity is that the innocent faith in God and law is the foundational element of Judaism. One woman who turned to Chabad Lubavitch, a branch of Hasidism, recounted her previous spiritual quest to the other women at the study house: "She'd taken drugs and begun to get involved with the guru Maharaj ji by attending classes and meditations. She had really wanted to become a 'premie' (the name for Maharaj ji's followers) and find higher truth."[51] Finally she found her home at the study house; the form of spirituality offered there answered her questions and made sense with her experience of the world. Another woman there explained her attraction: "I needed a spiritual community. There is a whole other level of spiritual reality ... so it's very fulfilling for me to be a part of the spiritual community where that part of me can get exercise."[52] She, too, had searched elsewhere, but found the spirituality she sought only in Chabad Lubavitch. Especially popular among young adults, the BT movement is a particularly visible example of two connected trends in American Judaism: increased spirituality and increased observance.

Orthodox women also began to form prayer groups, or *teffillot*. While most of these women use language indicative of feminist consciousness, they simultaneously use spiritual words to indicate that their primary concern is spiritual development through Judaism. In a characteristic account, one woman pronounced: "Souls have no gender. Our souls have the same desire and need to get close to God and the Torah through learning as do men's souls. Women's prayer groups bring us one step closer to God."[53] As another participant explained, "Experiencing the stirring spirituality and beauty of the prayer service has been my principal reason for belonging to the women's davening [prayer] group.... [It is] a more satisfying religious experience than membership in a traditional Orthodox synagogue."[54] For the most part, these women remain observant Jews, but they no longer rely exclusively on attendance at synagogues. Without the presence of men, they may read out loud from the Torah, pray most prayers, and even sing. Since women cannot speak or sing in most Orthodox services, and the women's section is frequently located in a crowded balcony with poor sight lines, they created a different atmosphere where they could participate fully in Jewish practice as women. From the secular Jew who found spirituality in his encounters with nature to the BT who prayed and studied mysticism, many American Jews across the spectrum looked to develop their connections within themselves and to higher powers. Once again, these American Jews were creating new groups and venues to fit their desires, all the while holding on to a form of tradition.

This is not to say that all lay Jews were desperately searching for spirituality, nor that all rabbis and denominational leaders were oblivious to such needs. As early as 1985, for instance, one prominent Orthodox rabbi, who willingly taught many students the art of Jewish meditation, explained: "If finding spiritual meaning is difficult for the uncommitted Jew, sometimes it is difficult for the Orthodox Jew as well.... When asked why they do not seek [meditation] within Judaism, they have the same answer as uncommitted Jews: they are not aware how such an experience can be found within Judaism."[55] But he was ahead of his time; it was not until nearly a decade later that synagogues began to incorporate more spiritual content into their services and programs.

RENEWED SPIRITUALITY IN THE SYNAGOGUES

As many practitioners noticed and commentators began to point out, the synagogues were not the forerunners in the trend of spirituality. Because of its American—as opposed to Jewish—origins, the spirituality "fad" made many Jewish leaders nervous. They were concerned that holding informal services and embracing practices such as meditation and spontaneous prayer would turn Judaism into a simply universalistic feel-good religion without the vital aspect of tradition. Complete accommodation of the requests of religious seekers would empty the content and distinctiveness of Judaism, leaving something equivalent to just another yoga class at the gym.

The story of spirituality since the 1990s is a story about the gradual development of the push and pull between the American spiritual quest and Jewish tradition. As time went on, rabbis and synagogues found creative ways to do both. As the historian Mark Lee Raphael explains, this emphasis on spirituality in America "began in the 1990s (perhaps as early as the late 1980s in some synagogues), intensifying at the end of that decade into a search for new depths of meaning in Judaism. When rabbis announced a class in Jewish thought, modest numbers attended; when they used the word *spirituality* in the title, the course was packed. It is the cry of our age."[56] For more liberal synagogues, this development is generally seen as a boon: more interest and maybe even more congregants. Orthodox and other traditional synagogues, while more wary, have viewed the increase in spiritual dimensions of religious life in terms of a return to traditional Jewish practices, such as the practices of the Hasidim and Jewish mysticism. But across denominational lines, both lay people and rabbis have incorporated a greater degree of spiritual emphasis in religious life.

As with many changes in American Judaism, the gradual incorporation of spirituality into the synagogues began earliest in the more liberal movements and latest in the most traditional communities. One obvious institutional change that contributed to the growth of spirituality in three movements was the decision to ordain women as rabbis and cantors. Since 1972 in Reform, 1974 in Reconstruction, and 1985 in Conservative Judaism, women have become rabbis, preaching, teaching, and serving as an example to their congregants. If women are perceived as more spiritual, members may sense an atmosphere of spirituality in the synagogue when they have a female rabbi, whether or not she intended such a consequence. The rabbi, as a role model, can also make others feel more comfortable pursuing and expressing spiritual thoughts and journeys when they feel that she is a spiritual person. Moreover, personal religiosity then receives a legitimate place in the synagogue. Women, who are traditionally branded "private" to men's "public," are perceived as bringing the personal into the communal. One female rabbi explained bluntly: "[W]omen rabbis, like all women, are often not viewed as having distinct public and private lives."[57] Whatever difficulties it may cause aside, this blurring of private or personal religious life with religious leadership further reinforces the welcome feelings of spirituality in the synagogue.

In addition to the more diffuse factors of the growing role of women, the contributions of individual women, and the blurring of private and public spheres for rabbis, the Reform movement has devoted attention to the roles of synagogues and rabbis in cultivating spirituality. In fact, the movement's annual conference in 1993 was organized around the theme of understanding and developing spirituality (and also dedicated to Sally Priesand, the first woman rabbi, on the twentieth anniversary of her ordination). The Dalai Lama, the honored guest speaker, plainly and eloquently explained the goal of the rabbis: "You all meet here, and the main purpose of your gathering is searching, searching, you see, for a deeper spiritual value."[58] One Reform rabbi at the denominational conference,

Steven Chester, lamented the past emphases of material society and called for a change in the rabbinate:

> [T]here has been an eclipse of God.... We were swallowed by the whale of success and materialism and we floated aimlessly. Suddenly, we were awakened to the realization that we needed more. We needed God, and God had been there all the time. We simply forgot how to relate to the *Shechinah* [the feminine, spiritual aspect of God]. We needed God to add a dimension to our lives, yes, even to our rabbinate.[59]

He went on to describe the former focus of the synagogue, explaining that it had overshadowed the "real" Judaism: "We stopped talking about God or preaching about God.... The Jewish people, Israel, Soviet Jewry, Social Action these became our sole reasons for occupying the pulpit. These were good reasons, but we forgot the cornerstone of our faith.... [We] banished God in the process."[60] American Jewry had spent so much time on external issues, he explains, that it had neglected issues of the soul. Chester went on to ask: "Why has 'spirituality' become the topic of so many conferences?" His answer was simple: Our people asked for it.

> I believe it is because we have been forced to deal with these questions, have been forced to look at and even explain our individual relationships to God because our congregants have demanded it of us.... Not too long ago our congregants stopped fleeing and began asking.... As they returned to synagogue life, they asked about their spiritual lives, about their place in the universe, and we had to respond, and many of us have. We have looked into our souls.[61]

The Reform congregants themselves began this return to spirituality, and the rabbis decided that they should follow. And follow they did: At a 2005 conference of Reform leaders, the sessions on spirituality were the most highly attended, and the *Houston Chronicle* reported on the "Yoga Minyan: Connecting Body and Soul to the Divine," a service consisting of prayers from the traditional liturgy matched to yoga poses. Rabbi Andrea London, who led the service, explained: "We took a service, and we embodied it fully."[62]

This new spirituality takes the form of changes in the regular service, as well as the addition of small groups and workshops offered in addition to it. Rabbis have begun to incorporate more time for personal reflection upon prayers and scripture. They encourage members to take time to consider what each word says to them during the service. Some have gone away from forward-facing pews in favor of circular formations or other more egalitarian arrangements. In addition to regular services, many synagogues offer extras, not only "yoga-minyan" types, but weekly spiritual growth workshops and small study groups focused on reconnecting with God.

Few heartily object to the new emphasis on spirituality, but those who do—mostly older members—explain the reason, ironically, is tradition. Reform Judaism, since its inception, has been based on a rational model of religion. Both leaders and individuals would decide whether or not to practice or believe in a certain way by using their own judgment. The founders and many following generations shunned what they saw as elaborate rituals based on mythic events. Return to observing outdated commandments and reinstituting "hocus-pocus" is a step backwards, offending the hard work to assemble a meaningful, rational religion for enlightened people, these dissenters think. One rabbi told the *Chronicle* that "spiritual stuff" was a charged issue that had the potential to spark some disagreement within the denomination.

Another institutional debate over a long-deliberated question also highlighted the turn to spirituality. The contentious "Who is a Jew?" question drives to the heart of defining Judaism itself. In years past, Judaism was passed on through the mother; a child with a Jewish father and non-Jewish mother would not be Jewish regardless of upbringing. But in a time of mix-and-match family units and personal choice, it was not uncommon to find people who felt Jewish, but were told that they must undergo conversion to be "truly" Jewish. In the last half-century, both Reform (1983) and Reconstructionist Judaism (1968) have decided that the answer should be in terms of spirituality rather than biology: Children of one Jewish parent, mother or father, are Jewish if they practice Judaism. The matter depends on inner person, not on maternal contribution to the DNA. One scholar points out: "The great majority of Jews ... have widely accepted patrilineal descent as the basis for Jewish identity."[63] This decision is immensely popular within these denominations despite the acrimony it causes with more traditional Jews; few disagree that religion is something other than a matter of the heart.

Taking a cue from disillusioned former members, synagogues in all four movements now organize their own study and prayer groups, some of which they even call *havurot*. Like the original intimate model, people form these groups based on similar interests or life situations. A Reconstructionist synagogue, for example, might sponsor a young adults' *havurah*, a gay and lesbian *havurah*, and a women's *havurah*. Unlike the unaffiliated *havurot*, the people who participate in these groups are also synagogue members who attend services.

Unlike Reform and Reconstructionist Judaism, which have embraced the popular growth of spirituality without significant concern, both Conservative and Orthodox branches worry about its authenticity. By 1999, Conservative Judaism in America decided that the still-growing issue demanded its time at the annual assembly of rabbis. Although some saw spirituality as "feel-good" Judaism without real content and found it threatening to substance, ritual, and commandments, the majority felt that a search for spirituality was worthy and traditional. In a discussion historically characteristic of Conservative Judaism, Jews looked to find a historical precedent for what they desired; once they found such a precedent, then they could embrace it through tradition. As Jewish Theological Seminary Professor Neil Gillman said, "There is nothing new about a meditative Judaism."[64] The Conservative movement was founded as a middle way, a way that held tradition highly, but also wanted to make Judaism accessible to Americans in a changing environment. For better or for worse, although many like Gillman think it for the better, a Conservative rabbi must respond to the demands of American culture and address the spiritual needs of members rather than the more broadly political issues of the past: "[The] agenda has shifted from a primary concern with the issues of Jewish peoplehood to the issues of Jewish religion, from concern with the State of Israel, Russian Jewry, and anti-Semitism to God, prayer, mitzvah, why 'bad things happen to good people,' and the afterlife."[65] The movement has begun to notice and take steps to accommodate the changing priorities among its members, but most rabbis think that the synagogue can and should do more to nurture spirituality among its members. One explained: "I think that we do not have an adequate space yet in our institutions and in our synagogues for the individual seeker."[66] Once leaders understand the idea of spirituality in Judaism as part of the tradition, they find it acceptable and want to help members by adding these elements, like slower prayer, directed meditation, and more silence, to their services.

Conservative objectors to this new spirituality, although in the minority, still have a significant voice. They think that the search for a warmer, fuzzier Judaism is a wasted effort because the result ceases to be Jewish. At the 1999 convention, Elliot Abrams contended: "What many people want is what you should not give them.... Many want the Conservative synagogue to be more like the rest of American culture—easy, relaxed, no standards, new lifestyles, get in touch with your feelings, get out a lot more than you put in."[67] What Conservative Judaism needs, he claimed, is not greater membership at the price of authenticity, but the cultivation of genuinely committed Jews. "Judaism should not be used to make us feel even better, which is what I think is often behind this call for more spirituality, instead of a call for more challenges, more observance, more Judaism."[68] Abrams, like most dissenters, would prefer renewed emphasis on study and observation of commandments instead of their opponents' interest in cultivating personal relationships with God.

The Orthodox movement is more significantly divided on the issue, but nevertheless recognizes its growing popularity. In 2005, the Orthodox Forum, the major body of leaders, chose as its topic the proper place of "spirituality" in Judaism, and the ambivalence in the movement was palpable. The Orthodox community, in its traditional stance, is wary of both change and "popular religion." The general American clamor for spirituality makes leaders concerned that "spiritual quests" and meditation are frequently inauthentically Jewish. Norman Lamm, an Orthodox scholar, claimed: "The contrast between the two—spirituality and law—is almost self-evident. Spirituality is subjective; the very fact of its inwardness implies a certain degree of anarchy; it is unfettered and self-directed, impulsive and spontaneous. In contrast, law is objective; it requires discipline, structure, obedience, order."[69] But even Lamm found the human impulse for spirituality and its traditional place within Judaism so apparent that he concludes that the spiritual must be given a place alongside the legal. In the same forum, Chaim Waxman declared that, given the pervasiveness of spirituality in America, rabbis ought to give positive attention to spirituality if they wanted to sustain membership: "Given the extent of the contemporary spiritual quest in American society, those seeking to, at least, stem the tide of defection from Orthodoxy if not attract others to it, would appear to be advised to foster and encourage this spiritualism within legitimate halakhic boundaries."[70] Once again, American Jewish leadership had to resourcefully balance American culture and its influences with Jewish tradition.

The place of spirituality in American Judaism remains in transition; it proliferates outside of synagogue walls, and has now begun to creep through the doors. Previously contained in the private sphere and the domain of the feminine, in the last three decades, American Jewish spirituality has crossed gender lines and come out in public. Some, like Lawrence Kushner, suggest that spirituality is the raison d'etre of the synagogue: "When we look into the eyes of our children and our grandchildren, ... we realize there is something beyond us. We are humbled and graced. We are reminded of our birth and of our death. We take our place in the long line. That is the root experience of religion. And that is why there are synagogues."[71] Others insist that Judaism is and always has been about law and tradition. Although the future of spirituality in American Judaism remains unknown, one thing remains certain: American Jewry will continue to grapple with both American culture and Jewish tradition to forge a creative solution that is both distinctly American and distinctly Jewish.

NOTES

1. Jonathan Sarna, *American Judaism: A History* (New Haven, CT: Yale University Press, 2004).

2. Zalman Schacter-Shalomi, *First Steps to a New Jewish Spirit* (Woodstock, VT: Jewish Lights Publishing, 2003).

3. Wade Clark Roof used the term to characterize the pick-and-choose nature of American religion. Wade Clark Roof, *Spiritual Marketplace: Baby Boomers and the Remaking of American Religion* (Princeton, NJ: Princeton University Press, 2001).

4. Hava Tirosh-Samuelson, "Jewish Spirituality: Past Models and Present Quest," in *Studies in Jewish Civilization XIII: Spiritual Dimensions of Judaism,* ed. Leonard Greenspoon and Ronald Simkins (Omaha, NE: Creighton University Press, 2003), 4.

5. For a discussion, see Marshall Sklare, *Jewish Identity on the Suburban Frontier* (New York: Basic Books, 1967).

6. Susan Alter, "The *Sefer Torah* Comes Home," in *Daughters of the King: Women and the Synagogue*, ed. Susan Grossman and Rivka Haut (Philadelphia: Jewish Publication Society, 1992), 281.

7. Dvora Weisberg, "On Wearing *Tallit* and *Teffilin*," in Grossman and Haut, eds., 283.

8. Paul Mendes-Flohr, "The Retrieval of Innocence and Tradition: Jewish Spiritual Renewal in an Age of Liberal Individualism," in *The Uses of Tradition: Jewish Continuity in the Modern Era*, ed. Jack Wertheimer (New York: Jewish Theological Seminary, 1992), 290.

9. Steven Cohen and Arnold Eisen, *The Jew Within* (Bloomington: Indiana University Press, 2000), 150–51.

10. Tirosh-Samuelson, 4.

11. David Ariel, *Spiritual Judaism: Restoring Heart and Soul to Jewish Life* (New York: Hyperion, 1998), 5.

12. Talya Penkower, "A Daughter's Decision," in Grossman and Haut, eds., 268.

13. Jerry Adler, "In Search of the Spiritual," *Newsweek* (August 29, 2005): 46.

14. Steven Cohen, "Are American and Israeli Jews Drifting Apart?" in *Imagining the Jewish Future*, ed. David Teutch (Albany: State University of New York Press, 1992), 119.

15. Ibid., 121.

16. Ibid., 122.

17. Chaim Waxman, "Weakening Ties: American Jewish Baby-Boomers and Israel," in *Envisioning Israel: The Changing Ideals and Images of North American Jews*, ed. Allon Gal (Jerusalem: Magnes Press, 1996), 377–78.

18. Arnold Eisen, "Theology and Community," in Teutch, ed., 248.

19. Susan Starr Sered, *Women as Ritual Experts: The Religious Lives of Elderly Jewish Women in Israel* (New York: Oxford University Press, 1992), 123.

20. Egon Mayer, "The Coming Reformation in American Jewish Identity," in Teutch, ed., 178.

21. Preface to *Jewish Identity in America*, ed. David Gordis and Yoav Ben-Horin (Los Angeles: University of Judaism, 1991), 14.

22. Martin Marty, "Religion in America Since Mid-Century," in *Religion and America: Spirituality in a Secular Age*, ed. Mary Douglas and Steven Tipton (Boston: Beacon, 1982), 273.

23. Ariel, 2.

24. Deborah Lipstadt, "Tradition and Religious Practice," in Teutch, ed., 40.

25. Arthur Green, "God, Prayer, and Religious Language," in Teutch, ed., 17.

26. Lipstadt, 43.

27. Ariel, 3.

28. Wertheimer, ed., ix.

29. Ariel, 3.

30. Steven Chester, "The Rabbi—The Nature of Religious Leadership Today," in *Central Conference of American Rabbis Yearbook*, vol. 104 (New York: Central Conference of American Rabbis, 1994), 53.

31. Sherwin Wine, *Judaism Beyond God* (New York: Ktav Publishing, 1985), 221.

32. Yaakov Malkin, *Secular Judaism: Faith, Values, and Spirituality* (London: Valentine Mitchell, 2004), 41.

33. Green, 13–14.

34. Mendes-Flohr, 283.

35. Michael Lerner, *Jewish Renewal: A Path to Healing and Transformation* (New York: Grosset/Putnam, 1994), 51.

36. Mendes-Flohr, 290.

37. Lerner, title of chapter 7.

38. Ariel, 285.

39. Lerner, 422.

40. Schachter-Shalomi, xxv.

41. Judith Plaskow, "God, Prayer, and Religious Language: A Response," in Teutch, ed., 32.

42. Arthur Waskow, "Social Justice: Reenvisioning Our Vision," in Teutch, ed., 201.

43. David Wortman, "Social Justice: Reenvisioning Our Vision: A Response," in Teutch, ed., 218.

44. Eisen, 254.

45. Rabbi Jeff Roth, personal interview with the author, December 15, 2005.

46. Ibid.

47. Mark Verman, *The History and Varieties of Jewish Meditation* (Northvale, NJ: Jason Aronson, 1996).

48. Malkin, 39.

49. Ibid., 37.

50. Wine, 221.

51. Lynn Davidman, *Tradition in a Rootless World: Women Turn to Judaism* (Berkeley: University of California Press, 1991), 24.

52. Ibid., 106.

53. Naomi Doron, "Building Synagogue Skills," in Grossman and Haut, eds., 261.

54. Susan B. Aranoff, "On Being a *Hazzanit*," in Grossman and Haut, eds., 263.

55. Aryeh Kaplan, *Jewish Meditation: A Practical Guide* (New York: Schocken, 1985), vii.

56. Mark Lee Raphael, *Judaism in America* (New York: Columbia University Press, 2003), 117.

57. Nancy Kasten, "Mi Li? Ma Ani? Our Public and Private Lives," in *Central Conference of American Rabbis Yearbook*, 21.

58. Dalai Lama, "Special Address," in *Central Conference of American Rabbis Yearbook*, 70.

59. Chester, 53.

60. Ibid., 53.

61. Ibid., 54.

62. Tara Dooley, "This is a Movement in Transition," *Houston Chronicle* (November 18, 2005).

63. Mayer, 180.

64. Neil Gillman, "The Renewed Yearning and a Search for God: A New Jewish Spirituality?" in *Proceedings of the Rabbinical Academy* (New York: Jewish Theological Seminary, 2000), 29.

65. Ibid., 20.

66. Ibid., 29.

67. Elliot Abrams, response to Neil Gillman, in *Proceedings of the Rabbinical Academy*, 26.

68. Ibid., 27.

69. Norman Lamm, *The Shema: Spirituality and Law in Judaism* (Philadelphia: Jewish Publication Society, 1998), 6–7.

70. Chaim Waxman, "Religion, Spirituality, and the Future of American Judaism," in *Jewish Spirituality and Divine Law*, ed. Adam Mintz and Lawrence Schiffman (New York: Yeshiva University Press, 2005), 514–15.

71. Lawrence Kushner, "The Synagogue and Caring Community," in Teutch, ed., 231.

SUGGESTIONS FOR FURTHER READING

Cohen, Steven, and Arnold Eisen. *The Jew Within*. Bloomington: Indiana University Press, 2000.

Greenspoon, Leonard, and Ronald Simkins, eds. *Studies in Jewish Civilization XIII: Spiritual Dimensions of Judaism*. Omaha, NE: Creighton University Press, 2003.

Lerner, Michael. *Jewish Renewal: A Path to Healing and Transformation.* New York: Grosset/Putnam, 1994.

Sarna, Jonathan. *American Judaism: A History.* New Haven, CT: Yale University Press, 2004.

Teutch, David, ed. *Imagining the Jewish Future.* Albany: State University of New York Press, 1992.

CHAPTER 5

Fundamentalism and Pentecostalism: The Changing Face of Evangelicalism in America

David G. Roebuck

On July 17, 2005, the Lakewood Church in Houston, Texas, taped its weekly television program that airs in more than 140 countries around the world on networks such as Black Entertainment Television and USA Network as well as the major religious networks such as Trinity Broadcasting Network. This Sunday was different, however. The eyes of many religious and secular observers were on this Pentecostal congregation that, under the leadership of Pastor Joel Osteen and his wife Victoria, had achieved celebrity status. Today they were in their new sanctuary—the Compaq Center, former home of the Houston Rockets. With more than $95 million of renovation, the now 16,000 seat sanctuary, complete with three jumbotrons, two waterfalls, and a large gold-colored rotating globe, was renamed the Lakewood International Center and became the home of America's largest church with some 30,000 members. New to much of the American public, this growing congregation has its roots deep within both the fundamentalist and Pentecostal traditions of American evangelicalism. But with only modest appreciation for its roots, it has quickly become the new face of evangelicalism in America.

THE EVANGELICAL MILIEU

Evangelicalism has had renewed influence in American life in the last quarter of the twentieth century and into the new millennium. This is evident in church attendance on Sunday mornings and in the polling places on election days. Although numbers are hard to come by, in his recent history of evangelicalism in America, the historian Douglas A. Sweeney suggests that one-tenth of the world's population is evangelical. Sweeney goes on to describe evangelicals as "gospel people," noting that the very label itself comes from the Greek word meaning "gospel" and that evangelicals are committed to sharing the gospel of Jesus Christ. Other more complex definitions of the word often look at a series of theological beliefs related to the nature of scripture, Jesus, salvation, and the role of the Christian in society. Yet Sweeney suggests that many definitions of evangelicalism tend to define little more than conservative, if not mainstream, Christianity.[1] Thus it is not surprising that the public often confuses and interchanges terms such as evangelicalism, fundamentalism, and Pentecostalism.

Contemporary evangelicalism began nearly 300 years ago, about the time of the Great Awakening, as Protestants who had previously been divided over issues that emerged from the Reformation began to join together for the promotion of revival, spiritual awakening, and common mission. Ministers such as John Wesley, Jonathan Edwards, and George Whitefield focused the attention of the English-speaking world on both sides of the Atlantic on the common goal of evangelism. Out of this emphasis came a broad cooperative Protestant Christianity that has come to be called evangelicalism. This new evangelicalism was particularly successful in those areas in which Christianity was separated from the idea of a state religion such as in the United States. According to Sweeney, "Disestablishment created a free market for religion in which evangelical entrepreneurs enjoyed unparalleled success."[2] Out of that success came the large variety of evangelical denominations that exist today in the United States. The nineteenth century proved to be a century of extraordinary growth for Methodists, and the twentieth proved to be just as successful for Baptists and Pentecostals. Of extraordinary importance in the twentieth century have been those segments of evangelicalism known as fundamentalism and Pentecostalism.

Although fundamentalism and Pentecostalism may be viewed as almost identical religious movements from a distance, this is not the line of sight used by those within these movements who are particularly aware of their differences. Further, these differences get exaggerated by insiders because one of the common characteristics of both of these movements is that they historically set themselves off from other Christians and from each other. Fundamentalists are quick to distinguish themselves from Pentecostals. And although some Pentecostals consider themselves fundamentalists, most in the last twenty-five years would disparage the connection. For our purposes in this chapter, I will suggest that fundamentalism and Pentecostalism can be considered the two extremes of the vast group of Christians in America today who call themselves evangelicals. But these are in fact the two extremes of evangelicalism that have had the growth and the most public attention in the last twenty-five years. Thus they cannot be ignored by observers of religion in America, including journalists and scholars. An example of this is that in his recent book on the emergence of pluralism in American religion, Charles H. Lippy acknowledged the resurgence and influence of these movements, even suggesting that "the major challenge to the hegemony" of mainline Protestantism came from those religious groups rooted in the Pentecostal movement that emerged at the beginning of the twentieth century.[3] According to Sweeney, the twentieth century saw an explosion of evangelicalism in the world. And the largest part of this includes Pentecostals and charismatics. Not to be outdone, fundamentalism continues to grow as well.

THE EMERGENCE OF FUNDAMENTALISM

The term "fundamentalism" is a broad category that is not limited to one or more denominations but is often used to refer to a variety of Protestant Christians who passionately emphasize what they identify as the fundamentals of the faith. Today it is often used by the public and the media to describe many conservative evangelicals—especially those who might be Baptist or on television or support the Right to Life movement. But the historical, theological, and social story of fundamentalism is far more complex and narrow. Although the list of "fundamentals" will sometimes vary, they most often refer to the authority of an inerrant Bible, the virgin birth of Jesus, the substitutionary sacrifice of Jesus to atone for sins, the bodily resurrection of Jesus, the authenticity of biblical miracles, and Jesus's return to earth to usher in a millennium of peace. But scholars such as George Marsden also note that while fundamentalists are deeply religious evangelicals, who hold to a specific set of doctrines, they have also been uniquely shaped by experiences in American culture.[4]

Fundamentalism as a more or less organized movement developed as a reaction against the growing modernism of the late nineteenth and early twentieth centuries. Modernism was the label attributed to liberal Protestants who increasingly accepted both evolution as an explanation for human origins and "higher criticism" as the dominant method of biblical studies. "Higher criticism" described the move away from a literal reading of the Bible in favor of a historical and symbolic reading of those texts that did not seem congruent with modern science and experience. Its proponents suggested that while the Bible was true in terms of faith, it should not be considered reliable in the areas of history and science. The use of higher criticism was highlighted in arguments that questioned the miracles related in scripture, the nature of Jesus, and the Genesis accounts of creation. Following the publication of Charles Darwin's *On the Origin of Species by Means of Natural Selection, or the Preservation of Favored Races in the Struggle for Life* in 1859, many scientists and Protestant theologians came to view some method of evolution—often theistic—rather than the Genesis accounts as a plausible model for understanding the emergence of life. By the 1880s college textbooks were beginning to include an evolutionary framework, and high school textbooks were not far behind. Such ideas also permeated the highest levels of theological training in America as well as some of the best known pulpits.

Those who would come to be called fundamentalists reacted against this defection from the faith and began to call for publications and organizations to stem the modernist tide. Denominations like the Presbyterian Church were split over the pronouncements of biblical scholars such as Charles Briggs at Union Seminary in New York. Opponents such as Charles Hodge and B.B. Warfield at Princeton Theological Seminary argued for an inerrant

Bible and traditional theology. Yet even Princeton eventually succumbed to new ways of thinking. The situation in America was exacerbated with societal changes that were taking place. As immigrants poured into the United States throughout the nineteenth century, cities began to explode with both people and problems. The Christian response varied, but some such as Washington Galdden and Walter Rauschenbusch critiqued the traditional evangelical gospel as inadequate because it failed to deal with the social problems of humankind. They called for a social gospel that gave primacy to solving the urban problems of the day rather than to saving men and women from their individual sins. This liberal approach was rejected by evangelicals, who appeared to abandon the hope of changing society in order to save some before the soon return of Jesus Christ.

In what has come to be called the "great reversal," evangelicals in large numbers shifted from a post-millennial view of Christ's return to a premillennial view. This premillennialism was bolstered by John Nelson Darby's dispensationalism, which taught that human history was divided into seven dispensations and that the church would be raptured before the Great Tribulation and the millennium.[5] Although neither side of the struggle between evangelicals and those who emphasized the social gospel was as one-sided as their opponents suggested, the social gospel's "liberal" approach to salvation was one more reason for fundamentalists to react against the changes of the time.

Sweeney suggests that fundamentalists are so well known in part because many of their battles took place among the educational and ecclesial institutions of America.[6] For example, the Presbyterian General Assembly called for all ordained ministers to subscribe to five fundamental Christian doctrines but abandoned that requirement in 1924. Princeton Theological Seminary began to become more tolerant when the presidency of J. Ross Stevenson began in 1914. In response to these types of changes, those calling for adherence to the fundamentals of the faith sounded the alarm. Three million copies of a twelve-volume set titled *The Fundamentals: A Testimony to the Truth* were sent to ministers and missionaries around the world. When more than 6,000 gathered for a conference of the World's Christian Fundamentals Association in 1919, fundamentalists had found an institutional home and signaled a renewed militancy. High on their enemies list was Darwinism, their most public spokesperson was former secretary of state and three-time presidential candidate William Jennings Bryan, and their most public battle in their war to call Americans to righteousness took place six years later in Dayton, Tennessee, in what has come to be called the Scopes Monkey Trial.[7]

Although the Dayton, Tennessee, trial should not be seen as the personification of fundamentalism, it brought to the public's attention a cultural divide that had been increasingly widening. With growing numbers of students involved in secondary education by the 1920s, anti-evolutionists became alarmed at the possibility of millions of American youth being exposed to evolution in their science textbooks. Beginning with Kentucky, legislative efforts to ban the teaching of evolution were at the forefront of the efforts of anti-evolutionists. In January 1925, primitive Baptist John

Washington Butler introduced a bill to prohibit teaching evolution in Tennessee's public schools. Butler's bill made it criminal to teach "any theory that denies the story of the Divine creation of man as taught in the Bible, and to teach instead that man has descended from a lower order of animals."[8] With support coming in countless sermons and newspaper articles, the Tennessee legislature passed the bill. Many Tennesseans, including Governor Austin Peay who had signed the bill into law, hoped the Butler law would allow time for the debate over evolution to subside. They expressed belief that the law would never be enforced.

Such hopes did not anticipate an active American Civil Liberties Union, however, who, believing the bill was a violation of free speech, advertised in Tennessee newspapers for someone willing to test the new law. On May 5, 1925, a group of Dayton businessmen asked substitute science teacher John Thomas Scopes to test the law. They hoped such a test case would bring both publicity and prosperity to the small town. The resulting trial, which became known as the "Trial of the Century," became a national display of both the best of public oratory and the best of American carnival. Joe Mendi, known as the "chimpanzee with the intelligence of a five-year-old child," was brought to Dayton so that, according to advertisements, "Every man has a perfect right to decide for himself as to whether his 'family tree' bore coconuts or not."[9] The famed attorney Clarence Darrow defended Scopes. Bryan argued the case for the state of Tennessee. Almost two hundred journalists, including H.L. Mencken, covered the proceedings, and by the time Scopes was convicted on a misdemeanor, many considered Dayton the epicenter of backward culture and religious fanaticism. Scholars now see the trial as the quintessential clash between culture and values in America: between the North and the South, between urban industrialization and rural agrarian economies, and between Protestant liberalism and fundamentalism.

With an onslaught of public ridicule, many erroneously believed that fundamentalism had experienced a death blow in American culture. Nothing was further from the truth, however. Rather, fundamentalist Christians quietly developed institutions and nurtured the faithful. Within denominations and independent congregations they formed networks and support groups. Indeed, the years since 1970 have seen an extraordinary surge of public activities of fundamentalists in American politics and a renewed public debate over the teaching of evolution in public schools.

THE EMERGENCE OF PENTECOSTALISM

Pentecostals are those Christians who emphasize the immediate work of the Holy Spirit in the life of the Christian. They claim an experience called the baptism of the Holy Spirit in which the Christian has a post-conversion encounter that is often accompanied by speaking in tongues and other gifts of the Holy Spirit. Pentecostals base their theology on biblical passages such as Joel 2:28–29 and Acts 2. According to Joel, the "word of the Lord" was: "Then afterward I will pour out my spirit on all flesh; your sons and your daughters shall prophesy, your old men shall dream dreams, and your young men shall see visions. Even on the male and female slaves, in those days, I will pour out my spirit." Following the ascension of Jesus, the disciples who gathered on the Jewish feast day of Pentecost experienced "a sound like the rush of a violent wind" and "divided tongues as of fire." According to Luke, "All of them were filled with the Holy Spirit and began to speak in other languages as the Spirit gave them ability" (Acts 2:4). When questioned about the event, Peter claimed that this was the fulfillment of Joel's prophecy (Acts 2:16–21).

The historian Edith L. Blumhofer has suggested that although fundamentalism was primarily a reaction against modernism, Pentecostalism was primarily an attempt "to reverse the overwhelming trend toward 'carnality' in the churches and among church members."[10] Although fundamentalists focused on the theological battle with modernism, Pentecostals engaged more in a pietistic protest. Pentecostalism is one of the fastest growing religious movements in the United States today. Just as important, it has influenced large numbers of Christians in most denominations.

Interpreters of Pentecostalism often talk about three waves of development. The first wave, or "classical" Pentecostalism, was born out of radical nineteenth-century perfectionism and restorationism. Those searching to perfect the soul and to restore the New Testament church turned to the language in the biblical book of Acts that describes the outpouring of the Holy Spirit on the day of Pentecost. They concluded that they were living in the "last days" and that God was granting a fresh outpouring of the Holy Spirit. The evidence of that outpouring was supernatural gifts of the Spirit. In particular speaking in tongues was seen as the biblical evidence that the believer was "baptized in the Holy Spirit." While the giving of the Spirit on the day of Pentecost was the "former rain" of the Spirit given to establish the church, this "latter rain" of the Holy Spirit was seen as the final preparation of the church in order to win the world for Christ in the last days.

Pentecostals look to two events as foundational to the movement. Under the tutelage of holiness preacher Charles Fox Parham, Agnes Ozman spoke in tongues at Parham's Bethel Bible School in Topeka, Kansas, on January 1, 1901. Although the history of Christianity has included others who have spoken in tongues, it was Parham who brought together the cluster of ideas that included the premillennial return of Christ, radical perfectionism, and the supernatural gifts of the Spirit. Parham concluded the Spirit was being poured out in the last days and that speaking in tongues was a supernatural impartation of a natural human language specifically to win the world before the soon return of Christ.

Although Parham's ideas and influence were limited, they were transmitted by one of his disciples to a revival in Los Angeles now known as the Azusa Street revival. William J. Seymour, an African American, attended Parham's Bible School in Houston, Texas, in 1905 and was later invited to Los Angeles to pastor a small holiness mission. When participants in a home prayer meeting on Bonnie Brae Street experienced speaking in tongues, the neighborhood was so inundated with seekers and onlookers that the small group moved to facilities at 312 Azusa Street.

There they established the Apostolic Faith Mission and conducted a revival that lasted from 1906 to 1913. News of events, bolstered in part by attempts to explain the concurrent San Francisco earthquake, spread quickly in both the secular and religious press, and many holiness denominations and independent ministries seeking spiritual gifts and some form of perfectionism were influenced by the revival. Already existing holiness groups, such as the Pentecostal Holiness Church of North Carolina and the Church of God in Christ, were swept into the Pentecostal movement. New denominations of Pentecostal believers, such as the Assemblies of God, soon formed as well. Parham's theology and Seymour's revival had ushered in what Vinson Synan describes as "the century of the Holy Spirit."[11]

THE PUBLIC TRANSFORMATION
OF PENTECOSTALISM

For the most part what we now call classical Pentecostalism remained hidden from public life in America during the first half of the twentieth century. Most congregations worshipped in small meeting houses on the other side of the railroad tracks or in storefronts that dotted downtowns. The occasional Pentecostal who garnered public notoriety such as Aimee Semple McPherson,[12] did little to endear Pentecostals to most Americans. Yet Pentecostalism turned out to be an extraordinary missionary movement that slowly but surely built networks and institutions both within and without the United States. Along the way, its message of a fresh outpouring of the Holy Spirit began to influence some in Roman Catholic congregations and mainline Protestant denominations who were seeking renewal of their own traditions.

This emphasis on renewal through the work of the Holy Spirit, which began in the second half of the twentieth century, came to be called the charismatic movement and is now referred to as the "second wave" of Pentecostalism. The beginning of the movement is generally attributed to Dennis Bennett who, as rector of St. Mark's Episcopal Church in Van Nuys, California, announced his personal experience of speaking in tongues to his congregation in 1960. Although Bennett was forced to resign from St. Mark's, "exile" to St. Luke's Episcopal Church in Seattle, Washington, gave him an opportunity to share his story and influence thousands of Christians in mainline denominations. A new openness to an emphasis on the Holy Spirit existed in part owing to the emergence of the "healing evangelists" in the 1940s and 1950s. Countless numbers of people who considered themselves as mainstream Protestants were exposed to Pentecostal theology through television programs and tent meetings of evangelists such as Oral Roberts and T.L. Osborn. Others were brought into the baptism of the Holy Spirit through parachurch ministries, such as the Full Gospel Business Men's Fellowship International, which began in Los Angeles in 1951 and quickly spread throughout the United States. Although those who emphasized the gifts of the Spirit at the beginning of the twentieth century had often found themselves ostracized by their denominations and thus organized their new Pentecostal denominations, fifty years later these new converts to the Pentecostal message remained within their mainline denominations and attempted to renew them. These Christians came to call themselves "charismatics" in order to distinguish themselves from Pentecostals.[13]

The charismatic renewal also grew rapidly among Roman Catholics in the United States. This was particularly facilitated by Pope John XXIII, who called for a new general council of the Roman Catholic Church. Vatican II looked for a "new Pentecost," recognized the work of the Holy Spirit in the "separated brothers" of Protestantism, and emphasized the charismatic gifts of the Holy Spirit—all of which opened doors for the newly emerging charismatic movement among Roman Catholics. The early development of the movement is attributed to events at two universities in 1967: Duquesne University in Pittsburgh, Pennsylvania, and the University of Notre Dame in South Bend, Indiana. At both, faculty and students alike read books with Pentecostal testimonies, studied the biblical book of the Acts of the Apostles, and sought for the baptism of the Holy Spirit. From these two universities interests in the charismatic renewal of the Catholic church grew rapidly, especially among those affiliated with Catholic higher education. The results included an extraordinary amount of theological reflection and the publication of a large number of books for both popular and academic audiences. In 1977 Protestant and Roman Catholic charismatic leaders joined forces to hold a conference on charismatic renewal in Kansas City, Missouri. About half of the 45,000 attendees were Protestant and about half were Catholic.[14]

The term "charismatic" is also used to denote many independent churches that emphasize the gifts of the Spirit, but are not a part of any denomination. These tend to look more like classical Pentecostal churches than do charismatics in mainline Protestant or Roman Catholic churches. Examples include Victory Christian Center in Tulsa, Oklahoma, and Crenshaw Christian Center in Los Angeles, California. Many of these large independent churches are in what is called the "Faith/Word" movement, which teaches that God desires Christians to have the faith to experience personal health and prosperity and that such blessings are realized by speaking words of faith.

The "third wave" or "neocharismatic renewal" is the most recent development in the history of Pentecostalism. This category is used to describe groups that emphasize the Holy Spirit, spiritual gifts and Pentecostal-like experiences, signs and wonders, and power encounters, but do not use classical Pentecostal terminology. Third-wave groups often do not see speaking in tongues as the evidence of Spirit baptism or as even a necessary part of the work of the Spirit in the life of the Christian. Most in the neocharismatic renewal are not historically or theologically linked to Pentecostals. The best known of these are Calvary Chapel Ministries and the Vineyard Christian Fellowship. Calvary Chapel Ministries began as a single congregation in Costa Mesa, California, under the leadership of Chuck Smith, who received national attention during the 1970s "Jesus

People" revival. Smith's emphasis on casual worship and Bible study led to rapid growth and the birth of more than 300 other congregations throughout the United States. Initially founded by Ken Gullichson, the Association of Vineyard Churches experienced extraordinary growth when John Wimber joined after leaving Calvary Chapel Ministries. Wimber was a former musician who had earlier formed the rock group, the Righteous Brothers. He was converted in 1963 and made a spiritual pilgrimage from the Society of Friends to Calvary Chapel and into the Vineyard. By 2005 the Vineyard reported about 600 congregations in the United States. Perhaps because of Wimber's musical background, they are particularly well known for a style of "praise" music that has influenced many churches across the evangelical spectrum.

Typical of many third-wave churches, both Calvary Chapel Ministries and the Association of Vineyard Churches emphasize divine healing, signs and wonders, and power manifestations in which a spontaneous work of the Holy Spirit leads to a supernatural event. Although there is a place for speaking in tongues it is not considered the sign of a Spirit baptism experience as it is among classical Pentecostals. In a more general sense, the term third wave is also used as a broad category to place groups that emphasize the work of the Holy Spirit but do not fit into either classical Pentecostalism or the charismatic movement. This is particularly true of groups outside the United States.

It is difficult to determine how many Pentecostals of all three waves there are in the United States and around the world. Pentecostals are not unique in that they count members or constituents in a variety of different ways and often to their best possible advantage. The statistics quoted most often are those generated by David B. Barrett, a research professor of missiometrics and global evangelization at Regent University in Virginia Beach, Virginia. In the year 2000 Barrett reported 523 million worldwide, divided into 65 million classical Pentecostals, 175 million charismatics, and 295 million third wavers. Of these only 32 percent were in the Western world and just over 75,000,000 were in the United States.[15]

However they are counted, Pentecostals have emerged as an important force in contemporary religious life and may well represent the most influential Christian movement of the last quarter of the twentieth century. The renewed emphasis on the work of the Holy Spirit, the millenarian missionary impulse, and vibrant worship style has led to extraordinary growth. This growth has undoubtedly been aided in part by the importance given to a personal expression of religious faith at a time when this has become a dominant value in the religious landscape. Although Christianity has always had the personal dimension, there emerged in the twentieth century what Charles H. Lippy calls an "astounding proliferation to the expression of personal spirituality."[16] This proliferation spanned the spectrum of religious faith in America from Pentecostalism to Neopaganism as well as secular movements such as Alcoholics Anonymous. Its presence has been particularly helpful to the growth of movements such as Pentecostalism and fundamentalism. Recent Pentecostalism is different from that of its roots, however. And this difference is directly tied to the rebirth of public fundamentalism.

THE REBIRTH OF PUBLIC FUNDAMENTALISM

Many observers of religion in America believed that fundamentalism had died with the legal victory but subsequent public discrediting in the Scopes Trial of 1925. Such was the opinion of the eminent editors of the famed *Christian Century* who touted the death of the movement they considered "hollow and artificial" and "lacking in qualities of constructive achievement or survival."[17] This belief was decidedly mistaken, however. The heirs to fundamentalism began to establish a potent network of non-denominational congregations, Bible institutes and colleges, youth camps, periodicals, and other parachurch ministries that enabled them both to separate from compromising Christians and to inculcate their faith into their own constituency. Fundamentalist heroes arose who encouraged and nurtured the faithful along with providing places of formation for their youth. Perhaps the best known of these were evangelists like Bob Jones, who founded what is today Bob Jones University, and John R. Rice, whose *Sword of the Lord* was read religiously by countless devotees for decades.

Instead of dying, fundamentalism divided into two primary camps. One camp withdrew from public life with the intention of remaining separate from those who had compromised and accommodated modernism. But another camp evolved and emerged with the intent of engaging and changing both religious and public life. Both of these camps remained hidden through the two decades that followed the Dayton, Tennessee, events, but neither remained dormant. Both emerged in the 1940s with public associations designed to give them presence and clout in the public arena.

The largest of these associations was the National Association of Evangelicals (NAE). Founded in 1941 under the leadership of J. Elwin Wright and Harold John Ockenga, the NAE adopted a position of "cooperation without compromise." They avoided the use of terms such as fundamentalist and preferred to be called "new evangelicals." Their stance can be seen in the title of their periodical, *United Evangelical Action*, and they encouraged participation in the public arena through a public affairs office and a humanitarian agency known as World Relief. Some even softened their position on scripture by jettisoning language referring to the inerrancy of scripture in favor of language that affirmed the authority of scripture.

Of particular importance was the development of a related organization, the National Religious Broadcasters, in order to capitalize on the airwaves as a means of spreading the gospel. These cooperating heirs to fundamentalism soon dominated Christian radio, and today they dominate Christian television, especially through cable and satellite networks such as the Trinity Broadcasting Network, the Christian Broadcasting Network, the Inspiration Network, and Daystar Television Network. In addition to broadcasting, the emergence of the magazine *Christianity Today*, which was the idea of evangelist Billy Graham, gave the new evangelicals a significant voice in the print media. Today publishing among the new evangelicals is big business. Outlets such as Family Bookstores occupy malls, and popular titles such as Tim LaHaye's *Left Behind* series sell millions and propagate fundamentalist theology among the masses. On television stations, in bookstores, and in pulpits across the nation these heirs of fundamentalism seemed in the last quarter of the twentieth century to have arrived. Particularly important to our story is that these fundamentalists-turned-new-evangelicals welcomed, even if sometimes begrudgingly, the inclusion of Pentecostals, and Pentecostals leaped at the chance to be inside the new evangelical establishment. Pentecostals have often served as leaders of the National Association of Evangelicals and its related organizations. And Pentecostal churches represent 50 percent of the organization in terms of membership.[18]

Many new evangelicals and especially Pentecostals have done remarkably well in television. Edith Blumhofer suggests that as a popular religion, Pentecostalism excels on television for several reasons. First the rhetoric of evangelism does well on television. Television provides what many Pentecostals believe is an efficient way to communicate the gospel. Second, television serves as a showcase for demonstrating the blessings of God with the display of fine clothes, jewelry, sanctuaries, and stage furnishings. This has been especially true among Word/Faith preachers, such as Kenneth E. Hagin, who have taught that God's people should expect physical and financial as well as spiritual prosperity.[19] Finally Pentecostals have always been fascinated with modern technology. Although Pentecostals at first resisted television, they have generally been open to the latest technology and comforts of American culture.[20] This openness to the modern has been a characteristic of Pentecostalism from its earliest days according to historian Grant Wacker in his extraordinary look at the early years of Pentecostalism, *Heaven Below: Early Pentecostals and American Culture.*[21]

Yet Billy Graham and his new evangelical colleagues have had their opponents among contemporary fundamentalists. Along with the National Association of Evangelicals (NAE), another group known as the American Council of Christian Churches was also founded in 1941. Its leader, Carl McIntire, sought to separate not only from the world but from those, such as Graham, who did not separate from the world. In pulpits and the printed page of his *Christian Beacon* he attacked not only the modernists and their representative voice, which at the time was the Federal Council of Churches of Christ, but he also attacked new evangelicals just as vigorously. Among other issues was the NAE's acceptance of the Pentecostals.

The results of this infighting are that fundamentalists and their heirs have continued to be divided over issues at the core of their faith. By 1957 the very popular Graham was criticized for including mainline Protestants on the stage during his evangelistic crusades. In the eyes of McIntire, Jones, and Rice, Graham was cooperating with the enemy and thus had become the enemy. When Fuller Theological Seminary, a bastion of evangelical thought, dropped language on the inerrancy of scripture from its statement of faith, it too was seen as having compromised with liberal Christianity. Perhaps the bloodiest battle has occurred among the

Southern Baptist Convention, in which a civil war broke out in the late 1970s between so-called "fundamentalists" and "moderates," over views of scripture. Once those in the "fundamentalist" camp had taken control over the major institutions such as the Baptist Sunday School Board (now LifeWay) and seminaries such as the Southern Theological Seminary in Louisville, many of the so-called moderates began to support the alternative Cooperative Baptist Fellowship. Along the way the Southern Baptist Convention has grown even more conservative in its rejection of social change, such as refusing to accept women in the ordained ministry.[22]

It is difficult to know how many heads to count when estimating the number of fundamentalists in America in the early twenty-first century, but the movement had a remarkable resurgence in the last half of the twentieth century. Most churches that identify themselves as fundamentalist are independent, having long left the confinement of denominations that they considered liberal and worldly. Many of these can be identified by the use of "Bible" in their name. A few fundamentalist networks have emerged. Larry Eskridge presents a narrow but helpful definition on the Web site of the Institute for the Study of American Evangelicals at Wheaton College. He notes that:

> since the 1940s, the term fundamentalist has come to denote a particularly aggressive style related to the conviction that the separation from cultural decadence and apostate (read *liberal*) churches are telling marks of faithfulness to Christ. Most self-described fundamentalist churches today are conservative, separatist Baptist (though often calling themselves "Bible Baptist" or simply "Bible" churches) congregations such as the churches of the General Association of Regular Baptist Churches (GARBC), or the Independent Fundamental Churches of America (IFCA). Institutions associated with this movement would include Bob Jones University (Greenville, SC) and Tennessee Temple (Chattanooga, TN); representative publications would be the *Sword of the Lord* and the *Biblical Evangelist*.[23]

Most definitions of fundamentalism revolve around the rigid adherence to a sacred text—in the case of Christianity, the Bible; and many new evangelicals and Pentecostals fit into that category. Yet most evangelicals eschew the term not for doctrinal reasons but because of past stigma or because of the rigid separation demanded by fundamentalists. Should Pentecostals be included in the numbers when counting fundamentalists? Certainly those of the second and third waves should not be included. But what about classical Pentecostals? Fundamentalists themselves tend to reject Pentecostals, yet most classical Pentecostals would pass a fundamentalist test related to doctrine. Although neither a view of scripture as inerrant nor premillennial dispensationalism is historically Wesleyan, even those Pentecostal denominations out of the Wesleyan tradition have adopted these doctrinal positions practically if not officially. The Church of God (Cleveland, TN) is a case in point. The Church of God's declaration of faith does not use the word "inerrant" in its discussion of the authority of scripture. Yet it can be argued that many of its members would use this term when discussing scripture and might even label themselves as fundamentalists. It is clear that the denomination officially avoids this characterization of the movement as fundamentalist, however. The movement's official history describes the Church of God as "foundational" in reference to the basic doctrines of Christianity. But when these foundation doctrines are listed they are in fact the five "fundamentals." This language is repeated on the denomination's Web site as well.[24]

However they are counted, fundamentalists have been very visible in American life in recent years and have often been credited with being key to the elections of Ronald Reagan and George W. Bush to the White House. They are also active participants in public discussion and policy making on a broad agenda that includes the availability of abortions, the selection of Supreme Court justices, the production of stem cells, and the use of school vouchers, as well as the ongoing place of evolution and creationism in public schools. It seems that politics have reunited the American religious right of all denominations, and fundamentalists seem to be at the heart of it despite their inability to cooperate with other evangelicals in other ways.[25] Certainly Pentecostals have not only joined with fundamentalists in promoting a conservative political agenda, but many have become active participants in government. For example, Assemblies of God members who have been part of the institutions of government include James Watt, Secretary of the Interior under Reagan, and John Ashcroft, who served as attorney general for George W. Bush after having served as governor of Missouri. M.G. "Pat" Robertson, a charismatic Baptist and one of the most public charismatic figures, made a significant run for the Republican nomination for president of the United States in 1988. One should not limit the appeal of fundamentalism to the power of a political agenda, however. Within fundamentalism are powerful attractions for some people. Charles H. Lippy has noted the power of informal worship and absolute stands in a culture that is rocked by ambiguity on many of the moral and theological issues of the day.[26]

PRESENCE AND POWER TODAY AND TOMORROW

Despite the emergence of fundamentalism in the last part of the twentieth century, the future of evangelicalism may lie with Pentecostalism or at least a Pentecostal-influenced evangelicalism. Although this influence is difficult to measure, it cannot be denied, even in those theological traditions most resistant, such as the Southern Baptist Convention (SBC). Congregations that practice speaking in tongues are sometimes barred from local or state Baptist associations, but the national convention has not ruled on this issue because it considers this a local matter rather than a national matter. Baptist missionaries will not be sent if they testify to speaking in tongues, however.[27] Despite such restrictions, there are significant numbers of Baptists who have been influenced by Pentecostalism in both subtle and overt ways. In her article, "Pentecostal Currents in the SBC," Helen Lee Turner attempts to suggest some of the ways that Southern Baptists have been influenced by Pentecostalism. Among those are a more open stance toward immediate divine intervention and at least in some places an emphasis on the preacher as a prophet. Characteristics of the latter include the preacher kneeling for prayer prior to the sermon and a lively, loud preaching style. Turner also concludes that worship space and style have been influenced by Pentecostals. Although she admits the difficulty of showing cause and effect, she points to the move toward radial rather than rectangular worship space, which creates more of a community atmosphere and allows for more space for the response of the people; the use of smaller and translucent pulpits, which seem to eliminate some distance between the congregation and the preacher; the use of a larger platform area, which gives more space for musical ensembles and dramatic presentations; and the trend toward singing courses rather than hymns, which allows for music that is easily learned and easily sung and also frees the hands for worship.[28] Despite Turner's suggestive examples, it is difficult to know to what degree these currents are "Pentecostal" and to what degree they are simply societal changes that are being adapted by Pentecostals as well as other Christian groups.

THE FACE OF PENTECOSTALISM IN THE TWENTY-FIRST CENTURY

However one determines cause and effect, Lakewood International Center in Houston is a revealing example of a congregation's move from fundamentalism to Pentecostalism and then to what may be the future look of evangelicalism. The Lakewood Church began under the leadership of John Osteen and his wife, Delores (Dodie). John Osteen, a Southern Baptist minister and pastor in Houston, experienced a personal baptism in the Holy Spirit in 1958 as well as the healing of his daughter from an injury she sustained at birth. When other church members received the baptism of the Holy Spirit, Osteen found it difficult to remain in his local church and launched a healing ministry. Then on Mother's Day in 1959 he started the Lakewood Baptist Church in an abandoned feed store just outside of Houston.[29]

The Osteens' youngest son, Joel, attended Oral Roberts University for a brief time and then in 1981 came to work for the church in order to produce a television program. The program became very successful and by 2005 aired on many Christian television networks in both a one-hour and half-hour formats. The show is unique in that it never solicits money as part of the program.

With John's preaching style and Joel's marketing abilities, the Lakewood Church achieved remarkable growth and became widely known in the Pentecostal and charismatic world. Six thousand people attended each Sunday by the time of John's death in 1999. Despite his lack of experience, Joel became the senior pastor of the Lakewood Church, and the church quickly rose to the top of the growing ranks of megachurches in America. Even the 8,000-seat sanctuary built in 1987 was unable to accommodate those who came to worship, and the church began to look for a place to relocate. When the National Basketball Association's

Houston Rockets vacated the Compaq Center, Lakewood Church leased the facility and turned it into a 16,000 seat sanctuary. Once again an abandoned facility was transformed into a worship center. "I don't want this to sound arrogant, but I believe one day we're going to have 100,000 a weekend," Osteen has said.[30] Currently the church has a Saturday evening service and multiple services on Sunday, including a Sunday afternoon Spanish-language service.

Lakewood is not a traditional Pentecostal church. Rather, it looks more like a third-wave congregation than a classical Pentecostal church. Neither is Joel Osteen a traditional Pentecostal preacher. He works hard to have a positive, upbeat, and relevant message. His signature theme is "Discover the Champion in You," and his preaching focuses on practical living rather than fine points of theology. The message is one of inclusion rather than separation. Yet when one looks closely, one sees that the church is clearly rooted in both the fundamentalist and Pentecostal camps. The first declaration in its seven-point statement of faith is "We believe the entire Bible is inspired by God, without error and the authority on which we base our faith, conduct and doctrine." One has to look more closely to find evidence of the charismatic movement, at least on the church's Web site. Although there is no doctrinal statement on speaking in tongues, there is the mention of a monthly class on the baptism of the Holy Spirit. The statement of faith also includes the call for each believer to yield to the Holy Spirit and the declaration that children of God "are overcomers and more than conquerors and God intends for each of us to experience the abundant life He has in store for us." This latter point fits well with the Word of Faith strand of Pentecostalism that had been preached by John Osteen, as does the declaration that the congregation recites aloud before each sermon:

This is my Bible.
I am what it says I am.
I have what it says I have.
I can do what it says I can do.
Today I will be taught the Word of God.
I boldly confess.
My mind is alert.
My heart is receptive.
I will never be the same.
I am about to receive the incorruptible, indestructible, ever-living seed of
   the Word of God.
I will never be the same.
Never, never, never.
I'll never be the same.
In Jesus' name.

As is typical in fundamentalist and Pentecostal churches of the past, each sermon ends with an altar call, in which dozens of people respond to the opportunity for salvation and dedication to Jesus Christ. There are some unique aspects of the Lakewood Church, however, including the fact that from its earliest days it has had nearly equal numbers of Hispanic,

African American, and Anglo members. Such multiculturalism has been rare in Pentecostalism since the revival at the Azusa Street Mission in 1906.

Like his father before him, Joel Osteen has become far more than a local pastor. His extensive television exposure has made him a religious celebrity. His book, *Your Best Life Now: 7 Steps to Living at Your Full Potential*, was widely promoted on television talk and news shows such as *Good Morning, America* and *Larry King Live!* and quickly rose to the top of the *New York Times* bestseller list. It has spawned a companion devotional book, *Daily Readings from Your Best Life Now*, so that the previous book can be consumed in ninety "bite-sized bits."[31] In July 2004, Joel and Victoria began to tour major cities of the United States to hold "An Evening with Joel Osteen." Hundreds of thousands have purchased $10 tickets through TicketMaster in order to have an evening with music, worship, and a motivational sermon complete with a traditional evangelical altar call. With its occupation of the Compaq Center, the Lakewood Church has greatly increased its visibility in Houston as well and is becoming a major player in the community. For example, in December 2005 the Lakewood Church hosted the Houston Symphony and Chorus, with the evening's program narrated by Pastor Joel Osteen and his wife Victoria.

Through megachurches such as the Lakewood Church, Pentecostalism will have even more influence on faith in America in the coming years. Megachurches are a new American phenomenon and are typically considered those churches with more than 2,000 in attendance on a given Sunday. Most of them are evangelical, and the largest number is Southern Baptist. But a growing number of them are Pentecostal—at least in background. Examples of Pentecostal megachurches include Brownsville Church (Assemblies of God) in Pensacola, Florida, Cornerstone Church in Houston, Crenshaw Christian Center in Los Angeles, First Assembly of God in Phoenix, Arizona, The Potter's House in Dallas, Texas, and World Harvest Church in Columbus, Ohio. Their worship is often very contemporary, with an emphasis on dynamic and lively music that is made possible through the services of paid musicians and the best sound and video equipment that money can buy. Congregations have usually been built around one central personality, although in the case of Lakewood Church the ministry of the father has been extended through the son. Although megachurches are currently most successful in the Sunbelt and can exist only in areas with lots of people and property, their influence reaches far beyond the driving distance of its membership because many of them have television programs viewed by large audiences and their pastors often host or attend conferences for ministers and laity around the world. Thus these megachurches have become a type of "cathedral," with the pastor serving as bishop of a large number of ministers.[32] With their public and powerful presence, Pentecostals are no longer a marginalized sector of American Christianity.

With the rise of neo-Pentecostalism and megachurches such as Lakewood Church, it is not surprising that Pentecostalism has had a major influence on evangelical Christianity. Douglas Sweeney calls attention to the fact that the casual "come as you are" style of the Calvary Chapels and Vineyard have been adopted by many congregations, as has a more casual and enthusiastic form of worship that includes heavy doses of folk and pop music. Sweeney concludes, "Now found in every Christian tradition in every corner of the world, uniquely Pentecostal passion for apostolic authenticity, the supernatural gifts, and energetic spirituality has excited the Christian piety and practices of billions. Perhaps the fastest-growing movement that the church has ever seen, holiness-Pentecostalism—as conveyed by charismatics—has given the one, holy, catholic, and apostolic church a facelift, rendering its features more evangelical in the process."[33] Corwin E. Smidt and his colleagues concur that Pentecostalism has made "inroads within American religious life" and go on to suggest that in addition to the influence at the institutional level, important changes have occurred at the individual level.[34] These include an increase in interaction between Pentecostals and other Christians, the fact that Pentecostals now come from a variety of social and cultural backgrounds, the cross-fertilization that the radio and television media has produced, and the apparent changes in worship styles across denominations.[35]

CHALLENGES FOR OVERCOMERS

Although both fundamentalists and Pentecostals declare that the Christian can be an overcomer and although these movements have had tremendous impact on faith in America in the last twenty-five years, the movements themselves face a variety of challenges. Many of these are the typical challenges that face most Christian denominations in the United States. These include, for example, an aging ministry. The youthful Joel Osteen is unusual in pulpits today. The Church of God reports that only 15 percent of its pastors are under the age of forty, and it is likely that similar statistics can be reported by most other Pentecostal denominations and independent churches. Another challenge is the shift from the prominence of small churches in rural America to churches that serve the growing populations of the nation's cities. As small towns decrease, so do the numbers of members of their churches. Yet those that remain need pastoral care. And planting churches in cities requires different strategies and increased resources.

Also typical of other Christian groups is the struggle to become more inclusive in an increasingly racially diverse America on a shrinking globe. Following the founding days of the movement, Pentecostals quickly divided along racial, ethnic, and doctrinal lines. It was not until they became part of the National Association of Evangelicals that Pentecostal denominations began to look beyond their differences toward the possibilities of cooperation not only among other evangelicals but among themselves. In 1947 many Pentecostal denominations gathered together in Europe for the inaugural meeting of the World Pentecostal Conference in Zurich, Switzerland. Then in 1948 representatives of several U.S. denominations formed the Pentecostal Fellowship of North America (PFNA). They adopted the statement of faith of the National Association of Evangelicals, with the addition of an article on the baptism of the Holy Spirit and speaking in tongues. All of the charter denominations and others that later joined were majority-white denominations. No denomination was invited to join that was a majority-black denomination.

When Bishop Bernard E. Underwood of the International Pentecostal Holiness Church was elected as chairperson of the PFNA in 1991, he moved toward the inclusion of other races in the organization. At their annual meeting in Memphis in 1994, members disbanded the PFNA and organized a new group that included both black and white denominations, along with independent charismatic congregations and networks. By the time the meeting ended, delegates were calling the event the "Memphis Miracle." Named the Pentecostal/Charismatic Churches of North America (PCCNA), this new organization has been led by black and white co-chairs. Bishop Ithiel Clemmons of the Church of God in Christ became the first African American co-chair.

Despite the powerful and groundbreaking beginning, the role of the PCCNA in the lives of its constituents remains uncertain. Attendance at large interdenominational gatherings both in the United States and abroad have tended to decline in recent years. There is also little evidence that the PCCNA has put forth an agenda that has helped to move Pentecostalism toward a more racially and ethnically inclusive posture in American life. Part of the issue is that organizations like the PCCNA have traditionally depended on well-attended events to promote their causes. With the proliferation of Pentecostal television and the popularity of evangelists, such as Benny Hinn, who routinely fill large auditoriums, the faithful are not as likely to be drawn to such events. In recent years, the PCCNA has attempted to focus on smaller gatherings of young leaders as it charts the future of the organization.

The challenge of becoming more racially and ethnically diverse is compounded for Pentecostal denominations by the fact that much of their growth in recent years has come among the expanding immigrant populations in the United States. Many of the new congregations are being planted among Hispanic, Korean, Haitian, Romanian, and other ethnic populations, while church plants among white and African American populations are relatively flat. Although these new congregations are welcome, incorporating them into the life of a denomination that is majority-white or majority-black will require new ways of thinking among the classical denominations. Added to this challenge is the reality that Christianity, including its Pentecostal forms, is growing far more rapidly in the Southern hemisphere and in the East than it is in the West. All Christians in the West may by the middle of this century understand what it means to be part of a minority.[36]

In light of the growing presence of neo-Pentecostalism, the identity and place of classical Pentecostal denominations are undergoing challenging changes. Edith Blumhofer has suggested that Pentecostals have modeled themselves after their television celebrities and have substituted a celebration of the Spirit for their earlier emphasis on the soon return of Jesus.[37] Although independent Pentecostal congregations may be growing, classical denominations are flat or declining. Edith Blumhofer has suggested that the Assemblies of God (and, I suggest, other denominations as well) are facing challenges that come to movements when they both conserve and expand. According to Blumhofer, the Assemblies of God began the last decade of the twentieth century by declaring it to be the "Decade of the Harvest," and its leadership looked forward to achieving important growth goals as the movement entered the twenty-first century. Despite their rhetoric, Blumhofer suggests that Assemblies of God leadership both failed to inspire their ministers and members and instead masked the reality of what was more akin to a stagnant decade with only modest gains. For Blumhofer, the fact that denominational leadership measured success in terms of numbers indicated that it was no longer interested in living in tension with this world but longed to be a part of the American mainstream. Underneath the call for increased numbers was a denominational leadership out of touch with many of its constituencies, including women ministers. For Blumhofer, the location of the denomination's U.S. headquarters in Springfield, Missouri, represents a cloistered reality out of touch with an increasingly urban America. She concludes that the few bright spots in Assemblies of God life are those megachurches that are successful numerically but do not represent the typical Assemblies of God congregation.[38]

At the heart of Pentecostal challenges regarding identity is the practice of speaking in tongues, which has most often been considered the evidence of Spirit baptism since the days of Charles Fox Parham's Bethel Bible School. Classical Pentecostals fear that growing numbers of their constituency do not testify to a Spirit-baptism experience accompanied by tongues speech. For example, Thomas Trask, general superintendent of the Assemblies of God, has lamented "that nearly 50 percent of the Assemblies of God laity did not have the experience." He concluded, "We may be Pentecostal in doctrine, but not in experience."[39] Trask is not far off the mark when compared to a study of 4,001 Americans of various denominations conducted by the Survey Research Center of the University of Akron in 1992. This study showed that 55.6 percent of white Pentecostals claimed to speak in tongues, while 33.1 percent of black Pentecostals reported tongues speech. Interestingly the percentage is much higher (74.6 percent) among nondenominational charismatics.[40] Although Trask may indeed be correct, no significant study has charted the experience among Pentecostals through the decades. So it is impossible to compare the contemporary scene with that of earlier generations with any degree of accuracy. Whatever the reality, Pentecostal leaders are convinced that they have a problem.

Their larger problem, however, may not be doctrine, but the very survival of the old denominations in an age that seems to favor megachurches and independent, personality-driven ministries. In her 1989 study *The Assemblies of God at the Crossroads: Charisma and Institutional Dilemmas*, Margaret M. Poloma suggested that although institutional success in the Assemblies of God has always been closely intertwined with charisma, there was evidence that charisma was being devalued by many of the denomination's leaders and ministers. Further, she suggested that marriage between Pentecostals and new evangelicals had led to a lessening of the charismatic and experiential theology in the movement. As a result, the heart and soul, the very reason for the existence of Pentecostalism, was being preserved not in the movement's institutional structures or even in many of its congregations. Rather, charisma was most often within the Assemblies of God seen in local congregations led by charismatic pastors and outside the Assemblies of God in the emerging charismatic and neo-charismatic movements.[41] If she were writing today it is likely that she would have included Joel Osteen and Lakewood Church on her list.

Since the days of Jonathan Edwards, evangelical Christianity in America has witnessed the ebb and flow of both the work of the Holy Spirit and the work of church leaders to conserve the results of revivals into human institutions. There is little evidence to believe that this will cease in this millennium. The tension between charismata and institution building will continue to challenge leaders and laity alike. Yet with today's immediacy of television and the inexpensive proliferation of publishing, events seem to be playing out on a much larger stage and in much greater numbers. Despite its call for separation, which seems to be part of its very essence, fundamentalism continues to play a major role in the public life of Americans as its challenges basic cultural values in the political arena. At the same time, Pentecostalism continues to influence the worship practices and vitality of Christianity far beyond the strength of its own numbers. There is much that classical Pentecostals can find to lament about their changing role in the Pentecostal movement and to complain about the emerging face of Pentecostalism in the twenty-first century. But as the movement enters its second century of existence it stands poised for yet another "century of the Holy Spirit."

NOTES

1. Douglas A. Sweeney, *The American Evangelical Story: A History of the Movement* (Grand Rapids: Baker Academic, 2005), 9, 17–21.

2. Ibid., 61.

3. Charles H. Lippy, *Pluralism Comes of Age* (Armonk, NY: M.E. Sharpe, 2000), 19.

4. George M. Marsden, *Fundamentalism and American Culture: The Shaping of Twentieth-Century Evangelicalism, 1870–1925* (New York: Oxford University Press, 1980), 3.

5. For a brief discussion of the role of premillennialism in the evangelical movement see Timothy P. Weber, "Premillennialism and the Branches of Evangelicalism," in *The Variety of American Evangelicalism*, ed. Donald W. Dayton and Robert K. Johnson (Downers Grove, IL: InterVarsity Press, 1991), 5–21.

6. Sweeney, 155, 165–69.

7. For an excellent discussion of the Scopes trial, see Jeffery P. Moran, *The Scopes Trial: A Brief History with Documents* (Boston: Bedford/St. Martin's, 2002).

8. Ibid., 21.

9. Ibid., 1.

10. Edith L. Blumhofer, "Introduction," in *Pentecostal Currents in American Protestantism*," ed. Edith L. Blumhofer, Russell P. Spittler, and Grant A. Wacker (Urbana: University of Illinois Press, 1999), ix.

11. Vinson Synan, ed., *The Century of the Holy Spirit: 100 Years of Pentecostal and Charismatic Renewal* (Nashville: Thomas Nelson, 2001). For a history of the Pentecostal movement, see also Vinson Synan, *The Holiness Pentecostal Tradition: Charismatic Movements in the Twentieth Century* (Grand Rapids, MI: Eerdmans, 1997).

12. For the best discussion of McPherson, see Edith L. Blumhofer, *Aimee Semple McPherson: Everybody's Sister* (Grand Rapids, MI: Eerdmans, 1993).

13. For a history of the healing evangelists, see David Edwin Harrell, Jr., *All Things Possible* (Bloomington: Indiana University Press, 1975). For information on the charismatic renewal in the Protestant churches see Dennis Bennett, *Nine O'Clock in the Morning* (Plainfield, NJ: Bridge Publishing, 1970); Michael Harper, *As At the Beginning: The Twentieth Century Pentecostal Revival* (London: Hodder and Stoughton, 1965); and Synan, *Century of the Holy Spirit*.

14. For information on the charismatic movement among Roman Catholics, see Kevin and Dorothy Ranaghan, *Catholic Pentecostals* (Paramus, NJ: Paulist Press, 1969); Edward O'Connor, *The Pentecostal Movement in the Catholic Church* (Notre Dame, IN: Ave Maria Press, 1971); and Francis A. Sullivan, *Charisms and the Charismatic Renewal* (Ann Arbor, MI: Servant Publications, 1982).

15. Actual numbers for the United States include 4,946,390 Pentecostals, 19,473,158 charismatics, and 50,736,451 neocharismatics. D.B. Barrett and T.M. Johnson, "Global Statistics," in *The New International Dictionary of Pentecostal and Charismatic Movements*, rev. ed., ed. Stanley M. Burgess and Eduard M. Van der Maas (Grand Rapids, MI: Zondervan, 2002), 277, 284, and 301.

16. Lippy, 93.

17. "Vanishing Fundamentalism," *Christian Century* (June 24, 1926): 799, quoted in Joel A. Carpenter, *Revive Us Again: The Reawakening of American Fundamentalism* (New York: Oxford University Press, 1997), xi.

18. Arthur H. Matthews, *Standing Up, Standing Together: The Emergence of the National Association of Evangelicals* (Carol Stream, IL: National Association of Evangelicals, 1992), 167–75.

19. During his lifetime, Kenneth E. Hagin wrote many booklets propagating his theological ideas which have spread among many independent Pentecostals in particular. Hagin's theology is often referred to as the Gospel of Health and Wealth. Some of Hagin's booklets include *The Believer's Authority* (Tulsa, OK: Faith Library, 1984); *Healing Belongs to Us* (Tulsa, OK: Kenneth E. Hagin, n.d.); and *Redeemed from Poverty, Sickness and Death* (Tulsa, OK: Faith Library, 1983).

20. Edith L. Blumhofer, *Restoring the Faith: The Assemblies of God, Pentecostalism, and American Culture* (Urbana: University of Illinois Press, 1993), 256.

21. Grant Wacker, *Heaven Below: Early Pentecostals and American Culture* (Cambridge, MA: Harvard University Press, 2003).

22. See Nancy Tatom Ammerman, *Baptist Battles: Social Changes and Religious Conflicts in the Southern Baptist Convention* (New Brunswick, NJ: Rutgers University Press, 1990).

23. Larry Eskridge, "Defining Evangelicalism," Web site of the Institute for the Study of Evangelicals, http://www.wheaton.edu/isae/defining_evangelicalism.html# Pentecostalism, accessed November 14, 2005.

24. Charles W. Conn, *Like a Mighty Army: A History of the Church of God*, definitive ed. (Cleveland, TN: Pathway Press, 1996), xxviii. See also http://www.churchofgod.cc/about/church_is.cfm, accessed November 15, 2005.

25. See Ed Dobson and Ed Hindson, *The Fundamentalist Phenomenon: The Resurgence of Conservative Christianity* (Garden City, NY: Doubleday-Galilee, 1981), 143–44.

26. Lippy, 33.

27. See John W. Kennedy, "The Art of Cooperation," *Christianity Today* (April 24, 2000): 24.

28. Helen Lee Turner, "Pentecostal Currents in the SBC: Divine Intervention, Prophetic Preachers, and Charismatic Worship" in Blumhofer, Spittler, and Wacker, eds., 209–25.

29. See, as examples, John Osteen, *The Confessions of a Baptist Preacher* (Houston: John Osteen, 1983); John H. Osteen, *How God Baptized Me in the Holy Ghost and Fire* (Houston: John H. Osteen Evangelistic Association, 1961); and John H. Osteen, *How You May Receive the Baptism of the Holy Ghost* (Houston: John H. Osteen Evangelistic Association, 1961).

30. Quoted in Ernest Herndon, "How a Big Church Grew Bigger," *Charisma & Christian Life* (June 2004): 42–50.

31. See Joel Osteen, *Your Best Life Now: 7 Steps to Living at Your Full Potential* (New York: Warner Faith, 2004); and Joel Osteen, *Daily Readings from Your Best Life Now* (New York: Warner Faith, 2005), vi.

32. For an excellent study of megachurches, see Scott Thumma, "Exploring the Megachurch Phenomena: Their Characteristics and Cultural Context," http://hirr.hartsem.edu/bookshelf/thumma_article2.html, accessed November 14, 2005.

33. Sweeney, 152–53.

34. Corwin E. Smidt, Lyman A. Kellstedt, John C. Green, and James L. Guth, "The Spirit-Filled Movements in Contemporary America: A Survey Perspective," in Blumhofer, Spittler, and Wacker, eds., 111.

35. Ibid., 111–12.

36. See Philip Jenkins, *The Next Christendom: The Coming of Global Christianity* (New York: Oxford University Press, 2003).

37. Blumhofer, 257.

38. Ibid., 264–74.

39. Quoted in Smidt, et al., 129n6.

40. Ibid., 116.

41. Margaret M. Poloma, *The Assemblies of God at the Crossroads: Charisma and Institutional Dilemmas* (Knoxville: University of Tennessee Press, 1989), 241–43.

SUGGESTIONS FOR FURTHER READING

Blumhofer, Edith L., Russell P. Spittler, and Grant A. Wacker. *Pentecostal Currents in American Protestantism.* Urbana: University of Illinois Press, 1999.

Burgess, Stanley M., and Eduard M. Van der Maas, eds. *The New International Dictionary of Pentecostal and Charismatic Movements,* rev. ed. Grand Rapids, MI: Zondervan, 2002.

Carpenter, Joel. *Revive Us Again: The Reawakening of American Fundamentalism.* New York: Oxford University Press, 1997.

Sweeney, Douglas A. *The American Evangelical Story: A History of the Movement.* Grand Rapids, MI: Baker Academic, 2005.

Synan, Vinson. *The Holiness Pentecostal Tradition: Charismatic Movements in the Twentieth Century.* Grand Rapids. MI: Eerdmans, 1997.

CHAPTER 6

Buddhism, Hinduism, Islam, and Sikhism in America: The Impact of World Religions

Khyati Y. Joshi

Throughout American history, Buddhism, Hinduism, Islam, and Sikhism have been represented on American shores by both immigrants—individuals born in or descended from those Asian and African countries where the religions predominate—and domestic converts. Indeed, immigrants and their families still constitute the majority of American Buddhists, Hindus, Muslims, and Sikhs. While the theologies of these four religions are varied, they share certain similarities both in terms of their impact on the United States and its culture and in terms of America's influence on their followers.

American followers of these faiths have been relatively few in number until recently. The waxing and waning of the population of adherents of these world religions in America have been primarily impacted by two "push/pull" forces: (1) U.S. immigration policy and (2) the sociopolitical situation in the adherents' countries of origin.

At particular historical moments, "pull" factors such as the need for certain types of labor have influenced U.S. immigration policy. "Push" factors may include the pre-immigration characteristics of an immigrant cohort, such as majority or minority status in the country of origin or status as a refugee from war, political instability, or economic distress in the home country. The experience of an early wave of Asian immigrants (including many Buddhists) illustrates the interaction of push and pull factors: In the mid-1800s, during the California Gold Rush, laborers were needed to provide services like construction of the transcontinental railroad. Tens of thousands of immigrants from China were welcomed for this purpose. Alongside this "pull" factor was a "push" factor: Most men who came to the United States were second or third sons in their families in China, where family property typically went only to the first-born son.

Also, China was then experiencing difficult economic times, and there was widespread poverty. This situation, combined with cultural traditions of inheritance, caused later-born male siblings to leave China to seek economic prosperity. Other religious communities, such as the relatively small number of Sikh agricultural workers from India, had similar experiences in the nineteenth century as a result of different "push" factors.

Although these Asian immigrants were allowed to enter the United States, after arrival they were restricted to a few types of jobs; federal law forbade them to own land, become citizens, or establish businesses. Many states—including California, Oregon, and Washington—where most of the Asian immigrants resided, passed their own separate laws making aliens ineligible for citizenship. Many Asian immigrants challenged these laws, but were successful in only a few cases, resulting in a handful of exceptions for people wanting to buy land to own a home or start a business.

The pendulum of support for Asian immigration soon swung in the opposite direction. Racial tensions increased as more Chinese created competition in the job market. By 1882, growing hostility against the Chinese resulted in the Chinese Exclusion Act. Initially written as only a ten-year ban on Chinese immigration, the law later was extended indefinitely and made permanent in 1902. Immigration from the rest of Asia was possible until the 1917 Barred Zone Act, which recognized an Asiatic Barred Zone—a geographic region encompassing much of southern and eastern Asia and the Pacific islands, but excluding American territories of Guam and the Philippines—from which no immigrants would be admitted to the United States. Because these geographic regions were then home to many of the world's Buddhists, Hindus, Muslims, and Sikhs, these religious groups were effectively shut out of the United States by the act. The Middle East was not included in the "barred zone," and Arab immigrants, some who were Muslim, were still allowed to enter the country until 1924. The National Origins Act of 1924, also known as the Johnson-Reed Act, dramatically slowed immigration by indexing foreign countries' immigration quotas to the number of Americans of that national origin as reported in the 1890 census. Known as the 2-percent rule because the law capped new immigration at 2 percent of those of a particular national stock already in the United States, the provision functioned to preserve the American demographic profile of 1890, allowing only a handful of Asian, African, and Middle Eastern immigrants and even a relatively small number of southern and eastern Europeans. Later the 2-percent rule was replaced by an overall limit of 150,000 immigrants annually with countries' proportions determined by "national origins" as revealed in the 1920 census.[1]

For more than forty years, most of these restrictions remained in place. The Asiatic Barred Zone was abolished by the McCarran Walter Act in 1952, which permitted up to one hundred people from each country in the world to immigrate each year and allowed a small number of individualized exceptions, such as the admission of two thousand Palestinian refugees in 1953. After 1924 there were other pieces of federal legislation that impacted selected Asian groups, but it was not until the Immigration

Reform Act of 1965 that Asians, Africans, and Arabs could enter the United States again in large numbers. This time the "pull" was the United States' need for physicians to supplement a medical workforce stretched thin by the Vietnam War and for engineers to bolster American efforts to keep up with its cold war enemy, the Soviet Union. Later, the "pull" was the technology boom of the 1990s. Immigration from Southeast Asia was expanded further by the Indochina Migration and Refugee Act of 1975, which established a program of domestic resettlement assistance for refugees from Cambodia and Vietnam. The post-1965 wave of immigration from former "barred zones" has resulted in substantial growth in the Buddhist, Hindu, Muslim, and Sikh populations in the United States.[2]

How many Buddhists, Hindus, Muslims, and Sikhs are there in the United States? It is virtually impossible to know the exact numbers. Whereas the decennial census affords us a clear look at the ethnic and racial makeup of the U.S. population, it does not provide the same with religion. The law expressly permits the Census Bureau to collect data on religious affiliation, but the Bureau declines to do so on the basis of a law that prohibits "mandatory" questions about religion.[3] Most nongovernmental research surveys that collect data on religion do so based on local congregations. These surveys are unlikely to yield reliable data especially for followers of Buddhism, Hinduism, and Sikhism, since for them religious observance is not centered around the house of worship or the regularized congregational practice typical of the Abrahamic faiths. Nevertheless, by relying upon several data sources it is possible to come up with an approximate (and likely accurate) number for each religion. In 2005, the United States was home to approximately 1.5 million Buddhists and between 5.5 and 6 million Muslims of all races. It is believed there were between 1 million and 1.3 million Hindus in the United States, and 250,000 to 500,000 Sikhs. All four religious populations continue to grow and are part of life across the country, in suburbs and small towns as well as major metropolitan centers.[4]

Although each of these religions has American converts of all races, most of the communities are made up of first- and second-generation Asian, Arab, and African Americans. Buddhists have come primarily from Japan, Korea, China, Tibet, Thailand, and other Asian nations. Approximately 75 percent to 80 percent of Buddhists in America are Asian American with the remainder being white American converts. The majority of Hindus in the United States are originally from India, and some are twice migrants. That is, they first immigrated to the British Commonwealth nations of Africa and the Caribbean or Canada and later arrived in the United States. Islam is a panethnic religion; its American adherents hail from East, Southeast, Central, and South Asia; from Africa; and from the Arab world. There are also African American and European American (e.g., Albanian) Muslims. The ethnic origins of the Muslim community in America in the early twenty-first century is approximately 26.2 percent Middle East (Arab), 24.7 percent South Asia, 23.8 percent African American, 10.3 percent Middle East (non-Arab), 11.6 percent Other, and 6.4 percent East Asia.[5] Most Sikhs are from the Indian subcontinent, specifically from a region called the Punjab that includes parts of present-day India and Pakistan.

National origin is relevant to adherents' religious experience in America in part because of the impact of social structures in country of origin. Consider, for example, the fact that Hindus arriving from India and Muslims arriving from countries such as Indonesia and Egypt were accustomed to being part of the majority community in their native lands, but on arrival in the United States suddenly found themselves part of a tiny minority invisible in the broader culture. By contrast, consider the experience of Sikhs and Muslims from India, who both left and arrived to a status as an arguably oppressed minority group. Finally, consider how all these immigrant communities' social interaction with the broader American milieu was affected by their status as non-native speakers of English and in many cases by their status as racial minorities.

While all four faiths have been present throughout the history of the United States, the most substantial impact on U.S. society and culture has come about because of the passage of the Immigration Act of 1965 that allowed immigrants from Asia in particular to come in unprecedented numbers. Unlike earlier waves, which were often comprised primarily of young single men, the post-1965 wave of Asian immigrants and refugees included entire families in many cases. Their children enrolled in American schools, and developing Buddhist, Hindu, Muslim, and Sikh communities established centers that functioned not only to maintain a religious and cultural identity, but also to transmit it to the next generation. Each religion, with its theology, global history, and encounters with the American milieu, gives unique characteristics to the experiences of its adherents and their place in contemporary American society. Although there are American converts to each tradition as well, the focus of this chapter will center on the experience of the new immigrant generation.

AMERICAN BUDDHISM: A HISTORICAL OVERVIEW

Siddhartha Gautama, also known as Sakyamuni (Sakya clan sage) or the Buddha, is credited with founding Buddhism over 2,500 years ago. He was born in the kingdom of the Sakayas, near the present-day border between India and Nepal. Fundamentally, the ultimate goal of Buddhism is to end the cycle of suffering and rebirth, samsara, and attain nirvana. Buddhists believe that one must rise above desires in order to reach a state of enlightenment. This can be accomplished by leading a virtuous life and gaining wisdom, which is attained as a result of long reflection and deep thought leading to insight into the nature of reality. Specifically it is the wisdom in following the Four Noble Truths: the truth of suffering, the truth of arising, the truth of cessation, the truth of the path. Siddhartha reached enlightenment at the age of 35 and became a supreme Buddha. Although the Buddha never claimed to be anything more than a man, he was idolized and subsequently deified in some Buddhist circles. Many Western scholars place the Buddha's lifetime from 563–483 B.C.E., while the Sri Lankan tradition believes the Buddha lived from 624–544 B.C.E.

The teachings of the Buddha were transmitted by oral tradition for several centuries. When written teachings emerged, they were in two different forms, the Pali canon of the Theravada tradition (written down in Sri Lanka around the middle of the first century B.C.E.) and the Sanskrit of the northern Mahayana tradition. The Tripitaka is considered to be the major scripture and is comprised of: the Sutra Pitaka, the discourses of the Buddha; the Vinaya Pitaka, accounts on the origin of the sangha and the rules of monastic discipline; and the Abhidharma Pitaka, scholastic treatises on Buddhist psychology and philosophy. The traditions of the faith have migrated from India to other Asian countries, where the majority of followers can be found. This migration of faith has, in the passage of time, resulted in three historical streams: Theravada, Mahayana, and Vajrayana.

America's first encounter with Buddhism occurred when Chinese laborers immigrated to the United States to build the transcontinental railroad. The immigration of these Buddhists came to a halt with the passage of the 1882 Chinese Exclusion Act, but until the Asian Barred Zone Act of 1917, other Buddhists continued to arrive from Japan and Korea. About the same time that Asian Buddhist immigrants were first starting to arrive in America, some American intellectuals had their introduction with Buddhism. Especially drawn to Buddhist philosophy were those called the Transcendentalists such as Henry David Thoreau and Ralph Waldo Emerson, who published the first English version of a portion of the Lotus Sutra. One of the most significant encounters between Buddhism and the United States was the 1893 World's Parliament of Religions held in Chicago. China, Japan, Thailand, and Sri Lanka sent Buddhist delegates. The parliament provided the first major public forum from which Buddhists could address themselves directly to the Western public.[6]

In the first half of the twentieth century, Buddhist teachers from Japan played the most active role in disseminating Buddhism to the American public. The largest and most influential ethnic-based Buddhist organization in the United States is the Buddhist Churches of America, which originally was the Buddhist Mission of North America (BMNA). Founded in 1914, it resulted from several Japanese Buddhist congregations coming together. The BMNA focused primarily on social and cultural activities for and ministry to the Japanese American communities. In the late 1920s, it first began to develop programs to train English-speaking priests for the benefit of the growing number of American-born parishioners. Things took a turn for the worse when Japanese and Japanese American Buddhists faced discrimination when President Franklin D. Roosevelt signed Executive Order 9066, placing people of Japanese descent into internment camps because they were perceived to be a threat during World War II. During the internment, the Buddhist Mission of North America took its current name in 1944. All of the Buddhist Mission's leadership, along with almost the entire Japanese American population, had been interned during World War II. The name Buddhist Churches of America was adopted at Topaz Relocation Center in Utah. The use of the word "church," which normally implies a Christian house of worship, was significant. After

internment ended, some members returned to the West Coast and revital-
ized churches there, although a number of others moved to the Midwest
and built new churches.[7]

Japanese Buddhists fought in the U.S. military, but were prohibited
from having their Buddhist faith imprinted on their dog tags, in one sense
erasing their Buddhist identities. Since passage of the 1965 Immigration
Act, the number of immigrants arriving from China, Vietnam, and the
Theravada-practicing countries of Southeast Asia has greatly increased.
Immigrant Buddhist congregations in North America are made up of followers from many Asian countries including China, Japan, Korea, Vietnam,
Thailand, and Cambodia, among others, and generally are mono-ethnic
communities/congregations.

Some scholars, such as Charles Prebish (1999), have suggested that
there are several broad types of Buddhism in America. The oldest and largest of these is "immigrant" or "ethnic Buddhism" described above. The
next oldest and arguably the most visible and best heralded type is referred
to as "import Buddhism" because it came to America largely in response
to the demand of interested American converts who sought it out, either
by going abroad or by supporting foreign teachers. Representative of such
is Henry Steele Olcott, who traveled to Sri Lanka in 1880 to learn about
Buddhism and then disseminated the information in the United States.
The three most notable trends of this type are Zen, Tibetan Buddhism,
and Vipassana, which is an outgrowth of the Theravada tradition. The
membership tends strongly to be drawn from among educated, white,
native English speakers. This is sometimes also called "elite Buddhism"
because its practitioners, especially early in the process, tended to come
from social elites. The third type of Buddhism in America is "export" or
"evangelical Buddhism," groups that are based in another country but
actively recruit members in America from various backgrounds. For example, the Hsi Lai Temple in California, Soka Gakkai, and the Buddhist
Churches of America are actively engaged in evangelical efforts in hopes of
recruiting converts from among the general public.

AMERICAN HINDUISM: A HISTORICAL OVERVIEW

The roots of Hinduism have been traced back to the Indus Valley civilization and the Indo-Aryan culture. Because residents of the Indus Valley
practiced a religion possessing several features common with modern Hinduism, the beginnings of Hinduism have been dated back to the time in
which the civilization flourished, approximately 2500 B.C.E. Indo-Europeans
extended the name of the province of Sindh, in the northeast of modern-
day India, to the whole country lying across the Indus River. The inhabitants were simply called Hindus, Persian for "sindh." The religion that
came to be known as Hinduism does not owe its existence to any single
historic event or person. Rather, it is a complex religion that has continually evolved and transformed over the course of millennia. Hinduism in its
belief, from manners of practice to regional differences in the names and
functions of various gods, is very diverse. The term and even the concept

of Hinduism as a singular religion on par with the other world faiths was the result of a confluence of forces, namely the British Raj, Christian missionaries in India, and Orientalist scholars, all of whom began to use the term Hinduism.

There are many different components of Hinduism, and there is wide variation in belief and practice, depending on the adherent's caste, region, and socioeconomic class. The Hindu house of worship is a *mandi,* or temple. While popularly thought of as a polytheistic faith, Hinduism is both monotheistic and polytheistic. Diana Eck described Hinduism as having a "polytheistic imagination"[8] that points to a myriad of avenues to approach the divine. Here multiplicity becomes a way of expressing unity and oneness. Many Hindus worship deities in a physical form, such as a *murti* (statue), but the deity is not perceived to be limited to that form.

There are many sacred texts in Hinduism, with none having an authoritative monopoly, particularly across all time periods. The sacred literature of Hinduism can be divided into two categories: *sruti* and *smriti.* Sruti refers to the manifestation of the divine in the world and, more specifically, to truths revealed by the deities to the early sages, or rishis. The shrutis include the Vedas, the four most ancient of the scriptures (Rig Veda, Sama Veda, Yajur Veda, and Atharva Veda); the Upanishads; the Brahmanas; and the Aranyakas. The Vedas, some of the most revered scripture, contain accounts of creation, information on ritual sacrifices, and prayers to the deities. Smriti is the other type of literature, that which is remembered or handed down. These texts are also considered to be based upon revealed truths, but composed by humans. The epics, the *Mahabharata* and the *Ramayana,* and the Puranas comprise the bulk of the Smriti literature. These sacred texts narrate episodes in the lives of the great warriors (the epics) or of the gods and goddesses (the Puranas).

Even before Hindu immigrants arrived in substantial numbers, America had its earliest encounters with Hinduism in the writings of the Transcendentalists Ralph Waldo Emerson and Henry David Thoreau, both of whose more philosophical works were significantly impacted by the Bhagavad Gita. Swami Vivekananda lectured on Hindu ideals in a public forum at the 1893 World's Parliament of Religions in Chicago. Vivekananda emphasized the Advaita Vedanta philosophy and later founded the Vedanta Society in New York. This group was the first Hindu organization primarily designed to attract American adherents and spread the tenets of Hindu philosophy worldwide.

Hindu immigrants first arrived on the West Coast before the beginning of the nineteenth century. Most pursued agrarian professions because the law forbade them as Asians to acquire citizenship or to buy, own, or lease agricultural land. The impact of Hinduism on American culture actually increased during the years after the 1917 Barred Zone Act. Still, until 1965 most of those attending Hindu religious centers in the United States were non-Indians. Prior to that watershed year, a slow trickle of Indians from Bombay and Calcutta were able to immigrate after passage of the 1946 Luce-Cellar Act. Most settled on the West Coast, and when San Francisco's "Old Temple" became too small for the growing population, a new temple was built to accommodate the growing number of Hindu immigrants. The next influx of Hindu immigrants was comprised mostly of students seeking graduate education in the 1950s and 1960s. By far the largest wave of Hindu immigrants has arrived in the years after 1965. Arriving with high educational capital, such as professional and advanced degrees, these immigrants—more likely than earlier waves to include entire families—have settled in cities across the United States. Subsequent waves of Indian Hindu immigration occurred after the Immigrant Reform and Control Act of 1986 liberalized "family reunification" policies to allow the parents and siblings of earlier immigrants to join their kin already in the United States. Yet another wave came about in the 1990s with the influx of high-tech workers from India. Today *mandirs* dot the American landscape and there are large Hindu communities in New York, Los Angeles, Chicago, Houston, Atlanta, and many other cities and towns.

AMERICAN ISLAM: A HISTORICAL OVERVIEW

Islam is the third Abrahamic and monotheistic religion, after Judaism and Christianity. Muslims believe they are the descendents of the Prophet Abraham's son Ishmael. Muhammad is credited with founding the religion in 620 C.E., in Mecca, Saudi Arabia. Muslims believe in a chain of prophets beginning with Adam and including Noah, Abraham, Ishmael, Isaac, Jacob, Joseph, Job, Moses, David, Solomon, and Jesus. Muhammad is the final prophet. Islam has a creed of faith, the *Shahada*: "There is no god but Allah and Muhammad is his prophet." This declaration of one's faith is one of the religion's five pillars, the others being prayer, charitable giving, fasting, and pilgrimage. Muslims acknowledge one god and believe all individuals will face the Day of Judgment and will be accountable for their actions.

Islam is a religion that focuses on the truth that God revealed to all his prophets throughout history. Most Muslims recognize two sacred texts, the Qur'an and the Hadith. The Qur'an is a collection of the scriptures of God as revealed to the Prophet Muhammad. Considered the direct word of God, it consists of 114 chapters that are arranged in order of length, not chronologically. The Hadith, the other major text in Islamic tradition, is a collection of Muhammad's sayings as well as a narrative of his actions.

Over time, various sects that interpret Islam's teachings differently have developed. This main schism in Islam dates back to Muhammad's death, when followers debated over who would succeed him as their spiritual leader. Two major subgroups developed: Sunni and the Shi'a. Sunnis, or "traditionalists," are the largest sect of Islam, comprising about 87 percent of Muslims worldwide. Sunnis are united in their belief in the legitimacy of the first three caliphs (successors to Muhammad), Abu Bakr, Umar, and Uthman. By contrast, the Shi'a, or "partisans of the faith," emphasize the importance of the descent from Muhammad's family and feel that the Prophet's first successor should have been Ali, the husband of Muhammad's only surviving daughter, Fatima. Eventually, Ali did become the fourth caliph, but was assassinated by a member of another Muslim sect. While

Sunnis accept Ali's caliphate, they do not consider him as important as the Shi'ites do. There are many sects within Shi'a Islam, such as Isma'ilism (a sect that recognizes the Aga Khan as its spiritual leader). Shi'ites are the dominant Islamic sect in Bahrain, Iran, and Lebanon.

There are a number of similarities between these two sects. However, there are two fundamental differences in their beliefs that have divided them for centuries. In addition to the dispute over Ali's status, there are philosophical differences between Shi'ites and Sunnis. Shi'ites approach Islam through the practice of *ijithad*, the interpretation of the law by individual scholars, whereas Sunnis strictly believe in the *ijma*, the consensus of Muslim scholars, in addition to *ijithad*. Also, Shi'ites are less strict in their adherence to the five pillars and do not accept the Hadith as sacred.

Prior to the twentieth century, Islam remained a relatively unknown religion and lifestyle to Americans. Some of the first Muslim adherents to arrive on U.S. shores were black Africans brought as slaves between 1530 and 1851. Yet the sole representative of Islam at the World's Parliament of World Religions in 1893 was a white American convert, Mohammed Alexander Webb (1847–1916). Islamic countries chose not to send representatives to the Parliament because of anti-Islamic sentiment of the time.

Thousands of Muslims had arrived in the United States in the 1870s, most from regions of the Ottoman Empire that comprise present-day Syria, Lebanon, Jordan, Israel, and the Palestinian Authority. These migrants were poorly educated laborers who came seeking greater economic stability; many returned, disenchanted, to their homeland. Those who stayed suffered isolation, although some managed to establish Islamic communities in unlikely places. For example, by 1920, Muslim immigrants worshiped in a rented hall in Cedar Rapids, Iowa, and they built a *masjid* (mosque) there fifteen years later. Lebanese-Syrian Muslim communities did the same in Ross, North Dakota, and later in Detroit, Pittsburgh, and Michigan City, Indiana. Many Muslims arrived at the end of World War I, with the demise of the Ottoman Empire. The first wave of Muslim immigration ended in 1924 when the Johnson-Reed Act allowed only a trickle of Africans and "Asians," a designation that included Arabs and South Asians, to enter.

In addition to pre-1924 Muslim immigration, the twentieth century saw a substantial increase in Muslim affiliation in the United States thanks to the Black Muslim movement. Throughout its history, the Black Muslim movement, which ultimately became the Nation of Islam, proclaimed that black nationalism and Islamic faith together would help African Americans obtain success through discipline, racial pride, knowledge of God, and physical separation from white society. Islam in the life of black America strengthened with the mass migrations of Southern blacks to northern cities beginning in the early decades of the twentieth century. Noble Drew Ali established a black nationalist Islamic community, the Moorish Science Temple, in Newark, New Jersey, in 1913. After his death in 1929, one of the movement's factions became the Nation of Islam, founded by Wallace D. Fard of Detroit who mysteriously disappeared in 1934. Elijah Muhammad then took control of the movement, attracting disenchanted and poor African Americans from the urban North. They converted for a variety of reasons. For some, the poverty and racism in those cities made the Nation of Islam's message about "white devils" and "black superiority" plausible. Whites also converted to Islam during the twentieth century, though in much smaller numbers than blacks.[9]

The majority of Muslim immigrants arriving in the forty years after 1924 came from now-former Soviet republics. With the arrival of Palestinian refugees after 1948 and the more general opening of America's doors in 1965, new waves of immigration from the Islamic world—including Muslims fleeing oppressive regimes in Egypt, Iran, Iraq, and Syria, and African and South Asian Muslims seeking economic opportunity—have dramatically increased the American Muslim population. In the 1990s Muslims arrived from the former Yugoslavia, Somalia, and Sudan. By the 1990s, Muslims had established more than six hundred *masjids* and centers across the United States.

AMERICAN SIKHISM: A HISTORICAL OVERVIEW

Sikhism is a monotheistic revealed religion founded in the late fifteenth century by Guru Nanak. Sikhs consider Guru Nanak their prophet and first religious teacher and recognize nine successor gurus over the two centuries following Nanak's death. *Guru* literally means the "light who dispels darkness" and comes from a Sanskrit word meaning "disciple," emphasizing the importance of learning and seeking truth. Born into a Punjabi Hindu family in 1469 in what is now present-day Pakistan, Nanak was deeply meditative throughout his life. Nanak was influenced by the devotional (*bhakti*) movement of Hinduism and Islamic Sufi mysticism. Evidence of such influence includes his belief in reincarnation, his monotheism, and his emphasis on spirituality. Though primarily containing teachings by the Sikh gurus, Sikh scriptures also contain verses from both holy Hindu scriptures and the Qur'an. However, Nanak differed with traditional religious thought by rejecting any sort of idol worship and believing in a casteless society without any distinctions based on birthright, religion, or gender.

The sacred text of the faith is the *Guru Granth Sahib*, which consists of hymns and writings by the first nine gurus. Guru Nanak emphasized the superfluous nature of tradition, preaching that there was a religion greater than the one embodied in tradition and rituals. Sikhs are prohibited from worshipping idols, images, or icons.

Another important facet of Sikhism involves the Khalsa, the Sikh brotherhood and sisterhood. In 1699, Guru Gobind Singh freed Sikhs from the caste system by ordaining that all Sikh males incorporate "Singh" (and women "Kaur") into their names, thus shedding their caste identity and signifying their membership in the Khalsa.

Sikhs wear a uniform to unify and bind them to the beliefs of the religion and to remind them of their commitment to the gurus at all times. This uniform serves as a highly visible marker, particularly for men, of a

Sikh identity. Commitment to the Khalsa is demonstrated by keeping five physical signs (sometimes called "the five Ks"):

1. Kesh (uncut hair),
2. Kanga (a wooden comb),
3. Kaccha (shorts worn under regular clothes),
4. Kara (a steel bracelet), and
5. Kirpan (a short sword, not ever used for violence but representing the Sikh's willingness to protect self and community).

Sikhs hold worship services in what they call *gurudwaras* ("gates to the gurus"), the most revered of which is the Golden Temple in the city of Amritsar, in Punjab, India. These services contain a mixture of singing, meditation (believed to foster communication with God), and readings from the Guru Granth Sahib by the officiant or *granthi*. Sikhs recognize no one day of the week as more holy than others, but worship services are typically held on Sundays out of convenience because both India and the United States observe the Western Monday to Friday work week. The first American gurudwara was established in Stockton, California, in 1915.[10]

The Sikh migration to the United States can be seen in four segments and in some cases parallels Hindu immigration to the United States. Some of the first Sikhs to immigrate were single young men who arrived on the West Coast more than two hundred years ago; they came from small land-owning families in the Punjab region of present-day India and Pakistan, and most of those who remained pursued agrarian lives. Most had been rural peasants, driven abroad, for instance, by land rights legislation that created unfavorable economic and social conditions in the early twentieth century.[11] Sikhs, like other Asian immigrants of the time, were ineligible to acquire citizenship or, in California and Oregon, to buy, own, or lease agricultural land. Many Sikh men married Mexican Catholic women, and their children grew up as Catholics.[12] Sikh immigration came to a halt with the 1917 Asian Barred Zone Act. The second wave of Sikhs, like Hindus, was comprised of students seeking graduate education in the 1950s and 1960s. The third wave of Sikh immigrants arrived after passage of the 1965 Immigration and Naturalization Act. For Sikhs, the fourth wave came about in the 1980s because of political persecution in India, East Africa, and Afghanistan. In 1984, the Indian military besieged and occupied the Golden Temple in response to domestic political unrest. In addition to causing an increase in Sikh emigration from India, this incident triggered a strong emotional reaction among Sikhs worldwide; it was interpreted as a threat to the community and caused many Sikhs to feel vulnerable. The attack thus also fostered a sense of collective fate, re-shaped the dynamics of Sikhs' religious identity, and weakened the attachment of Sikhs abroad to India as compared to their attachment to Sikhism itself and to their host country.

In this respect, Sikhs have a different relationship with India than Hindus. As a minority group in India that has faced persecution, Sikhs have been emigrating from India for centuries. Many Sikh communities in the

United States coalesced around the "Khalistan movement," which advocates an independent Sikh homeland in the Punjab. While some diasporic Sikhs have always supported the idea of secession, after the events of 1984 the community offered vociferous support for the formation of an independent Khalistan. Territory had not been a major element of Sikh political identity until recently, although the question of Punjab's independence was raised in 1948 when the British showed a willingness to let Hindus and Muslims divide up the Punjab and granted India and Pakistan separate statehood for essentially religious reasons. The rise of effective new leaders helped to sustain the movement beyond the initial phase of mobilization. Support for Khalistan by diasporic Sikhs is generally attributed to anomie or alienation from migration; the desire to establish power and credibility as a community; and the strong ties these Sikhs have consistently maintained with Punjab through kinship, culture, and economic links.[13]

THE LAST TWENTY-FIVE YEARS: WORLD RELIGIONS IN AMERICA TODAY

The story of these four religions in the United States really is one of newness. Although certain communities, such as Chinese and Japanese American Buddhists and Arab American Muslims, were present in substantial numbers by the end of the nineteenth century, the plurality (Islam, Buddhism) or even the majority (Hinduism, Sikhism) within each religious group is currently an immigrant and second-generation cohort. It was not until the years after 1965 that the United States saw the arrival of substantial numbers of immigrant families that established homes, built ethnoreligious communities, and sent their children into the American school system in substantial numbers. By dint of numbers and diversity, these new faiths now permeate American society across professions and trades in the workplace, in K–12 and collegiate classrooms, and increasingly (albeit haltingly) in the mainstream media. Just as important, these communities are becoming self-aware as groups with national reach and importance. While a small number of masjids, mandirs, temples, and gurudwaras was in existence before 1965, for example, their populations were relatively small and many adherents were neither aware of nor geographically proximate to them. Later immigrants constituted a highly educated group of professionals who arrived in the United States at a time when the world was "shrinking" and when cultural diversity was finding increased acceptance in the United States, as compared to the earlier migrants. They were able to break some barriers to economic and social success and, to a certain extent, influence the host community's opinions of them and of immigrants in general. They were able to insure good education for their children and also set up mechanisms for elementary religious education. While anti-immigrant sentiment remains and discrimination against minority religions can flare up in response to contemporary events, the United States has come a long way towards appreciating the value of ethnic and religious diversity, thereby enabling immigrant communities to retain salient cultural traits rather than merely "assimilating."

In light of each group's presence in the United States prior to 1965, scholars have reported that all three religious groups "had a presence" here and did not arrive to a country "without" Hindus, Sikhs, and Muslims. Indeed, Hindu organizations like the International Society for Krishna Consciousness ("Hare Krishna") and the Vedanta Society; a Sikh community in Yuba City, California; and ethnically white congregations of Buddhists did pre-exist the 1965 Act. However, these structures were of limited salience to the post-1965 immigrant wave, either because they were geographically distant or because the religious experiences and social capital available from older institutions were unappealing or irrelevant to new arrivals. During the first three decades after the Immigration Reform Act of 1965, immigrant Buddhist, Hindu, Muslim, and Sikh communities put down new roots; their religious structures and practice are now becoming visible to mainstream America.

Religion has a vital role in the Americanization process for immigrants. Just as social services and places of ethnic solidarity help in transition to life in the United States, temples, churches, gurudwaras, mosques, and the broader contours of religion have sustained individuals and families, even as the specific religion has undergone changes in the Americanization process, and helped maintain transnational connections. Raymond B. Williams (1992) describes religion as a "sacred thread" that binds the personal and group identity for immigrants.[14] Immigrants who arrived prior to about 1978 began laying the foundations for their respective religious communities. Initially individuals gathered in people's homes where religious classes were held. Temples were established in former churches, and meetings would be held at business offices. Immigrants thus met at first in living rooms or rented halls, then perhaps in a building acquired for the specifically religious and cultural use of the community. A church may be ideal because it is already zoned for religious use; the Richmond Hill gurudwara in Queens is a former Methodist church. When a certain "critical mass" of population was achieved in a particular geographic area, ethnically homogeneously houses of worship—or, in some cases, separate "ethnic" services in a shared facility—were created.[15]

Ethnoreligious communities have built houses of worship in cities, suburbs, and small towns from coast to coast. In the 1980s and 1990s, Sikh *gurudwaras* were built in Detroit, Birmingham, and Reno, Nevada. South Asian Muslims arrived in a country with many *masjids* (mosques) already in existence and often worshipped at these facilities, but many communities went on to establish mosques of their own geared specifically to their own ethnoreligious needs and interests. Although most mosques remain nominally multi-ethnic, in reality nearly two-thirds still serve one dominant ethnic group, usually South Asian or African American. Often traditional buildings sprang up to replace or supplement earlier establishments that, because they used pre-existing or rented facilities, did not bear an external resemblance to traditional structures.[16] For example, a *mandir* (Hindu temple) was established as part of the Indian Cultural and Religious Center in a former church building outside Atlanta in 1986. In 1993, the Hindu Temple of Atlanta, similar in architectural style of traditional Indian mandirs, started housing religious functions on an ongoing basis. Both mandirs continue to operate.

CURRENT ISSUES AND CHALLENGES

These four faith communities face many challenges in the United States and are dealing with a range of issues that affect transnational religious communities: the reformulation of the religions through their encounter with the American social milieu, including theological and practical changes; the transmission of religious belief to second-generation youth; language, including second-generation language loss; the influence of transnational experiences; and sometimes-troubled interactions with wider society. Common themes emerge, as do points of divergence among the religions.

We are seeing an American reformulation of these faiths, that is, the emergence of American forms of these faiths. The reformulation of these religions—the development, for example, of an "American Hinduism"—is a source of tension for members in each community. In particular, the notion of authenticity is of concern. The country of origin is still the reference point for authenticity; the notion of performing prayers and rituals the way it was done "over there" is seen as having a spiritual and theological importance in many communities. For example, communities in the United States are going to great lengths to create houses of worship that resemble those in the country of origin. Examples include the Hsi Lai Buddhist Temple in Los Angeles, with its Ming- and Qing-style architecture, and the soaring South Indian-style Sri Venkateswara Temple near Pittsburgh. The concern over authenticity reflects a popular misconception of religion as static—eternal and, therefore, unchanging. "Over there" comes to define not only a place, but also a time. It evokes the manner in which rituals were performed at the time when immigrants left the countries decades ago.

Competing with these concerns over authenticity are the needs of the contemporary community. Communities therefore also adapt to the American context. For example, when religious holidays fall during the work week, their observance is often scheduled on the weekend when it is more convenient for people to gather and celebrate. While necessary, these changes also contribute to the emotional link adherents make between geography and theology: Across these faiths, communities are struggling with issues of authenticity, and often comparing worship and ritual practices performed in the United States with those observed at "home." Practice in America has come to be seen as less authentic. They are probably observed on a small level at home; for example, fasts may be observed, but then the program held on the weekend. Yet at the same time there are authenticity issues where people want to "do it the way it's always been done." Immigration continues from these countries, while at the same time an American-grown version of the faith flourishes. Questions about who is a Buddhist or who is an "observant" Sikh abound.

Influenced by the dominance of some strains of belief within each community and by the influence of wider American society, these religions are also formulating what Raymond Williams describes, for example, as an "ecumenical Hinduism." The Hindu holidays and celebrations most celebrated in the United States are Diwali, Navaratri, Holi, and Raksha Bhandan, among others. Diwali in particular is becoming more important than its theology or its observance "over there" warrants. This is partly in response to Christian hegemony; Diwali, like the Jewish holiday Hannukah, is rendered important by its proximity to Christmas on the calendar. The Diwali phenomenon also represents the development of a "common ground" religion, a set of holidays and other cultural markers on which the broad range of American Hindus, otherwise divided by region, language, caste, and village traditions, can agree. The Chinese New Year has to a certain extent served the same function within the American Buddhist community, even to the point of providing common ground with Chinese American Christians. The phenomenon described above, whereby religion becomes frozen at the time and place of immigrants' departure from the old country, also exerts an influence here. Regional traditions as practiced in the 1960s and 1970s in the "home" country contribute to the development of a common American version of each faith.

At the same time, new immigrants of these four faiths have continued to arrive in the United States and often affiliate themselves with established religious and cultural centers. The arrival of new adherents with modern traditions and with social needs that differ from those of both older immigrants and the second generation is creating new challenges for houses of worship. To this challenge is added the fact that individual American houses of worship and cultural centers were built from the ground up, meaning in most cases that there are no over-arching religious structures that provide resources.

All these religions have nonimmigrant adherents, such as the Gora Sikhs, Black Muslims, and others. Among Muslims and Buddhists in particular, the panethnic nature of the religion intersects with religion's function as a tool for ethnic maintenance. That facet of the immigrant experience which is theologizing and drives immigrants to seek out others like themselves results, for example, in mosque communities where ethnic maintenance—speaking Arabic or Urdu, consuming ethnic or regional cuisine, and popular culture, and the like—is as important and attractive a function as worship. Thus, as noted earlier, although most mosques are nominally multi-ethnic, any given mosque will typically be dominated by a single ethnic group.[17] Ethnicity, in place of or in conjunction with theology, often distinguishes one community or house of worship from the next. Scholars who study the Buddhist community have noted that most Buddhist groups can be described as "ethnic" or "import" Buddhists by reference to their mono-ethnic memberships.

These four religions also face practical challenges with respect to preparedness and ability to provide appropriate services for the American milieu. For example, the Buddhist, Hindu, and Muslim religious institutions in the United States must often hire clergy from overseas because each religion has few or even no American institutions where one can undertake the necessary studies. This has a variety of effects. For example, American clergy are often called on to undertake duties such as counseling and other services that in the Christian context might be called "pastoral care." Pandits (Hindu priests) and Muslim imams trained abroad are often not prepared to undertake these tasks, nor to undertake the substantial tasks of facility management and fundraising for the religious community, tasks traditionally understood to be within the cleric's purview in America. Likewise, as non-native speakers of English, these religious leaders may have a more difficult time relating to and providing appropriate services for second-generation youth in the American religious community. The language barrier often hinders their ability to interact with the wider community, such as taking part in interfaith activities. It remains to be seen how the communities will respond to these challenges. Will domestic training facilities be created, similar to those serving some Buddhist faith communities? Will training programs overseas develop specialized language and management programs for religious leaders to be placed in the United States? Will individual American religious communities develop new structures that spread the "pastoral" burden to others in the organization?

The issue of language loss confronts all immigrant communities as the immigrant generation ages and second- and third-generation members raised in the American context demonstrate a range of language ability. The American reconceptualizations of Buddhism, Hinduism, Sikhism, and Islam all face a pair of language issues, one related to the language of scripture and worship and the other related to the transmission of the spoken vernacular language to the second generation. Across faiths, the understanding and retention of the scriptural language is an issue. Sanskrit, Hinduism's scriptural language, is not a spoken one; some Muslims speak Islam's scriptural language, Arabic; and although Gurumurkhi might be close to spoken Punjabi, most Sikhs do not understand the Sikh scriptural language. Sikh organizations have stressed the learning of Punjabi for the second generation, which has a social, familial, and religious purpose. For the Hindu second generation, even knowing one's family language does not mean one will understand the Sanskrit prayers and hymns. For Muslim Americans, debates continue on the significance of knowing Arabic, for example, versus relying on Urdu, which Indian Muslims have tried to pass on to the second generation.

Although it manifests itself differently in each community, the language issue leads to a series of questions over whether and how to retain the scriptural language as part of worship: Should we pray in English? When should we not pray in English? It is easy to see how this debate takes on theological importance. The answers, in turn, will lead to a host of practical challenges, from the transliteration of traditional prayers into the Latin alphabet to the translation of prayers and scripture into English.

Undertaking such efforts responds to the problem of language loss, allowing second- and subsequent-generation adherents to participate with a greater understanding of ritual meaning. At the same time, resistance to the idea has fed efforts to teach the scriptural languages of each faith through religious classes. Thus many communities have developed "Sunday schools," a term obviously borrowed from the Christian lexicon, to transmit ritual language and practice as well as other cultural traditions (often in translation) to each community's American-born children.[18]

International migration is no longer a one-way process. Contemporary migrants and their children maintain transnational connections—familial, economic, cultural, and political ties across international borders. New technologies, especially involving inexpensive long-distance phone calls, emailing, and the relative ease of travel, serve to connect such networks with increasing speed and efficiency. Most of these religious communities are involved in transnationalism, the frequent and widespread movement back and forth between communities of origin and destination and the resulting economic and cultural transformation[19] and religious transformation. For example, the Buddhist Churches of America is an affiliate of Japan's Nishi Hongwanji, a sect of Jodo Shinshu, which is a form of Pure Land Buddhism, itself a branch of the Mahayana tradition. Transnational ties thanks to technology mean also that one need not consult with a priest or speak a language other than English to identify a holy day; specialized religious calendars on the Internet abound. It is also easier for followers of the faiths to go on pilgrimages. Religious organizations in other countries can and do depend on the relative wealth of the United States to support many of their activities overseas. Many adherents engage in transnational religious practices. Hindus can now even do *darshan* online; major temples have Webcams that allow devotees anywhere to do *darshan*. For all these religions, transnationalism may also take on a political aspect, as it does through American Sikhs' support of the Khalistan movement and American Muslims' support of Islamic charities that direct funds to social services and other efforts overseas.

Buddhists, Hindus, Muslims, and Sikhs no longer face the strict limitations on their rights and overt public discrimination of the nineteenth and early twentieth centuries. However, even now, when they are on their way to becoming accepted and viewed as an important part of the religious mosaic of American life, followers of these four religions face challenges of social disadvantage. In particular, the majority of the followers are non-white immigrants. As racial minorities, they may face disadvantages and even violence. Moreover, because race is one of the preeminent organizing principles in U.S. society, adherents' race may become associated with a particular religion. This process, called the racialization of religion, exerts a particularly strong effect on Arab and South Asian people. In many cases, brown skin comes to be seen as associated with, and therefore a proxy for, a particular faith. Since September 11, brown skin is linked especially with Islam, and brown-skinned people may be seen not only as different but also as a foreign enemy's domestic "fifth column." Race may exert another effect on Asian and Arab Americans. Since the American racial understanding remains bipolar—literally black and white—these communities are seen as "other," ambiguous, and not fully American. Rather, these populations may be seen as perpetual foreigners, a status that often brings with it hostility from members of the dominant society in the form of xenophobia.

Living in a society that is dominated by another religion, Christianity, raises many issues for these faith communities. In American society, there are individuals and organizations that desire to restrict, exclude, or attack immigrants. Religion, particularly when racialized, adds another dimension for abuse. This abuse has taken many forms, ranging from verbal epithets against "foreigners" and restrictive legislation to vandalism of property and murder. The American creation myth insists that the Puritans sought religious freedom; indeed they did, but only for themselves. Anabaptists, Quakers, Mormons, Catholics, Jews, and others have each in turn discovered that "religious freedom" is enjoyed disproportionately by Protestant Christians. Moreover, "freedom of religion" is not the same as having that choice accepted and supported, rather than ignored, marginalized, exoticized, or demonized. This fierce commitment to English norms, values, and ways of operating begins the trail to modern nativism.[20] Contemporary non-Christian immigrants are simply its latest target.

Notwithstanding the long history of the presence of minority religions in the United States and the nation's self-image as a haven for those fleeing religious oppression, the reality of life in America for a devotee of a non-Western faith is one of misunderstanding, missed opportunities, and outright abuse. The followers of Sikhism, Islam, Hinduism, and other non-Western faith traditions encounter prejudice and discrimination because of religion. While the racialization of religion surely exacerbates the discrimination faced by adherents of these religions, it alone does not explain the discrimination. Nor does the excuse that the faiths are "Eastern" suffice. Islam, like Christianity and Judaism, is an Abrahamic faith with adherents of all ethnicities; yet Muslims in America face perhaps the most pervasive and virulent religious discrimination of the day, Islamophobia.

Religious oppression refers specifically to the systematic subordination of Buddhists, Hindus, Muslims, and Sikhs by the dominant Christian milieu. This subordination is a product of power and the unequal power relationships among religious groups within American society; it is supported by the actions of individuals (religious discrimination), cultural norms and values, institutional structures, and societal practices. Through religious oppression, Christianity and its cultural manifestations function to marginalize, exclude, and deny the members and institutions of Hindu, Muslim, and Sikh religious groups in society the privileges and access that accompany a Christian affiliation.[21]

At the societal and institutional level, these groups are subject to oppression and face conflict on the basis of injustices that spring from their racial status, their religious status, or from the combination of the two. The racialization of religion can render religious oppression both invisible and acceptable. For example, various Buddhist, Hindu, Muslim, and Sikh communities have encountered opposition when attempting to erect houses of worship. Gurudwaras have been fought by city councils and zoning boards steered by xenophobic sentiments: the fear of the foreign, the unknown, and the "strange."[22] Muslim and Hindu communities have encountered similar problems. At the same time, Hinduism and Buddhism struggle with their holy images being commodified and sold. Popular retail outlets sell statuettes of the Buddha or the Hindu goddess

Saraswati, body lotions called "Om," and even lunchboxes and underwear bearing holy images.[23]

Because American Buddhist, Hindu, Muslim, and Sikh communities are locally grown phenomena, their ability to participate on equal footing in national debates, without having unifying infrastructures like the National Council of Churches or even local or regional dioceses, is hampered. These communities are therefore underrepresented in interfaith conversations. They often struggle with questions of whether, when, and how to participate in mainstream civic life. Their presence as students and scholars in the educational arena is not yet reflected in chaplaincies.

Let us consider that last example. How should the educational arena adapt to the growing presence of Buddhism, Hinduism, Islam, and Sikhism? The existence of these "new" religions demands that teachers and administrators know how to identify and confront religious discrimination and to promote religious pluralism in classrooms; to develop an understanding of the actual Supreme Court rulings on "religion" in the classroom and acknowledge that the presence of these communities complicates the issue of separation of church and state in America. Teachers must become more comfortable with ethnoreligious items and concepts because of the substantial overlap between religion and "culture" in these faiths. The aim should not be to exclude religion from the classroom more vigorously. Such efforts effectively exclude only non-Christian religions. Rather, educators must recognize the challenge of avoiding the promotion, exclusion, or limitation of religion—the First Amendment's real mandate—while ensuring that when religion is present it encompasses the full diversity of contemporary America. For example, the debate over whether to teach "creationism" should involve not only the book of Genesis but also the creation stories of Buddhism, Hinduism, Islam, and Sikhism.

TRANSMISSION

The children of the post-1965 immigrants—the second generation—are now reaching adulthood and starting families of their own; many more immigrant and second-generation children are now rising through American school systems. This raises a new set of questions for these religious groups: Growing up as religious minorities in a culture where Christianity is pervasive, what will the second and subsequent generations know about their home faiths? How will they learn it? What can be transmitted and what cannot? Communities create the aforementioned "Sunday schools" to formalize the transmission process. Individual parents teach what they can, but because they often come from countries where it is as "easy" to be nominally Buddhist or Hindu or Muslim as it is to be nominally Christian in the United States, many of these immigrant parents did not develop the required knowledge base to convey the home religion to their children's satisfaction.

As a result, research indicates that some in the second generation are undertaking their own searches for information, such as through college coursework. Influenced by the dominant Christian milieu, some long for an easy explanation of "the ten commandments" of their home religion. Others, convinced that they cannot match the religiosity of their parents by eschewing alcohol (Muslims) or beef (Hindus) or keeping the five Ks (Sikhs) or praying in the scriptural language, consider themselves not religious.

All these phenomena offer hints, but only hints, about the future profile of Buddhism, Hinduism, Islam, and Sikhism in the United States. Descendant generations will seek knowledge through study and transnational experiences, but probably will still feel increasingly disconnected from the authentic, "over there" religion of their parents and grandparents. American reconceptualizations of the religions may be embraced by many, but the communities will also have to respond and relate to a continuing influx of new immigrants. The continuing challenge of race and resources, and the devaluation of the religion through commercialization and caricature, will remain barriers to full membership in American culture. But with large and rapidly growing populations, all these American religions are here to stay.

NOTES

1. These pieces of legislation were designed to bar certain ethnic and national groups from entering the United States; as a result, they also excluded certain religious groups—in particular, Buddhists, Hindus, Muslims, Sikhs, and other non-Christians. See Ronald Takaki, *Strangers from A Different Shore: A History of Asians in America* (Boston: Little, Brown, 1989).

2. Ibid.

3. At one point, the Bureau of the Census collected information in the Census of Religious Bodies from 1906–1936. This information was obtained from religious organizations. The Census Bureau says, "Public Law 94-521 prohibits us from asking a question on religious affiliation on a mandatory basis; therefore, the Bureau of the Census is not the source for information on religion" (http://www.census.gov/prod/www/religion.htm). In fact, the referenced public law, passed in 1976, doesn't bar questions about religion but rather prohibits the punishment of respondents who decline to state their religion because doing so would violate its tenets. The relevant law is found at 26 U.S.C. section 225(d): "Where the doctrine, teaching, or discipline of any religious denomination or church prohibits the disclosure of information relative to membership," a respondent may not be punished for "a refusal, in such circumstances, to furnish such information." Because of its unique effectiveness in the collection of population-wide data, the Census should include in future decennial and other surveys optional questions on religious affiliation. (It would remain free to include in its presentations of data a caveat regarding the number of respondents who declined to answer.)

4. See The Pluralism Project, "Statistics: The Pluralism Project and Harvard University," available at www.pluralism.org/resources/statistics/index.php, accessed February 3, 2004. Many social scientists often refer to the American Religious Identification Survey (ARIS). While ARIS tried to overcome congregational bias by using a random-digit-dialed telephone survey, its substantial undercount of Hindus (766,000), Muslims (1.1 million), and Sikhs (57,000) as compared to other estimates raises questions as to the degree of its success. See Barry Kosmin, Egon Mayer, and Ariela Keysar, *American Religion Identification Survey 2001* (New York: The Graduate Center of the City University of New York, 2001).

5. See Hussein Abdulwaheed Amin, "Islam in the United States," available at www.islamfortoday.com/historyusa4.htm, accessed July 9, 2005.

6. See Thomas Tweed and Stephen Prothero, *Asian Religions in America: A Documentary History* (New York: Oxford University Press, 1999).

7. See Richard H. Seager, *Buddhism in America*, Columbia Contemporary American Religion Series (New York: Columbia University Press, 1999).

8. See Diana Eck, *Darsan: Seeing the Divine Image in India*, 3rd ed. (New York: Columbia University Press, 1998), 22.

9. See Jane I. Smith, *Islam in America*, Columbia Contemporary American Religion Series (New York: Columbia University Press, 1999).

10. See Gurinder Singh Mann, *Sikhism*, Religions of the World (Upper Saddle River, NJ: Prentice Hall, 2004).

11. See Sripati Chandreshekar, "A History of United States Legislation with Respect to Immigration from India: Some Statistics on Asian Indian Immigration to the United States of America," in *From India to America: A Brief History of Immigration, Problems, of Discrimination, Admission and Assimilation*, ed. Sripati Chandrasekhar (La Jolla: Population Review, 1982), 11–29.

12. See Karen I. Leonard, *Making Ethnic Choices: California's Punjabi Mexican Americans* (Philadelphia: Temple University Press, 1992).

13. See Harnik Deol, *Religion and Nationalism in India: The Case of the Punjab*, Routledge Studies in the Modern History of Asia (New York: Routledge, 2000).

14. See Raymond B. Williams, "Introduction," in *A Sacred Thread: Modern Transmission of Hindu Traditions in India and Abroad*, ed. Raymond B. Williams (Chambersburg, PA: ANIMA 1992), 3–6.

15. For a history of the development of houses of worship for the different religions, see Diana Eck, *A New Religious America: How a "Christian Country" Has Become the World's Most Religiously Diverse Nation* (San Francisco: Harper Collins, 2001); Yvonne Yazbeck Haddad, *Muslims in the West: From Sojourners to Citizens* (New York: Oxford University Press, 2002); Vasudha Narayanan, "Creating the South Indian 'Hindu' Experience in the United States," in Williams, ed., 147–76; and Williams, "Introduction."

16. See Ihasan Bagby, Paul M. Perl, and Brian T. Froehle, *The Mosque in America: A National Portrait* (Washington, DC: Council on American-Islamic Relations, 2001), 63.

17. See Khyati Y. Joshi, *New Roots in America's Sacred Ground: Religion, Race, and Ethnicity in Indian America* (New Brunswick, NJ: Rutgers University Press, 2006).

18. See Nina Glick Schiller, Linda G. Basch, and Cristina Szanton Blanc, *Towards a Transnational Perspective on Migration: Race, Class, Ethnicity, and Nationalism Reconsidered*, Annals of the New York Academy of Sciences (New York: New York Academy of Sciences, 1992), 645.

19. See Joe R. Feagin, "Old Poison in New Bottles: The Deep Roots of Modern Nativism," in *Immigrants Out: The New Nativism and the Anti-Immigrant Impulse in the United States*, ed. J.F. Perea (New York: New York University Press, 1997).

20. In reality, religious oppression affects all non-Christian faiths. One well-known form of religious oppression is anti-Semitism. Indeed, even anti-Catholicism has not disappeared entirely from American culture. See Joshi.

21. See Jaideep Singh, "The Racialization of Minoritized Religious Identity: Constructing Sacred Sites at the Intersection of White and Christian Supremacy," in *Revealing the Sacred in Asian and Pacific America*, ed. Jane Naomi Iwamura and Paul Spickard (New York: Routledge, 2003).

22. See Joshi.

23. Ibid.; see also John Y. Fenton, *Transplanting Religious Traditions: Asian Indians in America* (New York: Praeger, 1988).

SUGGESTIONS FOR FURTHER READING

Eck, Diana. *A New Religious America: How a "Christian Country" Has Become the World's Most Religiously Diverse Nation.* San Francisco: Harper Collins, 2001.

Haddad, Yvonne Yazbeck. *Muslims in the West: From Sojourners to Citizens.* New York: Oxford University Press, 2002.

Joshi, Khyati Y. *New Roots in America's Sacred Ground: Religion, Race, and Ethnicity in Indian America.* New Brunswick, NJ: Rutgers University Press, 2006.

Prebish, Charles S. *Luminous Passage: The Practice and Study of Buddhism in America.* Berkeley: University of California Press, 1999.

Seager, Richard Hughes. *Buddhism in America.* Columbia Contemporary American Religion Series. New York: Columbia University Press, 1999.

Smith, Jane I. *Islam in America.* Columbia Contemporary American Religion Series. New York: Columbia University Press, 1999.

Takaki, Ronald. *Strangers from a Different Shore: A History of Asians in America.* Boston: Little Brown, 1989.

CHAPTER 7

Porous Borders: Mexican Immigration and American Civic Culture

Roberto Lint Sagarena

On Christmas Eve 1969, Chicano-rights attorney Ricardo Cruz led a march of several hundred Mexican-origin Catholics to a protest at the newly completed, multimillion-dollar St. Basil's Church in Los Angeles. The group picketed the church during mass, demanding that the clergy become more engaged with the religious and social concerns of Mexican-origin communities. Although the protest would eventually spark a series of reforms, initially the church was cool to the demands of the demonstrators and the protest resulted in twenty-one arrests, including that of Cruz himself.[1]

The St. Basil's demonstration and the hostile reaction to it on the part of church officials made public a long-standing rift between Mexican-origin Catholics and the American Catholic church. This rift was a result of more than a century of national, ethnic, and religious conflicts, which had long resulted in Mexican-origin Catholics being marginalized within the American church. However, neglect by the institution of the church fostered innovation in the expressions of religious faith by immigrant Catholic laity. And, as demographic changes have increased the Mexican-origin population of the United States, their religious culture has, in turn, come to greatly influence the mainstream church itself.

RELIGION IN THE BIRTH OF THE SOUTHWEST

Mexican immigration is unique compared to any other group entering the United States, including other groups from Latin America, in that the main geographic locus of their migration (the U.S. Southwest) is a region that was taken from the immigrants' home country by American military conquest. This conquest has largely been naturalized within American civic life and national history, but memories of the loss of the U.S. Invasion of Mexico remain strong on the Mexican side and have had great consequences on Mexican American émigrés' views of migration and acculturation as well as on the shape of their religious lives.

After Mexico's independence from Spain in 1821, Catholic clergy were sparse in the nation's northern frontier. As a result, the piety of Mexican people in this place and time can be characterized by the prominent role played by the laity in the creation and perpetuation of religious traditions. During Alta California's Mexican period (1821–1848) the bulk of the territory's numerous missions was secularized and lands fell into private hands. Similarly, in New Mexico during this period, Mexican priests were vastly outnumbered by lay Catholics.[2] In their absence, lay penitential brotherhoods organized groups of male laity as religious and civic authorities. And, although seminaries were established in both Santa Barbara and Taos in an attempt to foster the birth of an indigenous clergy, this project was interrupted by war. Ultimately, the maintenance of religious belief among Mexican-origin people in the region remained in the hands of lay practitioners for much of the nineteenth century.[3]

The war between the United States and Mexico (1846–1848) resulted in an American conquest of the region and sparked massive demographic and social changes in what became the Southwestern States. Mexican immigration to the United States in any recognizable numbers began with the end of the U.S. Invasion of Mexico in 1848. Prior to the war, migration had largely run towards Mexico as considerable numbers of Americans migrated into the Mexican territories of Tejas and Alta California. These American Mexicans became Mexican citizens, often converted to Catholicism, often married into prominent Mexican families, and ultimately alarmed Mexican civil authorities with their growing numbers and political influence. Although the war between Mexico and the United States had many secular causes—struggles over the expansion of Southern slavery, the popularization of the idea of America's manifest destiny, and the relatively undefended condition of Mexico's northern frontier among many others—in many ways it was perceived on both sides as a religious and cultural conflict. Both sides often understood it as a larger cultural war between Anglo Protestantism and Latin American Catholicism.[4]

In the decades preceding war with Mexico, the arrival of huge waves of Irish Catholic immigrants in the United States precipitated the fiercest period of anti-Catholic nativism in the history of the nation. As immigration rose sharply after the 1830s (mostly from Ireland and Germany) nativists demonized immigrants for allegedly importing crime and disease, stealing jobs, and practicing a long list of imagined moral depravities. Since the majority of these new Americans were Catholic, they were often denounced as "Papist" adherents to a religion that was antithetical to American democracy. The rites of the Catholic church were seen as dangerous idolatry; Catholic rituals and iconography were caricaturized as sensuous earthly distractions that weakened the will, ultimately eroding America's moral fabric and inviting catastrophe. For nativists, Catholicism symbolized all of the evils of the old world. By mid-century they had fostered a popular sentiment, articulated perhaps most clearly by Lyman Beecher and Samuel Morse, in which immigrants and unchecked immigration became culpable for a good number of the evils that threatened "orderly and godly" Americans. In time, many Catholic immigrants would themselves come to adopt and perpetuate this form of nativism as other ethnic and religious groups arrived after them.[5]

Unsurprisingly then, most American perceptions of Mexican Catholic religiosity prior to the war tended to be negative. For example, Josiah Gregg, one of the first American travelers to comment on Mexican religious practice was unsparing in his critique of Mexican veneration of the Virgin of Guadalupe. Gregg saw Mexican Catholics as having been duped by clergy with the pious legend of Guadalupe's apparition to the neophyte Juan Diego, now recently canonized as Saint Juan Diego. Rather than appreciating the complex role of Guadalupe in newly forming Mexican nationalism, Gregg saw veneration of a mixed-race virgin and the strongly devotional cast of Mexican religiosity as primitive and heretical. Although Gregg was a Protestant, it is noteworthy that much of the American Catholic clergy tended to agree with the tenor of his negative assessment of Mexican religious life.[6]

Nearly immediately after the end of the war, the California Gold Rush of 1849 precipitated a massive influx of immigrants from the world over to the newly Americanized territory. But the largest immigrant group heeding the call of gold was miners from northern Mexico. Thanks to this first wave of Mexican immigration to the United States in the 1850s, the Mexican-born population of California would actually be higher after losing the territory than before. These immigrants would create the first *barrios* (Mexican neighborhoods) in the United States. Americans would call them "Sonora-towns" after the Mexican state that most of the immigrant miners came from. This appellation, as well as the enactment of foreign miners' taxes and brutal racist violence, worked to reinforce an American understanding of the Mexican-born population as foreign and unwelcome to a region that had been part of their nation just a few years prior.[7]

Anglo Americans came to dominate the region politically and culturally, and Mexican-origin peoples were cast as alien to the region. For much of the nineteenth century, native-born Mexican-origin people in Texas and California were referred to by Americans as Texans (Tejano) and Californians. But, as early as the 1880s, Americans began to claim the title of "Texan" and "Californian" for their own native-born population. This shift in ethnic ascription finally marked those of Mexican origin as outsiders in much of the Southwest.

Mexican citizens living in the newly conquered region were given the option of American citizenship or exile to Mexico. But because of the problematic relationship between Mexican immigrants and territories that had only recently been Mexican, the initial Americanization of the region was predicated largely on the assumption that Mexican-origin residents would not assimilate. Rather, for American claims to place to be normalized, Mexicans would be expected simply to "fade away" as Native

Americans had or "return" to neighboring Mexico, out of the way of the advance of American culture and civic institutions.[8]

Changes in secular authority in the region also resulted in changes in religious authority, as Mexico's northern frontier became the Southwestern United States, political transformations brought about religious transformations. Catholic authority in the region was ceded to the American church, itself an embattled institution at the time of war with Mexico as this was the high point of American anti-Catholic nativism. As American Catholic clergy entered the region after the war they tended to perpetuate this understanding of American citizens of Mexican origin as inassimilable and focused their ministerial efforts towards the needs of arriving European American Catholics.

Upon arrival in California, Bishop Alemany, the first American bishop of the state, made the creation of a new physical infrastructure to serve American Catholics his first priority. Alemany was successful in lobbying the U.S. government to intervene and transfer ownership of secularized missions to the American Catholic church from private hands. These colonial buildings became public monuments that connected early Spanish pioneers to contemporary American Catholics. The fact that these missions had been secularized under Mexican rule allowed Americans to cast secular Mexican authorities as enemies of the "civilizing" project of the Spanish missionaries, again reinforcing a divide between the church and the Mexican-origin laity.[9]

In New Mexico, Jean Baptiste Lamy, the first American bishop there, implemented a host of reforms (most controversially, the institution of a tithe) aimed squarely at curbing lay authority. Lamy's reforms were resisted by powerful penitential brotherhoods as well as a resistive clergy (most notably Father Antonio Martinez of Taos), creating deep and abiding rifts between himself and the Hispano community. Ultimately, Lamy was successful in limiting the power of the local clergy by recruiting sympathetic priests and nuns from the seminary that trained him in France to replace the few indigenous clergy. Although there has been a long and vibrant continuation of *penitente* and *santero* traditions among New Mexico's Hispano laity, the Catholic clergy in the state was almost entirely of French origin until the early 1970s, maintaining rifts between Hispano laity and the American church for almost a century.[10]

MEXICAN AMERICA

Mexican immigration to the United States increased dramatically during the 1910s as the Mexican Revolution ravaged the country and tens of thousands fled for their lives; one out of every eight Mexicans was killed by the war's violence. In the 1920s, Mexican immigration intensified even further with the explosive growth of agribusiness in the American West. American firms actively and illegally recruited cheap Mexican labor to come to work in the United States. Census data show that between the years of 1900 and 1930, the Mexican-born population of the United States grew from 103,000 to 1,400,000, with the largest waves of immigration occurring in the 1920s.[11]

American Catholics credited their church with a central role in the settlement and Americanization of the Southwest. By favorably contrasting American Catholic traditions against Mexican Catholic traditions, American Catholicism could be understood as a unified tradition that was unquestionably American. In the late nineteenth and early twentieth centuries, many American Catholics supported an unprecedented displacement of prejudices. Mexican-origin Catholics were burdened with the same negative attributes that had been previously applied to Catholics by Protestant writers during the most virulent peaks of nativism. Mexican laity was cast as the dupes of tyrannical, despotic priests with questionable sexual mores. Thus, by negatively describing Mexican Catholicism and assuming the foreignness of Mexican culture in the Southwest, many promoters of a unified American Catholic culture appropriated anti-Catholic rhetoric in an effort to define the church's boundaries and limit the divisiveness of ethnic and cultural pluralism.[12]

Although a great number of Mexico's Catholic clergy also came to the Southwest during the 1910s and 1920s, their travels northward were largely a result of involuntary exile and their principal concern was in returning to Mexico as soon as possible, not the spiritual well-being of Mexican congregations in the United States. With the exception of limited Americanization campaigns and the funding of Sunday schools for Mexican children, Mexican and Mexican American communities were largely neglected by the American Catholic clergy well into the 1940s. But the neglect often went both ways. Although Mexican immigrants were still nominally Catholic, the anti-clerical violence of the war had left many of them unaccustomed to regular church attendance and others were themselves staunchly anti-clerical.[13]

Although Mexican participation in American Catholic services was low, domestic piety in the form of home altars and prayer groups maintained connections to the Catholic faith, much as it had for earlier Catholic immigrant groups. The proximity of the Mexican border and the speed of rail travel further limited incentives to actively assimilate or convert. These factors, combined with racism and segregation, resulted in fairly insular Mexican and Mexican American communities in California in the early twentieth century; from 1910–1930, only 5–13 percent of Mexican nationals in the United States applied for permanent residency or citizenship.[14]

In the early 1930s, global economic depression fanned the flames of anti-immigrant sentiment in the United States and spurred on the creation of a program designed to rid the United States of unwelcome Mexican immigrants. Los Angeles, the American city with the largest Mexican-origin population at the time, became a focal point for repatriation efforts. Roughly 50,000, or about a third, of the city's Mexican residents returned to Mexico from 1920 to 1939, many forcibly, some voluntarily. Although repatriation campaigns were largely fueled by racist rhetoric and nativist legislation, for much of the decade the American Immigration Service was aided by Mexican consular officials in carrying out the campaigns. The Mexican government was eager to facilitate the homecoming of its citizens; the return of those who had left in the aftermath of the Mexican Revolution would not only increase the ranks of Mexico's skilled laborers, it would also ease the embarrassment of Mexican nationalists at having such a large émigré community in the United States.[15]

By the mid-1930s, most Mexicans wishing to repatriate had done so; those who chose to stay in California continued to face the risk of forced repatriation as well as a steady increase in anti-Mexican sentiment. Immigrants attempting to create more settled lives for themselves in the United States and no longer intending to return to Mexico faced serious issues surrounding their identity; they were now more *de afuera* (of the outside) than Mexican, and yet unable to integrate into American society, as they were ostracized by wealthy and poor migratory whites alike.

But Mexican repatriation efforts would not last. Beginning in 1942, just three years after the end of the repatriation campaigns, the United States government initiated a bi-lateral labor agreement with the Mexican government to recruit poor rural Mexican workers; with the advent of World War II and the end of the Great Depression, Mexican labor was needed once more. This agreement, known as the *Bracero* program, brought more than 220,000 Mexicans to the United States, more than half of them coming to the agricultural fields of California. Although most *Braceros* would eventually return to Mexico, their presence greatly increased the size of the region's Mexican American communities. More importantly, the *Bracero* program firmly established a virtually tidal pattern for Mexican immigration to the United States that would last through the rest of the twentieth century; during times of plenty, Mexican laborers would cross the border, and during lean times, they would return to Mexico, resulting in prolonged cultural exchanges between Mexican and nascent Mexican American cultures.[16]

In the midst of this renewal of Mexican cultures within the United States, the American Catholic church launched its first concerted Americanization campaigns among Mexican-origin peoples. These campaigns can be characterized as a combination of English language lessons and a catechism that was largely hostile to Mexican lay devotional traditions. Perhaps the most successful Catholic outreach of the mid-twentieth century was the *Cursillo* movement. Originating in Majorca, Spain, in 1947 and brought to the United States a decade later, the *Cursillo* phenomenon has had a great impact on Mexican-origin Catholics throughout the Southwest. Participants in the *Cursillo* undertake three-day "retreats" for religious renewal and dedication. Although the clergy would often participate in organizing the retreats, the aim of the *Cursillo* was to stress greater responsibility among lay persons in the maintenance of the church and their own spiritual lives. Further, the *Cursillo* movement had a significant impact on larger American culture because it fostered social activism among Mexican-origin Catholics. The *Cursillo* movement can be credited with influencing Catholic leadership during the civil rights era. Cesar Chavez of the United Farm Workers (UFW), for example, became a *Cursillista*.[17]

During the 1950s, Mexican Americans became encouraged by the advent of the civil rights movement; as they witnessed African Americans' successes through demonstrations, picketing, and direct confrontations with racism, they began to emulate these tactics in both the political and religious spheres. Beginning in 1958, Reies Tijerina, a Pentecostal minister, radicalized questions of land ownership in New Mexico. Citing the oft broken provisions of the Treaty of Guadalupe Hidalgo that guaranteed the retention of lands by Mexican citizens remaining in the annexed territories, Tijerina called for the return of property that had been taken through American deception and fraud, including large tracts that were now under the management of the United States Forestry Service.[18] In 1965, César Chávez headed the first attempts by Mexican agricultural workers in California to unionize under the banner of the United Farm Workers (UFW). During Lent of 1966, members of the new union undertook a 300-mile march of "Pilgrimage, Penitence, and Revolution" from Delano to Sacramento under the banner of the Virgin of Guadalupe and both Mexican and American flags.

The use of the image of Guadalupe by the UFW was in part an expression of ethnic identity and in part a strategic use of symbolism to counter accusations of communist subversion from the right. Criticism of the union helped to foster communication and dialogue between field workers and American Catholic clergy as both sides reached out to each other, with union leaders seeking protection from cold war nativism and a new generation of activist clergy seeking to participate in the moral renewal of the civil rights movement. In Chávez's own words, "we had the Virgin with us. And people, see, people said no they're not communists, once they saw the church around us. That was the way we broke the red-baiting."[19] As a result of the prominence given to the symbol of the Virgin of Guadalupe by the UFW, one of the most innovative and lasting legacies of the union is the transformation of Guadalupe into more than an emblem of Mexican nationalism. In the context of the American civil rights movement, the image of Guadalupe at once became a radicalized religious symbol for popular protest and also an emblem for Chicano nationalism.

NEW CHURCH, NEW IMMIGRATION

Although the civil rights movement provided an opportunity for some reconciliation between the American Catholic church and Mexican-origin laity to occur, the relationship continued to be contentious well into the next decade. Protests such as the one at St. Basil's are credited as a source of the political pressure that prompted the church to commission the first Mexican-origin bishops and cardinals in the 1970s. And ultimately, the confluence of several factors in the late 1960s would change the public character of American Catholicism (especially in the Southwest).

Many reforms instituted by Vatican II, such as the vernacular mass, provided powerful new methods for outreach in ethnic parishes. In the early 1970s, Spanish language services became increasingly popular and took inventive new forms such as the "mariachi mass" that featured Mexican musicians in the performance of the liturgy.[20] Although Mexican-origin Catholics welcomed the integration of Mexican cultural elements into services that targeted them, churches that sponsored these types of masses faced considerable criticism from many American Catholics who were wary of the rise of ethnic particularism within *their* church.

At the same historical moment that Mexican culture and Mexican-origin Catholics were making inroads into the American Catholic church, the study of race and ethnicity was being formalized within the academy. Early ethnic studies programs fostered a politicized sense of identity for Mexican-origin peoples as Chicano\as and promoted active resistance to American-ization. Like members of the early UFW, Chicano\a nationalists often employed religious iconography, most importantly that of the Virgin of Guadalupe, as emblems of ethnicity.

Chicano\a artists have reinvented Guadalupe in a variety of forms sym-bolizing political and cultural autonomy. Although the image of Guada-lupe has retained its sacredness, many artists depict the Virgin in a manner that radically departs from Catholic orthodoxy. Chicano\a artists often depict Guadalupe in ways that stress her connection to the Aztec goddess *Tonantzin* in an attempt to valorize and claim continuity with the indige-nous cultures of Mexico. Further, Chicana feminists have re-imagined Guadalupe in a host of forms suggestive of feminine strength and sexual-ity. Among a multiplicity of forms, Guadalupe has been cast as a black-belt karate practitioner, as jogger, as factory worker, as a powerful nude, and as the subject of countless tattoos.[21]

As Chicano\as embarked on the project of creating a culture betwixt and between Mexican and American cultures, the liberalization of Ameri-can immigration laws resulted in a massive influx of Mexican-origin peo-ple. In the 1980s, large-scale immigration from Mexico became one of the largest elements of what scholars of immigration to the United States have come to term "the new immigration." In specific consideration of Mexi-cans, this immigration is characterized by large-scale flow of documented and undocumented immigrants that intensified rapidly after 1980. In the 1990s there were more legal immigrants to the United States from Mexico than from all of the countries of Europe combined.[22]

Many of these "new" Mexican immigrants in the United States are transnational citizens rather than simple transplants. These recent arrivals are emerging as important actors in American society and civic life while still participating in Mexico's religious, economic, political, and cultural spheres, a situation that is not lost on Mexican politicians. Mexican Presi-dent Vicente Fox toured the border region in December 2000 to welcome back personally a few of the estimated 1 million Mexicans traveling south for Christmas. The popularity of Fox's dual nationality initiative, whereby Mexican immigrants becoming U.S. citizens retain a host of political rights in Mexico, suggests an emerging transnational framework for the identities of "new" immigrants.[23]

Although contemporary immigrants have found the American Catholic church more sympathetic than earlier generations did, Protestant denomi-nations (especially charismatic churches) have had significant success in their conversion efforts. Many of these churches make use of transnational networks to establish satellite congregations in Mexican hometowns thereby creating important support networks for their members and religious cultures that are American and Mexican all at once.[24]

The transnational character of the religious lives of many new Mexican immigrants has also led to great innovations in Catholic devotional life in the borderlands. Among the most noteworthy is the existence of two separate cults of patron saints of undocumented Mexican immigrants, Juan Soldado and San Toribio Romo.

Although not recognized by the Catholic church, Juan Castillo Morales, commonly known as Juan Soldado, has long been understood to be a patron saint of undocumented Mexican immigrants. Morales served as a soldier in Tijuana when he was accused of the rape and murder of an eight-year-old girl, a crime for which he was executed in 1938. His hagiography claims that he was framed by a superior officer who was actually guilty of the horrible act. As he was led to his execution, he swore that his innocence would be proven when miracles were asked and granted in his name after his death. "Juan Soldado" is buried in Tijuana's Panteon 2, which has become a pilgrimage spot for the faithful to ask for intercession in issues of immigration: crossing the border safely, dealing with the border patrol, and negotiating permanent residency and citizenship. Devoted followers have built a chapel on the site of his grave that is decorated with thanksgivings in the form of photographs, letters, gifts, candles, flowers, and copies of green cards.[25]

In 2000, Pope John Paul II canonized twenty-four martyrs killed in Mexico's Cristero revolt, an insurrection against a repressively anti-clerical Mexican government that occurred in the late 1920s. One of these newly minted saints is Father Toribio Romo, a priest shot and killed by government forces in an ambush in Tequila, Mexico. Since canonization, Romo has gained considerable popularity among Mexican migrants and is credited with leading many lost or injured people safely across the border. Although Romo's relics reside in a church in central Mexico, it is significant that all of Romo's surviving relatives have emigrated from Mexico and live in the United States.

A CHURCH REBUILT

In California, the Northridge earthquake of 1994 damaged Los Angeles's St. Vibiana's Cathedral badly enough to warrant its condemnation by structural engineers. However, plans for a grander cathedral were quickly drawn up and by the following year the campaign to build a new structure was well under way. In September 2002, the massive new cathedral of Our Lady of the Angels was dedicated and opened to the public.

Like St. Basil's Church noted earlier, the new cathedral makes use of a simple, modern, and very controversial architectural vocabulary. However, the design of Our Lady of the Angels is radically different from that of its predecessor. In some ways the architecture of the new cathedral can be read as a compensatory gesture by the American church to ethnic and national Catholics. Its architect and the clergy very self-consciously created the building as an emblem of a pluralistic vision of American Catholicism and civic culture. The entrance to the cathedral is surmounted by a statue of Mary that "does not wear the traditional veil. Her arms are bare, out-stretched to welcome all. Her carriage is confident, and her hands are strong, the hands of a working woman. From the side can be seen a thick braid of hair down her back that summons thoughts of Native American or Latina women. Other characteristics, such as her eyes, lips, and nose convey Asian, African, and Caucasian features."[26] Below the multiracial statue of Mary are monumental cathedral doors designed by a Mexican-born artist and emblazoned with fifteen distinct Marian images from around the world.

As the laity enter the cathedral, they pass a series of side-chapels that are designed to house and acknowledge the important role of the diverse ethnic parishes of the city. The interior walls of the cathedral are decorated with large tapestries that depict the communion of saints. Catholic saints, revered individuals, and children of all nationalities and epochs are present in an eclectic mix. But of these symbols of inclusivity, the one that would be most striking to the Chicano\a protesters of 1969 at St. Basil's is the installation of a full-scale replica of Our Lady of Guadalupe placed just outside the exit of the cathedral. This Mexican Virgin is visible both to all visitors and to the thousands of commuters passing the cathedral on the 101 freeway that runs adjacent to the building.

The tremendous array of ethnic religious emblems that adorn the new cathedral marks a dramatic change in the American Catholic church. The church seems to have come full circle to an ethnic parish model, but as a more complex American church made up of many transnational ethnic par-ishes, not as a church that stands over and against ethnic particularity. Given that the cathedral's design and its location near government offices in downtown Los Angeles promote its use as a ceremonial and public cen-ter for the city, it seems likely that the religious culture and symbols of immigrant ethnic Catholics, most notably Mexican-origin Catholics, will only come into greater prominence in the civic life and culture of the city. In doing so, they may well represent the future for Mexican influence on the whole of American religious life.

NOTES

1. The events of this protest are treated in Oscar Zeta Acosta's autobiography, *The Revolt of the Cockroach People* (New York: Vintage, 1973).

2. See David J. Weber, *The Spanish Frontier in North America* (New Haven, CT: Yale University Press, 1992), for a clear treatment of missionization and secularization.

3. For examples, see Mary Montaño *Tradiciones Nuevomexicanas: Hispano Arts and Culture of New Mexico* (Albuquerque: University of New Mexico Press, 2001); and Timothy Matovina and Gary Riebe-Estrella, eds., *Horizons of the Sacred: Mexican Traditions in U.S. Catholicism* (Ithaca, NY: Cornell University Press, 2002).

4. For discussions of perceptions of the war on the U.S. side see John Eisen-hower, *So Far From God: The U.S. War with Mexico, 1846–1848* (Norman: Univer-sity of Oklahoma Press, 1989); and Robert W. Johannsen, *To the Halls of the Montezumas* (New York: Oxford University Press, 1985).

5. See John Higham, *Strangers in the Land: Patterns of American Nativism, 1860–1925* (New Brunswick, NJ: Rutgers University Press, 1955). For a primary example see Lyman Beecher's widely reprinted sermon, "Plea for the West."

6. Josiah Gregg, *Commerce of the Prairies* (1845; Norman: University of Oklahoma Press, 1990).

7. See Kevin Starr and Richard Orsi, eds., *Barbarous Soil: People, Culture and Community in Gold Rush California* (Berkeley: University of California Press, 2000); Susan Lee Johnson, *Roaring Camp: The Social World of the California Gold Rush* (New York: W.W. Norton, 2000); and Douglas Monroy, *Thrown Among Strangers: The Making of Mexican Culture in Frontier California* (Berkeley: University of California Press, 1990).

8. See Reginald Horsman, *Race and Manifest Destiny: The Origins of American Racial Anglo-Saxonism* (Cambridge, MA: Harvard University Press, 1981).

9. John Bernard McGloin, *California's First Archbishop: The Life of Joseph Sadoc Alemany, 1814–1888* (New York: Herder and Herder, 1966).

10. See Ray John De Aragon, *Padre Martinez and Bishop Lamy* (Las Vegas: Pan American, 1978); and Alberto Lopez Pulido, *The Sacred World of the Penitentes* (Washington, DC: Smithsonian Institution Press, 2000).

11. See George Sanchez, *Becoming Mexican American: Ethnicity, Culture and Identity in Chicano Los Angeles, 1900–1945* (New York: Oxford University Press, 1993).

12. Consider the enthusiastic response of American Catholic clergy to Willa Cather's *Death Comes for the Archbishop*, a novel that portrays the struggle between American and Mexican forms of Catholicism.

13. See Mathew Butler, *Popular Piety and Political Identity in Mexico's Cristero Rebellion: Michoacan, 1927–1929* (London: British Academy, 2004).

14. See Sanchez.

15. See Francisco E. Balderrama and Raymond Rodriguez, *Decade of Betrayal: Mexican Repatriation in the 1930s* (Albuquerque: University of New Mexico Press, 1995).

16. See Ernesto Galarza, *Merchants of Labor: The Mexican Bracero Story* (New York: McNally and Loftin, 1964).

17. Richard Etulain, *Cesar Chavez: A Brief Biography with Documents* (New York: Palgrave/Macmillan, 2002).

18. See Rudy Busto, *King Tiger: The Religious Vision of Reies López Tijerina* (Albuquerque: University of New Mexico Press, 2005).

19. F. Arturo Rosales, ed., *Testimonio: A Documentary History of the Mexican American Struggle for Civil Rights* (Houston: Arte Publico, 2000), 283.

20. See Martin McMurtrey, *Mariachi Bishop the Life Story of Patrick Flores* (San Antonio, TX: Corona Publishing, 1988), on post–Vatican II Spanish-language liturgical changes in the Southwest.

21. The classic article on the topic is Shifra Goldman, "The Iconography of Chicano Self-Determination: Race, Ethnicity, and Class," *Art Journal* 49, 2 (1990): 167–73. See also Marie-Pierre Colle, *Guadalupe Body and Soul* (New York: Vendome, 2005); and Carla Trujillo, "La Virgen de Guadalupe and Her Reconstruction in Chicana Lesbian Desire," in *Living Chicana Theory*, ed. Carla Trujillo (Berkeley: Third Woman Press, 1998).

22. For a broad discussion of the contemporary effects of Latin American immigration see Marcelo Suraez-Orozco and Mariela M. Paez, eds., *Latinos: Remaking America* (Berkeley: University of California Press, 2002).

23. See Carlos Veles-Ibanez and Anna Sampaio, eds., *Transnational Latino/a Communities: Politics, Processes and Cultures* (Oxford: Rowman and Littlefield, 2002).

24. See Luis Leon, *La Llorona's Children: Religion, Life, and Death in the U.S.-Mexican Borderlands* (Berkeley: University of California Press, 2004); and David Maciel and Maria Herrera Sobek, eds., *Cultures Across Borders: Mexican Immigration and Popular Culture* (Tucson: University of Arizona Press, 1998).

25. See the first book-length treatment: Paul J. Vanderwood, *Juan Soldado: Rapist, Murderer, Saint* (Durham, NC: Duke University Press, 2004).

26. From the Los Angeles Cathedral Web site, available at http://www.olacathedral.org/cathedral/art/doors1.html; accessed January 20, 2006.

SUGGESTIONS FOR FURTHER READING

Cantu, Norma, and Olga Najers-Ramirez, eds. *Chicana Traditions: Continuity and Change.* Urbana: University of Illinois Press, 2002.

Isasi-Diaz, Ada Maria. *Mujerista Theology.* Maryknoll, NY: Orbis, 1996.

Leon, Luis. *La Llorona's Children: Religion, Life, and Death in the U.S.-Mexican Borderlands.* Berkeley: University of California Press, 2004.

Sandoval, Moises. *On the Move: A History of the Hispanic Church in the United States.* Maryknoll, NY: Orbis, 1990.

CHAPTER 8

The Shifting Role of the Latter-day Saints as the Quintessential American Religion

Ethan Yorgason

Many Americans know the Church of Jesus Christ of Latter-day Saints, the largest and most prominent body in the Mormon tradition,[1] as one of the country's fastest-growing churches. Somewhat less commonly known is this movement's label as "the quintessential American religion."[2] Since its establishment some critics have decried Mormonism as not even a legitimate faith. How then, this chapter asks, have many others viewed it as the quintessential American religion? This chapter also poses questions of why and whither. Why has Mormonism been given this designation? Whither the relationship between Mormonism and the American-essence label?

In ancient Greek and medieval European philosophy, "quintessence" meant aether, the fifth element of the universe along with fire, earth, air, and water. By the nineteenth century, aether named the invisible element that permeated the universe. Mark Twain famously linked this aether with Mormonism when he called the *Book of Mormon* "chloroform in print."[3] The pun alluded both to aether's supposedly gaseous nature as well as to the capacity of the *Book of Mormon*—of which the book of Ether forms a part—to induce sleep, like chloroform gas. Not many years later, aether became the Achilles heel of Newtonian physics, as scientists famously abandoned the search for this quintessence. This chapter raises the question of whether the label of Mormonism as the quintessential American religion might similarly evaporate. Could this label, like aether, become more of a reminder how people used to think than a notion that provides insight? The label of Mormonism as the quintessential American religion gained greatest resonance in the mid-to-late twentieth century. I ask whether the label will have staying power into the twenty-first. It is probably too soon to provide confident answers. Yet I think the question deserves to be posed.

Peter Williams recently wrote, "Mormonism has been called the most American of religions, and at times has been treated as subversively un-American. It is clearly a community of apparent paradoxes...."[4] This chapter does not concentrate on arguments that Mormonism was un-American, but such charges were almost constant during the nineteenth century because of polygamy, prophets, theocracy, denial of traditional Christianity, and communalism; and some continue to make such charges today.[5] On the other side of the paradox, the "quintessential" label is somewhat shallower than it might appear. Many fewer people fully endorse the argument than note that it has been made by others. There are shades to the "quintessential" argument; some use the precise label and straightforwardly argue that Mormonism is the most American religion, while others merely make suggestions in that direction. In what follows, before more fully posing the staying-power question, I explore arguments that approach the "quintessential" claim without directly endorsing it, as well as those that more fully make it.

DOCTRINAL AND FORMAL FOUNDATIONS OF THE "QUINTESSENTIAL" ARGUMENT

The "quintessential" claim draws on various aspects of Latter-day Saints (LDS) history. I wish, however, to suggest first that this claim depends on a foundation of Mormonism's doctrinal and formal characteristics. Basic LDS teachings are relevant to the United States. The *Book of Mormon*, for example, tells of ancient inhabitants of the American continent. Mormons typically interpret those inhabitants' prophecies for "this land" and "this nation" as referring to the United States. Mormonism's canonized "Articles of Faith" include the enjoinder to be subject to the rulers of the land and the prophecy that Zion, the New Jerusalem, will be built on the American continent. Joseph Smith identified western Missouri as the actual site of the biblical Garden of Eden, the place to and from which Christ will return and rule at the Second Coming. As well, Mormons have held the United States Constitution to be divinely inspired, perhaps even revealed. It was not simply the best possible outcome at the historical moment, but the universally paramount guide for a nontheocratic world. The United States, throughout much of LDS doctrinal history, was not just *a* promised land. It was, along with Palestine, *the* promised land.

Four basic formal elements also ground most "quintessential" arguments. First and perhaps most simply, though not most trivially, Mormonism's numerical success bolsters the "quintessential" claim. Mormonism was not unique in many of the impulses we today regard as novel. But it is the movement among those that advocated such novelty that succeeded and continues to succeed. Other movements that seemed to be better candidates for much of the nineteenth century, such as the Disciples movement, have stagnated numerically by comparison.[6] They seem to lack the vitality the quintessential American religion should possess. Mormonism's strong and fairly consistent growth implies vitality.

Second, Mormonism possesses manifestly American origins. Observers have historically given priority to origination over adaptation. Protestantism, in its many varieties, dominates American religious life numerically and ideologically. Its nonsectarian form is the de facto basis for the presumed common religious values that have grounded and continue to permeate American public life.[7] It has proven highly adaptable to and supportive of American nationalism.[8] Yet most Protestant denominations, and Protestantism as a whole, have European origins. Many observers thus seem to imply that these groups cannot constitute pure American essence. Similarly, Catholicism, by far the dominant single religious institution in the United States, exists in America because of immigration, and its institutional loyalty is still exported.

Third, and related, Mormonism, according to many accounts, created something distinct from earlier religious categories. It was novel. "Our deep [American] need for originality gave us Joseph Smith even as it gave us Emerson and Emily Dickinson, Whitman and Melville, Henry and William James, even as it gave us Lincoln...."[9] Mormonism did not claim allegiance to Protestantism, nor did outsiders often place it there.[10] Mormonism claims to be Christian, but it does not claim the institutional Christian tradition, as never-ending debates over Mormonism's qualifications to be called Christian demonstrate.[11]

Finally, Mormonism created strong, tightly integrated leadership and membership. Mormonism has often been labeled a cult in part because of its influence throughout the breadth of its members' lives. Mormonism has not been simply a loose coalition of similarly minded believers. The movement's novelty and strong integration have led many observers to find Mormonism more essentially American than the Pentecostal movement, for example, which is both numerically large (much larger than Mormonism), vital, and American in origin.

Thus Mormonism can be characterized as a large, consistently vital movement springing from American soil without obvious connections elsewhere,[12] one with manifestly distinctive content and one that motivates high levels of loyalty and comradeship. To the extent that those looking for the quintessential American religion find these formal characteristics attractive, few religions in America can match Mormonism. Add Mormonism's theological statements about America, and the LDS church becomes the quintessential American religion by near default. These doctrinal and formal elements, whether left implicit or made explicit, typically ground arguments about Mormonism as the quintessential American religion. Without these building blocks, the claim would be difficult to sustain. Yet those who make the "quintessential" argument often insist that there is much more.[13] Mormonism, they say, profoundly participates in, manifests, or shapes something of the American ethos. Just how it does so varies, depending on who makes the argument.

QUINTESSENTIAL THROUGH AMERICANIZATION

Many scholars have argued that the Americanization period of Mormonism (1880–1930) led to conditions that allowed Mormons to be subsequently regarded as super-Americans.[14] Some of my own work has followed this basic theme.[15] Strong late-nineteenth-century non-Mormon pressure—of legal, social, political, and cultural varieties—induced Mormons generally to accept a narrow form of Americanness, more narrow in fact than that which existed in America or even Protestantism as a whole.[16] By the twentieth century, strict Victorian ideals replaced greater gender tolerance. The nascent LDS feminist movement was a casualty of the pressure as much as polygamy was. Commitment to capitalism and its cultural logic assumed priority over egalitarian economic ideals. And a nearly axiomatic jingoism pushed aside carefully considered national loyalty, with its capacity for critique.

With early Mormonism's strong millennial expectations of retreat from the world having faded substantially, Mormons moved beyond simple declarations that God inspired the U.S. Constitution and that Mormons would build Zion within the boundaries of the United States. Mormons came to see the American nation as an active agent in spreading God's agenda, rather than just as an entity providing place and protection for the church to grow. Mormons explicitly argued that they were spreading the gospel of Americanism as much as that of Mormonism.[17] Although not unique among churches in making such professions, Mormonism espoused doctrines that added a more direct theological claim to them. Mormons did not have to tenuously rely on the Bible to support beliefs in American exceptionalism. As Leonard Arrington and Davis Bitton put it: "By the end of World War I in America, if not before, the Mormons were more American than most Americans. Patriotism, respect for the law, love of the Constitution, and obedience to political authority reigned as principles of the faith."[18]

Thus one sense of Mormons as the quintessential American religionists asserts that the Latter-day Saints deeply embraced basic American values, ideologies, and practices near the turn of the twentieth century. As this process continued throughout the century, some observers began to label Mormons "super-Americans" or "model Americans."[19] Ideologically, Mormons approached mainstream American society most closely from about 1920–1965.[20] Utah voting patterns largely mirrored national trends then.[21] Mormonism's racialized priesthood and conservative gender tendencies fit mainstream moods. Capitalism took strong hold in Utah, and mainstream Protestantism extended social, if not theological, tolerance toward Mormons. Growing economic and nationalist conservatism within parts of LDS leadership matched broader American cold war tendencies.

At times, this notion of Mormons embodying American values slid into assertions that Mormon culture represented the essence of traditional, rather than contemporary, America.[22] Mormonism's presumed community-mindedness, patriarchal gender roles, and strict sexual morality reminded many of an America that used to exist.[23] Mormonism, in this variation, offers little insight into contemporary or future American life; instead it provides a living heritage museum that helps America access its past.

Other observers, however, found Mormonism a leader in many aspects of contemporary American life. Such areas include health-consciousness (the LDS Word of Wisdom), corporate-mindedness (business-oriented church leadership and membership), and international awareness (due to Mormonism's missionary program).[24] I suspect that scholars and other observers may in the future look more in this vein to Mormonism for insight into American globalization.[25] Mormonism offers possibilities for analyzing global attraction or rejection of things with American origins.[26] Mormonism also has apparently taken on a prototypical American challenge within globalization, managing and accommodating itself to international diversity, even while maintaining both the priority of key American-born ideologies and practices and also the perpetuation of American institutional primacy and hierarchical focus.

QUINTESSENTIAL THROUGH WESTERN EXPERIENCE

Another common argument locates Mormonism's essential Americanness at an earlier point in history. In this regard, Mormonism represents America not so much because of twentieth-century cultural accommodation, but because of its nineteenth-century flight from mainstream America. Mormonism thus participated centrally in the creation of the American frontier. Or, alternatively, Mormonism's experience provides insight into America's obsession with Western space.

According to the first version, Mormonism shaped, and was shaped by, the frontier through its migrations toward and settling of the Salt Lake Valley.[27] Positive and negative shadings of this version exist. On the one hand, Mormonism's saga, especially its westward movement, demonstrates the nobility, tenacity, and success of the principled American quest for freedom. Alternatively, Mormonism offers a cautionary tale of the degradation produced on the wild frontier. In either case, Mormonism functions as a central element within the American frontier mythos. Since the frontier itself stood for many years as a key symbol of American uniqueness, it was only a short step to calling Mormonism the quintessential American religion.

In recent years, scholars have critiqued mythologized interpretations of the frontier. Nevertheless, many continue to suggest that America's obsession with the frontier and with the Western United States more generally was a key element of nineteenth- and early-twentieth-century America. In this more sophisticated version of the West's role in American life, Mormonism at times remains central.[28] A recent and particularly interesting account argued that to early-nineteenth-century Americans, "the notion of America as an ideal of freedom was in many respects removed from the concrete realities of the landscape itself." Western space only became symbolically important to America after religious dissidents, Mormons among the foremost of these, first "saw the potential of the landscape itself to become redemptive."[29] Perhaps, then, Mormons were key shapers of the American geographical mythos. Others similarly called Mormonism a signal marker for the American characteristics of migration, mobility, and the capacity for social and individual renewal. Still others read Mormonism as enacting American Manifest Destiny historically and theologically.[30]

Another interpretation holds Mormonism as quintessentially American because it created a people. This assertion goes beyond typical observations that Mormonism created a tightly knit religious group. It additionally suggests that Mormonism's integration had staying power over generations. Both insiders and outsiders recognized and cultivated its sense of distinctiveness. It created a separate culture—or at least a subculture, not just a tightly organized voluntary association—complete for a time with its own economy and spatial boundaries. According to one highly influential formulation, Mormonism not only created a people, but also at certain historical moments became nearly a nation.[31]

Laurence Moore recently made this argument. He found Mormonism's peoplehood little diminished even in the late twentieth century. Mormonism, he suggested, originated out of a desire for distinctiveness, and this distinctiveness has been cultivated ever since:

> The Mormons have retained the main quality of sect-like behavior, which is insistence on a difference that *matters* between themselves and everyone else.... Many non-Mormon Americans living in western states continue to believe that present-day Mormons in secret councils hatch conspiratorial schemes against other Americans. Objective differences persist of the very same sort that laid the basis for the Mormon controversy in the nineteenth century. Mormons are ... a singularly concentrated group. Mormons have not abandoned the *Book of Mormon*; they give a great deal of deference to their church authorities; and they proselytize aggressively. A sense of difference has persisted so strongly among Mormons that they have probably gained an ethnic as well as a religious identity, thus becoming like the Jewish people they have always emulated.[32]

Moore recognizes that difference does not, at first blush, sound like an argument for centrality. But, he asserts, it is precisely this creation of difference that constitutes the American essence:

> Mormons taught *the* American religion, or at least a vital aspect of it, but not because their doctrines somehow sprouted naturally out of the American frontier and provided a domestic alternative to faiths imported from Europe. Mormons followed a lesson, already by their time well established in American experience, that one way of becoming American was to invent oneself out of a sense of opposition.... In defining themselves as being apart from the mainstream, Mormons were in fact laying claim to it. By declaring themselves outsiders, they were moving to the center.[33]

QUINTESSENTIAL THROUGH ORIGINARY IMPULSES

Finally, another category of "quintessential" arguments claims that Mormonism, usually through Joseph Smith's originary teachings, tapped into deeply rooted American cultural/religious longings and habits. To Klaus Hansen, one of the most perceptive observers of the Mormon–American relationship, the *Book of Mormon*'s physical setting plays only a minor role in Mormonism's Americanism. Instead:

> More typically American is the optimistic, progressive, "materialistic" nature of Mormon theology; its denial of original sin and its Arminian thrust. But

perhaps most typical of all is its practical, nonutopian emphasis, not only in its social thought ... but also in its metaphysics. Mormon cosmology [of uncreated matter, eternal progression, etc.] fits readily into the framework of nineteenth-century American science—at least as it was perceived in the popular mind.[34]

Others variously argued that Mormonism fundamentally typifies America's republican heritage, its search for authority amid conflict, or its populist and democratizing sensibilities (with a lay priesthood of most male believers and populist economic rhetoric, for example).[35] Others suggested that Mormonism reenacts America's Puritan heritage, distills and attempts to resolve key early debates from the Northeast United States, or provides an authentic declaration of independence for America from religious tradition.[36]

The Yale literary critic Harold Bloom gave probably the most provocative and insightful recent example within this category of argument.[37] Although he also presented some highly original claims, Bloom's argument pulled together many earlier assertions in this "originary" category. Joseph Smith, Bloom flatly stated, was a "religious genius."[38] Though he insisted that no single group wholly embodies "the American Religion," Bloom regarded Mormons and Southern Baptists as those that come closest. Given recent fundamentalist trends among Southern Baptists, he thought, Mormonism may offer the most insight for the future.[39] For Bloom, "our unofficial but pervasive national faith ... does not believe or trust, it *knows*, though it always wants to know more."[40] Mormons, he implied, know their place in the cosmos. "The God of the American Religion is not a creator-God, because the American never *was* created, and so the American has at least part of the God within herself."[41] Thus, the Mormon God is fundamentally American by being subject to time and space.[42]

> The Mormon Gods are a sequence of American fathers, each progressing from human to divine on the basis of hard work and obedience to the laws of the universe, which turn out to be the maxims of the Latter-day Saints Church. Organization, replacing creation, becomes a sacred idea, and every good Mormon indeed remains an organization man or woman.[43]

Bloom thus argued that much of what makes Americans *Americans* at the deepest levels is celebrated and developed within Mormonism.

As it turns out, there is more to Bloom's image of Mormon centrality in American religion. Bloom wrote in 1992 with what, as a geographer, I characterize as a geopolitical vision. To him, Mormonism's Americanness also lay in its currently sublimated drive—in, through, and beyond America and its ideals—to produce the Kingdom of God on earth. This drive for power over American space made the LDS manifestation of American religion simultaneously attractively audacious and frightening to Bloom. Mormonism, he was certain, will become the de facto religion of the American West, just as the Southern Baptist Convention is for the South:

> I surmise ... that the heirs of Smith and of Brigham Young have not altogether given up the aspiration to achieve the Mormon vision of the

Kingdom of God in America. No one really knows what portion of the liq-
uid wealth in America's portfolios is held by the Latter-day Saints Church.
Yet it is clear that Mormon financial and political power is exerted in Washington to a degree far beyond what one would expect from one voter in
fifty. The Republican regimes of Reagan and Bush have enjoyed fierce Mormon financial and moral support, and the Salt Lake City hierarchy in turn
can make itself heard in the White House. The nation will not always be
only two percent Mormon. The Saints outlive the rest of us, have more children than all but a few American groups, and convert on a grand scale, both
here and abroad.... [M]y own guess is that by the year 2020 ... they could
well form at least ten percent of our population, and probably rather more
than that. Their future is immense: the Mormon people consistently are the
hardest-working, most cohesive bloc in our society; only Asian-Americans
rival them in zeal, ambition, and intensity. Salt Lake City may yet become
the religious capital of the United States.[44]

Nevertheless, Bloom also frequently argued that contemporary Mormons
have forgotten or downplayed Smith's original vision. He never entirely
reconciled that assertion with his confidence that church leadership could
easily call the geopolitical scenario into existence. His membership predic-
tions also wildly mislead, as we shall see below. Yet here is a highly
respected non-Mormon scholar suggesting that the Mormonism of past,
present, and future is central to understanding American religious essence.

ORIGINS AND BACKGROUND OF THE
MORMONISM-AS-QUINTESSENTIAL ARGUMENT

Let us now turn to the issues of who has made these "quintessential"
arguments and why they were made. Factors extending beyond the content of Mormonism and American essence have provided the background
upon which the "quintessential" argument flourished. Both Mormons and
non-Mormons had reasons at various times to make the "quintessential"
argument. In the twentieth century, particularly its second half, these
motivations converged: Mormon desires to be seen as American, and non-
Mormon American scholarly and cultural yearnings to identify a quintessential American religion.

Mormons, as noted earlier, had from Joseph Smith's day valued America
and its Constitution. They felt the country operated under the world's
best possible system, in spite of arguing in the nineteenth century that
Americans did not extend religious freedom to the Saints and in spite of a
theology that expected the Kingdom of God to supersede America and all
other nations. Throughout the nineteenth century, they claimed to be
loyal Americans. Repeated flights from what they perceived as religious
persecution reminded them of the Pilgrims and Puritans, to whom many
Mormons explicitly claimed direct lineage.[45] They regarded the Mormon
Battalion's service in the Mexican War as more recent proof of their patriotism. Yet Mormons seem to have had little sense until the late nineteenth
century that they might be enacting something essential to the American
experience. Earlier, they had more regularly explained their originality and
contributions to the world in religious terms: They were following in the

model of the great Protestant dissidents, or they were breaking from Protestantism altogether and returning to Christ's original church.

But near the turn of the twentieth century, Mormons developed a sense of themselves partaking centrally in the American experience based in part on claims made in written sources. In 1888, five years after the statement first appeared in print, LDS Apostle George Q. Cannon quoted in his biography of Joseph Smith from Josiah Quincy's *Figures of the Past*:[46]

> It is by no means improbable that some future textbook, for the use of generations yet unborn, will contain a question something like this: What historical American of the nineteenth century has exerted the most powerful influence upon the destinies of his countrymen? And it is by no means impossible that the answer to that interrogatory may be thus written: *Joseph Smith, the Mormon Prophet*. And the reply, absurd as it doubtless seems to most men now living, may be an obvious common-place to their descendants. History deals in surprises and paradoxes quite as startling as this.[47]

Americans do not yet regard Joseph Smith in quite this manner, of course, but Quincy was remarkably prescient nevertheless.

However, the prediction very probably helped to create the situation it described. To say that Quincy wrote self-fulfilling prophecy is an overstatement. Many people with little personal stake in bolstering Joseph Smith's reputation took part in the process. But a relationship exists between the fact that these words were written and the extent to which they came to pass. Mormons repeated the quote over and over in the twentieth century, mostly for internal consumption.[48] Mormons undoubtedly came to consider Joseph Smith, and Mormonism by extension, as fundamentally important to America partly because of this quote. It cannot help but have led Mormons to find pride in the "quintessential" argument, a pride many Mormons certainly still feel today.

Non-Mormons more often came to the "quintessential" argument through a "Leo Tolstoy" quotation. But even here, Mormons preceded them. And here, the history becomes messy. According to the common version of the story, Tolstoy once told Dr. Andrew White, who served as both U.S. ambassador to Germany and president of Cornell University:

> Catholicism originated in Rome; the Episcopal Church originated in England; the Lutheran Church in Germany, but the [American religion] ... is commonly known as the Mormon Church.... The Mormon people teach the American religion; their principles teach the people not only of Heaven and its attendant glories, but how to live so that their social and economic relations with each other are placed on a sound basis. If the people follow the teachings of this Church, nothing can stop their progress—it will be limitless. There have been great movements started in the past but they have died or been modified before they reached maturity. If Mormonism is able to endure, unmodified, until it reaches the third and fourth generation, it is destined to become the greatest power the world has ever known.[49]

Factually, the story seems to be largely mistaken. But few people realized the problem.[50] Mormon scholars and apostles, non-Mormon scholars and journalists, and many others took the story at face value. Laurence Moore and Harold Bloom, to mention examples noted above, supplemented their own interpretations of Mormonism as quintessential by frequently stating that Tolstoy had it right.

Calling the story wholly false is too strong. We may never know the precise details. What we do know comes primarily from Leland Fetzer's research.[51] Tolstoy did indeed speak with White about Mormonism. Also, he did modestly compliment Mormons in an area or two. But the supremely flattering assessment of Mormonism and its fortunes is very probably a figment of LDS imaginations.

According to Fetzer, Susa Young Gates, Brigham Young's daughter and an important actor in Mormonism's transition into the twentieth century,[52] read that Tolstoy had decried America's oppression of both the Chinese and the Mormons. On the strength of that information, she initiated a brief correspondence in 1888–1889 with Tolstoy and his daughter. Along with the correspondence, she sent him a *Book of Mormon* and a copy of Cannon's biography of Joseph Smith, the book quoting Josiah Quincy's assessment of Joseph Smith. The letters to Gates from the Tolstoy family have apparently been lost, but Tolstoy recorded short notes about the correspondence and the two books in his journal. He was as appalled by the deception he thought Mormonism encompassed as by that of any other organized religion. But he regarded such deception, as with other organized religions, as a necessary social myth. When Tolstoy spoke with White about Mormonism, five years after the last Gates correspondence, he wryly said that he preferred deception that comes from the earth (Joseph Smith's golden plates) over that which comes from the heavens. He also expressed interest in the church's women and its success in enjoining chastity.[53] Nevertheless, Fetzer found no direct evidence that Tolstoy either speculated on Mormonism's future or regarded Mormonism as a whole in positive terms.

Fetzer tracked LDS modifications to this presumably accurate account of the conversation. Gradually, he argued, storytellers added elements that favored Mormonism, until the currently popular version emerged in a church magazine in 1939.[54] This version came from an LDS former Cornell student who reported to have received his information from White himself more than 30 years earlier. For various reasons, Fetzer strongly distrusts the 1939 version, but it nonetheless became dominant among both Mormons and non-Mormons. Whether Josiah Quincy's concern about the future reputation of Joseph Smith led Tolstoy to express positive interest in the future of Mormonism or whether such interest was simply imputed to Tolstoy by Mormons may be impossible to finally determine.[55] It seems highly likely, however, that the specific prognosis of Mormonism usually assigned to Tolstoy did not originate from him. In reality, it matters little where the historical truth lies. Mormons believed and told the story of Tolstoy, and non-Mormons also came to believe it. The story served important interests for both groups.

Mormons near the turn of the twentieth century yearned to interpret LDS history as acceptably American. But so, too, did some non-Mormons.

Even before much attention was given to Tolstoy, Mormon and non-Mormon interpretations converged within Utah's early-twentieth-century popular culture on the conclusion that Mormon colonization of the Great Basin importantly participated in the American story of Western colonization. This joint interpretation aided regional peace.[56] As Mormons felt ever less harassed in the twentieth century, the boldness and breadth of the American claim increased. By 1933, for example, John Henry Evans could release with a national publisher his *Joseph Smith: An American Prophet*.[57] As the twentieth century progressed and American nationalism became more dominant in Mormonism, stronger statements arose. These included more frequently a recollection of a statement of Joseph Smith. The Latter-day Saints, he is reported to have prophesied, will save the U.S. Constitution during an hour in which it hangs by a thread.[58] Mormons, in many LDS minds, were not only historically American, but were also destined to become saviors of the nation.

Twentieth-century non-Mormons outside of Utah gradually freed themselves from the interpretive strangleholds of polygamy and heresy, and likewise found something uniquely important in Mormonism. A relatively few nineteenth-century non-Mormon writers had looked beyond the usual condemnatory interpretations to provide more balanced accounts of Mormonism.[59] But at that point, those writers had little incentive to do more than situate Mormonism within the American experience: It was something unusual or interesting, perhaps, but not vital to the understanding of America.[60] The situation for non-Mormons changed in the twentieth century, although more slowly than in Utah. Perhaps most important was the 1903 assessment by the economist Richard Ely that Mormonism constituted the most perfect social organization outside of the German army.[61] Ely did not directly link Mormonism to American essence, but his conclusion gave Mormons and non-Mormons scholarly authorization to speak of Mormonism as enacting something fundamentally important. From the other side of the admiration spectrum, the scathing, sarcastic story of Mormonism by historian/essayist Bernard DeVoto, a non-Mormon Utah native who had since left Utah, hardly constituted a full argument for Mormonism as the quintessential American religion. Yet his account did have Mormonism searching misguidedly for "the perfect American religion."[62]

By the 1940s and 1950s, the theme of Mormonism as representative of America became prominent among scholars.[63] Particularly influential were Thomas O'Dea, who strongly argued that Mormons were a fundamentally American people, and David Brion Davis, who located Mormonism's roots in early New England culture. Significant numbers of Mormon and non-Mormon observers thereafter joined in portraying Mormons as quintessentially American at some level. Discussion then flourished on what the American essence was that Mormonism had tapped into.

Where did scholars and other non-Mormons outside of Utah find such underlying motivation to view Mormonism as the quintessential American religion? Cultural historians tell us that twentieth-century America was obsessed with diversity. Theorists early in the century formulated models of American pluralism, and the rest of that century can be interpreted as an attempt to work through the implications of diversity.[64] Americans eventually saw diversity as essential to the American spirit. Thus elements from beyond the mainstream could encompass something essentially American, especially if they had American origins.[65] The nineteenth century had not regarded diversity in this manner. When Mormonism was considered in an American sense then, writers used Mormonism to illustrate unfortunate, twisted, and marginal American offspring rather than American essence. In the twentieth century, a tendency to celebrate diversity arose, though an ambivalent one. Chiung Hwang Chen helped us understand this tendency by charting the development of two "model minority discourses" that paralleled each other in content and chronology.[66] She showed that American news and popular magazines portrayed both Mormons and Asian Americans as model minorities, groups that supposedly partook substantially of the American essence, especially in producing economic success, even though they were not incorporated into the mainstream culturally. The "model minority" label itself is much more commonly applied to Asian Americans, of course, but the magazines found model aspects in Mormons a bit earlier (the 1930s) than they did for Asian Americans (after World War II). The diversity Mormonism provided the country, I would thus like to suggest, ironically aided its interpretation as quintessential.[67]

Equally important motivation exists in the country's basic, long-standing, and taken-for-granted search for essences. Though the general urge to identify essences has been a part of general Euro-American thought for centuries, the quest for the national society's essence is an especially modern phenomenon, one that accompanies the equally modern phenomenon of nationalism. America realized by the twentieth century that it could not call upon a single ethnic identity as essence. And so ethos and mythos became especially valuable as markers of essence. This search for American essences helped the nation locate its place in the world.[68] In fact, much of the twentieth century's scholarly project on America centered on identifying such essences.[69] The fear has been that without such unifying themes—myths as we often call them today—America stands in danger of disintegrating.[70] Unity through diversity, in fact, is one such myth.[71]

This drive for essences, when combined with the American tendency to value diversity and the Mormon need to feel sufficiently American, produced fertile ground. By planting the LDS movement's characteristics in this soil, Mormonism's observers made the "quintessential" argument bloom. "Tolstoy's" quotation became believable. Josiah Quincy became a prophet.

PROSPECTS FOR CHANGE?

LDS growth rates increased after World War II, producing a ten-fold increase in membership in fifty years, as did the Mormon presence outside its traditional core; church leaders explicitly drew on early-twentieth-century statements recommending that converts not gather to Utah and

America, but instead build up the church where they were. Hence, by the 1960s, this growth was clearly international, with rapid increases in Latin America and East Asia. The church embarked on a program of "correlation" during that decade, a program designed to regularize administrative and theological control of Mormon practice. The church has since famously excommunicated a relatively small handful on both its left and right wings. Most Mormons remain conservative, however. By the 1960s and 1970s, Mormon conservatism prompted complaint from some quarters that Mormonism was fundamentally racist, sexist, anti-liberal, jingoistic, and perhaps even anti-intellectual.

Although Mormonism's racialism has diminished substantially over the past three decades, many argue that LDS leaders have fortified gender distinctions. During the twentieth century, the church developed a principle of acting politically only on moral issues.[72] The church thus agitated on topics such as prohibition, gambling, and abortion. More recently, the church spoke out on matters that concern (in currently popular LDS parlance) "the natural family." It sanctioned advocacy against the Equal Rights Amendment during the 1970s and 1980s, efforts some regard as decisive. In the past decade, Latter-day Saints have opposed gay marriage.[73] These political actions indicate a social move toward the conservative wing of American Christianity. Some observers have also discerned an increased recent LDS insistence that its Christian origins be recognized as such.[74] This may in part be a response to the increased religious attacks from the many conservative Protestants who regard Mormonism as a dangerous cult. Meanwhile church membership continues to grow. It now contains more than 12 million members, a bit more than half of whom live outside the United States. Latin Americans comprise close to 40 percent of church members. Activity levels in the United States are substantially higher than those elsewhere, however. The hierarchy is still overwhelmingly American.

Given this situation, will this "quintessential" label flourish in the twenty-first century? This chapter initially raised the question of whether the label might vanish as quickly and completely as did aether. At this point, that comparison seems overblown. It would be foolhardy to predict any sudden change. Too much scholarship, tradition, and perhaps even validity exist for the label to disappear quickly. Observers variously advocate the label for one or all of three major periods in Mormon history—origins, Western pioneering, and twentieth-century American accommodation.[75] In an era where religious and socially conservative nationalists seem to determine elections, the "quintessential" interpretation may still be on the rise. Scholars might also find an essential match between Mormonism and America as both entities participate in a globalizing world. Nevertheless, some modest, potentially counter trends deserve attention. They leave many of the factors that led to the "quintessential" label undisturbed at this point. If the trends strengthen, however, it is possible to imagine the label withering to some degree.

First, and most widely commented upon, Mormonism's membership composition is rapidly changing.[76] Mormons are no longer 80–90 percent

American. Depending on how one reckons, the LDS church may not be a majority American religion anymore. Central LDS leadership may even lose its American majority at some point over the next several decades, though this will surely lag behind membership shifts. Many American Mormons may not have noticed it yet, but church leaders are expending substantial effort to dampen some flagrantly American aspects of LDS practice in response to international growth. The adjustments may not be fast or deep enough to suit those desiring less nationalistic content from Mormonism, but change is occurring. If the early-twentieth-century transformation is an appropriate comparison, the process could produce unexpected ideological results.[77] Perhaps just as importantly, the international membership growth adds to the complexity of creating and maintaining a people. If Mormonism appears as simply another denomination on the international religious landscape,[78] rather than as a people rooted in the American physical and social landscape, will its American quintessentialness fade?

Other aspects of LDS membership trends may come into play.[79] Growth rates slowed substantially over the past decade—by approximately 40–50 percent. The sociologist Rodney Stark predicted in the 1980s and early 1990s, just before LDS growth rates declined, that Mormonism would become the world's next great global religion. He gave a qualified estimate that it would reach 265 million members by 2080.[80] Harold Bloom wrote in 1992 and understandably relied on these or similar estimates. Contrary to Bloom's extrapolations, however, Mormonism is not even now a full 2 percent of the U.S. population, and at 5.7 million in 2005 it most certainly will not reach more than 30 million U.S. members in 2020.[81] Also, for the first time since the early twentieth century, the percentage of LDS Americans who live outside of Utah dropped between 1980 and 2000 very slightly, from just over to just under 70 percent of all American Mormons. The last decade of this decrease also saw Utah's percentage of Mormons, compared to the total state population, fall as well. This is not to say that Mormons are declining in the United States; Mormonism's growth rate still exceeds the American growth rate, but now by less than seven-tenths of 1 percent. In any case, Harold Bloom's population-based geopolitical vision of Mormonism in the United States does not offer a realistic forecast for the near- and medium-term future. If the trends toward slower growth and U.S. concentration in Utah continue, observers might find reason to rethink LDS quintessentialism.

Beyond the issue of sheer numbers, it is not yet clear where observers will find continued American vitality within Mormonism. Mormonism's "quintessential" label often stemmed from proactive programs or doctrines that seem to expand the American spirit: new American scriptures, potential to become gods, the Mormon flight and fight for religious freedom, the Mormon welfare program, family home evening, the health code, temples, and genealogy, etc. Perhaps global growth will allow Mormonism to demonstrate continuing vitality.[82] Nevertheless, one dominant image of the current Mormon agenda within the United States, whether merited or not, is of a reactionary movement most concerned with protecting narrowly conceived traditional social relations.[83] Mormonism has often faced this charge, but if growth becomes less dependable, it might be harder to observers to see beyond the negative image.

There may also be shifts in the underlying motivation to declare Mormonism the quintessential American religion. Mormonism's doctrinal scholarship seems increasingly disinclined to read Mormonism as basically American. Thomas Alexander noted that Mormonism's critics often use the Mormonism-as-Americanism argument to discount the validity of the *Book of Mormon* and other early LDS doctrines.[84] Those critics suggest that LDS doctrine seems designed to answer questions that directly confronted people in 1820s upstate New York and is thus limited in time, space, and scope. Terryl Givens observed that the *Book of Mormon* contains a built-in rebuttal in its claim that its prophets saw the latter days; Mormons thus expect the *Book of Mormon* to address debates of nineteenth-century America.[85] Yet that answer may ring increasingly hollow to an ever more international LDS audience. American Latter-day Saints have an increasingly ambivalent attitude toward the "quintessential" label. Although it can still produce pride where it seems to be a compliment, especially among the general membership in the United States, many non-American Mormons are ever more wary of the label's potential to work against contemporary Mormon objectives. LDS doctrinal scholars on the whole increasingly emphasize more universalistic themes instead.[86]

Finally, just as Mormons may have reasons to play down the "quintessential" label, so too may non-Mormon scholars and observers. The postmodern turn in certain quarters of the academy has severely critiqued the search for essences, particularly social essences.[87] There is no such thing as a historically transcendent national essence, many scholars argue. Where there are dominant themes within the nation or trends that might be called a dominant American spirit, they are always historically constituted. More typically, there may at best be historically changing myths, ideas and ideals that will be constantly subject to evaluation to determine whether they still resonate. The myths may not apply across large spans of time. Others go further and suggest that any search for essences masks a drive for power and justifies oppression against those who do not seem to conform. Humanists and social scientists, the groups that will make most of the judgments about Mormonism, have been particularly influenced by these arguments. Could assessments of Mormonism as the quintessential American religion decline simply because scholars shy away from discussion of essences? Or, alternatively, will a changing Mormonism of the twenty-first century once again have to prove that its dominant trends match those of a changing America?

Similarly, historians remind us that histories are always interpretations with contemporary considerations in mind.[88] Ultimately, to some very real extent, the label of some *x* as quintessential to *y*, has more to do with what people think *y* is than what *x* is. The arguments for Mormonism as quintessentially American may tell us more about America than about Mormonism. The historical considerations—perhaps even cultural needs— that allowed Mormonism to be viewed as the quintessential American religion might not persist. Even if scholars continue to look for essences, their evaluation of what constitutes American essences will undoubtedly shift over time. It is entirely possible, for example, to imagine the American concern for diversity passing Mormonism by. It is hard to argue that America's obsession with diversity has diminished or stands poised to decrease. Increasingly, many leading scholars now concern themselves more with minorities that have not apparently prospered in America than with those who seemed to thrive.[89] America's cultural needs that lead it to find particular types of essences will not remain static; will Mormonism of the future be able to fill these needs? Thus, factors having little to do with the content of Mormonism could lead to the "quintessential" label's decline.

However, none of these trends is definitive at this point. A continued shift toward a higher proportion of international LDS membership may be the safest bet, but it could lead to fresh arguments for Mormonism as quintessentially American as much as it works against the label. The recent slowdown in growth rates may simply be a temporary aberration. Mormonism could exhibit vitality in latent or unanticipated emphases. The political climate may change such that both non-Mormons and Mormons are prouder to emphasize the movement's American origins. Anti-essentialism may prove to be nothing more than a brief intellectual footnote to much more powerful scholarly trends. Certainly many scholars pay little attention to it now. Shelves and shelves of recent books at university libraries continue attempts to discern American essence.[90] Or the momentum of the "quintessential" label may simply overwhelm any or all of these potentially contrary trends. After all, most of its fundamental bases remained unchanged. Yet, the trends bear watching. The history of aether testifies that quintessence may not be eternally valid.

NOTES

I should like to thank Davis Bitton, Chiung Hwang Chen, and Laurence Yorgason for their helpful suggestions.

1. Although Mormonism may be said to include all the churches that give loyalty to the teachings of Joseph Smith, I use the label here for convenience to refer to the Church of Jesus Christ of Latter-day Saints (I also use "LDS"). It is that Mormon body toward which observers use the "quintessential" appellation.

2. Of course, many observers disagree with this label. Perhaps even more simply ignore the label. Alternative categorizations toward Mormonism have included, for example: heresy, universal truth, stupidity, a unique but marginal footnote to American religious history, a sect within the American denominational framework, or a quest for power disguised as religion. Many volumes written on American religion hardly mention Mormonism at all or give no hint of it as the quintessential American religion. A couple of important recent examples: Robert Wuthnow, *The Restructuring of American Religion: Society and Faith since World War II* (Princeton, NJ: Princeton University Press, 1988); Harry S. Stout and D.G. Hart, eds., *New Directions in American Religious History* (New York: Oxford University Press, 1997).

3. Mark Twain, *Roughing It* (Hartford, CT: American Publishing Company, 1886), 127.

4. Peter W. Williams, *America's Religions: From Their Origins to the Twenty-First Century* (Urbana: University of Illinois Press, 2002), 398.

5. Of course, most of these same charges later were used to argue for Mormon Americanism. The best treatment of anti-American charges is Terryl L. Givens, *The Viper on the Hearth: Mormons, Myths, and the Construction of Heresy* (New York: Oxford University Press, 1997).

6. Although he does not quite make this argument, see Richard T. Hughes, *Myths America Lives By* (Urbana: University of Illinois Press, 2003), 158–62.

7. Robert N. Bellah, *The Broken Covenant: American Civil Religion in Time of Trial* (New York: Seabury, 1975); Robert T. Handy, *Undermined Establishment: Church-State Relations in America, 1880–1920* (Princeton, NJ: Princeton University Press, 1991); Noah Feldman, *Divided by God: America's Church-State Problem—and What We Should Do about It* (New York: Farrar, Strauss and Giroux, 2005). Those who do not consider Mormonism the quintessential American religion usually find America's religious center in Protestantism, or perhaps the Protestantism-Catholicism-Judaism triad.

8. Wuthnow, 241–67.

9. Harold Bloom, *The American Religion: The Emergence of the Post-Christian Nation* (New York: Simon & Schuster, 1992), 127.

10. Jan Shipps verified this sense of difference, though also took it a bit further in arguing that Mormonism constitutes a religious tradition that stands in relation to Christianity as Christianity stands to Judaism. Jan Shipps, *Mormonism: The Story of a New Religious Tradition* (Urbana: University of Illinois Press, 1985).

11. Jan Shipps, *Sojourner in the Promised Land: Forty Years among the Mormons* (Urbana: University of Illinois Press, 2000), 335–57.

12. For an intriguing, controversial attempt to establish such links, see John L. Brooke, *The Refiner's Fire: The Making of Mormon Cosmology, 1644–1844* (New York: Cambridge University Press, 1994).

13. Sydney Ahlstrom, *A Religious History of the American People*, vol. 1 (Garden City, NY: Image Books, 1975), 614.

14. Shipps, *Sojourner*, 308. Recent work that supports this thesis to various degrees and in quite different ways includes, among many others: Gustive Larson, *The Americanization of Utah for Statehood* (San Marino, CA: Huntington Library, 1971); Mark P. Leone, *Roots of Modern Mormonism* (Cambridge, MA: Harvard University Press, 1979); Klaus J. Hansen, *Mormonism and the American Experience* (Chicago: University of Chicago Press, 1981); Thomas G. Alexander, *Transition in Mormonism: A History of the Latter-day Saints, 1890–1930* (Urbana: University of Illinois Press, 1986); Sarah Barringer Gordon, *The Mormon Question: Polygamy and Constitutional Conflict in Nineteenth Century America* (Chapel Hill: University of North Carolina Press, 2002); Kathleen Flake, *The Politics of American Religious Identity: The Seating of Senator Reed Smoot, Mormon Apostle* (Chapel Hill: University of North Carolina Press, 2004).

15. Ethan R. Yorgason, *Transformation of the Mormon Culture Region* (Urbana: University of Illinois Press, 2003).

16. Though John Sorenson might differ in whether the resultant change is properly labeled Americanization, he is precisely correct in arguing that Mormonism's version of Americanism did not mean that Mormons became indistinguishable from other contemporary Americans. The point instead is that Mormons profoundly internalized traits and habits of political thought that were seen by many, both Mormons and non-Mormons, as the essence of good Americanness. John

Sorenson, "Mormon World View and American Culture," *Dialogue: A Journal of Mormon Thought* 8, 2 (1973): 17–29.

17. Yorgason, 164–68.

18. Leonard J. Arrington and Davis Bitton, *The Mormon Experience: A History of the Latter-day Saints* (New York: Knopf, 1979), 184.

19. Chiung Hwang Chen, *Mormon and Asian American Model Minority Discourses in News and Popular Magazines* (Lewiston, NY: Edwin Mellen, 2004).

20. Armand L. Mauss, *The Angel and the Beehive: The Mormon Struggle with Assimilation* (Urbana: University of Illinois Press, 1994).

21. James B. Mayfield, "Electoral Patterns," with maps by Deon C. Greer, in *Atlas of Utah*, ed. Wayne L. Wahlquist (Provo, UT: Weber State College and Brigham Young University Press, 1981), 170–71.

22. Tony Kushner's famous play (and now HBO special) *Angels in America* has been interpreted in this way. Mormonism, according to Mario DePillis, serves as the hidebound, intolerant symbol of traditional America in contrast to a promising, progressive future American ethos that might be imagined. Mario S. DePillis, "The Emergence of Mormon Power since 1945," *Journal of Mormon History* 22, 1 (1996): 5–9. For an interesting partial dissent, one that reads Mormonism's theology as much more central to Kushner's American progressivism, see Michael Austin, "Theology for the Approaching Millennium: *Angels in America*, Activism, and the American Religion," *Dialogue: A Journal of Mormon Thought* 30, 1 (1997): 25–44. Among other arguments, Austin notes (29) that Kushner himself called the angel Moroni (of Joseph Smith's gold plates) the "prototypical American angel."

23. For example, see Robert Lindsey, "The Mormons: Growth, Prosperity and Controversy," *New York Times Magazine* (January 12, 1986): 24.

24. Malise Ruthven, "The Mormons' Progress," *Wilson Quarterly* 15, 2 (1991): 22–50. The Hasbro game company began promoting "Family Game Night" in recent years. To Mormons, this sounds much like the Family Home Evenings the LDS church has advocated since the early twentieth century. While I have not found evidence of direct connection between these phenomena, this is the kind of parallelism-based evidence Mormons use when they argue that Mormonism leads in wholesome American trends.

25. Philip Barlow, "Jan Shipps and the Mainstreaming of Mormon Studies," *Church History* 73 (2004): 425.

26. See Robert Remini's comments in "The Worlds of Joseph Smith," a 2005 conference co-sponsored by the Library of Congress and Brigham Young University. While the proceedings are expected to be published in *BYU Studies*, an online recording can be utilized through the LDS church's Web page at http://www.lds.org/library/display/0,4945,510-1-3067-1,00.html.

27. Ronald W. Walker, David J. Whittaker, and James B. Allen, *Mormon History* (Urbana: University of Illinois Press, 2001), 43–44; see also the critique of such frontier interpretations of Mormonism by David Brion Davis, "New England Origins of Mormonism," *New England Quarterly* 26 (1953): 148.

28. Though for an argument about the marginalization of Mormonism in Western history, see Shipps, *Sojourner*, 17–44.

29. Laurie F. Maffly-Kipp, "Routing the Republic: Religion and the American West," in *Lectures on Religion and the Founding of the American Republic*, ed. John W. Welch with Stephen J. Fleming (Provo, UT: Brigham Young University Press, 2003), 125–36; quotes from 128, 130.

30. Hughes, 160; Remini, "Worlds of Joseph Smith."

31. Thomas O'Dea, "Mormonism and the Avoidance of Sectarian Stagnation: A Study of Church, Sect, and Incipient Nationality," *American Journal of Sociology* 60 (1954): 285–93.

32. Laurence R. Moore, *Religious Outsiders and the Making of Americans* (New York: Oxford University Press, 1986), 44.

33. Ibid., 45, 46.

34. Hansen, 82.

35. Kenneth H. Winn, *Exiles in a Land of Liberty: Mormons in America, 1830–1846* (Chapel Hill: The University of North Carolina Press, 1989); Marvin S. Hill, *Quest for Refuge: The Mormon Flight from American Pluralism* (Salt Lake City: Signature Books, 1989); Nathan O. Hatch, *The Democratization of American Christianity* (New Haven, CT: Yale University Press, 1989), 113–22.

36. Davis, "The New England Origins"; Hughes, 158–59; Remini, "Worlds of Joseph Smith."

37. See Bloom, *The American Religion*.

38. Ibid., 80. Bloom also made the rather remarkable argument that Judaism, Catholicism, and traditional Protestantism are not truly biblical. Instead, Mormonism comes much closer. Smith, Bloom suggested, produced a biblical reading so powerful (a "creative misreading," as Bloom called it) that he broke through all extant orthodoxies and intuited much of the essence of ancient Jewish religion.

39. One could perhaps argue that fundamentalism (in its loose, technically inaccurate, but more popular sense as deeply conservative religion) has much to do with helping us understand quintessential American religion of the future. And some have come close to making this argument, suggesting that understanding the future of American religion lies in understanding the social (if not theological) convergence between groups such as conservative Protestants, conservative Catholics, and Mormons. Bloom, however, brooked none of this argument. What makes American religion, for him with aesthetic sensibility, is not numerical or simply political domination but authentically innovative extensions of the American spirit.

40. Bloom, 31.

41. Ibid., 114.

42. Ibid., 115.

43. Ibid., 116.

44. Ibid., 112–13.

45. See, for example, George A. Smith's declarations in *Journal of Discourses* (London: Latter-day Saints' Book Depot, 1854–1886), 2:24, 5:110.

46. Josiah Quincy, a former mayor of Boston, had made a visit to Joseph Smith in Nauvoo before the latter's death. Josiah Quincy, *Figures of the Past: From the Leaves of Old Journals* (Boston: Roberts Brothers, 1883).

47. George Q. Cannon, *The Life of Joseph Smith, The Prophet* (Salt Lake City: Deseret Book, 1986 [1888]), 346–47.

48. A word search on the LDS database, *Gospel Link 2001*, published by Deseret Book confirms that Mormons used the quotation frequently during the century.

49. LeGrand Richards, *A Marvelous Work and a Wonder* (Salt Lake City: Deseret Book Co., 1950), 413.

50. To his credit, the *New Yorker* writer, Lawrence Wright was one of the few to recognize that the facts may be elsewhere than the usually quoted narrative. Lawrence Wright, "Lives of the Saints," *New Yorker* (January 21, 2002): 57.

51. Leland A. Fetzer, "Tolstoy and Mormonism," *Dialogue: A Journal of Mormon Thought* 6 (Spring 1971): 13–29.

52. Yorgason, 200.

53. The account of this conversation comes from notes White took as they were interpreted in a magazine article and a book he subsequently wrote.

54. Thomas J. Yates, "Count Tolstoi and the 'American Religion,'" *Improvement Era* (February 1939): 94. For an important accretion Fetzer missed, see Ben E. Rich, *Conference Reports of the Church of Jesus Christ of Latter-day Saints, 1880, 1897–1973* (Salt Lake City: Deseret News, April 1913): 24. For an early LDS expression of Mormonism as "the American religion"—sentiment that may have made its way into the "Tolstoy" quotation, see Nephi Anderson, "Are We Americans?" *Improvement Era* (October 1900): 933–36.

55. Perhaps it was simply that since Mormons knew, from Susa Young Gates, that Tolstoy would have had access to Quincy's assessment, they mistakenly began to conflate the stories about these two famous men who had surprisingly spoken on Mormonism.

56. Yorgason, 159–61.

57. John Henry Evans, *Joseph Smith: An American Prophet* (New York: Macmillan, 1933). Isaac Russell also furthered the Mormonism-as-America notion by asserting that Joseph Smith intentionally sought to fulfill America's manifest destiny. Isaac Russell, "Joseph Smith and the Great West," *Improvement Era* (published serially, 1925–1927).

58. Among a whole genre that deals with such issues, see *"The Constitution Will Hang by a Thread": Prophecies on the Constitution, Quotes from* Journal of Discourses (Salt Lake City: Hawkes Publishing, 1975).

59. Walker, Whittaker, and Allen, *Mormon History*, 9–11, 18–21.

60. Alexander Campbell may have inadvertently started this tradition in 1832 when he condemned the *Book of Mormon* for repeating "every error and almost every truth discussed in New York for the past ten years." Alexander Campbell, *Delusions. An Analysis of the Book of Mormon; with an Examination of its Internal and External Evidences, and a Refutation of its Pretences to Divine Authority* (Boston: Benjamin H. Greene, 1832), 85.

61. Richard T. Ely, "Economic Aspects of Mormonism," *Harper's Monthly* (April 1903): 668. A church leader elaborated on Ely's comment nearly a decade later, using the term "quintessence," but like Ely without linking the notion to anything essentially American. Orson F. Whitney, *Gospel Themes* (Salt Lake City: n.p., 1914), 80–81. I should note that I have not been able to track down the origins of the precise term "quintessential" to describe Mormonism's relationship to American religion. A possibility: Whitney's gloss on Ely's quote and Tolstoy's ascribed label became conflated over time.

62. Bernard A. DeVoto, "The Centennial of Mormonism," *The American Mercury* (January 1930): 1–13. DeVoto, in locating Mormonism specifically in American culture, can be read as carrying on the tradition of nineteenth-century travel writers, many of whom were European and visited Utah in search of American novelty. However, see also DeVoto's comment about Mormonism's irrelevance to America noted in Barlow, 424.

63. Marvin S. Hill and James B. Allen, "Introduction," in *Mormonism and American Culture*, ed. Marvin S. Hill and James B. Allen (New York: Harper & Row, 1972), 4–5. They identify Ralph Henry Gabriel, *The Course of American Democratic Thought: An Intellectual History Since 1815* (New York: Ronald Press, 1940); Alice Felt Tyler, *Freedom's Ferment: Phases of American Social History to 1860* (Minneapolis: University of Minnesota Press, 1944); Whitney Cross, *The Burned-over District: The Social and Intellectual History of Enthusiastic Religion in Western New York, 1800–1850* (Ithaca, NY: Cornell University Press, 1950); Davis,

"The New England Origins of Mormonism," 147–68; and Thomas O'Dea, *The Mormons* (Chicago: University of Chicago Press, 1957). Whether Davis knew of the much less sophisticated popular LDS arguments that Mormonism recapitulated early American Puritanism, he endorsed a similar conclusion.

64. Werner Sollors, *Theories of Ethnicity: A Classical Reader* (New York: New York University Press, 1996).

65. Stephen Stein may be largely correct in suggesting that for many historians of American religion, the diversity encompassed by "indigenous sectarian religion movements," Mormonism included, could not be considered in non-condemnatory terms until nearly the 1980s. Until then, he argued, heresy and eccentricity were dominant interpretive motifs. I would, however, argue that Mormonism's twentieth-century social accommodation allowed scholars whose primary emphasis was not *religion* per se to begin to discern an acceptable Mormon Americanness several decades earlier. Stephen J. Stein, "History, Historians, and the Historiography of Indigenous Sectarian Religious Movements in America," in *Religious Diversity and American Religious History: Studies in Traditions and Cultures*, ed. Walter H. Conser Jr. and Sumner B. Twiss (Athens: University of Georgia Press, 1997), 128–29.

66. See Chen, *Mormon and Asian American*.

67. Diversity may be a double-edged sword. Although some commentators probably consider Mormonism as particularly important because it has been a minority (the Disciples movement offers an instructive example, by contrast, in its mainstreaming), others point to increasing Mormon power in the American mainstream as an additional sign of its quintessentialness. Richard N. Ostling and Joan K. Ostling, *Mormon America: The Power and the Promise* (San Francisco: Harper Collins, 1999). Jan Shipps has begun to consider some of the possible consequences of LDS mainstreaming in *Sojourner*, esp. 112–16.

68. An outside observer who can point to such essences, such as Tocqueville, becomes invaluable to the nation. Tocqueville's role in America, of course, parallels that played by Josiah Quincy, "Tolstoy," Thomas O'Dea, Jan Shipps, and Harold Bloom in Mormonism.

69. Browsing the American history section of any decent library demonstrates this.

70. Hughes, 4.

71. Judith Goode, "Teaching against Culturalist Essentialism," in *Cultural Diversity in the United States: A Critical Reader*, ed. Ida Susser and Thomas C. Patterson (Malden, MA: Blackwell, 2001), 435.

72. This category of morality is, of course, highly plastic. LDS defenders and critics have argued for decades about where the boundaries between proper and improper church political action lie.

73. For partially dueling perspectives on this political action, see Jan Shipps, "The Persistent Pattern of Establishment in Mormon Land," and D. Michael Quinn, "Exporting Utah's Theocracy Since 1975: Mormon Organizational Behavior and America's Culture Wars," both in *God and Country: Politics in Utah*, ed. Jeffery E. Sells (Salt Lake City: Signature Books, 2005). I suspect that the next candidate for LDS scriptural canonization is the 1995 Proclamation on the Family, which, among much else, asserts that gender differences, not just the physical facts of sexual difference, and gender roles are God-given.

74. Shipps, *Sojourner*, 346–47. For a controversial argument that LDS *theology* is approaching conservative Christian ideals, see O. Kendall White, *Mormon Neo-Orthodoxy: A Crisis Theology* (Salt Lake City: Signature Books, 1987).

75. Richard Hughes does not quite make the argument that Mormonism thoroughly incorporated each of his six American myths at one point or another during

its history, but I suspect he would endorse the claim (mythic elements of capitalism, plus myths of chosen nation, nature's nation, Christian nation, millennial
nation, and innocent nation). Hughes, *Myths*. See also his comments in "Worlds of
Joseph Smith."

76. For example, Philip Barlow, "Shifting Ground and the Third Transformation of Mormonism," in *Perspectives on American Religion and Culture*, ed. Peter
Williams (Malden, MA: Blackwell, 1999), 140–53; Alan Wolfe, *The Transformation
of American Religion: How We Actually Live Our Faith* (New York: Free Press,
2003), 149–51; Terryl L. Givens, *The Latter-day Saint Experience in America*
(Westport, CT: Greenwood, 2004), 260–69.

77. Though it is occurring for reasons that go beyond international growth, a
more recent example of unexpected ideological results might be the gradual and
ongoing de-emphasis in assigning *Book of Mormon* origins to Native Americans in
the United States, while LDS native peoples elsewhere take on that lineage to a
greater extent. Many scholars similarly argue that the removal of racial barriers in
the LDS priesthood had much to do with LDS growth in Brazil and Africa.
Armand L. Mauss, *All Abraham's Children: Changing Mormon Conceptions of Race
and Lineage* (Urbana: University of Illinois Press, 2003).

78. Douglas J. Davies, *The Mormon Culture of Salvation* (Aldershot, Eng.:
Ashgate, 2000), 245. See also Davies's comments in "Worlds of Joseph Smith."

79. My membership analyses rely on figures published by the *Deseret News
Church Almanac* series (Salt Lake City: Deseret News), as well as U.S. Census data.

80. Rodney Stark, "The Basis of Mormon Success: A Theoretical Application,"
in *Mormons and Mormonism: An Introduction to an American World Religion*, ed.
Eric A. Eliason (Urbana: University of Illinois Press, 2001), 207–42. Current
growth rates translate to a 2080 worldwide LDS population of closer to 75 million.
Needless to say, forecasting growth for a church that does not yet proselytize in
China or the Middle East and has barely begun the process in India, the former
Soviet sphere, and Africa, is a tricky exercise.

81. One poll even indicates that the percentage of self-identified Mormons, as
opposed to those reported by the church, may have *fallen* from 1.4 percent of the
U.S. to 1.3 percent between 1990 and 2001. American Religious Identification
Survey, conducted by the City University of New York, reported in "America
Growing More Secular," from Web page of Freedom from Religion Foundation,
http://www.ffrf.org/timely/ARISsecular.php, accessed September 6, 2005. The
current annual church-reported growth rate of Mormonism in the United States
(just under 1.9 percent) would produce 7.6 million American Mormons by 2020.
The 1990–2000 decade was the first decade since 1910–1920 in which the LDS
growth rate in the United States has been less than double the U.S. population
growth rate.

82. The Perpetual Education Fund is a program that provides such potential,
even though it is not well known outside the church. By financing the education
of many members outside the United States, much as Mormons financed immigration for Northern European converts in the nineteenth century, the recently instituted fund has the potential to greatly strengthen the LDS sense of community, as
well as benefit individual members. It is much too soon to evaluate the PEF's
actual impact, however. Additionally, Douglas Davies, more than most commentators, finds potential for continued vitality in LDS teachings about salvation, over-
coming death, and family life. However he finds as much possibility for such
vitality to break down Mormonism's American content as to accent it. Douglas J.
Davies, *An Introduction to Mormonism* (New York: Cambridge University Press,
2003), 248–54.

83. Even a new set of essays that argue against one another in various ways about Mormonism's political project in Utah seems to at least share elements of this common conception: Sells, *God and Country.* A much more positive view, though one that focuses more directly on teaching sexual morality than on political movements, sees continuing vitality in the church's moral stances: Wolfe, 143–45.

84. Thomas G. Alexander, "The Place of Joseph Smith in the Development of American Religion: A Historiographical Inquiry," *Journal of Mormon History* 5 (1978): 3–17.

85. Terryl L. Givens, *By the Hand of Mormon: The American Scripture that Launched a New World Religion* (New York: Oxford University Press, 2002), 166.

86. See especially the first session of "Worlds of Joseph Smith." In that conference Richard Bushman said that Mormonism is a globally significant movement with an "American accent." To be fair, it must be admitted that *individual* Mormon scholars began this process decades ago.

87. I use the term postmodern in the broad sense to include poststructuralism, postcolonialism, postmodernism, and some other types of recent critical social/cultural theory.

88. For Richard Bushman, "histories are detachable." Mormonism's story will not apply in the future in the same way it has in the past. "Worlds of Joseph Smith."

89. Among those who discerned this trend early, see Bellah, *The Broken Covenant,* 144–51.

90. On the need to find a "center" of the study of American religion, see also Barlow, 424.

SUGGESTIONS FOR FURTHER READING

Arrington, Leonard J., and Davis Bitton. *The Mormon Experience: A History of the Latter-day Saints,* 2nd ed. Urbana: University of Illinois Press, 1992.

Bloom, Harold. *The American Religion: The Emergence of the Post-Christian Nation.* New York: Simon & Schuster, 1992.

Davies, Douglas J. *An Introduction to Mormonism.* New York: Cambridge University Press, 2003.

Givens, Terryl L. *The Latter-day Saint Experience in America.* Westport, CT: Greenwood, 2004.

Ostling, Richard N., and Joan K. Ostling, *Mormon America: The Power and the Promise.* San Francisco: Harper Collins, 1999.

Shipps, Jan. *Sojourner in the Promised Land: Forty Years among the Mormons.* Urbana: University of Illinois Press, 2000.

Yorgason, Ethan R. *Transformation of the Mormon Culture Region.* Urbana: University of Illinois Press, 2003.

CHAPTER 9

The Continuing Influence of Region on American Religious Life

Randi Jones Walker

Anyone who has perused Phil Barlow and Edwin Gaustad's *New Historical Atlas of Religion in America* (2001) will see that some characteristics of American religion need to be discussed in terms of geography and region. In any given period, the maps clearly show that religious groups tend to concentrate in particular regions. Those patterns of concentration are remarkably persistent over time.

The establishment of generally Catholic majorities in the Spanish colonial areas of the Southern coast and the Southwest and in the French colonial areas around the Great Lakes, the St. Lawrence River, and the Mississippi Valley, and of Protestantism in the English colonial areas, overlaying or overturning Native American traditions, provide patterns of religious demographics that changed little through the history of the United States. So, too, do the impact of African religious traditions and African-influenced Christianity, notably in the South but also in the North. The Catholic Southwest, the Baptist South, the Methodist middle states, the Lutheran north central region, and the Reformed Protestant Northeast persist on the map of American religion despite the increasing religious diversity caused by large-scale movement of people from one region to another. Looking at the religious developments in each region over time, the cultural influence of distinctive regional forms of religious life on religious institutions will emerge.

Thinking about the distinctive regional cultures discernable in American religion will illuminate other topics in these anthologies on faith in America: the erosion of mainline Protestant denominations; post–Vatican II Catholicism; sexual misconduct scandals in Roman Catholic and other churches; Judaism as religion, ethnic identity, and/or culture; the resurgence of fundamentalism and Pentecostalism; the impact of world religions such as

Hinduism, Buddhism, and Islam in America; the Hispanic presence in American religious life; the growth of the Latter-day Saints and their role as the quintessential American religion; megachurches and emerging churches that have changed congregational understanding; the story of African American religious institutions; as well as the ongoing role of new and alternative religions.

THE DEVELOPMENT OF REGIONAL CHARACTERISTICS: THE COLONIAL PERIOD

The earliest layers of religion in North America were closely related to physical geography and the ways of life best suited to each particular climate and topography. For instance, the people living in the Pacific Northwest coastal areas recorded their religious stories by carving them into the trunks of the tall conifers abundant in the coastal forests. In addition, their religious symbols include the salmon, a major item in their diet, and the eagle. Since rain is abundant, it does not play the central role in the cycle of rituals as it does in the desert religions of the southwestern United States and northern part of Mexico. There, adobe is the material for building religious ritual sites. Various manifestations of rain as well as corn, their major staple food, play the central roles in belief and ceremony. Similarly, the rivers and lakes of the north central region of the continent, the Great Plains, the warm waters of the Gulf Coast and Caribbean, the arctic snow and tundra, and each of the other distinctive combinations of topography and weather shaped the religions of the people who lived in these areas before the Europeans. They often still do.

Europeans contributed a complex set of traditions to the religious landscape of North America, beginning in the sixteenth century and continuing to today. Here, too, geographical patterns emerged as religious developments reflected colonial settlement through the beginning and later waves of immigration. The Spanish colonies very early in this period pushed north from Mexico and the Caribbean into the southern part of what eventually became the United States. Spain was a Roman Catholic nation and imposed that form of Christianity on all inhabitants of its colonial empire. The French established their colonies along the major river systems of the central continent, along the St. Lawrence, the Great Lakes, and the Ohio, Mississippi, and Missouri valleys. France, too, was Roman Catholic, and so were its colonies. However, France did not foster the huge population growth of the Spanish colonial enterprise with its haciendas, ranches, and mines. French traders tended to establish economic empire without making large settlements or imposing great changes in the life of the subject peoples. All were encouraged, though, to be Roman Catholic.

The English and Dutch colonies brought Protestant Christianity to the Atlantic coast. The Dutch, as the French, had a trading establishment, but not a substantial residential colonial population. The English sent their religious dissenters freely to their North American colonies. Several types of

Protestant Christianity that formed tiny minorities in Europe found themselves flourishing in the English American colonies. Puritans, Baptists, and Quakers—who did not necessarily get along with each other—nonetheless found room in North America to pursue the growth of their religious points of view and ways of life. So, too, did Jews find uncommon toleration in the Dutch and English colonies in particular. In the eighteenth century, the Russians added Orthodox Christianity to the mix, creating a layer of Eastern Christianity along the West Coast from Alaska down to California.

Spanish colonial policy included official state-supported efforts to proselytize the native peoples as well as to require Catholic religious practice from the Spanish themselves. At the beginning of Spanish imperial expansion, Jews and Muslims had just been driven out of Spain or forced to convert to Catholic Christianity. This compulsory Catholicism stamped any area influenced by the Spanish colonial enterprise with a Catholic religious character. Since the Spanish encouraged settlement of their colonial empire, this Spanish Catholicism grew. The area that eventually came to be the southwest part of the United States was the northern periphery of the Spanish empire, and the population of Spanish colonists and Native Americans was roughly balanced. The Spanish Catholic church had no means of enforcing its principles of uniformity of practice, and in this region native religious practice mixed freely with Roman Catholic practice, creating a distinctive kind of religion. In addition, the Spanish colonists themselves were isolated and developed strong lay-led folk practices based on Catholic doctrine, but independent of the hierarchy. The Penitentes of New Mexico are an example of such lay creativity. Jews and perhaps also Muslims continued to exist in Spanish colonial societies, but practiced their faith in secret. African slaves were less common in the northern parts of Spanish territory, but where they were present, they easily imported their African religions and adapted Native American practices into their own versions of Catholic beliefs and rituals.

The French colonial enterprise was quite different, and therefore the religious character of their areas of influence in North America was also different. In areas where the French established colonial immigrant settlements, such as in the St. Lawrence River Valley, Quebec, Acadia, and New Orleans, French Roman Catholic parishes developed. When the British took over Canada in 1763 after the French and Indian Wars, many French Catholics were forced to migrate to New Orleans, augmenting the Catholic population in Louisiana. In addition to Roman Catholics, early French settlements included Huguenots or Reformed Protestants. Pierre du Gua, a wealthy Huguenot, in cooperation with Samuel de Champlain, had a trade monopoly in Canada and a guarantee of freedom for Huguenot immigrants from the persecution they experienced in France.

Franciscans carried out the first French missionary efforts to convert the Native Americans. As in the Spanish colonies, they established mission settlements, primarily villages under the governance of France. Further west in the Great Lakes region, Native Americans such as the Huron resisted this approach. Jesuit missionaries undertook proselytizing ventures in the French-claimed territories around the Great Lakes and along the river valleys of the Ohio, Missouri, and Mississippi, and into nearby areas in central Canada, following the fur trade into the Native American Huron, Chippewa, Iroquois, Miami, and other communities of the region. As in places where the Spanish empire claimed hegemony over Native American people, a few converted to Catholicism and remain Catholic today. However, the French colonial enterprise did not go to the same lengths as the Spanish to enforce the conversion of the Native American peoples in their territories.

The map of European-imported forms of Protestant Christianity in the English colonies shows that certain groups were already dominant in recognizable regions by 1790 when the first census of the new United States was conducted, officially marking the end of the British colonial period.[1] New England had a Reformed Protestant and Congregational majority.[2] Pennsylvania, parts of western Virginia, and both North and South Carolina had developed Reformed majorities—Presbyterian mainly from Scotland in western Pennsylvania and the Appalachian valleys; Dutch Reformed in the Hudson Valley; and German Reformed especially in central Pennsylvania and parts of the western Carolinas. Episcopalians or Anglicans of the Church of England prevailed along the Atlantic coast south of Pennsylvania. Baptists held Rhode Island, where they first established a colony in the seventeenth century. By the end of the eighteenth century, they were also growing rapidly in the western areas of the southern states. Lutherans, refugees from religious wars in Europe, settled early in the river valleys near to the Appalachians; the Quakers held majorities in small areas of southeastern Pennsylvania (a colony founded by the Quaker William Penn and noted as a refuge for any number of small Protestant groups facing persecution in Europe) and in parts of New Jersey, North Carolina, and Georgia; and by the end of the eighteenth century, the Methodists had a foothold in Delaware and were growing fast. Roman Catholics and Jews, though present in many places, were not in the majority anywhere. Maryland was established as a Roman Catholic colony in 1634 and retained a Roman Catholic majority for a short time. In New York and Pennsylvania, Catholics also enjoyed relative toleration, as did Jews in New York. Despite increasingly tolerant policies, especially in the eighteenth century, Roman Catholics continued to be singled out as a threat to English and afterwards American Protestant assumptions, values, and political structures.[3]

The Act of Toleration of 1691 opened the British colonies to all religious groups, thus beginning the context in which people of various Protestant religions were allowed to move and settle freely anywhere in the colonies. Roman Catholics continued to face restrictions in Great Britain, but in the colonies, especially Maryland, they could find a measure of freedom to organize their churches as they wished. The principal effect of the Act of Toleration was to allow several minority traditions to develop free from restriction. For instance, whereas in Europe under a state church system Baptists were nearly everywhere a suppressed minority, in the British colonies they began to flourish and finally became the dominant Protestant tradition in the United States.

The Native American population in the British colonies, though still present, was completely obscured in terms of religious influence by European settlement by the end of the eighteenth century. The English showed comparatively little interest in converting the Native Americans to Christianity. Certainly it was not the policy of the English government to compel their conversion. Native communities, Christian and otherwise, persisted, and many survive to the present. In the area represented by the former British colonies, the marked decline of Native American population because of exposure to European diseases and outright warfare continues to show in sparse communities, in contrast to the higher and more concentrated population of Native Americans in the West, especially in the Spanish colonial areas where the Native American population has recovered in some measure from the initial onslaught of disease and violence, although it is still plagued by poverty and lack of social services.

With the European colonial enterprises came also African slavery. The Spanish first and then the French and the English imported slaves from Africa to do hard labor, especially in the Caribbean and the southern English colonies. The slaves brought with them their African religions. Although the slave owners tried to suppress these traditions, they persisted and emerged to shape later African American Christianity. Wherever the French, English, and Spanish had colonies, African slaves and thus African religious traditions appear and persist.

By the end of the colonial period in the eighteenth century, there were already several layers of religion: Native American religions, European Christianity—Catholic, Protestant, and Orthodox, Judaism, and African religions. It is tempting to think that these can be neatly categorized and recognized in their respective regions. However, they were in a constant state of blurred boundaries. People from one tradition living beside people from another one borrowed freely from each other. In spite of attempts on the part of many religious leaders to keep their traditions pure and unaffected by the rapidly increasing pluralism, it is rarely possible to extricate one tradition from another simply without finding some exchange of belief or practice with another.

THE DEVELOPMENT OF REGIONAL CHARACTERISTICS: THE NINETEENTH CENTURY

The character and demographics of American religion changed rapidly in the nineteenth century.[4] This century can be divided into periods based on a number of factors influencing the growth and change of religion. The first period, from about 1789 to 1830, marks the early national period and is characterized by the steady movement of people from the original colonial areas to the West. The second period, from about 1830 through the Civil War, is characterized by continuing movement West, but also by a large influx of immigrants from Europe, the annexation of the northern provinces of Mexico, and the division of the nation into North and South. The period from the end of the Civil War to 1893 is characterized by the still continuing movement to the West; immigration not only from Europe, but also from Asia, Mexico, and other areas of Latin America; the persistence of the division into North and South despite political reunification; and the impact of the building of the transcontinental railroad. The development of distinct religious regions in the United States still evident in the early twenty-first century began in this period. These regional distinctions were shaped by the complex history of territorial expansion in the United States, patterns of religious settlement and missionary activity, and the migration of people from one place to another.

By 1830, the United States had reached the Mississippi River in its westward national expansion. Although the Native American religious traditions persisted wherever tribal populations remained, they were quickly overshadowed by forms of European Christianity. The pressure upon the Native Americans by the expansion of the United States was not of great concern to the churches in the new nation. Some of these European Christians attempted to convert the Native Americans to Christianity, but most concentrated on the conversion or reconversion of their own people because they showed a tendency to leave their religious practice behind as they moved West. Congregationalism was still the predominant tradition in New England, but the most characteristic developments of the period were the explosive expansion of the Methodist churches; the annexation of predominantly Catholic territories in the upper Great Lakes region, Louisiana, and areas along the Mississippi and Ohio rivers with the Louisiana Purchase; and the growth of the Baptists along the Appalachians, in the Ohio River Valley, in Maine, and in the newly opened trans-Mississippi West. In both the South, where slavery formed the backbone of the economy, and in the North, where Africans, both slave and free, were present, what became characteristically African American religious traditions began to take shape during this period. Regionally, they particularly gave the South a distinctive evangelical identity. To understand regional characteristics in religion in this period, it is also important to note that in 1790 in Virginia, South Carolina, and Georgia, the African American population was predominant, sometimes accounting for more than 70 percent of the total. In North Carolina, Maryland, Kentucky, and Tennessee, African Americans constituted at least 20 and as much as 50 percent of the population. By 1830, the whole of the South was predominantly African American, although nearly all were slaves.

While the recognized regions of the United States were still in development, already the religious characteristics of New England were clear in the 1830s. Maine and Rhode Island were strongholds of Baptist churches, but New England itself west to the Hudson River was Congregational. During this early period of the nation's history, the founding mythology of the United States centered in New England stories about the Pilgrims' fleeing religious persecution to found colonies in the name of liberty, about the first Thanksgiving, and about the Revolution, the Boston Tea Party, Paul Revere's ride, and the political exploits of Samuel and John Adams. The Congregational tradition in Christianity became so intertwined with this national mythology and the new industrial capitalism of New England's economy that Congregational Christianity became virtually synonymous with Yankee. Congregationalists claimed that their democratic ecclesiology set the stage for the development of the republican ideals of the U.S. Constitution. Although the Presbyterian and Reformed Protestants probably have a better claim to have influenced the political fervor of the nation, New England Congregationalists shaped the popular images with which much of white America thought about its religious identity. New England religious culture expanded westward through New York into the Western Reserve, creating a Congregational majority in northeastern Ohio and in a few places in Illinois where a Congregational band of missionaries settled. In the Hudson Valley, in Pennsylvania, and in numerous scattered western areas, Reformed Protestants, Lutherans, and Presbyterians held sway. Together these churches from the European Reformation traditions joined the Congregationalists in shaping the civil religion of the United States. They had not yet suffered divisions over the issue of slavery and with the Methodists, to whom we next turn our attention; they forged the predominantly evangelical Protestant character of the westward migrations of people in the United States.

By 1830, Methodists had largely replaced Episcopalians as the predominant religious group in the former British colonies where once the Church of England held sway or where the Baptists had not established hegemony. Although the Methodists no longer predominate in the United States except in a band of counties from the northern Ohio Valley westward to Nebraska, in the early national period, Methodism was also the most widespread religious tradition in the then western states. The Methodist system of itinerant clergy and lay-run congregations was ideal for starting new churches, supporting them, and keeping them connected to the larger denomination. Where the Congregationalists and Presbyterians claimed the mythology of national origins, the Methodists claimed the mythology of the frontier. The circuit rider carrying a saddlebag full of Bibles, books, and tracts, and unafraid to preach in a saloon, carry a gun, or travel miles to perform a wedding or funeral, became a stock character in the story of the settlement of the West.

Methodism joined the more enthusiastically evangelical of the Reformed, Congregationalists, Baptists, and Presbyterians in the great revivals of the period. The most famous at Cane Ridge, Kentucky, and in what came to be known as the "burned-over district" in upstate New York created a religious ethos in what was then the West marked by emotional fervor, a sense of personal contact with the divine, a zeal for missions both foreign and domestic, and a strong expectation that the religious person was obligated to better society. An enormous outpouring of volunteer labor forming organized societies to address mission concerns or social reform issues resulted from this western revival passion. Where the Reformed, Congregationalists, Presbyterians, and Baptists were often divided on the wisdom of the revivals, especially their emotional enthusiasm, the Methodists were generally supportive of them. Regionally, Methodists and revivalism occupied the same territory.

African Americans, whether slave or free, were attracted to Methodism. The African Methodist Episcopal Church, formed in 1816 by free African Americans in Philadelphia, was the first of several such denominations founded because of the racial prejudice in the white Methodist churches. Some of these African Methodist churches were short-lived, but three remain strong: the African Methodist Episcopal Church; the African Methodist Episcopal Zion Church; and the Christian Methodist Episcopal Church. An even greater number of African Americans were attracted to the Baptist churches. The radical congregationalism of the Baptist traditions allowed for the easy establishment of new churches and offered freedom to organize the local church as the people saw fit. Both the Baptist and Methodist churches in the African American community created an amalgamation of African religious ethos and Protestant institutional and cultural forms of religious life.

With the Louisiana Purchase in 1803, the infant United States incorporated lightly settled but strongly Roman Catholic, French-language territory that by 1830 gave birth to the states of Louisiana, Arkansas, and Missouri. In addition, old French colonial territory in northern Michigan and the Wisconsin territory was already part of the United States. Some Native Americans in these regions had converted to Christianity under French Catholic missions, and some of these Roman Catholic native communities persisted. In addition, several Roman Catholic settlements along the Mississippi River, such as St. Louis, developed into major cities with Roman Catholic majorities. The Congregational presence in western Illinois by 1830 is in part a sign of East Coast Protestant anxiety about the annexation of Catholic territory and the early signs of increasing Catholic immigration from Europe. The region west of the Appalachians, in the Ohio and Mississippi valleys, became a contested area between Roman Catholics and Protestants as the nineteenth century wore on, and Protestants encouraged in-migration to contain presumed Roman Catholic influence. As well, Catholic immigration allowed Roman Catholicism to become the largest single religious body in New England.

The Baptists characteristic of the South and of the African American Protestant community were also beginning to spread elsewhere. Predominant as well in Maine, a frontier area at this time, and their historical stronghold in Rhode Island, they were the majority mostly in areas in the West where the Methodists or the Presbyterians were not already strong. Like the Methodists, they were able to spread rapidly, although for different structural reasons. Having a completely congregational form of organization, small churches could establish themselves quickly, independent from any larger denominational structure, and carry on their affairs without having to be in communication with others. Later they could associate with other Baptist congregations as the need arose. They shared several characteristics nonetheless, including the practice of adult baptism and the reliance on the Bible alone rather than on traditional creedal formulations for their theological positions.

The concentrations of the major denominations are only one way to look at regional differences in this period. The patterns discussed above derive largely from studies of white Christian church membership. This view mutes the fact that African Americans were in the majority in many areas of the South and Gulf Coast regions. The African American majority in these areas, largely living in slavery, had not yet developed institutional forms of religious expression; the emerging separate African American denominations had not penetrated into slaveholding areas. Nonetheless the melding of Christianity and African and Native American religious thought and practice was already underway and contributed to the distinctive ethos of Southern religion.[5] The presence of minority religious traditions, such as the Brethren, the Amish, or utopian communities of various kinds, as well as new American denominations such as the Christian churches, the Mormons, and those coming from the Holiness movement, began to emerge in the older western areas of New York and Pennsylvania and in the Ohio Valley. A few of them later gained enough prominence to become characteristic of an entire region.

Finally, in the early national period the United States was almost wholly Christian, at least nominally. New York and the East Coast cities held a handful of synagogues, but the greater part of Jewish immigration was yet to come. Native American religions remained prominent where the United States had yet to expand. Immigration from Asia bringing Buddhism, Hinduism, and other Asian religions had not yet begun.

Although the main cultural developments in American religion in this period were felt across regional lines, there were regional differences in the way religious institutions participated in these new movements. The experiment in disestablishment was resisted most strongly in the Northeast, where older forms of colonial establishment persisted. The freedom of expression, communal energy, and sense of individual agency characteristic of the revivals became more characteristic of the West than of the more established coastal areas of the old colonies. In all of the colonial areas—British, Spanish, French, and Russian—the sense of establishment, if not of a state church, persisted. The placement of churches in the civic center, the sense of access of those in political office, and the sense of entitlement to participate in public policy debates all derive from older colonial patterns of religious organization.

The period from 1830 to the end of the Civil War, just a generation, saw three major regional developments in religion in the United States: the annexation of the Catholic Southwest, the Mormon establishment in Utah, and the division of much of American Protestantism into Northern and Southern bodies over the issue of slavery. In 1848, the United States annexed much of northern Mexico; Texas and California almost immediately became states; and the large territory of New Mexico (including Arizona), Colorado, Utah, and Nevada became a new region of the country characterized by Spanish language, Mexican culture, and well-established Roman Catholicism. In spite of efforts on the part of mainline Protestant missionaries, few of the new citizens converted from Catholicism. The Southwest region to this day is largely Roman Catholic, and Spanish persists as a common language. Within American Roman Catholicism, this area remained a distinctive region. Mexican Catholicism, developed for four hundred years in contact with strong indigenous native religions, was a very different Catholicism from the Irish, German, and French Catholicism common in the rest of the United States.

This period also embraces the beginnings and early growth of the Church of Jesus Christ of Latter-day Saints. The Saints, following the teachings of their prophet Joseph Smith, began to move West, settling first in the Ohio Valley and then in Illinois and Missouri. They began to experience opposition and persecution, and finally in the mid-1840s most moved to Utah to establish the political state called Deseret. From their center in Salt Lake City, the Mormon Saints spread north into Idaho and south into the Arizona Territory and established a chain of towns leading toward the coast in California. For the Mormons, the area around the Great Salt Lake was their Palestine.[6] The Great Salt Lake was the Dead Sea, Utah Lake was the Sea of Galilee, and the river running between them was the Jordan. Salt Lake City was located in a site analogous to the site of Jerusalem in Palestine. In 1850 the area became a U.S. territory. The Mormon character of the region was already established and persists to this day.[7]

At the same time, immigration and in-migration created Catholic majorities in the major cities of the Midwest. By 1890, Chicago, Cleveland, St. Louis, and other urban areas were solidly Catholic. In the northern Midwest, Catholics and Lutherans (many from Germany, Ireland, and countries of Scandinavia) vied for predominance. The older French Catholic presence from the colonial era was subsumed by the later arrivals, although it may still be detected in the place names. Catholics continued to predominate in other territories acquired from Mexico, especially along the Gulf coast of Louisiana and Texas, forming a ring around Mormon Utah and outlying Mormon corridors in Arizona, Idaho, and Nevada. The north central region of the country remained predominantly Methodist and the South about evenly divided between Baptists and Methodists. The African American majorities in the former slave states meant that much of the Baptist and Methodist South was actually predominantly African American Baptist and Methodist. These five denominations—Roman Catholic, Methodist, Baptist, Lutheran, and Latter-day Saints—remain the predominant five religious groups in these areas to the present. One or two of them together account for the majority of religious adherents in most states both in 1890 and in 1990. Their geographical distribution into the Roman Catholic regions of the Northeast and West, the Lutheran upper Midwest, the Methodist middle, Mormon Utah, and the Baptist South creates persistent religious cultures in those regions, although the Roman Catholics have never participated to the degree the Protestants have in influencing the public or civil religious ethos of the nation. That ethos remained Protestant in flavor even in areas where the Catholics were in the majority in part because of the concentration of Catholic immigrants among the working class, but also in part because of strong earlier and still persistent anti-Catholic sentiment among Yankee Protestants.

Although most immigration during this period was from Europe and therefore mostly Christian—whether Protestant, Catholic, or Orthodox— European Jews arrived in large numbers in both the East Coast cities and in San Francisco and Los Angeles on the West Coast. By the 1890s, San Francisco came to rival New York as a center of Jewish life and influence in American culture. The West Coast was also home to adherents of an increasing variety of other religious traditions, such as Buddhists, Sikhs, and Taoists, while Hindus came to the West Coast to participate in the economic booms that followed the Gold Rush and the building of the railroads. During this period also the West Coast became increasingly diverse in its religious character, thanks to the complex nature of migrants from the eastern states who brought their religious traditions with them. These many traditions became rivals with each other in the new western territories. Where large numbers migrated from the same areas, they developed small cultural pockets in their new homelands, such as the Church of the Brethren colony in La Verne, California, or the Quaker community in northwestern Oregon. Usually many small competing congregations grew up in the same town. But just as characteristically, people moving to the far West left their religious adherence behind, joining a growing number of religiously unattached people in the region.

Regional understandings of religious dominance persisted. The churches in the older states still understood their religious culture as a higher, more developed form, and through the agency of home missions spent countless resources to shape the West to the models of New England or the old South. In the former Mexican provinces of the Southwest, the once-established Roman Catholic Church waged a culture war with the Anglo-Protestants over the control of public schools, where the culture of the next generations would be shaped. In a larger frontier pattern, Protestant church schools and colleges dotted the West long before public education was well established. Roman Catholic parish schools sprang up everywhere to contest Protestant hegemony.

The World's Parliament of Religions in Chicago in 1893 provides a convenient symbol to close discussion of the nineteenth century. This meeting of world religious leaders and teachers was organized by American Christians largely for the purposes of showing the superiority of Christianity to other religions and of educating Christian church members about other religions in order to devise strategies for missionary appeal. The effect was more complex. The parliament served as well to introduce Americans to a number of religious options they had never considered. After 1893, increasing numbers of Americans were attracted to Buddhism, particularly the Zen variety, and to Hinduism, and many converted. For those already disenchanted with the divisions of Christianity, the parliament merely underlined the inability of any religion to enforce its claim of unique authority.

The effects of the parliament are not immediately apparent in religious population statistics, but the gathering does serve to mark the end of the possibility of understanding the United States as a solidly Christian nation. The 1890s also mark the end of the United States' wars against the Native Americans, although not an end to efforts to control or eliminate them. In this decade, the Native American population hit its low point. In religious terms, almost none of the native peoples was able to practice their religions without interference in some form from white society. Nonetheless, regionally Native American traditions remained alive and part of the religious life characteristic of the area in Oklahoma, where a number of tribes were concentrated together; in the Southwest, where most tribes still inhabited traditional lands, however truncated by U.S. appropriation; in the Dakotas; and on many other local reservations throughout the West. In addition, Native American communities persisted in the East, although in much smaller numbers. The presence of Native Americans and their religious traditions, the concentration of immigrants from Asia bringing their religious traditions with them, and the mixture of migrants from the distinctively Baptist, Methodist, Lutheran, and Catholic regions of the Eastern United States created the diverse religious landscape of the American West. During the twentieth century, this Western diversity played an important role in shaping all of American religion.

INTO THE TWENTIETH CENTURY

As noted, in 1893 the World's Parliament of Religions held in Chicago in conjunction with the Columbian Exposition or World's Fair introduced a large number of people to the religions of Asia. The parliament ushered in a century of growing interest in traditions outside of the European Judeo-Christian mainline American religious groups. From 1893 to the end of World War II in 1945, the religious characteristics of the major regions of the country became more complex. Especially in the West and in the larger cities, religious demographics shifted as religions of new immigrants and also new religious movements such as Pentecostalism appeared on the scene. The final period from the end of the Second World War to the present represents a definite shift in religious demographics, carrying forward the growing religious diversity, but also revealing a fault line between those who are more religious than ever and those who are increasingly secular in their outlook. The decline of mainline Protestant churches and the rise of nondenominational megachurches represent a particularly significant trend in this latter period. Nonetheless, during the twentieth century the religious regions that developed in the United States during the nineteenth century remained the template for what was new. The main trends came in increasing diversity within the regions, especially in urban areas, and in the thinning out of religious adherence, especially in the West.

In 1910, 1920, and 1930, the United States collected religious data in its regular census, publishing the results in 1916, 1926, and 1936. After the government stopped gathering such data, first the National Council of Churches (1952) and more recently the Glenmary Research Institute (1970, 1980, 1990, and 2000), the National Atlas of Religion in America (an online database), and various opinion poll research projects continued the endeavor. The quality of the data has steadily improved. In the early years, the researchers categorized religion only in terms of the familiar Christian denominations and Judaism. Even more recent data, although acknowledging many new kinds of Christianity (Pentecostal churches, nondenominational evangelical congregations, and independent mega-churches), exhibit categories only for the recognized world religions, tend-ing to dismiss tribal religions, New Age groups, and small religious communities. In addition, little of the data about racial and ethnic minor-ity religions is completely reliable. In earlier studies, researchers did not think to differentiate white Methodist denominations from the African American Methodist churches, for instance. In later studies, researchers did not count those groups that did not respond to their forms of inquiry. Numbers of adherents reported by religious institutions can be difficult to compare, since different religious bodies count members and adherents by different criteria. In addition, some of the later data is derived from opin-ion polls. Individuals' self-identification may differ from the institutional identification of a person as a member. Increasingly, individuals may iden-tify with more than one religious tradition.

Until after 1990, the denominational character of the various regions changed very little from the patterns formed in the nineteenth century. The South remained solidly Baptist; in fact, the number of counties with a Baptist predominance increased over the course of the twentieth century. New England remained predominantly Roman Catholic, as did the Gulf Coast, Southwest, and the area of the West surrounding the predomi-nantly Mormon area centered in Utah. The upper Midwest remained pre-dominantly Lutheran; the band separating the Catholic and Lutheran North from the Baptist South retained its Methodist predominance.

By 1990, two new denominational trends became clear. First, an increas-ing number of counties reported a Pentecostal predominance. Second, an increasing number of counties reported the predominant group as having less than 50 percent of the religious adherents in the county. This latter trend signifies either that the county had become increasingly unaffiliated—in other words, that 50 percent or more of the population is not affiliated with any religious group—or that the county has become more diverse, with several groups vying for predominance and none having more than 50 percent of the population in its ranks.

In institutional terms, the influence of the movement of people to the West and the diversity of religion that characterized the Western region were both factors in the weakening of church life. Not only churches but other civic organizations suffered. People who think of themselves as sojourners, as temporary residents planning to move on, rarely put much energy into the establishment of civic institutions. In addition, where there are small populations of diverse religious adherence, there are simply not enough people to sustain individual religious institutions over a long time. The weakened character of religious institutions in the West contributed to the disinclination of people to join what seemed to be a lost cause. Churches from the old established denominations situated in the West found themselves isolated from the centers of denominational life and became both more independent in their thinking and at the same time more dependent on the resources of the larger organization. The weakness of established religious organizations also contributed to the flourishing of new religious movements in the West. It is no accident that Pentecostalism got its start on the West Coast. The enormous diversity of the population and the lack of religious establishment created a good environment for a new movement that helped people find a way to be at home in a rapidly changing society.

THE ROLE OF REGION IN THE TWENTY-FIRST CENTURY

By 1990, one could frame the religious regions of the United States in a completely different way. Looking at the percentage of the population that claims church membership or which churches claim as members, a new regional configuration emerges.[8] A broad band of highly affiliated population extends from the Dakotas down through Nebraska, Kansas, and Oklahoma to west Texas and eastern New Mexico. There it meets another band of dense religious affiliation running from Georgia west to Texas. This more-or-less L-shaped region is characterized by the presence of a strongly evangelical Protestantism and Roman Catholicism. Within this region, much of the religious adherence follows racial and ethnic lines. Thus several subregions exist within it. African Americans in the South particularly have a high level of church affiliation and a historical sense of the church as an institution providing both identity and community and as a vehicle for promoting a common voice in the public arena. The Roman Catholic and Lutheran church members of the upper Midwest also have a strong sense of the connection of church affiliation and ethnic identity. Some of these churches still preserve the original language of the immigrant communities that started them. Finally, the persistence of the oldest Roman Catholic communities in the country in New Mexico, along the Rio Grande, and in Louisiana, is also tied to a strong ethnic tradition with deep roots.

The particularly strong level of church affiliation in Nebraska, Kansas, Oklahoma, and west Texas reflects the predominantly evangelical piety introduced into the area in the nineteenth century by denominational home missionary societies. The character of this "evangelical" religious culture was delineated by one historian of the home mission movement, Colin B. Goodykoontz: "It was practical rather than mystical; it put emphasis on individual righteousness and personal salvation after death rather than on social righteousness and community salvation now; it did not entirely escape the unchristian notion that men [and women] may attain goodness by the observance of rules rather than by a change of heart; it was strongly orthodox in its theology, which meant more specifically that it was Trinitarian, that it believed in the literal interpretation and the verbal inerrancy of the Bible, and that it visualized heaven as a city of gold and hell as a place of eternal torment."[9]

Two generations later, another student of American evangelicalism, George Marsden, included much the same characteristics in his definition of this religious culture, still central to the Midwest and South, and growing rapidly at the dawn of the twenty-first century. However, Marsden looked at evangelicalism from several points of view, resulting in a more complex definition. Conceptually, Marsden notes that evangelicals empha-size the "Reformation doctrine of final authority of scripture, the real, his-torical character of God's saving work recorded in scripture, eternal salvation only through personal trust in Christ ... the importance of evan-gelism and missions, and the importance of a spiritually transformed life."[10] Marsden also observed that in addition to a conceptual definition, we must also understand that evangelicalism is a dynamic movement rooted in the sixteenth-century Reformation, a perennial effort to return to the pure Word of God in scripture as the ultimate authority. It is also a common cultural experience growing out of a democratic society in which personal choice is significant, and whether persons in the culture are com-pletely committed believers or not, they share a common hymnody, styles of prayer and worship, and behavioral mores. These customs and mores may be organized in institutional forms, churches, voluntary societies, publications, mission and educational institutions, and charitable and social reform societies.[11] Finally, Marsden is careful to claim that one cannot equate evangelicalism with fundamentalism, dispensationalism, premillenni-alism, anti-modernism, or Pentecostalism, but that evangelicals often hold to one or more of those positions or practices as well.

In addition to this L-shaped region in the center and South, a few other well-affiliated areas occurred in the United States at the close of the twentieth century. The area surrounding Utah forms one of the solidly affiliated regions; in this case, more than 75 percent of the population in some areas are Latter-day Saints. New England and New York City form another such relatively well-affiliated area. Roman Catholics are a solid ma-jority of the population in every county. In addition, mainline Protestants maintain a solid presence, along with newer Pentecostal and nondenomi-national evangelical groups. Fewer scholars have attempted to define the cultural characteristics of mainline Protestantism, primarily because for so long it was assumed to be synonymous with American religious culture in general. Although in the nineteenth century the mainline tradition was solidly evangelical, in the twentieth century the mainline churches often took a liberal or modernist direction. For this reason, by the end of the twentieth century, we can understand the mainline tradition as distinct from the evangelical cluster in some senses. Leonard Sweet characterized mainline Protestantism as modernist, that is, as willing to embrace mod-ernity. In addition to trying to take the findings of science into account in formulating its theology, modernist Protestantism also embraced the cul-ture and values of modern business, concern for quantity and increased ef-ficiency (including creating flexible public spaces), a consumer orientation, and the use of market analysis and advertising. Mainline religion in Amer-ica looked forward rather than to tradition for its cues.[12] Wade Clark Roof and William McKinney point out that the mainline influence in American culture reflects traditions rooted in the Protestant Reformation and the co-lonial experience, a positive engagement with modernity, an ecumenical vision, often but not always staying within a broad understanding of orthodox Christian confession, a strong social conscience, and a tendency to emphasize nurture rather than conversion.[13]

Unlike the regions of solid religious adherence, the predominantly Catholic, doughnut-shaped region surrounding Mormon Utah is actually thinly populated with religious adherents, fewer than 50 percent in all cases and in some areas much less than that. Its Catholicism is thinned out, existing in religiously diverse contexts where nonaffiliation is the norm. Although Catholics may show up as predominant when using the denominational lens, it would be difficult to call them predominant when they are simply the largest group within a minority of church members. The Northeast, outside the region mentioned above, also is an unaffiliated region, with Catholics usually being the largest group within a minority of adherents. Florida is a similarly unaffiliated region, perhaps taking its character from the large number of residents who hail from the unaffiliated Northeast region. Alaska and Hawaii have generally a minority of church members. Hawaii's large percentage of immigrants from Asia and the Pacific Islands bring their own Asian religions with them and do not necessarily convert to Christianity. Data from Alaska are difficult to interpret because the population is so thinly spread and the Native American traditions are not well represented in the counts. The Pacific Northwest is so strongly unaffiliated that Patricia Killen has dubbed it the "none zone," meaning that when people respond to researchers' inquiries about their religious affiliation, they respond, "none."[14]

These several trends underway by the end of the twentieth century seem likely to shape the immediate future of religious regionalism in the United States. Given the regional persistence of the five predominant Christian denominations over more than a century, it would seem likely that their predominance will continue at least for a time—Catholics in the Northeast and in the West surrounding Utah, Baptists in the South, Latter-day Saints in Utah, Lutherans in the northern Midwest, and Methodists in the central band between the South and North. However, if the trend of the last thirty years holds, the continuing phenomenon of nonaffiliation will thin out the religious population overall, so that although denominational patterns of predominance may persist, their thinning overall numbers in relation to the population as a whole will pose changes in the religious ethos and political strength of many of these groups. Increasing religious diversity is also a trend likely to continue into the foreseeable future.

Both as people move around the country, taking their religious cultures with them into new areas, and as immigrants continue to bring to the United States new forms of religious practice, areas particularly affected by these kinds of migration—notably the coasts and the larger metropolitan areas—will also exhibit increasing religious diversity. Already religious demographers are more aware of and better able to count religious traditions outside the older Christian and Jewish denominations recognized by nineteenth-century students of American religion. For instance, as the Buddhist population grows, the various denominations of Buddhism will find increased recognition. A Buddhist American will not simply be lumped with other Buddhists, but have her or his own kind of Buddhism recognized. Buddhist regionalism in the United States will then be more apparent. Proximity to alternative religious options in these areas of increased diversity will also most probably show increased dual affiliation or mixing of traditions. For example, a hypothetical Buddhist American, such as mentioned above, may be a convert from Judaism and have a personal sense of adherence to both traditions, whether or not those traditions recognize such double adherence. As well, the myriad of new religious movements in the United States, from Jehovah's Witnesses to Scientology, do not currently appear in studies of religious demography. Whether they shape the ethos of any region of the country will become evident in time. If religious demographers continue to use denominational and world religions categories, these new populations of mixed religious practice and commitment will not show up, although they may come to characterize regions of significant population growth.

Finally, increasing influence of standardization will also create new categories and hence reshape the picture of religious regionalism. The 2000 surveys of religious preference began to provide data on evangelical and mainline Protestantism, for instance, rather than the previous denominational categories alone. Most mainline Protestant churches, however, have a mixture of self-consciously evangelical congregations, self-consciously nonevangelical (or perhaps self-categorized as liberal or progressive) congregations, and congregations somewhere along that spectrum. The religious map looked at in this way bears some similarity to the "red state, blue state" map of recent national elections. Regions that are strongly evangelical in religious culture tended also to vote strongly Republican, whereas regions that are religiously diverse or where the percentage of nonadherence is high tended to vote Democratic.[15] The kind of process Marsden and other scholars have noted that characterizes evangelical culture (worship forms, behavior, common reading, common television preferences) make evangelical congregations of whatever denomination more similar to each other than they are to more mainline congregations that may be in the same denomination. The marketing of religious identity, whether evangelical, progressive, or some other category, will serve to blunt older regional cultures, just as the marketing of national brand products has blunted regional product identity.

The fast-growing Pentecostal churches are only now becoming visible in the studies of demography and region. In many former Roman Catholic strongholds, particularly in the borderlands with Mexico, Pentecostal numbers are overtaking Catholics. Similarly, in the Baptist South, Pentecostalism is a growing presence and may change the religious character of the region before long, and Pentecostalism is also appearing as a dominant tradition in some parts of the "none zone" in areas previously thin to religious adherence. How Pentecostalism will shape the culture over time remains to be seen.

The influence of region on the character of American religious life stems from the way land shapes basic economies, from the collection of immigrants who have moved into an area over time, and from the interaction of older religious traditions with a new environment. Much of the shape of religious regions in the United States stems from older European colonial church establishments. However, distinctive American factors, such as the separation of church and state, have led to the flourishing of religious traditions that were suppressed in Europe, the Baptists being an outstanding example. Anyone wanting to understand a particular instance of religious life in the United States will do well to study the underlying layers of regional religious history. The life of a Jewish community in New York will be quite different from one in Atlanta or in Lawrence, Kansas. A Methodist may feel comfortable in the mainline of American religion in Ohio, but be an outsider in Utah. Religious institutions of the same denomination in Pennsylvania face a different level of acceptance in society than they do in Washington. Although the long-term trends may suggest that regional differences in religious culture will become less obvious as the twenty-first century wears on, for now region is important for understanding the variety of American religious experience.

NOTES

1. In this essay I refer primarily to the maps in Edwin Scott Gaustad and Philip Barlow, *A New Historical Atlas of Religion in America* (New York: Oxford University Press, 2001). In this case, I am using Fig. 1.42, p. 50, "Roman Catholic Missions in the West 1776," and Fig. C.1, p. 357, "Regional Denominational Predominance 1790." As in all the data used for this atlas, the reliability can be questioned, and the findings should be used only for broad generalization. In making use of any particular piece of data for more in-depth study, the researcher would want to look closely at the collection methods and limitations of the original sources of any of the figures.

2. Reformed Protestant refers to those Protestants closely related to the sixteenth-century reforms in the Swiss city states. Particularly influential was John Calvin in Geneva. Early in the history of the Reformation, these Protestants became distinguished from Luther's Reformation in Germany and later from the more radical reformers on the one hand and the growing Catholic reform movements on the other. In England, after Elizabeth I's Anglican reform, the Reformed-influenced Puritans became increasingly vocal in their opinion that she had not gone far enough in the reformation of the English church. During periods when the English church and state actively tried to suppress the Puritans, they migrated to the American colonies, establishing locations of Reformed presence in New England. The majority of these Puritans organized their churches according to a congregational style of polity, different from the presbyterian polity developed in Calvin's Geneva. Congregational polity locates the main authority for making decisions about belief and practice in the congregation, although these congregations most often affirmed the need for fellowship, cooperation, and mutual recognition. Presbyterian polity, on the other hand, locates authority in the presbytery, the gathering of pastors and elders from the congregations. In this polity, the congregations are subject to the authority of the presbytery. These Congregationalists were for two centuries the dominant religious group in New England. Later Reformed Protestants from other places in Europe—namely Scotland, France, and Germany—joined earlier Dutch Reformed Protestants in establishing what became the Presbyterian and Reformed churches in Pennsylvania and New York.

3. In part this reflects the ongoing national conflict between Spain and England and also the polarization of Roman Catholics and Protestants in Europe.

4. The sources of information regarding religious adherence in the nineteenth century are limited, as are the means of comparing data from one religious tradition to another. In general, scholars rely on two common sources of information. The first is the self-reported membership numbers contained in denominational records, and the second is data collected by the United States in its census every ten years until after 1930, when the government stopped including questions about religious affiliation in the census surveys. This limits our understanding of religious demography in this period somewhat, but for the purposes of this overview, we can use the figures that have informed the makers of atlases of American religion. Any deeper study would require more care.

5. A useful summary of this situation can be found in Cheryl Kirk-Duggan, "African-American and Native-American Folk Religion: Down But Not Out," in *Religion and Public Life in the Southern Crossroads: Showdown States*, ed. William Lindsey and Mark Silk (Walnut Creek, CA: AltaMira, 2005), 127–60. Longer classic works on the subject include Albert J. Raboteau, *Slave Religion: The "Invisible Institution" in the Antebellum South* (New York: Oxford University Press, 1978).

6. An illustration of this geographical interpretation can be found in Gaustad and Barlow, Fig. 3.16.

7. Kathleen Flake, "The Mormon Corridor: Utah and Idaho," in *Religion and Public Life in the Mountain West: Sacred Landscapes in Transition*, ed. Jan Shipps and Mark Silk (Walnut Creek, CA: AltaMira, 2004), 91–114. See also Jan Shipps, *Mormonism: The Story of a New Religious Tradition* (Urbana: University of Illinois Press, 1985).

8. See Gaustad and Barlow, "Church Membership as a Percentage of Total Population: 1990," Fig. 4.17, p. 352.

9. Colin B. Goodykoontz, *Home Missions on the American Frontier* (Caldwell, ID: Caxton Printers, 1939), 425.

10. George Marsden, ed., *Evangelicalism and Modern America* (Grand Rapids, MI: Eerdmans, 1984), ix–xvii.

11. Ibid., xvi–xvii.

12. Leonard Sweet, "The Modernization of Protestant Religion in America," in *Altered Landscapes: Christianity in America, 1935–1985*, ed. David W. Lotz, Donald W. Shriver, Jr., and John F. Wilson (Grand Rapids, MI: Eerdmans, 1989), 19–41.

13. Wade Clark Roof and William McKinney, *American Mainline Religion: Its Changing Shape and Future* (New Brunswick, NJ: Rutgers University Press, 1987).

14. Patricia O'Connell Killen and Mark Silk, eds., *Religion and Public Life in the Pacific Northwest: The None Zone* (Walnut Creek, CA: AltaMira, 2004).

15. The maps showing religious affiliation for 2000 can be found on at least two Web sites: www.thearda.com (the American Religion Data Archive) and www.religionatlas.com (the National Atlas of Religion in America NARA run by the Polis Center). Maps showing the results of the 2000 and 2004 presidential elections can be found in a number of places; I used ones at www.interventionmag.com.

SUGGESTIONS FOR FURTHER READING

Carroll, Brett A. *The Routledge Historical Atlas of Religion in America*. New York: Routledge, 2000.

Gaustad, Edwin, and Philip Barlow. *A New Historical Atlas of Religion in America*. New York: Oxford University Press, 2001.

Silk, Mark, and Andrew Walsh, series eds. *Religion by Region*. Published in cooperation with the Leonard E. Greenberg Center for the Study of Religion in Public Life at Trinity College, the series is in process. When finished, it will include nine volumes covering the following regions: Pacific Northwest, Mountain West, New England, Midwest, Southern Crossroads, the South, the Middle Atlantic, and the Pacific Region, along with a volume on religion and public life in the United States. At the time of this writing, the following had appeared:

Killen, Patricia O'Connell, and Mark Silk, eds. *Religion and Public Life in the Pacific Northwest: The None Zone*. Walnut Creek, CA: AltaMira, 2004.

Lindsey, William, and Mark Silk, eds. *Religion and Public Life in the Southern Crossroads: Showdown States*. Walnut Creek, CA: AltaMira, 2005.

Shipps, Jan, and Mark Silk, eds. *Religion and Public Life in the Mountain West: Sacred Landscapes in Transition*. Walnut Creek, CA: AltaMira, 2004.

Walsh, Andrew, and Mark Silk, eds. *Religion and Public Life in New England: Steady Habits, Changing Slowly*. Walnut Creek, CA: AltaMira, 2004.

CHAPTER 10

The Shape of Things to Come: Megachurches, Emerging Churches, and Other New Religious Structures

Scott L. Thumma

"Here is the church. Here is the steeple. Open the door, and see all the people."

Most of us fondly remember this childhood game we learned in Sunday school. The realism of that game, however, is slowly losing its footing. Not only are most churches seldom filled with people, but also fewer new congregations are being built with steeples and most of what passes for "church" seldom resembles the congregations in which many of us grew up. In fact, the rhyme of the future might well be more like "Is this a church? Where is the steeple? Open the door and, where are all the people?" Or in the case of the megachurches, "Here are no symbols. Here is no steeple. Yet open the door and see 10,000 people!"

Although organized religion in the United States hasn't changed quite that dramatically yet, the structures are in flux both for local congregations and for national denominations. It is still true that the vast majority of churches in the country are imbedded in a traditional model and tied to a denominational organization that has shifted very little in the past fifty years. In recent years, however, newer congregational forms have offered substantial challenges to this landscape. These forms include the popularity of the house church movement in the 1970s and a recent resurgence of interest in these; the growth of niche, cell, and emergent churches; and the proliferation of megachurches (congregations with two thousand or more attenders each week) in the past few decades. Each of these offers new models for the organizational structuring of religious expression. Likewise, the quasi-denominational networks of congregations that have evolved around these megachurches and a multitude of parachurch organizations present new forms of national cooperation that were once provided only by traditional denominational forms.

It should not be surprising that new forms of religious life are developing; organizational structures adapt and change over time in response to societal and cultural shifts. Nor should these new forms be considered entirely unique and original; variations on megachurches, house and independent churches, and networks or "fellowships" of congregations have existed for centuries. Nevertheless, what seems distinctive about these organizational forms is that they have a particular fit or "elective affinity" with the shifts taking place in the religious identity of individuals.

Many scholarly writings in the past few decades have indicated that religious identity for an individual is presently less tied to tradition, history, and organizational forms such as a denomination, local church, religious camp, or parochial school.[1] A vast majority of Americans report that the content of religious faith can be constructed apart from or independent of a church or other traditional religious authority.[2] Religious identity is seen as something an individual can pick and choose. It makes sense that in this evolving context, new religious structures that fit with the flexible, individualist beliefs of self-created religious consumers would arise or become more prominent in the religious marketplace.

Yet even within a situation of radical personal spiritual negotiation, there is still a sociological need for physical structures to contain this "individualized" religious identity. The "spirit" is not sustained without some organizational form. A spiritual treasure requires some earthen vessel in which to contain it, even if this vessel looks very little like the vases and ceramics of past decades. It isn't necessary that these vessels are completely unique and avant-garde for them to work; they just have to be customized to fulfill the purpose. Many congregations have adapted to the new context by a shift in function and a reorientation in their approach and understanding of what they offer "the spiritual consumer." Together, however, all these structural alterations amount to the beginnings of a reshaping of the religious organizational landscape.

This is not to argue that contemporary consumers necessarily are making conscious decisions on the choice of religious alternatives. Often, such decisions are anything but rational selections. However, this chapter argues that the new structural forms available allow for different ways of engagement with religious communities based on the interests of the individual. It will provide a glimpse into the characteristics of these new forms and then assess their implications for the future direction of religion in America.

WHAT HAS CHANGED?

What counts as a legitimate congregation? Recently in Rockaway Township, New Jersey, lawyers representing the township argued that a growing megachurch, Christ Church, was in fact "not a church." This counterintuitive argument was proposed when the megachurch wanted to move into the area. Township commissioners balked at the idea and hindered its efforts. The case eventually went before the courts. In a limited sense the assertion was true, Christ Church wasn't "a church" according to the definition of "church" in the minds of the town's nineteenth-century founding fathers. Likewise, most people who might walk into a contemporary house church or visit the Web site of an emergent church gathering would be hard-pressed to call what they see a "congregation." Then again, does a group of Wiccans who gather in a chat room or on a discussion board to discuss sacred texts and exchange methods of ritual practices constitute a religious community? What of hundreds of gay men routinely coming to a drag show in a gay bar to sing gospel hymns and praise God? And do the Willow Creek Association, the Fellowship of Christian Assemblies, the Apostolic World Christian Fellowship, the Vineyard Christian Fellowship, or Potter's House Network count as denominations? At the very least, the definitions of these religious structures are being stretched and pulled.

Over the past forty years there has been considerable experimentation with the structure of religious expression to fit and undergird a highly individualized approach to religion. Major shifts in an individual's perspective of religion in the 1960s and onward have created many "Sheilas," or persons constructing a religion of their own.[3] In a sense, religious belief has become customizable to an individual's tastes, experiences, and interests. Religious identity is less one that is ascribed or inherited and is instead more one that the individual creates. But the changes go even beyond just the achievement of an identity. The decades since the 1960s are characterized by cultural unsettledness and mark, as Wuthnow describes, a shift from a spirituality of habitation and dwelling to one of seeking:

> In the newer view, status [and, I would add, both identity and spirituality] is attained through negotiation. A person does not have an ascribed identity or attain an achieved identity but creates an identity by negotiating among a wide range of materials. Each person's identity is thus understandable only through biography. The search that differentiates each individual is itself part of the distinct identity that person creates. A spirituality of seeking is closely connected to the fact that people increasingly create a sense of personal identity through an active sequence of searching and selecting.[4]

The changes, sparked by major shifts in our society, have also begun to reconfigure our structured religious forms. The freedom that has enabled Americans to experiment and take control of their own individual belief systems, to wrestle the control of their faith from the gods and the forefathers, has also allowed them collectively to create religious organizational forms that fit this reality. The structures that have arisen likewise support this "a la carte" approach to belief in several different ways evident in major trends in American religion.

One major shift of adaptation in this spiritual consumer reality is the "niche approach," an organizational reduction in scale with a specificity of focus. This approach fractures traditional religious structures into narrowly focused niche congregations with specific and well-defined particular religious interests or subcultural characteristics. In economic language, it is essentially a "specialty store" approach to a particular slice of the American religious market.

This effort is evident in a number of developments from the 1960s onward, beginning with efforts to express a distinctive religious perspective. Small informal charismatic fellowships, gatherings of new religious organizations, discipleship groups, and house churches all fit this model. Other manifestations of this trend focus on quasi-political aims. They include intentional peace and justice communities, social activist and worker house communities, traditional mainline congregations that emphasize ancient rites and rituals of their tradition (such as Rite One Episcopal churches or Latin mass Catholic congregations), and Base Communities, modeled on a Latin American example. More recently this niche approach is seen in the emergent church movement. This approach segments the market into individual interest enclaves whereby religious persons can select specific groups to suit their needs and then travel between them as their interests change. Intimacy, integrity, and an intentionally narrow focus are key spiritual values in this organizational form.

A second counterintuitive adaptation to personal religious customization is the "megachurch approach," an organizational increase in scale in which multiple choices are offered within a large all-encompassing entity. This approach follows the "mall mentality" of offering countless boutiques and specialty stores, large anchor stores, and kiosks all under one large organizational reality. The megachurch offers a choice of individualized spiritual customization within small interest groups, while also embracing a larger mass worship experience in a highly professionalized, bureaucratic, and publicly prominent religious organization. Many of these megachurches are pushing the bounds of customization by creating multiple, simultaneous "venue worship services" and tailored branch campuses to appeal to the distinctive tastes of cultural subgroups within the larger membership. Likewise, it could be argued that the networks of likeminded churches centered around these megachurches are reforming larger national religious collectives as well as the local congregational reality. The values of this organizational expression are personal choice on a number of levels, a quality religious experience, and involvement in a prominent, successful endeavor.

Although this chapter will not focus on it, the Internet constitutes a third major adaptive structure to this customizable religious reality. The virtual structures of countless Web sites, chat rooms, blogs, listservs, and discussion boards allow users both to engage in online shopping for religious beliefs and also to discover communities of support and even create places to practice their rituals. There are a large number of Internet-based efforts by individuals and social collectives to support virtual religious quests. This approach is especially critical for individuals when no physical faith community of their liking exists in geographic proximity to them. The Internet is seldom recognized as a legitimate religious structure, but for many individuals of faiths on the fringe, it may provide their only tangible community. Persons within Christian, Jewish, Muslim, and Buddhist traditions who are gay and lesbian may know others of similar faith perspectives only through their Internet connections, especially if they are located in rural or small town settings away from major urban centers.

Persons interested in Wicca or Santeria, Hinduism or Rosicrucianism, or any combinations of the thousands of established religious beliefs can much more readily find virtual structures of communication, knowledge, writings, and fellowship to support such beliefs in the world of Internet technologies than in the physical realm.

Even though it is very difficult to state conclusively that denominational loyalty is nonexistent, according to many indicators, the salience of the denominational identity is waning. The prevalence of denominational switching and success of nondenominational congregations attest to the fact that many consider involvement in a particular denominational tradition a secondary value in choosing a local congregation.

American religion is now less institutionally bound. Persons can craft faith systems that fit them, as well as construct unique forms that fit these systems. Spiritual persons are able to customize not only their beliefs, but also their encounters with religious structures. This may not necessarily be a conscious decision. We are not purely rational customers of religious products or ideas. We do not search the spiritual marketplace with a "consumer guide" in one hand and our list of personal desires in the other. Nevertheless, contemporary Americans have the institutional freedom to shape their religious beliefs, worship experiences, and organizational forms to their personal tastes and cultural norms and values. They don't need to worship at the altars of their ancestors or adopt the "faith of our fathers." The words of the gospel hymn are not entirely true anymore; what was good enough for mama and good enough for papa is no longer good enough for me.

SPECIALIZED BOUTIQUE RELIGION: NICHE-BASED STRUCTURES

The approach of niche-based religious organizations is to focus narrowly upon a specific and well-defined religious interest or subcultural identity. Niche religion, then, attempts to attract persons to fit that distinct focus. As such, these congregations are small, intentional, and often sectarian in their flavor. In recent decades several major movements of congregations within this model can be identified, including the house church movement, cell groups, cell church, intentional activist communities, and more recently, the emergent church movement. Each of these distinctive groups has its own reality; however, taken as a whole, they exemplify a niche model that allows individuals to select among multiple lifestyle options, picking the group that most meets momentary personal tastes and needs for music, fellowship, and involvement in the larger Christian community.

In 1970, I worshipped in a small charismatic fellowship in central Pennsylvania. This group of fifteen to twenty teens and young adults met in a small storefront Christian bookstore. We sat on the floor on cushions and sang scriptural praise songs to music provided by an acoustic guitarist. We didn't have a leader per se. Each person took turns offering a lesson that "God laid on our hearts." We celebrated the Lord's Supper when we met, using a chunk of bread and any kind of juice we could find. We often did community service projects, such as picking up trash along the streets, helping the elderly shop for groceries, and donating food and money for the homeless in our town. We always spent hours each week witnessing to strangers and our friends, trying to convert them to our way of seeing the truth of the Bible. Everyone in the group knew of the larger charismatic movement, since most of our songs, evangelistic tracts, and reading material came from these national sources. We didn't, however, have any contact with other groups, except for the occasional regional mass spiritual rallies that were common in the early 1970s. All we knew was that we were worshipping God in a way that seemed correct to us, and most of us moved on to other religious groups when the charismatic fellowship group no longer filled our spiritual needs.

This was my first introduction to the house church movement. Later I came to understand that those of us who participated in the charismatic movement were not the only group to assert a return to an anti-institutional form of church based on what was seen as an authentic recapturing of New Testament worship. In fact, my own ancestors in the Mennonite tradition worshipped in much the same way for many of the same reasons, as had many other traditions throughout the centuries since the founding of the Christian church.[5] In our charismatic fellowship group we were able to worship in a way that our "home" congregations wouldn't allow. We wanted intimacy, lay leadership, a distinctive style of music that expressed a unique understanding of spirituality, and the freedom to praise God as we saw fit.

The larger charismatic movement drove this house church movement of the late 1960s and throughout the 1970s. Ideas of spiritual baptism and expression of the gifts of the Spirit were forbidden in many congregations. If Spirit-filled Christians wanted to gather and worship God, they often had to do it in homes or small fellowships outside the established traditional churches. These house churches were formed around a distinctive theology or worldview. They were characterized also as a distinct organizational form and had a different cultural style, as described by Hadaway, Dubose, and Wright:

> House churches are more inclusive, more dynamic, and more engaging of members' time, energies, and resources than other types of house groups. Persons who join such groups seek to involve their whole lives in church and community. The compartmentalization of religious and secular activities tends to dissipate. Commitment and identification with the group is pervasive.[6]

Often house churches looked to national leaders, such as Christian Growth Ministries, to help them structure their fellowships, organize their participants, disciple them in Christian truth, and connect with other similar groups. A number of these house churches formed into communal groups such as the one that Stephen Warner described as Antioch ranch.[7] The vast majority, however, were mostly autonomous entities that gathered for worship and fellowship as small groups for several years.

Eventually, some of these fellowships were accused of excessive discipleship, labeled as cults, and then disbanded. It is evident from the history of these small gatherings that leadership weaknesses both in terms of exercising undue authority and also maintaining an acceptable religious orthodoxy were continual difficulties. More often, house church fellowships eventually folded when participation dwindled because more established churches began to adopt many of the charismatic practices into their worship. Other members drifted away when their spiritual needs were no longer being met by the charismatic fellowship.

Another weakness this form of religious organization has is fragility as a structure. House churches are prone to instability and a short life span. Occasionally, some of these house church groups attracted larger numbers. If it grew, the group would begin to institutionalize, often becoming an established congregation. A few such congregations have even grown to megachurch status. Several of the larger congregations and networks of churches that came out of the Jesus People and charismatic movements (such as the Vineyard Fellowship and Calvary Chapel) began as small house church gatherings. However, by the mid-1980s, whether owing to some widely publicized scandals or to assimilation and institutionalization, the movement had waned considerably.

Several other types of house church congregations existed throughout these decades. These are supportive of small but vibrant movements on the part of more liberal Protestant and Catholic Christians with quasi-political aims. Some create small house-based intentional peace and justice communities, social activist missions, or, following a Latin American model, local base communities.

The conservative Protestant house church movement has not disappeared completely. Countless small fellowships continue, and new congregations have started since the waning of the charismatic movement. Many persons remained convinced that the most authentic model of church is the independent, intimate gathering in homes rather than in "institutional churches."

The Internet has in many ways been a boon to this movement. The potential to create virtual networks of these congregations in an effort to publicize their existence, proclaim their understanding of the house church model as the most genuine religious structure, and share resources among groups has been greatly enhanced by the Internet. A number of Web sites, discussion boards, blogs, and listservs support the contemporary house church movement. Sites such as www.housechurch.org/ (with a discussion board, worldwide registry, email lists, and a newsgroup) and www.hccentral.com (with a directory of over 1,400 house churches), www.house2house.tv/, and www.house-church.org/ provide structures of support to individual house churches and persons wanting to form new ones. In fact, these rich Internet resources have sparked a resurgence of interest in and acceptance of the house church model. Additionally, the recognition of the power of the house church to spread the Christian gospel in places such as China and Russia has prompted the model to be seen as a potent evangelistic strategy.

A similar but distinctive movement was developing in the 1970s through the influence of one of the largest churches in the world, Yoido Full Gospel Church in Seoul, Korea. Its pastor, Paul Yonggi Cho, created a structure of small home cell groups within his massive congregation. These cell groups, meeting throughout the week in different homes, allowed trained lay deacons and elders to teach and minister to large numbers of people in small intimate gatherings on a more personal level, while also sustaining mass worship gatherings in the tens of thousands. This structure is qualitatively different from the anti-institution house church movement. These small groups are seen as having a supportive role within a larger congregation. Cell groups were intended for meeting personal needs, individual spiritual development, and intimate fellowship with the ultimate goal for the church to grow larger. This model became very popular in the United States in the 1980s, with many very large congregations adopting it.

Many congregations of all sizes have begun adopting small group fellowships to encourage interaction among members as well as to deepen individual spiritual practices. A number of congregations have made this cell approach integral to their character. They have shaped their "traditional church" around the cell idea. The congregation's focus is on the life of the cell group, rather than on the weekly worship of the gathered community. The cells may come together each week for worship but the center of the congregation is seen as the cell groups. Individuals in these cells conduct worship, do ministry, evangelize unbelievers, provide pastoral care, and mentor each other spiritually. Often the cells within a given church have evangelism strategies to target specific social groups such as nurses, lawyers, or the police. When cell groups function this way, the model borders on being a network of house churches. As such, it has often been called a "cell church."

The newest entry into the niche model market is not only intentionally small and anti-institutional but also includes a radical embrace of the contemporary youth culture. The emerging/emergent church movement, as it has come to be labeled, often builds on a house church organizational form and claims a distinctive theological perspective, but is also very much about expressing the faith in diverse Gen X styles and using postmodern cultural idioms. This approach appeals to a segment of the religious market in which young religious persons can select new enclave groups to suit their personal spiritual needs. As noted earlier, intimacy, integrity, and an intentionally narrow focus are key values.

The ideals expressed by the lead figures within the emerging church movement are sophisticated and well-reasoned analyses of contemporary society and the role of both God and the church in a changing reality. The approach is the opposite of a consumer-driven, style-sensitive commercialization of the Gospel. As the emerging church movement's foremost spokesperson, Brian McLaren, claims, "It's not about the church meeting your needs, it's about you joining the mission of God's people to meet the world's needs."[8] Another emerging church leader and pastor of a very successful church, Rob Bell, further emphasized the distinctiveness of the approach. "People don't get it … they think it's about style. But the real question is: What is the gospel?"[9]

From the perspective of the congregation, however, the various emerging church forms seem radically open to individualistic interpretation and focused on a distinct cultural niche. Although there are a wide variety of types of worship, emerging church services are often held in nontraditional spaces, such as recreational halls and warehouse space. Instead of pews, couches, recliners, lounge chairs, or even pillows scattered on the floors of the worship space provide seating. The service is technological, multisensory, and participatory. Images flash on video screens, constantly changing in rapid succession. Music plays, as a DJ uses a computer and turntable to mix and control the sound. Attendees are invited to express themselves spiritually through poetry, art, or other creative acts. The expressed spiritual practices blend together elements from diverse religious traditions, including Catholicism, Eastern Orthodoxy, and Celtic practices. "Some are discovering medieval mystical practices such as walking the labyrinth, but adding decidedly modern twists. It's a pick-your-own-mix approach that also stresses community and social justice."[10]

The congregations are comprised mostly of middle class whites in their twenties and thirties. The pastors, if there are pastors at all, or leadership teams are almost all educated white males. The theology tends to be evangelical Protestant in nature but often with a progressive perspective regarding social issues. However, even this theological stance is somewhat open to negotiation. As one young woman in an emerging congregation told a *Religion and Ethics Newsweekly* reporter, "There is no set doctrine; there is no set theology. There are things we question and things we believe." Another claimed the emerging church is "a place where individuals can express their understanding of who God is either in new ways or in artistic ways or even reaching back and reclaiming some ancient ways of expressing their relationship with God, their love for God and connecting with him."[11]

More than anything else, this form of religious organization is seen as a culturally relevant expression of faith. It takes its cues from contemporary youth culture, much as the Jesus People movement of the 1960s did, and attempts to create forms and practices that conform to the needs of that specific generation. "Emerging church with a mission heart is different. It does not start with a pre-determined mould and expect nonchurchgoers to compress in. It begins with the people church is seeking to reach, and asks 'What might be an appropriate expression of church for them?'"[12]

Many of the key leaders deny that the emerging church phenomenon is a definable movement. As McLaren comments, "Right now Emergent is a conversation, not a movement. We don't have a program. We don't have a model. I think we must begin as a conversation, then grow as a friendship, and see if a movement comes of it."[13] There is no doubt that with leaders, literature, Web sites, conferences, and a directory of congregations worldwide it certainly looks like a distinct religious movement. Some of these emerging churches are likewise no longer small, but have grown to a thousand or more members. The questions are how the movement will routinize, exactly what larger organizational forms it will take, and whether it will remain responsive to contemporary cultural ideals, especially as its members grow beyond their current musical tastes and cultural values.

MEGACHURCHES: GENERALIZED MALL RELIGION

There is great appeal to the small intimate gathering. It offers rootedness in a highly mobile society and a safe place among "people just like us" in which to do spiritual work. This small-scale approach, however, lacks a resonance to the lives many Americans lead. Our lives are replete with large institutional forms, media images, and interest-driven choices from major office complexes, malls, and food warehouses, to Disney, Las Vegas casinos, and multiplex theaters. In certain ways, the megachurch is the complete opposite of the house church, but with hundreds of ministries, programs, and fellowship groups, it offers intimacy and choice in one package.

Megachurches have come to dominate the religious landscape in modern American society. Their profound influence is less the result of the numbers of these large congregations than it is of their public prominence and of their being an exemplary model for the new ways churches are restructuring themselves and implementing new forms of religious life. This religious organizational form represents a strategy that is the complete opposite of that of the niche. It is all things to all people, every religious necessity under one roof, within one structure. Think Wal-Mart Super Store or a regional mall rather than upscale center-city boutique.

Imagine driving through downtown Houston, Texas, just west of the Galleria on a Sunday morning, when you come upon a traffic jam. You sit in a long line of late model cars waiting to turn into a vast parking area under a huge sign announcing the presence of Second Baptist Church and eventually decide to follow them. Actually you are at the church's Woodway Campus, one of three that constitute the 18,000-attender church. Mostly what you see sitting on a 25-acre plot of land is beautiful landscaping, hundreds of cars, parking lot attendants directing traffic, and a distant dome atop a cream-colored sandstone building that resembles an office building. After being directed to a parking space, you follow the steady stream of people, couples and families mostly, toward large inviting doors held open by several smiling greeters in green vests. Passing through the doors, you enter an amazing four-story atrium complete with marble and polished wood floors, fountains, and huge potted plants all combined into a distinctly mall-like feel. Immediately, another clean-cut young adult, also wearing a green vest, pleasantly greets you, offers a packet of information, and directs you to a massive visitor kiosk of dark rich wood with video screens; more pleasant attendants hover nearby. You notice signs for the bookstore, for Jane's Grill, and for dozens of classes, ministries, children and adult educational groups, and the family life center offering a weight-training program.

After getting your packet of welcome materials, which includes a tasteful cloth lapel sticker indicating you are a visitor, various brochures, a magazine, and a CD of messages and screen savers from the attendant, you follow the hundreds of others into the sanctuary. This is no ordinary church sanctuary. The cavernous building has seating for several thousand in many rows of pews on the main floor with additional seating on two floors of balconies, for a total seating capacity of more than 5,500. But what catches your eyes immediately are the massive stained glass walls of windows to the left and right of the front of the sanctuary and the spectacular dome glass artwork in the ceiling. Behind the pulpit area, organ pipes rise to the ceiling. Between these sits a 300-person choir, and above the choir is a baptismal that is flanked by two immense video projection screens. After a number of upbeat songs and an occasional traditional Baptist hymn, Ed Young, Sr. takes the pulpit and mesmerizes the congregation with a down-to-earth, biblically-based sermon, complete with audio and video clips on the screens for emphasis.

Welcome to the megachurch model of church. No verbal description of walking into a megachurch can ever capture the experience sufficiently. Fortunately, Second Baptist's Web site provides a virtual tour of their buildings so interested readers can experience it for themselves at www.second.org/global/virtual_tour.aspx.

The megachurch is more than just an ordinary church on steroids. The size of the organization has altered the features and characteristics of these congregations that make them distinctive; they bear little resemblance to smaller traditional congregations. The characteristics described below are shared by many, but not all, of the nation's megachurches. Although these congregations are quite similar in approach and appearance, there is also considerable variety among them.

A megachurch is defined as a Protestant church with an average weekly attendance of 2,000 or more. Although large congregations have existed throughout Christian history, there has been a rapid proliferation of churches with massive attendance since the 1970s. Some researchers suggest therefore that this church form is a unique collective response to distinctive cultural shifts and changes in societal patterns throughout the industrialized urban and suburban areas of the world. Prior to 1970 there were less than a few dozen very large churches, while in the 1970s that number increased to around fifty. By 1990 the total number has increased to roughly 350 and to over 600 by 2000. Five years later it was estimated that there were at least 1,200 megachurches in the United States. As such, these congregations combined represent less than one-half of 1 percent of all the congregations in the country, but possibly account for as many as 4 million weekly attenders, equal to 7 or more percent of all weekly attenders.

Not only have the numbers of churches increased but the size of the largest ones has as well. In 1990, the ten largest megachurches ranged from 7,000 to 12,000 in weekly attendance. Fifteen years later, the largest church, Lakewood Church located in Houston, Texas, claimed an attendance of over 30,000. Dozens more hover near the 20,000 mark. Together these massive congregations collectively generate annual revenue of approximately $6 billion and routinely expend nearly that much. Megachurch pastors dominate religious television and cable channels as well; their books occasionally sell hundreds of thousands of copies (with Rick Warren's *The Purpose-Driven Life* an unbelievable more than 26 million copies), and they are looked upon as major religious celebrities. Most religious persons in the country, regardless of denomination, could name several of these larger-than-life pastors, and many other pastors have sat at their feet in teaching sessions and conferences or have devoured their program materials and sermon tapes. There is no doubt that these mammoth congregations and their leaders have an impact on the American religious landscape in an unmistakable way and their efforts have reformed the shape of religious organizations.

Size is the most immediately apparent characteristic of these congregations; however, the Protestant megachurches in the United States generally share many other traits, ones that are increasingly trickling down to smaller churches. The majority of megachurches (over 60 percent) are located in the southern Sunbelt of the United States, with California, Texas, Georgia, and Florida having the highest concentrations. Most megachurches are located in suburban areas of rapidly growing sprawl cities such as Los Angeles, Dallas, Atlanta, Houston, Orlando, Phoenix, and Seattle. These large churches often occupy prominent land tracts of fifty to one hundred acres near major traffic thoroughfares.

Virtually all these megachurches have a conservative theology, even those within mainline denominations. Not surprisingly, the majority of Protestant megachurches are affiliated with either the Southern Baptist Convention or the Assemblies of God or else are nondenominational. When asked to select a theological label that best fit their congregation, 88 percent of those megachurches surveyed chose a conservative theological identifier. Forty-eight percent claimed to be evangelical, 11 percent chose Pentecostal, another 14 percent selected the label of charismatic, 8 percent simply claimed "traditional," 3 percent said they were seeker, 2 percent said fundamentalist, and 3 percent chose "other." Only 12 percent of those surveyed described their church's theological identity as "moderate," and none claimed to be "liberal."[14]

Megachurches tend to grow to their great size within a very short period of time, usually in less than ten years, and during the tenure of a single senior pastor. One of the largest African American congregations in the country exemplifies this rapid and tremendous growth. In Atlanta, Georgia, World Changers Ministries, under the leadership of Creflo Dollar, began in 1986 with eight members and in ten years time had nearly 8,000 attenders and by 2005 claimed more than 20,000 attenders. In a northern suburb of the same city, Andy Stanley, son of the famous Southern Baptist megachurch pastor Charles Stanley, began a ministry in 1999, and within four years it grew to 5,000. In 2005 this church had over 15,000 attenders. Two other instances include New Hope Christian Fellowship O'ahu led by Wayne Cordeiro, which grew to 10,000 in its first nine years, and Mars Hill Bible Church with Rob Bell as pastor, which began in 1999 and five years later had over 10,000 in attendance. In 1996, T.D. Jakes, one of the most sought-after megachurch pastors, founded the Potter's House as a nondenominational church in the southern sector of Dallas, Texas, with just fifty families. Less than ten years later it had more than 18,000 attenders and well over 30,000 members.

Nearly all megachurch pastors are male and are viewed as having considerable personal charisma. The senior minister often has an authoritative style of preaching and administration and is nearly always the singular dominant leader of the church. Approximately 20 percent of megachurches have been exceptionally large for longer than the tenure of their current minister. Evidence suggests that although these churches often suffer some decrease in attendance with the change of senior ministers, this decline is likely to be reversed within a year. Megachurches can remain vital following a shift in leadership from the founder to his successor.

Supporting these senior pastors are teams of five to twenty-five associate ministers, and often hundreds of full-time staff. Of the 153 megachurches surveyed in the *Megachurches Today* report, the average workforce included thirteen full-time paid ministerial staff persons, and twenty-five full-time paid program staff persons. The average number of volunteers who gave five or more hours a week to the church was 297.[15]

Worship is one of the central drawing cards that anchor the church. The worship service in a megachurch is a high-quality, entertaining, and well-planned production. Given the congregation's size, this service cannot be left to "the flow of the Spirit," especially if there are multiple services on a Sunday morning. As a megachurch grows, worship becomes more professional and polished, but also more planned and structured. The vast majority of these worship experiences, even if they include extensive congregational singing, are focused around the preaching. Megachurch sermons are often inspirational, motivational, and well delivered. The message empowers members with the challenge that everyone has choices, but also that they are responsible for what they choose. The listener is instructed, "You can do it, make a change, and make a difference." Sermons are almost always powerful, practical, down to earth, and relevant.

The leadership of megachurches throughout the country is experimenting with several modes of worship service configuration. Many congregations have gone to multiple services throughout the week. Whether this is owing to space considerations or to an intentional strategy, it has allowed churches to offer a variety of formats and worship styles within one location and to address a diverse set of musical and cultural tastes of their members. It is quite common for a megachurch to have a Friday evening young adults' service with rock music and a laid-back format; likewise, an early Sunday service for older adults might include traditional organ music with hymns and a formal liturgy. Megachurches hold prayer services, Bible studies, singing services, and perhaps healing or charismatic praise services. The diversity offered at a megachurch extends even to the choice of the style, form, and time of a worship event that best fits one's needs and tastes.

Some congregations have modeled their efforts after multi-screen movie theaters and now offer distinctive worship venues at the same time in the central church campus. For example, the main sanctuary of a megachurch might have worship marked by contemporary praise music, with a worship team and a traditional order of worship. Concurrently in the fellowship hall there may be a parallel service for those who prefer a very expressive praise service with guitars for music, a healing time, and a younger set of leaders. In the youth wing, a group of teens might be drinking soda and eating doughnuts while rock or grunge music, lights, and video accompany free-form worship. When it is time for the sermon, however, people in each of the venues simultaneously see the senior minister deliver the sermon on video screen.

This characteristic of choice underlies the efforts of all megachurches. A congregation of thousands encompasses many diverse tastes and interests that must be addressed. Not only does this diversity influence the multiple styles of worship, preaching, and music offered, but it also affects the array of ministries available within a megachurch. In many ways, the megachurch functions like the mall owner providing stability and a common roof under which diverse ministries, seen as specialized boutiques, can operate. In addition, several core ministries, like anchor stores, offer a continuous draw to this spiritual shopping center.[16]

This organizational arrangement allows the larger church programmatic ministry structure to remain unchanged, while the lay-driven specialized offerings rise or fall, depending on changing needs. This system provides the entire membership with a continuous supply of appealing choices that fit their tastes. It also offers highly committed members a choice of places to serve. Finally, it ensures that the church as a whole appears relevant and vibrantly active at a minimum of cost both structurally and financially. This mall-like approach enables the megachurch's leadership to maintain a stable worship environment, yet exhibit flexibility in serving a changing clientele by continuously altering their ministry choices.

Nowhere is the characteristic of programmatic choice more evident, however, than in the range of internal ministries and the diversity of groups offered by megachurches. Some of these ministries are oriented specifically to religious and spiritual issues, such as age-graded Bible studies, prayer groups, new member sessions, and religious education classes. Other ministries focus more on enhancing interpersonal ties and strengthening fellowship and social interaction through home groups, covenant communities, recreational activities, sports events, and organized celebrations. There are always groups that train church volunteers both to assist in the functioning of the church and in the performance of its ministries. Often programs address the physical and psychological well-being of members with health fairs, preventative health clinics, employment support, vocational training, job fairs, various twelve-step-type recovery groups, and individual counseling services. In addition, there are any number of interest groups and activities, from music lessons and choir rehearsals to political action committees and auto repair clinics. Over 40 percent of megachurches support elementary and secondary private schools, with a much larger percentage hosting daycare centers, scout troops, Head-Start programs, and countless teen and young adult activities.[17] These large churches may even provide roller rinks, pools, gymnasiums, racquetball courts, and weight rooms.

Megachurch leadership realizes that given the size of the congregations, members must be strenuously encouraged to become involved in ministries and programs. Hence, 96 percent of congregations surveyed strongly pressure all their participants to volunteer in church ministries. Over three-quarters of churches required new members to take an informational class prior to or after joining. A third of those megachurches surveyed assign a pastor or lay leader to mentor new members as a way to incorporate them into the life of the church. These intentional efforts pay off, given that nearly three-quarters of surveyed megachurches thought that new members were very or quite easily incorporated into the life of their church.[18]

Somewhat surprising for these massive congregations, nearly 50 percent of the *Megachurches Today* respondents said the statement "their church feels like a close-knit family" described them very or quite well. This results in part from the extensive use of small group fellowship in megachurches. Half the surveyed churches say their use of small groups is central to their strategy for Christian nurture and spiritual formation. Another 44 percent have such groups but say these are not central to the church's program. These groups may be formal and highly structured prayer or fellowship cells, or they may be informal and activity driven such as small groupings of parking attendants, police officers, lawyers, or business persons. However, they reflect how members are able to customize their interactions with the church to fit their needs and interests. Over 80 percent say they have an organized program to keep up with members' needs and provide ministry at the neighborhood level.[19] There is no doubt that these organizational forms enhance community and build social networks even as they allow for a tailored spiritual experience based on an individual's needs and desires.

Most megachurches are either newly established churches or older congregations that moved into new buildings prior to their explosive growth. Brand-new congregations clearly have an edge over older churches; they have no existing patterns to revamp. In essence new congregations can choose to adopt whatever organizational model, or for that matter building structure, that works best with the size they anticipate becoming. It is a dynamic evolutionary strategy of growth versus a revisionist effort to expand. This lesson is not lost on many national denominational leaders who have recently engaged in concerted efforts at planting new churches. Given this advantage, it is not surprising that one finds numerous accounts in the early history of many megachurches when they were housed in "temporary structures"—school auditoriums, abandoned shopping centers, and even circus tents, before they considered building their "own" sanctuary.

Perhaps the best-known example of maintaining a fluid congregational form during its most rapid growth period is Rick Warren's Saddleback Community Church. This congregation met in a high school, then in countless satellite locations around the Mission Viejo, California, area, before it built its current sanctuary. However, there are many other examples of this from both the earliest megachurches to the more recent. Many of these churches report that every move to a new structure generated a rapid influx of persons to fill the building to capacity.[20] Megachurches describe this as "living at the limits of capacity." Those surveyed in the *Megachurches Today* report had an average seating of over 2,000, with

40 percent of them claiming to have moved into their building since 1980, and 85 percent of them describing the physical condition of their building as excellent or good. Nevertheless, over half the congregational leaders described their structures as inadequate for their current needs.[21]

A large number of megachurches are beginning to realize that having multiple campuses within one organization has strategic advantages. Churches needing to grow are becoming more intentional about establishing satellite locations at a distance from but still a part of the main congregation. In the 2001 *Megachurches Today* survey over 20 percent of churches said they had branch campuses or satellites of their home church elsewhere in their city.[22] Interest in this strategy has increased dramatically in recent years, with several major megachurches, including Willow Creek, creating multiple campuses. Megachurches draw from an extensive area of any city, with members often driving from forty-five minutes to an hour to attend. This brings many diverse cultural and social groups together under one roof. The challenge facing any megachurch is how to address this diversity of cultural styles or worship tastes. By creating satellite congregations in other parts of the city, the leadership is able to customize the worship style and format and tailor the message to each unique constituency within the congregation. This approach also allows a church to diminish the travel time of a portion of its membership, while also circumventing the need to construct ever larger and more expensive buildings and simultaneously deal with the shortage of land, inadequate parking, and restrictive zoning laws and yet continue to address diverse ministry situations. These efforts have introduced innovations of structure not only into megachurches but also smaller congregations are learning from these distinctive ways of being church.

NEW NETWORKS OF INTERCONNECTION

Given the rapid growth of many megachurches, there is a continual need to consider expansion. Creating multiple sites within one larger organizational entity is one solution to the need for expansion. A second is to emphasize planting new independent congregations that duplicate the mother church's model of ministry, essentially creating a franchise.

Creating daughter churches as independent congregations is a way of continuing to build God's kingdom. The leadership of most megachurches also reaps many other benefits from this strategy. This planting strategy is another effective way to customize the message to a much broader audience. It spreads the reputation and market for a distinct style of ministry, as well as expanding the influence of the mother church. In the *Megachurches Today* survey, nearly 70 percent of churches reported they had planted other congregations, with nearly a third having founded six or more churches. Eighty percent of these megachurches stated that their ancillary congregations had distinctive styles or missions compared to the mother church.[23] Such a strategy also has the added benefit of providing new positions in church leadership for promising young members who otherwise might become disgruntled at the mother church because of the limited number of leadership roles.

Another consequence of planting new congregations is that it creates an informal network of like-minded churches that look to the mother church for inspiration and resources. This "familial network" often shares the tasks of training pastors, developing resources, organizing conferences, and reinforcing a common identity. This model, found most prominently in the Calvary and Vineyard Networks, produces unique relational ties and accountability as if to a parent, with an emphasis on the independence of the offspring. A Calvary Chapel pastor claimed in an interview: "Each church is autonomous and each church is self-governing. It is, however, an association of churches.... It is an association of like-minded fellowships that associate with each other because they have the same philosophy."[24] These familial ties within the informal association are fertile grounds for the recruitment and training of new clergy. Often, promising lay leaders are nurtured into official leadership positions, mentored by existing clergy, and then encouraged to "plant a daughter church," occasionally with the financial support of the "sending" congregation.

Many large megachurches have expanded these "familial networks" to create networks open to all like-minded congregations. This connectional arrangement has been popularized by and heavily employed by megachurches over the past three decades. Certain researchers have interpreted these associations to be proto-denominations, implying that they will eventually organize into forms similar to contemporary national denominations.[25] However, these efforts at creating structures of interconnection are quite disparate from those found in traditional denominations.

Unlike traditional denominations, megachurch networks are loosely structured, de-centralized, nonhierarchical, and lacking bureaucratic structures. They are based on relationships, personal ties, and an affinity of interests and mission purpose. The network offers a skill or a strategy, an expertise or an identity, that other congregations or pastors find helpful. Many networks provide the opportunity to "belong to something bigger," while offering fellowship events, resources, and training as well as some minimal pastoral oversight, accountability, and identification with a successful ministry. A pastor in the Potter's House Network described the relationship this way:

> The Potter's House is more defined as a fellowship—not the denominational or legal ties, but strong relational ties are what binds us, with a common vision or goal. And so, while we as pastors are in essence independent ... yet we're not entirely independent—because of relationship. And so we link together and we keep the contact through laboring together and through area-wide conferences. It's the relationship that brings, if you will, the pressure point of things—I don't mean manipulation.... But as a denomination you have the guidelines and rules that you function under. In the fellowship, it's the relationship—so there are standards, guidelines, principles, ethics.... There are some very distinct relational connections. Typically it's kind of like a family.[26]

The networked relationship is so informal that a church may not know its pastor is associated with one or several networks. These networks are often loose affiliations of like-minded ministers who may or may not formally represent their congregations. The church membership might not even overtly recognize the influence of these networks. Often these connectional influences slip into the congregation unobtrusively through the music, teaching resources, and educational events offered by the network.

Unlike denominations, these networks are not exclusive. They are not restricted only to independent congregations or those churches a megachurch has planted. Any congregation can join one of these networks, even if they are part of an official national denomination. Likewise, networks do not demand singular loyalty. Any congregation may belong to multiple networks at the same time. They can just as easily dissolve a relationship with a network, as the church's needs change. There are few formal ties, with minimal obligations to join and even less sacrifices to disaffiliate.

The proliferation of these networks or associations of churches is almost as significant a change in religious structure and organization as are the megachurches and niche congregations over the past forty years. Twenty percent of megachurches in the 2001 study reported they were part of a network, fellowship, or association of churches. These networks ranged anywhere from fifteen members to several thousand. The median network size was six hundred churches.[27] The majority of networks that have arisen in recent years center on the megachurches but include primarily churches of much smaller size. But megachurches are not the hubs of all networks. Quite a few networks exist that interconnect and support groups of house churches, cell churches, and emerging churches. These connectional structures are developing across multiple forms of religious organizations.

There is no official count of such networks (although some such as the Association of Vineyard Churches, the Association of Calvary Chapels, or the Cooperative Baptist Fellowship occasionally get catalogued in official handbooks of denominations). Nevertheless, hundreds of these information structures exist and include well-known organizations such as the Willow Creek Association and the network of Purpose Driven Churches. A list of networks includes the Fellowship of Christian Assemblies, Morning Star Ministries, Potter's House Fellowship, Victory Outreach Network, International Communion of Charismatic Congregations, the Full Gospel Baptist Fellowship, and countless others.[28]

If these new networks and associations function as quasi-denominations at all, it is certainly with different characterizations of authority and agency than traditional denominations. The dominant basis of authority functioning in these networks is relational—grounded in a unity of vision and purpose—rather than charismatic, bureaucratic, or traditional. If a network member's direction of ministry changes, then, as a Vineyard Association judicatory pastor hypothetically counseled in an interview, "we are not walking together down the same path. I still love you as a brother in Christ, but perhaps you should think about finding a different group as your primary fellowship."[29] Likewise, the agency structure of these networks appears to be relatively informal in organization and minimal in the scope of functions performed. Finally, in nearly every case, the network does not function as the sole source of either religious authority or agency for the associated clergy member or the affiliated local church.

To some extent, these network structures expand the customization of religious identity at the congregational level. The networks allow individual congregations to choose their affiliational ties based on their momentary interests and needs rather than having it be denominationally-fixed, or permanently committed. These churches are able to select with whom they want to associate and to whom they choose to submit and be accountable. It is the same identity pattern, just written at the congregational level.

THE RELIGIOUS MARKETPLACE OF THE FUTURE

The various religious organizational forms addressed in this chapter represent a very small percentage of congregations and active participants in organized American religion. However, this number is continually growing, fueled both by the popularity of these alternatives and by the disillusionment of persons with traditional religious structures. Nevertheless, the likelihood of the religious landscape being filled with megachurches, emerging congregations, and house churches anytime in the first quarter of the twenty-first century is highly unlikely. Much of the impact of religious organizational forms described here is more likely to be felt by a vastly larger percentage of congregations of all theological persuasions in more indirect and subtle ways. The changes to these congregations are effected more slowly over time, as these distinctive organizational practices and habits become integrated into more traditional congregational forms, gradually altering them beyond recognition.

A reflection on the changes that have already diffused into contemporary religious culture and organizational reality is instructive. Changes in casual dress, music style, and worship formats wrought by the charismatic, the Vineyard, and Calvary Chapel movements prove the power of these glacier-like alterations to the religious landscape. One has to wonder what influence the Willow Creek Community Church's network and conferences have had in disseminating the gospel of seeker-sensitive worship to tens of thousands of churches, or how Rick Warren's hugely successful "purpose-driven" campaigns have reconceptualized church organization at the congregational, pastoral, and individual levels. In addition to these influences, many smaller churches have already adopted structural characteristics of megachurches learned at the countless pastors' conferences offered by nearly 50 percent of megachurches.[30]

Careful ethnographic investigations in all sorts of congregations have begun to show that many individuals no longer relate to traditional religious communities as they once did. Melissa Wilcox found this to be the case in her study of lesbians in the Los Angeles area.[31] The persons she interviewed and observed were attenders in a church but not necessarily shaped by the church; rather, their spirituality was rooted in their own quest, in their own exploration of the sacred. A similar dynamic can be seen in broad national studies of U.S. Catholics and their beliefs. Based on their lack of acceptance of papal teachings, these Catholics are in the church but do not embrace the church's pronouncements, traditions, and doctrines.[32] Many studies of members within specific denominations show considerable variation of attitudes, practices, beliefs, morality, and theology. The questions of what counts as a "good" Catholic, Presbyterian, Baptist, or Jew and who decides this are up for grabs.

To complicate this dynamic further, numerous other venues for spiritual development outside of traditional religious organizations abound. These parachurch realities offer ways for persons to structure their personal quest for the Spirit without necessarily subscribing to a larger religious tradition. Groups as diverse as the Women's Leadership Institute at Hartford Seminary and the "Gospel Hour" drag show in a gay bar in Atlanta, Sunday morning Gospel brunches in the suburbs of several Southern cities, or retreat centers, labyrinths, and Tai Chi exercises in public parks, spiritual weight loss clinics, even twelve-step programs grounded in a spirituality based on one's own understanding of a higher power all contribute to a radical reworking of religious organizational life beyond just those discussed in this chapter.

It could be argued that the large percentage of persons who claim a spiritual faith, even a religious tradition, and yet very seldom attend an organized faith community are essentially the masters of their own vessels. They implicitly follow their horoscope, learn "truth" from *The Da Vinci Code*, hold to a "prosperity gospel" taught by television preachers, practice yoga, explore Native American spirituality at Borders, burn incense, wear crystals, and chat in the interfaith rooms on Beliefnet. These same folks might even be found visiting a local megachurch or dropping in on a service at an emerging congregation. It is more likely, however, they are among the millions of anonymous believers who spend most Sundays worshipping at flea markets and malls, at youth soccer and baseball games, or in a local running and hiking trail communing with nature.

Societal and cultural changes took place in the decades of the 1950s through the 1970s that set in motion radical alterations to our understanding of spirituality and religion. These shifts began to separate personal beliefs and attitudes about faith from customary organizational forms, historic traditions, and established religious authorities. Over time religious organizations evolved or were created that embody an approach to the spiritual life, either niche- or mall-like in reality, that caters to the individual as captain of his or her own spiritual ship.

Some of the more obvious organizational forms have been discussed in this chapter, but these house churches, emerging congregations, and megachurches with cell groups and multiple venue worship services only scratch the surface of the diversity. Internet virtual communities are an example of this variety but other forms of spiritual organizations hinted at above abound and remain to be researched fully.

To identify and explore this spirituality variety we must broaden our conceptual definition of what constitutes a religious organization. Traditional congregational organizations will continue to exist as a path for pursuing spirituality but, as Robert Wuthnow suggests, "the congregation is less aptly characterized as a safe haven; rather, it functions as a supplier of spiritual goods and services."[33] However, all of this entails reversing our approach to understanding a life of faith. Religion is no longer only that which is being disseminated from "on high," coming down the mountain or through a denominational chain of command, to dwell among the people. Spiritually in the United States, individuals are now scaling the mountain on their own quest for the gods. At times they are following well-worn organizational paths, but more often they are forging their own trails with their own unique goals in mind.

NOTES

1. See various descriptions of the changes in religious identity and the corresponding cultural shifts in the works of Robert Wuthnow, *The Restructuring of American Religion: Society and Faith since World War II* (Princeton, NJ: Princeton University Press, 1988); Dean Hoge, Benton Johnson, and Donald Luidens, *Vanishing Boundaries: The Religion of Mainline Protestant Baby Boomers* (Louisville, KY: Westminster John Knox, 1994); and Wade Clark Roof, *A Generation of Seekers: The Spiritual Journeys of the Baby Boom Generation* (San Francisco: HarperSanFrancisco, 1993); and idem, *Spiritual Marketplace: Baby Boomers and the Remaking of American Religion* (Princeton, NJ: Princeton University Press, 1999).

2. Wade Clark Roof and William McKinney, *American Mainline Religion* (New Brunswick, NJ: Rutgers University Press, 1987), 57, indicate that as many as 80 percent of those asked responded in this manner.

3. The religious faith of one interviewee, Sheila, in Robert Bellah, Richard Madsen, Ann Swidler, and Stephen M. Tipton, eds., *Habits of the Heart: Individualism and Commitment in American Life* (Berkeley: University of California Press, 1985), named her religion after herself, claiming it was her own private faith.

4. Wuthnow, 9–10.

5. The historical use of house church gatherings is traced by C. Kirk Hadaway, Francis M. Dubose, and Stuart A. Wright, *Home Cell Groups and House Churches* (Nashville, TN: Broadman, 1987).

6. Ibid., 109.

7. See Stephen Warner, *New Wine in Old Wineskins: Evangelicals and Liberals in a Small-Town Church* (Berkeley: University of California, 1988).

8. See the interview with Brian McLaren in Andy Crouch, "The Emergent Mystique," *Christianity Today* (November 2004), at www.christianitytoday.com/ct/2004/011/12.36.html, accessed October 15, 2005.

9. This quote is part of an interview with Rob Bell in ibid. This *Christianity Today* article offers an excellent overview of the emerging church movement, as does Brian McLaren's commentary on this article at http://www.anewkindofchristian.com/archives/000271.html, accessed October 15, 2005.

10. Kim Lawton, "The Emerging Church," *Religion and Ethics Newsweekly* (July 8 and 15, 2005), episodes 845–46, available at www.pbs.org/wnet/religionandethics/week845/cover.html, accessed October 25, 2005. Interviews with several emerging church participants done by this reporter shed light into why these churches are so popular.

11. Ibid. An interesting summary of characteristics based on how one person within the emerging church envisions the movement to be can be found at www.emergingchurch.info/reflection/stevetaylor/index.htm, accessed October 25, 2005. Also see the many works of Brian McLaren. Another place to uncover information about the movement is, not surprisingly, on the Internet at sites such as www.emergingchurch.info, www.emergentvillage.com, www.anewkindofchristian.com, and www.theooze.com.

12. Michael Moynagh, "How Is Emerging Church Different?" (November 2004), at www.emergingchurch.info/reflection/michaelmoynagh/index.htm, accessed November 7, 2005.

13. Crouch, "Emergent Mystique."

14. Scott Thumma, *Megachurches Today: Summary of Data from the Faith Communities Today Project*, http://hirr.hartsem.edu/org/faith_megachurches_FACTsummary.html, accessed October 20, 2005.

15. Ibid.

16. Nancy Eiesland, *A Particular Place: Urban Restructuring and Religious Ecology in a Southern Exurb* (New Brunswick, NJ: Rutgers University Press, 2000).

17. Thumma, *Megachurches Today.*

18. Ibid.

19. Ibid.

20. Donald E. Miller, *Reinventing American Protestantism: Christianity in the New Millennium* (Berkeley: University of California Press, 1997), 168.

21. Thumma, *Megachurches Today.*

22. Ibid.

23. Ibid.

24. Scott Thumma, "What God Makes Free is Free Indeed: Nondenominational Church Identity and its Networks of Support," http://hirr.hartsem.edu/bookshelf/thumma_article5.html, accessed October 15, 2005.

25. Les Parrott and Dale Robin Perrin, "The New Denominations?" *Christianity Today* 34 (March 11): 29–33.

26. Thumma, "What God Makes Free."

27. Thumma, *Megachurches Today.*

28. Miller, *Reinventing American Protestantism*, begins to explore the nature of the Calvary Chapel, Hope Chapel, and Vineyard Associations. Les Parrott and Dale Robin Perrin, "The New Denominations?" is still the best overview of these quasi-denominational structures.

29. Thumma, "What God Makes Free."

30. Thumma, *Megachurches Today.*

31. Melissa M. Wilcox, *Coming Out in Christianity: Religion, Identity, and Community* (Bloomington: Indiana University Press, 2003).

32. William V. D'Antonio, James D. Davidson, Dean R. Hoge, and Katherine Meyer, *American Catholics: Gender, Generation, and Commitment* (Lanham, MD: AltaMira, 2001).

33. Robert Wuthnow, *After Heaven: Spirituality in America since the 1950s* (Berkeley: University of California Press, 1998), 15.

SUGGESTIONS FOR FURTHER READING

Bass, Diana Butler. *The Practicing Congregation: Imagining a New Old Church.* Washington, DC: Alban Institute, 2004.

Loveland, Anne C., and Otis B. Wheeler. *From Meetinghouse to Megachurch: A Material and Cultural History.* Columbia: University of Missouri Press, 2003.

Miller, Donald E. *Reinventing American Protestantism: Christianity in the New Millennium.* Berkeley: University of California Press, 1997.

Sargeant, Kimon. *Seeker Churches: Promoting Traditional Religion in a Nontraditional Way.* New Brunswick, NJ: Rutgers University Press, 2000.

Sweet, Leonard, ed. *The Church in Emerging Culture: Five Perspectives.* Grand Rapids, MI: Zondervan, 2003.

CHAPTER 11

In Search of the Promised Land: Post–Civil Rights Trends in African American Religion

Stephen C. Finley and Torin D. Alexander

Several significant institutional and noninstitutional trends have presented themselves in African American religion as of the post–civil rights era. Africentrism, for example, can be seen in the black church and the Nation of Islam, two religious movements that distinguished themselves as dominant African American religious expressions during and after the civil rights movement. As a result, both of these movements command significant attention in order to elucidate their changing dynamics.

On the one hand, the black church, for instance, has experienced an increase in the numbers of megachurches and a proliferation of evangelical movements, which tend to be politically conservative and socially conservative with regard to issues of sexuality, cultural/racial identity, and gender. Another important trend in the black church is the growing proportion of female members, though women still face sexism and discrimination when it comes to positions of power and leadership. On the other hand, the Nation of Islam has undergone considerable changes in this era regarding its identity, since many organizations now claim the name "Nation of Islam." Then, too, the Nation of Islam has evolved into various groups with differing theological and social agendas. In addition to the Nation of Islam, however, there have been numerous other movements, many of which resulted in the emergence of black religions that have more recently gained visibility. Many of these groups have long existed in black communities and reflect religious ideas and sentiments that have long existed in America, rather than "new" religious movements literally. At the same time, we want to be careful not to privilege one movement over another by implying that one development exists only in relation to another. Because of this, this chapter will discuss numerous traditions.

Finally, this chapter will offer an overview of academic developments in the study of black religion and explore the ways in which black intellectual trends are impacted and challenged by developments in African American religion and changing historical and cultural realities. This chapter will understand "black or African American religion" as orientation, or the ways in which African Americans make sense of their world. This orientation is characterized by a quest or a push for more fullness in life, to be known and find meaning over a variety of life factors and indicators. Anthony Pinn suggests that this push and search for meaning comprise the core characteristic of African American religion.[1] This central feature is the impetus for black religion, in its various forms including the form most studied, namely the black church.

THE BLACK CHURCH: NATURE AND DEVELOPMENTS

For the most part, the study of religion and religious experience in African American communities has revolved around the study of the black church, but what is meant by the term "black church"? Narrowly construed, the nomenclature "black church" refers to such historic black denominations as the African Methodist Episcopal Church, the African Methodist Episcopal Zion Church, the Colored (Christian) Methodist Episcopal Church, the National Baptist Convention, USA, Inc., the National Baptist Convention of America, the Progressive National Baptist Convention, and the Church of God in Christ. However, as noted by C. Eric Lincoln and Lawrence H. Mamiya in their monumental work, *The Black Church in the African American Experience*, the black church is also a kind of sociological and theological shorthand for the pluralism of black Christian churches in the United States.[2] Put in a slightly different fashion, the black church might be conceived of as a heuristic category that assists in discussing African American churches as a whole, while in reality they defy phenomenological objectification.

In many respects, that the black church garners so much attention is not that odd, for without question the black church has been the dominant and most significant historical, cultural, and social expression of the religious consciousness of African American people. Thus, it is often assumed, in the words of Joseph R. Washington, Jr.:

> In the beginning was the black church, and the black church was the black community. The black church was in the beginning with the black people; all things were made through the black church, and without the black church was not anything made that was made. In the church was life, and the life was the light of black people. The black church still shines in the darkness, and the darkness has not overcome it.[3]

Yet, as a historical, cultural, and social representation of African Americans, the black church has undergone substantive and in some instances radical changes and transformation in the post–civil rights era as has the African American community. Some of the most significant of these developments would include the rise of the black megachurch; the influence of white evangelicalism and conservative Christianity on African American churches and their resultant changes with respect to issues of sexuality, gender, cultural/racial identity, and politics; and finally the position of women in the black churches. We shall examine each.

Probably the most definitive study of the megachurch phenomenon has been done by Scott Thumma of the Hartford Institute for Religion Research. Thumma and the institute define a megachurch as a non-Roman Catholic congregation that has two thousand or more attenders per week, with such attendance being reached over a relatively short period of time. This last characteristic is significant, notes Thumma, for historically there have always been large churches. The megachurch, however, constitutes a new social, cultural, and "spiritual" organization that has developed only in the last thirty years.

Moreover, these congregations share a number of significant characteristics. First, they tend to be geographically situated in the southern and western regions of the United States. In part, this results from the availability of resources necessary for such churches, like large tracts of land for their substantial campuses. Second, these churches are likely to be theologically conservative, adhering strictly and rigidly to defined sets of dogma such as biblical inerrancy and Christian exceptionalism. Third, the dominant model of leadership is highly authoritarian and charisma driven. Fourth, they offer a diverse array of ministries to meet the needs of a broad range of potential attenders. Finally, these churches, though in many instances retaining some form of denominational connection, are essentially autonomous entities, that in many respects are organized along the lines of modern corporations with respect to their technological sophistication and structural diversification in order to effect with marketing, promotion, publishing, and recording efficiently.

This trend has manifested itself in several African American congregations. As stated above, while there have been African American churches with memberships in the thousands historically, particularly in metropolitan areas with large African American populations, there has been an eruption of mega-congregations of rather recent vintage. Though the Hartford Institute data are not broken down by race, the names of the pastors and their congregations are quite well known to many in the African American community. A few of those included in the Hartford database with average weekly attendance of more than ten thousand include T.D. Jakes's Potter's House in Dallas, Texas; Creflo Dollar's World Changers Ministries in College Park, Georgia; Eddie L. Long's New Birth Missionary Baptist Church in Decatur, Georgia; and Fred Price's Crenshaw Christian Center in Los Angeles, California.

In the wake of the civil rights movement in the 1960s, many came to view the black church as a liberal, even progressive, institution. In reality, however, only a minority of black clergy and black congregations were energetically engaged in the civil rights movement. One need only recall that the Progressive National Baptist Convention came into existence when the National Baptist Convention, USA, Inc. rejected the civil rights agenda, as well as clergy associated with it such as Gardner C. Taylor and Martin

Luther King, Jr. As Gayraud S. Wilmore notes in *Black Religion and Black Radicalism*, the black church had for the most part lost its radical orientation during the early portion of the twentieth century.[4] The civil rights movement saw radicalism resurrected only partially, and only for a limited period of time. A majority of the black church would embrace a social posture with an emphasis on self-preservation, often through assimilation of what was deemed socially acceptable and normative (read: "white norms"). This was manifest as a kind of social conservatism.

In the decades immediately following the 1960s, some African Americans would experience previously unknown social and professional success. This is not to imply that racism was eradicated. It persisted, often in more subtle, although perhaps no less detrimental, forms. Yet, there would develop a new black middle-class who often found greater commonalities with their white peers than poorer members of the African American community. Many of these African Americans, desiring perhaps to be recognized for their accomplishments, began to promote the American myths of meritocracy and rugged individualism. Representatives of such an orientation (e.g., Walter E. Williams, Thomas Sowell, Shelby Steele, and Glen Loury) would in fact begin to call into question the effectiveness of various policies such as affirmative action and programs such as welfare. It is important to note, however, that such transitions did not take place in a vacuum. Indeed, the late 1970s and 1980s would see a national turn to the political right, and the visibility of individuals such as Clarence Thomas, Condoleezza Rice, Colin Powell, and Alan Keyes marked the inclusion of African Americans in the conservative movement.

This period would also see a significant transformation for the American religious landscape. The once prominent mainline (liberal) Protestant denominations (American Baptist Churches, USA; Presbyterian Church, USA; United Methodist Church; United Church of Christ; Evangelical Lutheran Church in America; and the Episcopal Church) would experience significant decline in their memberships while denominations that are more conservative were experiencing increases.[5] With growth in numbers and growth in influence, these new style conservative and evangelical Christians, unlike their early twentieth century predecessors, articulated a vision of national reform and redemption. In such a context, they began to reach out to the black church as allies in their mission. As mentioned earlier, there was a strong tradition of social conservatism within the black church. Further, in keeping with the changing worldview and life situation of their congregants, many black churches had come to emphasize issues of personal piety and responsibility over expressions of faith associated with social justice. White conservative Christians, perhaps for the first time, identified shared values with African American Christians.

The 1990s would see movements such as the Promise Keepers and the Christian Coalition express commitments to racial reconciliation and denominations such as the Southern Baptist Convention publicly repent for slavery and "past racism." Hence, by the early twenty-first century, many black churches and white conservative congregations find common cause in matters of faith and politics.

As noted by various African American scholars, the black church, as most churches in America, has historically had a rather parochial view with respect to sexuality. Although there have always been gay and lesbian members within these institutions, even in positions of leadership, they were often tolerated as part of de facto "don't ask, don't tell" policies. This peace, however, would be disrupted with the sexual revolution of the 1960s and 1970s. While elements of American youth culture embraced "free love," thanks to the introduction of the pill, other marginalized communities and constituencies, taking inspiration from the black civil rights movement, also began to seek redress for their omission with respect to equality under the law. Thus was born the modern women's movement that included the campaign for women's reproductive rights, and the gay, lesbian, bisexual, and transgender movement.

As with the rest of the country, many in the black community felt that such groups were indicative of moral decay. Compounding and potentially exacerbating this impression in the African American community was a perceived growth in single-parent homes headed by females, given credence in part by the now famous Moynihan report, "The Negro Family: The Case For National Action." Although there were those who offered etiological analyses based on social and structural factors such as economic and educational opportunities, drugs, and the growing number of black males being incarcerated, many simply saw this as a breakdown of values.

Though mainline denominations have taken steps toward greater inclusion and affirmation with respect to sexuality within Christian churches as well as the body politic, many African American clergy have joined their conservative white counterparts in opposition to such trends. In March 2004, for example, several dozen black clergy in Atlanta, Georgia, publicly voiced their opposition to gay marriage and pressed the legislature for a constitutional ban on the practice.[6]

As previously mentioned, the identification of middle-class African Americans with their white peers as opposed to members of their racial ethnic group has led to new issues with respect to identity and loyalties. Many persons of color, not only African Americans, have expressed a desire to be viewed simply as Americans, taking literally Martin Luther King, Jr.'s famous words admonishing that people be judged not by the color of their skin, but by the content of their character. This has resulted in a tendency by some African Americans to shun notions of identity predicated on concepts of race or ethnicity, preferring rather to be identified with the larger common culture and nation.

Also, as noted, many of these positions have led to greater cooperation among conservative white politicos and members of the black community. For example, several high-profile African American clergy were visible participants in support of Republican congressional and presidential candidacies in the 2000, 2002, and 2004 campaigns. In addition to so-called issues of morality, such as same-sex marriage, abortion, or the president's faith-based initiatives funding, prominent black clergy have taken stands in favor of tax cuts, the ending of affirmative action, and appointment of conservative nominees to the federal courts, including the Supreme Court.

Walk into almost any predominantly African American church in recent years and one will find the majority of the attenders are female. Indeed, women have always had a significant presence within the black church. Often referred to as the backbone, the heart, or the foundation of the institution, not until fairly recently have significant numbers of them acquired access to ecclesiastical positions of power.

The first black denomination to ordain a woman to the ministry officially was the African Methodist Episcopal Zion Church (AME). As noted by Lincoln and Mamiya, Bishop James Walker Hood ordained Julia A. Foote a "deacon" in 1894. A year later, Mary J. Small was ordained a deacon by Bishop Alexander Walters. Small would be the first woman ordained an elder in 1898, to be followed by Foote in 1900. The AME church would not bestow this status on women again until 1948, followed by the Colored Methodist Episcopal (CME) church in 1954.[7]

One might expect, given the polity of Baptist churches—namely the autonomy of the local church—that there would be more opportunities for formal leadership by women. Unfortunately, although women fulfilled certain functions and offices, such as deaconesses and heads of Christian education and mission boards, to a large extent the road to the pastorate has remained closed. Of the three major black Baptist denominations, women have fared only marginally better in this regard among Progressive National Baptists than others.

With respect to the black Pentecostal tradition, however, one finds a great variety of orientations with respect to women and the church. By far the largest denomination associated with this tradition, the Church of God in Christ, maintains a firm stance opposed to the ordination of women. Unlike Baptist and Methodist conventions, however, many women have founded their own Pentecostal and Holiness congregations. Following the examples of such charismatic women pastors of the 1930s and 1940s such as Elder Lucy Smith, initiator of the All Nations Pentecostal Church in Chicago, and Bishop Ida Robinson, founder of Mount Sinai Holy Church of America, Inc. in Philadelphia,[8] are women such as Rev. Dr. Barbara L. King of Hillside International Truth Center in Atlanta and Rev. Johnnie Colemon of the Christ Universal Temple in Chicago.

The result of this state of affairs with respect to the historic black denominations has been that in 1990 females constituted only an estimated 5 percent of black clergy. Further, the vast majority of these likely served small storefront, independent, and Pentecostal/Holiness churches. Lincoln and Mamiya did note, nevertheless, a 240 percent increase in the number of women entering the professional ministry between 1930 and 1980.[9] Even more interesting is the set of data collected by Delores Carpenter that documents an increase in the number of black females graduating from accredited theological programs increasing some 676 percent between 1972 and 1984.[10]

As Lincoln and Mamiya note from Carpenter's study, such numbers have led to black women seeking ordination and leadership positions among the white mainline Protestant churches. More than 50 percent of the African American women in Carpenter's sample made just such a choice because of greater receptivity. Those seeking confirmation of such openness would no doubt point to the consecration of an African American woman, Leontine Kelly, in 1984 as a bishop of the United Methodist Church, a scant four years after the denomination ordained Marjorie Swank Matthews as the first female bishop. In 1988, an African American woman, Barbara Harris, was ordained a bishop in the Episcopal Church.

By the beginning of the twenty-first century, however, there were indications of greater receptivity to women in authority within historically black denominations and religious associations. In July 2000, the AME church elected Vashti McKenzie as its first female bishop. Four years later, AME called as presiding prelates Carolyn Tyler Guidry for the Sixteenth Episcopal District and Sarah Frances Davis for the Eighteenth Episcopal District. In addition, 2002 witnessed the election of Dr. Suzan Johnson Cook as the first female president of the Hampton Ministers' Conference, a national clergy conference held annually at Hampton University in Virginia.

THE NATION OF ISLAM

In addition to the black church, the Nation of Islam (NOI), which had established itself as a major black religious institution prior to the civil rights movement under the leadership of its founder, the Honorable Elijah Muhammad, became more well known to the American public. Those who study history in America or who are familiar with black popular culture would have surely heard of the iconic Malcolm X, the most famous member of the Nation during his time. They may also be familiar with other famous members of the NOI such as the former heavyweight champion of the world, Muhammad Ali, or the current leader of the NOI, Louis Farrakhan. Even Michael Jackson claimed to have converted to the NOI during his child molestation case of 1994. Nonetheless, prior to the civil rights movement it is appropriate to speak of the Nation of Islam as a single organization. Afterwards, in particular after the death of its founder the Honorable Elijah Muhammad, one has to speak properly of the "Nations" of Islam. Perhaps a brief historical sketch will contextualize and further elucidate this discussion.

Discussion of the founding of the NOI requires a look beyond Elijah Muhammad to engage the antecedents of the movement. A good place to begin is with Noble Drew Ali, the founder of the Moorish Holy Temple of Science, later changed to Moorish Science Temple of America (MSTA), since "it was the first mass religious movement in the history of Islam in America," according to Richard Brent Turner.[11] Born Timothy Drew in North Carolina in 1886, Noble Drew Ali founded the MSTA in Newark, New Jersey, in 1913. Once a Baptist minister, Drew had attempted to build a militant black Baptist movement, but it was short lived.

Turning his attention to "Islam," he established the MSTA based on the authority that he derived from several alleged experiences. One claim, for example, maintains that he made a pilgrimage to Morocco where he received a mission from the king of Morocco to teach Islam to "Negroes" in the United States. Accordingly, the king bestowed upon him the name "Ali," an Arabic word that means "above" or "over" as in rank. Another legend claims that Drew had to pass a test to prove that he was a prophet. The test required him to find his way out of a labyrinth in the pyramids of Egypt, a test which he apparently passed. Drew Ali died in 1929, either from police brutality or by the hands of those who were loyal to his rival within the MSTA.

The next major figure in NOI history is Master Fard Muhammad, also known as W.D. Fard. Fard claimed to be a reincarnation of Noble Drew Ali, as did John Givens-El. Whether or not Master Fard was a member of the MSTA is a disputed point. Notwithstanding, those who followed him would become the NOI in 1930, and those who followed Givens-El became the present-day MSTA. Master Fard's race or ethnicity was ambiguous. Some thought he was Arab, since he claimed to have been born in Mecca on February 26, 1877. He also claimed to be of royal ancestry as a descendent of the tribe of "Kareish," the same tribe as the Prophet Muhammad, the founder of Islam. He reportedly sold silks and performed magic tricks in Detroit, Michigan, teaching African Americans there about their true identity. Reportedly, one such magical feat was when he told several of his followers to take strands of their hair and place them in a pile. Master Fard then pulled a single strand of hair from his head and with it lifted the entire pile of hair belonging to his followers. Master Fard continued to build a following, and in 1931 the burgeoning movement apparently attracted Elijah Muhammad, then Elijah (or Eli) Poole, to one of his religious services.

Elijah Muhammad was born in Sanderville, Georgia, in October 1897. Like Timothy Drew, he was formerly a Baptist minister. He became one of Fard's star disciples. In 1932, however, he left Master Fard in Detroit in order to begin NOI Temple #2 in Chicago, Illinois, the location of the present international headquarters of the NOI. In 1933, Fard was ordered out of Detroit by the authorities and migrated to Temple #2 in Chicago, where he was again arrested by authorities there. Fard subsequently withdrew from the movement and eventually disappeared. Muhammad began to teach his followers that Master Fard was God in person and that his disappearance was due to his ascension to the mother ship, literally a space ship, from which he would exact judgment and retribution on the devil (whites). Henceforth, Muhammad assumed absolute authority in the NOI.

The NOI favored well under Muhammad's leadership from 1933 through 1975. The NOI started temples and study groups all over the country. They also built a sizable economic empire, including property, publications, bakeries, grocery stores, and restaurants. Yet, the group was largely unknown to the American public until the 1960s. It was then that they became known primarily through the public image of Malcolm X and his responses to the civil rights movement and to Martin Luther King, Jr., and by the very public schism between Malcolm and Mr. Muhammad in 1964. On the surface, the schism erupted over Muhammad's alleged sexual improprieties with several of his secretaries, while at the same time demanding sexual purity and marital fidelity of NOI members.

The reality may have been, however, that Malcolm X was becoming increasingly popular, both in the NOI and in the American media, and the NOI was flourishing as a result. Although Malcolm was totally loyal to Muhammad by most accounts, others in the NOI were perhaps jealous of his standing and his relationship with Muhammad. Many of them seemingly instigated the division between the two of them, causing Mr. Muhammad to be suspicious of Malcolm, who was the most likely NOI minister to succeed Muhammad as the leader of the group. Instead, Louis Abdul Farrakhan would succeed Malcolm X as the national minister of the NOI but not as leader of the NOI initially.

Malcolm's expulsion and secession from the NOI and his later assassination would pave the way for an intense struggle for power as Elijah Muhammad grew in age. This struggle for power would culminate in 1975 when Muhammad died, at which time the most crucial post–civil rights developments within the NOI occurred. Initially, Muhammad's son, Warith Deen Muhammed, would take over as the leader of the NOI, but almost immediately he sought to move the NOI toward the global community of "orthodox" Islam. Born Wallace D. Muhammad, Imam Warith D. Muhammed changed the name of the NOI to the World Community of Al-Islam in the West, signifying a movement away from the separatist and black nationalist program of the NOI. Imam Muhammed's loyalty to the NOI was suspect earlier, which resulted in his excommunication for philosophical, theological, and ideological reasons.[12] He had returned to the NOI perhaps because of the threat of violence and retribution against prominent members who apostatized. Now, given the opportunity to lead the group, he wasted no time disbanding significant NOI organizations and rituals. For example, he dissolved the Fruit of Islam, the security auxiliary, and he discontinued prominent rituals like the dress codes in which the men of the NOI wore bowties.

"NATIONS" OF ISLAM

In 1977, tension from conflicting perspectives came to a boil, tension that had existed between Elijah Muhammad and his son Warith concerning the "true" nature of Islam. Previously, Warith had secretly confided in Malcolm X about his misgivings, but he had no power to institute any of his convictions. Now that his father was dead, he had the freedom to move on his divergences and to deconstruct the ideological foundations of the Nation. Factions that had existed in the NOI prior to the death of Muhammad erupted, claiming that Imam Warith Deen Muhammed had strayed from the true teachings of his father, Elijah Muhammad. The result was the splintering of the movement in 1977 into three distinct and separate entities, each claiming the legacy of Elijah Muhammad. The three Nations of Islam would be led by Silias Muhammad, John Muhammad (son of Elijah Muhammad), and Louis Farrakhan. Clifton E. Marsh intimates that Farrakhan was excommunicated from Warith Deen Muhammed's group in 1977.[13] The NOI group led by Farrakhan would be the movement that most would associate with the NOI, since it seemed to be the largest and most well known, although scholars have been unable to quantify its membership. Then, too, Farrakhan continued to teach the racial consciousness and black economic uplift that had characterized Elijah Muhammad's movement.

Farrakhan's NOI is one that has itself undergone an evolution. First, Farrakhan reinstituted the Fruit of Islam and the dress codes and continued to build the NOI economically. Second, since the 1990s, the NOI has engaged in active conversation with Arabs and others of the world Sunni community. In fact, Mohammar Khadafi, the Libyan president, reportedly offered as much as a billion dollars to Louis Farrakhan and the NOI to start an independent bank for African Americans, which outraged the U.S. government. Furthermore, Farrakhan has traveled the world, meeting with such Arab leaders as Saddam Hussein of Iraq. Likewise, trends since the 1980s have brought the NOI in conversation with other Muslim leaders globally.

Perhaps more than anything else, the Million Man March of 1995 solidified Farrakhan's place as a global figure and leader as he spoke of an ideal world community made up of people of all colors. But such movement toward the ideals of a world community and Sunni Islam has had other consequences. For instance, Farrakhan has had to downplay very skillfully the doctrines of Elijah Muhammad and Master Fard Muhammad, whose legacy he claims. He has had to reinterpret or eschew the notion that white people are the devil collectively or the idea that Elijah Muhammad and Fard Muhammad are in the mother ship, literally a UFO, preparing to judge the world in a cataclysmic and violent intervention that is meant to punish the devil for its treatment of African Americans. Moreover, women's role in the NOI has become much more significant, evidenced by the fact that women are allowed to be temple ministers and members of the national leadership.

While Farrakhan and the NOI have become more liberal and more global in perspective, this has not guaranteed that the movement would gain mainstream or mass appeal. Sensing Farrakhan's liberal turn, the NOI under the leadership of Silis Muhammad and the United NOI of Kansas City, Missouri, led by Royall E. Jenkins, for instance, have taken a critical stance against Farrakhan, maintaining that he has distorted the teachings of the Honorable Elijah Muhammad and that their movements represent a more pure adherence to his doctrine. To our understanding, Royall of the United NOI is said to be the re-embodiment of Master Fard Muhammad, and he and his followers consider him to be "Allah in Person," a title that Elijah Muhammad bestowed upon Fard Muhammad after Fard's "disappearance." In other words, Royall is to the United NOI what Master Fard was to the NOI under Elijah Muhammad.

Likewise, one of the more interesting groups is a small group of individuals who meet around the Coalition for the Remembrance of Elijah (C.R.O.E.) in Chicago. All of these Muslims continue to consider themselves disciples of Elijah Muhammad but have no allegiance to Farrakhan or any other NOI mosque. Led by Munir Muhammad, they hold periodic religious meetings at C.R.O.E. headquarters and perpetuate the legacy of

Elijah Muhammad through television programs, videos, publications, and public education sessions, all of which they produce. C.R.O.E., Silis Muhammad's NOI, and the United NOI are all offshoots of Elijah Muhammad's NOI; however, they are separate entities from the NOI led by Farrakhan. On the other hand, at least two distinct movements broke away directly from Farrakhan's NOI, namely, the Five Percent NOI, lead by Clarence 13X and the NOI of Baltimore, Maryland, headed by Emmanuel A. Muhammad.

The direction the NOI will take under Louis Farrakhan seems uncertain. Nevertheless, four patterns seem apparent. First, the NOI is on the decline in terms of its membership. Second, the movement is acquiring features of "orthodox" Islam in terms of its rituals, like the practice of observing Ramadan and its shift toward the centrality and importance of the Five Pillars of Islam as a defining factor in what makes it "Islamic." The Five Pillars of Islam are the core practices of Islam, namely, the shahada, or the confession of faith in Allah as the only God; the Salat, or the obligatory daily prayers; the Zakat, or monetary offerings to the poor; observing Ramadan, or the month of fasting that celebrates the "revelation" of the Qur'an; and the Hajj, or the pilgrimage to Mecca that every able-bodied Muslim is required to make once. The NOI has evidenced each of these apparently except the Hajj.

Third, Farrakhan has somewhat relaxed the strongly moralistic interdictions of Elijah Muhammad, and, fourth, women continue to be more prominent in the movement. The last results perhaps from changes in the composition of NOI membership; it has proportionately more female and middle-class members than it did under Muhammad. Other factions of the NOI continue to exist, but with limited success in terms of membership and public recognition. It should be noted, however, that although this chapter describes developments in African American religion, many of the religious traditions of African Americans have been present in black culture for centuries. To that end, that numerous Africans sold into slavery in America were already Muslim has been well documented. The same has been argued regarding the Hebrews.

"NEW" BLACK RELIGIOUS MOVEMENTS

As stated earlier, although the dominant religious institutions in the African American community are the black church and the Nation of Islam, African Americans have founded and been drawn to a host of sectarian movements. Many of these groups rely heavily on iconic use of biblical images and motifs such as Ethiopia, Egypt, Exodus, and the Promised Land.[14]

Surprising numbers of these groups would choose to build upon the African American identification with Israel by founding Jewish or Hebrew religions.[15] Early expressions of this religious impulse would be associated with the likes of William Saunders Crowdy (1847–1908), founder of the Church of God and Saints of Christ, and Prophet (Rabbi) F.S. Cherry, founder of the Church of God in Philadelphia. Using the Exodus motif,

Crowdy consolidated elements of Judaism and Christianity and then infused them with a black nationalism.[16] Conversely, Cherry, relying solely on the Hebrew Bible and the Talmud, taught that God and Christ were black, that African Americans were the descendants of Jacob, and that white Jews were the descendants of Esau.[17]

Contemporary "Jewish" groups include the Original Hebrew Nation, a sect that emerged in Chicago in the mid-1960s. Under the leadership of one of its elders, Ben Ammi Carter, several hundred members migrated to Liberia in 1968. After some two years, a remnant undertook a second migration to Israel. The group is now officially known as the Original African Hebrew Israelite Nation of Jerusalem.[18]

In addition, the Nation of Yahweh, also called the Hebrew Israelites or the Followers of Yahweh, was founded in the 1970s by Yahweh ben Yahweh, who was born Hulon Mitchell, Jr. Yahweh ben Yahweh teaches that there is one God, whose name is Yahweh and who is black. As his adopted name would suggest, Yahweh ben Yahweh proclaims that he is the son of God, who has been sent to save and deliver the black people of America. Black people are considered to be the true lost tribe of Judah.

Over the last several decades, there appears to be a move toward greater unity among African American Jewish and Hebrew communities in the form of the International Israelite Board of Rabbis. This organization has as its express mission the strengthening of relations among the rabbinic sects that bear the closest resemblance to conventional expressions of Judaism, the Karaites or "Torah Only" groups, and finally the Messianic communities, which believe that Jesus is the messiah and include the New Testament in their religious canon.[19]

Similar in genre to the Hebrew groups is the Pan-African Orthodox Church (PAOCC). The PAOCC in 1953 began as a socially and racially conscious, African American religious institution under the name, the Shrine of the Black Madonna. The first shrine, formally known as the Central Congregational Church, was founded in Detroit, Michigan, by the Reverend Albert B. Cleage, Jr. The second shrine was established in Atlanta, Georgia, in 1975. The Southwest region's, and third shrine, was founded in Houston, Texas, in 1977. Finally, the fourth shrine, known as Beulah Land Farms in Calhoun Falls, South Carolina, was founded in 1999.

It was at their very first Pan-African Synod, that is, their national meeting, in Houston, Texas, in 1978 that the church adopted the name Pan-African Orthodox Christian Churches after having been known for a short time as the Black Christian Nationalist Church. The name was taken from Marcus Garvey's African Orthodox Church, affirming their belief that African peoples must have their own view of God. It was also at this gathering that Cleage was designated as the First Holy Patriarch and adopted the name Jaramogi Abebe Agyeman: *Jaramogi* meaning "leader of the people," *Abebe* meaning "defender," and *Agyeman* meaning "blessed man." With the death of Agyeman in February 2000, the church called as its new Holy Patriarch Cardinal Demosthene Nelson, who adopted the name Jaramogi Menelik Kimathi.

The principal tenets of the PAOCC revolve around black Christian nationalism that asserts that black people are the chosen people of God as revealed in the Old Testament in God's dealing with the black nation Israel. Jesus, as the black messiah, was a revolutionary leader who came to free a black Israelite people from the oppression of white Gentiles. The PAOCC also claims that God continues to work with God's people to help them find a way to freedom through building community and shunning individualism.

ADDITIONAL MOVEMENTS

There are numerous other groups that could be mentioned that do not readily fit into any of the categories above. For example, there is the United Nation of Nuwaubian Moors. With roots in a drug-infested community in Brooklyn, this body has been led by the charismatic Dwight "Malachi" York for over three decades. His followers refer to him as Dr. York, Isa Muhammad, Baba, the Master Teacher, and the Savior. One of the more eclectic new black religious movements, York's teachings integrate elements of Christianity, Islam, and Judaism with stories of extraterrestrial beings and ancient Egypt. In 1993, the group moved to a 476-acre farm near Eatonton in Putnam County, Georgia, where they constructed series of pyramids, obelisks, and statues. However, the last few years have been rough for Nuwaubians. On April 22, 2004, a federal judge sentenced York to 135 years in prison for racketeering and child molestation.[20]

Another group that defies neat categorization is the Ausar Auset Society. Founded in New York in 1973 by Ra Un Nefer Amen I (formerly Rogelio Straughn), it is an African-Kemetic-centered spiritual community with branches in twenty-four major cities in the United States, as well as in London, Toronto, Trinidad, and Bermuda. The members, initiates, students, and community participants study and implement spiritual practices ascribed to ancient Kemet (Egypt) and the Indus Kush (India), two ancient black civilizations. It is their belief that the Ausarian religious system is the world's oldest, going back over five thousand years. The branches replicate the structural archetype established by Ra Un Nefer Amen I, Shekem Ur Shekem ("king of kings") of the Ausar Auset Society in New York. There are kings (Ur Aua) and queen mothers (Ur-t Aua-t) who reign in other regions. The sacred text for the sect is the Metu Neter (divine word or God's word), of which Ra Un Nefer Amen I is the author.[21]

The last several decades have seen a growth in Old and New World African religious traditions in the United States. With an increase of immigrants from Africa, the Caribbean, and Central and South America, African Americans had the opportunity to become familiar with a variety of nonindigenous religious traditions. Perhaps the most prominent of these are orisha-based traditions such as Vodun, Santeria, and Candomble, and Yoruba traditional religion/Ifa. This is not to say that there were no practitioners of these traditions earlier. As Anthony Pinn notes, persons from the Caribbean have been immigrating to the United States since the nineteenth century.

Yet it was not until after 1950 that substantial numbers of immigrants began to arrive, some fifty thousand from Cuba alone prior to 1970, and Orisha worship became established in the United States.[22]

There are also those African Americans who exemplify a particularly modern religious posture and who identify themselves as religious humanists. Religious humanists reject theism and view religion as a human construct. This orientation has been given an intellectual presence through the work of scholars such as William R. Jones and Anthony B. Pinn, as well as symbolically with the election of William G. Sinkford as president of the Unitarian Universalist Association in 2001. In lieu of a transcendent imposition of norms, religious humanists emphasize human responsibility and creativity in the establishment of meaningful ways of being in the world as individuals and community.

Additionally, the last several decades have seen a growth in African Americans who express an interest in Eastern spiritual traditions as well as traditions that have been characterized as New Age. More and more, African Americans are adopting traditions such as Buddhism, Hinduism, and Taoism, as well as practices such as meditation, astrology, numerology, and holistic medicine.

APPROACHES TO THE STUDY OF BLACK RELIGION

First, contrary to the European roots of religious studies, African American religious studies has its most immediate roots in the history and development of African American studies based primarily in history and sociology. Second, those early studies were almost exclusively concerned with the black church. The classic texts include W.E.B. Du Bois, *The Negro Church* (1903); Carter G. Woodson, *The History of the Negro Church* (1921); Benjamin Elijah Mays and Joseph William Nicholson, *The Negro's Church* (1933); and E. Franklin Frazier, *The Negro Church in America* (1963). Although Arthur Fauset's work is not generally cited among the development of African American studies and the study of black religion, one should mention his *Black Gods of the Metropolis: Negro Religious Cults of the Urban North* (1944) at least parenthetically, since it was among the first anthropological studies of African American religion that sought to explicate religious movements beyond the black church.

In the later twentieth century, however, the primary methodology shifted from sociological and historical to the theological, with the appearance of James Cone's *Black Theology and Black Power* (1969). Black theology received its classic expression in Cone's *A Black Theology of Liberation* (1970), and many of his students continue to reiterate his basic theological formulations.[23] The most obvious limitation of this approach is that black theology is not relevant to any African American religious movement other than those derived from the black church.

Two additional critiques are noteworthy. The first comes from William R. Jones in his *Is God a White Racist?: A Preamble to Black Theology* (1973).[24] Jones maintains that the central doctrine in black theology, as in all theology, is theodicy, the apologetic attempt to justify the attributes of God, such as God's beneficence and omnipotence, in the presence of evil and human suffering and to determine the causes of suffering. At the same time, Jones argues that black theology fails in its response to evil because in its response it basically ignores the most logical explanation, that of divine racism. In other words, the eschatological theodicy of black theology with its emphasis on the exaltation-liberation event known as the crucifixion and resurrection of Jesus in Christian theology is evidence of what God will do in the future of black people, that is to say, liberate them from suffering.

Jones rejects this notion, suggesting that the only way to have a basis for determining what God will do in the future is based on what God has done in the past, and he argues that the events that have been interpreted as divine benevolence can just as easily be viewed as divine racism. One cannot demonstrate from history objective evidence that shows God's benevolence and liberation from evil. One can find just as many, if not more, events that demonstrate the opposite. Anthony B. Pinn, in his book *Why, Lord: Suffering and Evil in Black Theology* (1995), makes a similar critique of black theology, arguing that its responses to suffering in fact challenge the Christian God's basic attributes, God's goodness and omnipotence.[25] Pinn suggests that the only way to avoid this pitfall is to be willing to bracket the existence of God. Only this method resolves the problems of theodicy for black theology. Even Jones, Pinn argues, tacitly maintains the goodness of God by attempting to develop a humanocentric theism that locates the cause of evil with human agency and so fails to resolve the problem.

The second critique of black theology comes from womanist theology, which is in reality another form of black theology in which the subjects are African American women. In it, black women consider questions about God's activity in their lives and the meaning of God for them. Womanist theology was inaugurated with the publication of Jacquelyn Grant's *White Women's Christ and Black Women's Jesus: Feminist Christology and Womanist Response* (1989). The womanist critique argues that black theology is androcentric and sexist in its analysis of white theology and American culture. It focuses on the issue of racism and to a lesser extent on classism but fails to address sexism, including its own. Womanist theology claims to do theology from the "tridimensional experience" of racism, sexism, and classism.[26] Moreover, womanist theology reports as a primary source the lives and voices of ordinary black women and thus offers a variation on black theology in its study of African American religion.

On the other hand, some approaches to the study of black religion address critical and foundational issues. Some of the perennial questions addressed by African American religionists are concerned with the meaning of the term "African American or black religion." They are interested in other crucial questions as well. For instance, what is the nature of black religion? Is there something unique or distinctive about black religion that distinguishes it from other expressions and manifestations of religion? The answers to such questions, however, are determined to a large extent by the theories and methodologies employed by the diverse domains of inquiry in the field. In addition to the black and womanist theologians and ethicists, scholars associated with other academic discourses have brought forward a myriad of perspectives in an effort to explain more fully, describe, interpret, and understand the phenomena of African American religion.

The first theoretical and methodological approach to be considered is that associated with the field history of religions. In the decades following the civil rights era, the chief African American religionist associated with this field has been Charles H. Long. As a historian of religion, Long understands religion as orientation in the ultimate sense, particularly regarding one's place in the world.[27] Moreover, religion is understood as the fundamental element in the constitution of human consciousness and human community. Long maintains that African Americans, as people who have been oppressed, possess a religious consciousness that offers something unique with respect to what it means to be human. With such an understanding, Long is an advocate for the study of religion as essentially a hermeneutical or interpretative discipline.

Second, as a subfield of religious studies, philosophy of religion can be broken down still further into divisions corresponding to the areas of philosophy on which they depend. Thus, continental philosophers of religion traditionally make use of methods such as phenomenology, existentialism, hermeneutics, Marxism, and structuralism. Today, this category is often associated with those approaches characterized as postmodern: poststructuralism, deconstruction, post-colonial theory, and critical theory. African American scholars associated with this tradition would include William R. Jones, whose work was noted above and who draws on the thought of Jean Paul Sartre to challenge black theology's assumption of a benevolent deity, and Theophus Smith, whose interdisciplinary study of religion employs a hermeneutical analysis informed by Paul Ricoeur as well as an understanding of religion influenced by the work of Rene Girard.[28]

A third tradition that has seen much growth in the last several decades is philosophy of religion influenced by American pragmatism. Scholars such as Cornel West, Victor Anderson, and Eddie Glaude represent individuals whose study of religion is strongly informed by the legacy of Ralph Waldo Emerson, Charles Peirce, William James, John Dewey, and W.E.B. Du Bois, as well as neo-pragmatist philosophers such as Richard Rorty.[29] As the name would suggest, these scholars approach the study of religion in terms of how it is used as opposed to strictly the conceptual content, or ideas to which persons profess allegiance. Pragmatist theories of religion tend to be functional instead of substantive in orientation.

Fourth, in recent decades, a growing number of African American scholars have been influenced by the philosophical tradition of Alfred North Whitehead and Charles Hartshorne known as process philosophy or neoclassical metaphysics. Such scholars, including Theodore Walker, Jr., find the ideas of ultimate reality understood in terms of becoming, unfolding, and growth coherent with the African American experience of struggle in pursuit of liberation and freedom.[30]

Last, given the dominant presence of Christianity in the African American community, one would be derelict in omitting the work of African American intellectuals engaged in biblical studies. Such scholars have employed the tools of this discipline such as form, rhetorical, source, and historical criticism in their study of texts to uncover various relationships between the textual tradition and African peoples from antiquity to the modern context. Indeed, biblical scholarship into the early twenty-first century has called attention to the African presence in the Bible as well as exploring the use and function of the Bible by African Americans. Scholars of note in this area include Cain Hope Felder, Vincent Wimbush, Brian Blount, Clarice Martin, Randall Bailey, Stephen Breck Reid, and Renita Weems.[31]

FUTURE DIRECTIONS

African American religion is broad and complex. It comprises multiple and diverse religious traditions, linked together by a search for meaning and more life fullness, made necessary by the terrors of slavery, a history of oppression that is characterized by attacks on black bodies, racism, classism, and sexism. Historically, African Americans have developed and chosen numerous religious expressions in order to organize and make sense of the resulting absurdities of life. As a result, the black religious terrain is comprised of Buddhists, Muslims, Christians, Hebrews, Spiritualists, Humanists, Africentrists, and more. Although their truth claims often conflict, they have much in common. In a fabulous and wonderfully complicated way, they all make up the rich and yet under-explored fabric of black religious culture in America.

It is true that the majority of the studies and discussions of black religion still focus on some aspect of the black church and more recently on the Nation of Islam and many of its related movements. And those exposés, documentaries, essays, and reports are valuable in terms of the knowledge that they make available to us. Notwithstanding, it is our hope and push that the richness of diversity that is African American religion gains more recognition in American culture and the academy. Given that many of the religious traditions have roots in American and African cultures that are centuries old, it will be fascinating to explore what they might reveal about the history of America and the attempts of people to make sense out of changing historical, political, and cultural contexts.

Appropriately, approaches to the study of African American religion in the post–civil rights era reflect the polyvocality that is inherent in black religion. As American colleges and universities continue to recognize the importance of African American religion, the study of religion will necessarily reflect the diversity and orientations of various departments and disciplines. Traditionally studied from sociology, history, and theology, it can benefit from the insights and methods of other forms of inquiry such as psychological, philosophical, and other creative and complex methods of interpretation. At the same time, the study of black religion can transcend the narrowness of parochial interests of area studies and find depth and richness in interdisciplinary approaches. Furthermore, black religion will need new conversation partners. Often omitted from the curricula of Africana studies and African American studies programs, despite its apparent centrality to African American life and culture, black religious studies must show its relevance to obvious partners and develop new and creative relationships with departments such as art and art history. This will keep black religious studies fresh and innovative.

In the end, the study of black religion will have to keep in step with changes in African American religion, indeed with American culture and world cultures. As old identities are deconstructed and new identities are forged, religion will ask new questions or variations of existing ones. Therefore, since the world is becoming more global, the questions will be modified. The central question of African American religion regarding what it means to be black and religious may have to shift to accommodate changing historical realities like globalization. Instead, it may become "What does it mean to be black and religious in a global community?" African American religion may also have to be dichotomous, being able to speak to the pressing needs of American life and at the same time giving meaning to new global realities.

Finally, African American religion will reflect the tension of managing the tendency in religion to resist change while simultaneously participating in a changing world. Reevaluations of evolving social locations will be critical. Critical, too, will be the responses to important questions that arise from these changing dynamics. For instance, what happens to movements that were started in response to poor or working-class challenges when many of their members move into the middle-classes? How does globalization change racism and questions of race? How will black religion respond to insights regarding sexuality and gender that might be gained from new developments in the sciences and humanities? How will developments in technology affect our understanding of what is ultimate? African American religion will have to wrestle with these and other issues if it is to remain viable in the lives of its constituents.

NOTES

Stephen Finley wishes to acknowledge the help and support of his wife, Dr. Rachel Elisabeth Finley, advisors Elias K. Bongmba and Anthony B. Pinn, and members of the Theta Chi chapter of Omega Psi Phi. Torin Alexander wishes to acknowledge his wife, Charvonne Alexander, and Anthony B. Pinn.

1. Anthony B. Pinn, *Terror and Triumph: The Nature of Black Religion* (Minneapolis, MN: Fortress, 2002), 173.

2. C. Eric Lincoln and Lawrence H. Mamiya, *The Black Church in the African American Experience* (Durham, NC: Duke University Press, 1990), 1.

3. Joseph R. Washington, Jr., "How Black Is Black Religion," in *Quest for a Black Theology*, ed. James J. Gardiner and J. Deotis Roberts, Sr. (Philadelphia: Pilgrim, 1971), 28.

4. Gayraud S. Wilmore, *Black Religion and Black Radicalism: An Interpretation of the Religious History of African Americans*, 3rd ed. (Maryknoll, NY: Orbis, 1998), 163–95.

5. According to data from the National Council of Churches, such losses have been between 0.05 percent and 1.5 percent annually. See *Yearbook of American and Canadian Churches* (Nashville, TN: Abingdon, 2004).

6. Mark Niesse, "Black Pastors Rally Against Gay Marriage," Associated Press, March 23, 2004, available through Lexis Nexis.

7. Lincoln and Mamiya, 285, 286.

8. Ibid., 288. See also Arthur Huff Fauset, *Black Gods of the Metropolis: Negro Religious Cults of the Urban North* (1944; Philadelphia: University of Pennsylvania Press, 2001), chap. 2.

9. Lincoln and Mamiya, 298.

10. Delores Causion Carpenter, "The Effects of Sect-Typeness Upon the Professionalization of Black Female Masters of Divinity Graduates, 1972–1984" (Ed.D. diss., Rutgers University, 1986), 136. See also Lincoln and Mamiya, 298.

11. Richard Brent Turner, *Islam in the African American Experience*, 2nd ed. (Bloomington: Indiana University Press, 2003), 71–72.

12. Clifton E. Marsh, *The Lost-Found Nation of Islam in America* (Lanham, MD: Scarecrow, 2000), 101.

13. Ibid., 107.

14. Theophus Smith, *Conjuring Culture: Biblical Formations of Black America* (New York: Oxford University Press, 1994), 130, and Charles H. Long, *Significations: Signs, Symbols, and Images in the Interpretation of Religion* (Philadelphia: Fortress, 1986), 153.

15. Use of the term "black" here is actually redundant, since the Hebrews believe that the biblical Hebrews were black and that they have a literal, physical relationship to them. They reserve the term "Jewish" for white European Jews, who are not the original people of Judaism, but instead are converts. We use the term "black" here only for clarification. We should note, however, that some African Americans do consider themselves Jewish.

16. As in the case of certain Old Testament prophets, Crowdy would attest to having a vision in which the angel of the Lord presented him with a Bible such that the Holy Scriptures were then a part of his very being. See Hans Baer, "The Role of the Bible and Other Sacred Texts in African American Denominations and Sects: Historical and Social Scientific Observations," in *African Americans and the Bible: Sacred Text and Social Texture*, ed. Vincent L. Winbush (New York: Continuum, 2000), 95.

17. Ibid., 96.

18. The group made headlines when singers Whitney Houston and Bobby Brown made a trip to the community's center in Dimona, located in southern Israel's Negev desert. The group got more media attention in the summer of 2005 when the Israeli government, after more than thirty years, agreed to grant permanent residency to members of the group. Residency, which carries the right to vote in municipal elections and volunteer for military service, is the first step to becoming an Israeli citizen.

19. For further information about these movements, see http://www.blackjews.org/. There is also a great deal more about this phenomenon in the African American community that is worthy of analysis and further study.

20. Bill Tropy, "Judge Throws Book at Cultist: 135 Years in Prison Ordered," *Atlanta Journal-Constitution*, April 23, 2004, Metro Edition.

21. Regina Jennings, "Ausar Auset Society," in *Encyclopedia of Black Studies*, ed. Molefi Kete Asante and Ama Mazama (Thousand Oaks, CA: Sage, 2005), 104–5.

22. Anthony B. Pinn, *Varieties of African American Religious Experience* (Minneapolis, MN: Augsburg Fortress, 1998), 78.

23. James H. Cone, *Black Theology and Black Power* (New York: Seabury, 1969), and idem, *A Black Theology of Liberation* (Maryknoll, NY: Orbis, 1970).

24. William R. Jones, *Is God a White Racist? A Preamble to Black Theology* (Garden City, NY: Doubleday Anchor, 1973).

25. Anthony B. Pinn, *Why, Lord? Suffering and Evil in Black Theology* (New York: Continuum, 1999).

26. Jacquelyn Grant, *White Women's Christ and Black Women's Jesus: Feminist Critique and Womanist Response* (Atlanta: Scholars Press, 1989), 209.

27. See, for example, Long, *Significations.*

28. See the previously cited works for Jones, *Is God a White Racist?* and Smith, *Conjuring Culture.*

29. See, for example, Cornel West, *Prophesy Deliverance: An Afro-American Revolutionary Christianity* (Philadelphia: Westminster, 1982); idem, *The American Evasion of Philosophy: A Genealogy of Pragmatism* (Madison: University of Wisconsin Press, 1989); Victor Anderson, *Beyond Ontological Blacknets* (New York: Continuum, 1999); and Eddie S. Glaude, Jr., *Exodus! Religion, Race, and Nation in Early Nineteenth-Century Black America* (Chicago: University of Chicago Press, 2000).

30. See, for example, Theodore Walker, Jr., *Mothering Connections: A Black Neoclassical Metaphysics and Black Theology* (Albany: State University of New York Press, 2004).

31. Cain Hope Felder, ed., *Stony the Road We Trod: African American Biblical Interpretation* (Minneapolis, MN: Augsburg Fortress, 1991), includes essays from each of these biblical scholars.

SUGGESTIONS FOR FURTHER READING

Chireau, Yvonne, and Nathaniel Deutsch, eds. *Black Zion: African American Religious Encounters with Judaism.* New York: Oxford University Press, 1999.

Cleage, Albert B., Jr. *Black Christian Nationalism: New Directions for the Black Church.* Detroit, MI: Luxor Publishers of the Pan-African Orthodox Christian Church, 1987.

Fulop, Timothy E., and Albert J. Raboteau, eds. *African-American Religion: Interpretive Essays in History and Culture.* New York & London: Routledge, 1997.

Lincoln, C. Eric, and Lawrence H. Mamiya. *The Black Church in the African American Experience.* Durham, NC: Duke University Press, 1990.

Pinn, Anthony B. *The African American Religious Experience in America.* Westport, CT: Greenwood, 2005.

Pinn, Anthony B. *The Black Church in the Post–Civil Rights Era.* Maryknoll, NY: Orbis, 2002.

Turner, Richard Brent. *Islam in the African-American Experience.* 2nd ed. Bloomington: Indiana University Press, 2003.

Wilmore, Gayraud S. *Black Religion and Black Radicalism: An Interpretation of the Religious History of African American.* 3rd ed. Maryknoll, NY: Orbis, 1998.

CHAPTER 12

New and Alternative American Religions: Changes, Issues, and Trends

Sean McCloud

The chapters in this volume attest to dramatic transformations in American religion over the last several decades. New religions and alternative spiritualities in the United States have been part of these changes. At the same time, blanket generalizations about the subject are impossible. The period from the late 1970s to the present witnessed the tragedies of the Jonestown mass suicide, the Branch Davidian/ATF conflagration, and the Heaven's Gate suicides. In part, the period from 1978–2005 could be narrated through a series of so-called "cult controversies" in which a loosely organized anti-cult movement charged certain new religions with brainwashing and fought to impose legal restrictions on them. But at the same time, the period saw the significant expansion and growing acceptance of new religions like Mormonism and Neopaganism, as well as a decline in anti-cult activities. The last quarter century or so also signaled a shift in the types of American new religions attracting members, moving from totalistic communal organizations to loosely organized movements with permeable group boundaries. This style of alternative religion, exemplified in the activities often subsumed under the vague category "New Age," follows a larger trend of combinative, "pick-and-mix" spirituality seen across the contemporary American religious spectrum.

In this chapter, I present an historical overview of new religious movements in American history, focus on developments in the last several decades, and discuss current issues and trends. I argue several claims. First, I suggest that new and alternative religions are a constant in American history and have been marked by several heightened periods of growth and public attention. Second, I argue that the last three decades have witnessed not only the explosion and cessation of public controversies concerning new religions, but also significant changes pertaining to what kinds of new religions are gaining members and acceptance in the United States.

MATTERS OF DEFINITION

Definition must be the first task in any discussion of new and alternative religions. For the purposes of this chapter, a "new religious movement" is a group that has been founded in the last three hundred years and offers something new that differentiates it from pre-existing religious traditions. The new religion may—and historically often does—derive many of its beliefs and practices from an established movement. At the same time, it offers a new religious prophet, sacred text, or set of rituals and beliefs that causes it to depart significantly from other religions. For example, Mormonism, officially named the Church of Jesus Christ of Latter-day Saints, is based in Christianity and uses both the Hebrew Bible and the New Testament. Many Mormon beliefs and practices resemble those of theologically conservative American Protestantism. At the same time, it is not a branch of Christianity but a new religion because it offers a new prophet (Joseph Smith, Jr.), new sacred texts (*The Book of Mormon, The Pearl of Great Price*, etc.), and various new beliefs and practices.[1] Using this definition, all religions start as new religious movements. Christianity, for example, was once a new religion emerging from Judaism, Islam a new religion with Jewish and Christian sources, and Buddhism a new religion coming out of popular and elite Indian religious traditions. Unlike most new religions, however, these movements did not disappear, but grew to be the three largest world religions today.

Historically, the phrase "new religious movement" has replaced "cult" as the preferred scholarly term for new religions. Stemming from the Latin term "cultus," meaning an organized system of worship, the term cult is at once sociological, theological, and popular parlance. Sociologically, it refers to a small, unstable group often focused around one or a set of charismatic leaders. The organization is often weak and the group usually does not last long. The term is part of a church, sect, and cult classification system that focuses on institutional structures and tensions with the environing culture. An example of the sociological meaning of cult can be seen in the writings of J. Milton Yinger, particularly *Religion, Society, and the Individual* (1957).[2]

Theologically, cult has historically been a term twentieth- and twenty-first-century evangelical Protestants used to distinguish "true" Christians from "false" ones. In his 1962 book, *Cults and Isms*, Russell Spittler gave the classic evangelical definition of the term when he wrote that a cult "is any group that claims to be Christian but falls short of an evangelical definition of Christianity."[3] Perennial favorites in evangelical cult books included the Mormons, Jehovah's Witnesses, and Christian Scientists, but liberal Protestants and Roman Catholics also sometimes appeared.

In terms of popular usage, cult has lost any original sociological meaning and now brings to mind charges of brainwashing, coercion, deception, and abuse. Beginning in the early 1970s and growing in the latter part of the decade and through the 1980s, the image of a cult as a volatile, dangerous group of fanatics dominated American media and popular culture. Elsewhere I have argued that for many Americans, these associations were and still are so taken for granted that they have become doxa, those socially constructed opinions, assumptions, and inclinations so ingrained they appear commonsense and natural.[4] Because of the negative associations "cult" now holds for many Americans, scholars use "new religious movement" or "alternative religion" as value-free terms to describe particular new movements.[5]

NEW RELIGIOUS MOVEMENTS IN AMERICAN HISTORY: A BRIEF OVERVIEW, 1800–1977

New religious movements have been a constant in U.S. history. At the same time, periods of particular interest and ferment have occurred. Historian Jon Butler has called the first period, stretching through the first half of the nineteenth century, the "Antebellum Spiritual Hothouse."[6] Concurrent with the Second Great Awakening and respondent to the new nation's free exercise and disestablishment policies concerning religion, these decades saw the birth and growth of a number of new religious movements, as well as the appearance of evangelical Protestantism. Much of the action in the period occurred in western New York State, which became known as the "Burned-Over District" because of its propensity to be set ablaze by the fires of revivalism. Mormonism, Spiritualism, and the Oneida Community were all born in the Burned-Over District. Other new religions such as the Shakers, officially the United Society of Believers in Christ's Second Appearing, had been founded decades earlier, but gained members in the antebellum Burned-Over District. Even this early period reflects the diversity in styles of new religious movements that still exists today. Some groups, such as the Shakers and Oneidans, were communal and totalistic. Others, such as Spiritualism, were more loosely organized movements that occurred both within and without religious institutions.

The second period, from the end of the Civil War in 1865 to the end of the nineteenth century, saw a rise in a number of occult, new thought, and harmonial religious movements. In brief, "new thought" and the more general term "harmonial religions" are names given to belief systems that stress God's immanence within individuals, coupled with the notion that bad things like illness, violence, poverty, and even death result from negative thinking that separates humans from the spark of divine within them.[7] "Occult" refers generally to matters that are hidden in some way from everyday perception.[8] In this respect, certain information and knowledge, powers, and groups can fall under the occult rubric. Starting in the 1860s, numerous groups that fell under either or both the new thought and occult framework formed, including American Rosicrucianism, Christian Science, Unity, Theosophy, and the Order of the Golden Dawn. In addition to these movements, December 1890 witnessed a tragic late-nineteenth-century "cult controversy": the massacre of Wounded Knee. The Ghost Dance was a pan–Native American new religious movement that combined native and Christian rituals, symbols, and beliefs with an end-time prophecy. Participants believed that the world as known was about to end and that those taking up the Ghost Dance movement's rituals and lifestyle would survive the apocalypse and see a new paradisiacal era ensue. In December 1890, federal soldiers who were attempting to stop the movement among the Lakota Sioux Ghost killed over two hundred Ghost Dancers.

The period from the 1910s to the 1940s was marked by the birth of a number of predominantly African American new religions. These groups appeared in the context of the migration of African Americans out of the rural Jim Crow South and into urban industrial Northern cities. Flanked by World War I and World War II, the period of the Great Migration and Great Depression was marked by "tribalisms" that came in the form of heightened racial, class, ethnic, and religious conflicts. This was the period in which the religious, white supremacist Ku Klux Klan reached its numerical height, Henry Ford published anti-Semitic literature, and the Scopes trial popularly dramatized divisions between theologically liberal and conservative Protestants.[9] Given the time period, many African American new religions were forced to address the issues of race and fell into one of two categories. The first, integrationist new religions, theologically downplayed the importance of race and welcomed all into the fold. Examples of such movements include Sweet Daddy Grace's United House of Prayer for All People and Father Divine's new thought-inspired Peace Mission Movement, which explicitly argued that race was a falsity produced by negative thinking. The second style of African American new religion was nationalistic, meaning that the religious messages of such movements were meant exclusively for people of color and encouraged racial separatism. While Noble Drew Ali's Moorish Science Temple, founded in 1913, is an early example, the most well-known group is the Nation of Islam, founded in 1930 in Detroit. The "Black Muslims," as the media called them, preached a racialized theology of black divinity and white diabolicism. In practice and belief, the Nation combined elements of Islam and Christianity with the new teachings and practices of founder W.D. Fard and later leader Elijah Muhammad.

Following World War II, the United States saw a religious revival that entailed increases in church affiliation, church construction, and religious tithing. Polling from the 1940s through the 1990s showed that belief in God or a universal spirit was at an all-time high in the mid-1950s at 99 percent.[10] New religions of the 1950s included occult movements devoted to messages that founders had received from UFOs, such as the Aetherius Society and the Christ Brotherhood Incorporated. The decade also witnessed the early stirrings of groups that would later become well-known, such as Scientology and the Unification Church. While the 1950s was a decade in which some new religions flourished, the period from 1965–1977 saw more public and media attention given to them for at least four reasons.

First, in 1965 the Johnson administration lifted the Oriental Exclusion Act, an anti-immigration law from the 1920s that had severely curbed East and South Asians from entering the United States. Coinciding with this was the appearance and/or growth of Asian-based new religions such as the Hare Krishnas (officially known as ISKCON, standing for the International Society of Krishna Consciousness), Divine Light Mission, Transcendental Meditation, Nichiren Shoshu, and the aforementioned Unification Church.

Second, the youthful Jesus Movement, sometimes referred to as "Jesus Freaks," appeared in the late 1960s and early 1970s as an evangelical Protestant version of the larger youth counterculture. One of the earliest Jesus movement groups, the Children of God, was a semi-nomadic, communal troupe founded by prophetic leader David "Moses" Berg. Early members traveled throughout America, criticizing institutional Christianity and American capitalism through street preaching and occasional church service disruptions. By the mid-1970s, the group became even more controversial with the introduction of free love and "flirty fishing," a form of missionizing in which women in the group witnessed to unconverted men through sex. Along with free love among members, investigations and admissions later revealed that some in the group had even engaged in illegal sexual activities with minors in the commune. As the decade progressed, the Children of God, later renamed the Family, would be one of several movements viewed by some as a dangerous "cult."[11]

A third factor in the growing interest given to new religions from 1965–1977 was the heightened commercial and media attention given to the occult and occult movements. Movies such as *Rosemary's Baby*, television shows such as *Dark Shadows*, mass market books such as John Godwin's *Occult America*, and even popular board games like Parker Brothers' *Ouija* made the occult a visible part of American popular culture. In California, Anton LaVey's Church of Satan attracted celebrities like Sammy Davis, Jr. and Jayne Mansfield. It also received media attention from the reporters of *Time*, *Newsweek*, and other venues. Likewise, Neopagan witches appeared in the press at the same time as the new religion was becoming more prominent in the United States. Journalists depicted what they viewed as an "occult revival" with a contradictory mixture of exoticism, banality, and danger—at times with language hinting toward the "cult menace stories" that would appear frequently by the end of the 1970s.[12]

The fourth element, the one most crucial to the cult controversies of the late 1970s and beyond, was the development of grass roots organizations of parents, pastors, psychiatrists, and "deprogrammers" that opposed and lobbied against new religions. The first of these groups, founded by William Rambur in 1971, was FREECOG, short for "Parents Committee to Free Our Sons and Daughters from the Children of God." It was this group, and others like it, that fomented the brainwashing accusations that came to be iconic in popular media coverage of new religions. By the mid-1970s, charges of brainwashing, deception, fraud, and various other improprieties appeared in most stories about communal groups like the Unification Church, Children of God, and Hare Krishnas. By the late 1970s, the associations between such negative things and "cults" in general had become unquestioned truths for many Americans.[13]

NEW AND ALTERNATIVE RELIGIONS, 1978–2005: CHANGES AND DEVELOPMENTS

Two print media reports, one from 1978 and the other from 2004, represent the broad spectrum of events and attitudes concerning new and alternative religions in the last several years. On December 4, 1978, *Time, Newsweek*, and *U.S. News & World Report* published nearly identical stories on the mass suicide of 918 members of the Peoples Temple, an American group living communally in the jungles of Guyana. Both *Time* and *Newsweek* featured now iconic images of the dead and titled their covers "Cult of Death." Inside, all three magazines suggested that leader Jim Jones brainwashed his followers into committing suicide. *U.S. News* aptly summed up what one scholar has called the "cult menace" motif dominating late 1970s and 1980s mass media, writing that "in the end, only a cult's bizarre regimen of fear, violence, and unthinking devotion" could explain the tragedy.[14]

The second report, appearing on the Religion Newswriters' Association's "Tips" Web page for journalists on October 11, 2004, was titled "Wicca Moves into the Mainstream." The report described how Wicca, the largest branch of Neopaganism, had grown dramatically since the 1960s, and offered reporters a number of practitioners, academics, and other contacts.[15] While the "mainstreaming" of Wicca and Neopaganism suggested in the article might have been uneven in different regions of the country, the story was certainly supported in the marketplace of American popular culture, where positive images of Wiccans were appearing on the shelves of chain bookstores, in movies, and in children's shows such as Cartoon Network's *New Scooby Doo* and Disney's *W.I.T.C.H.* series.

Together, these media stories suggest the highly varied and occasionally contradictory images of new and alternative religious movements in the late twentieth and early twenty-first centuries. Because the umbrella term "new religion" features radically different groups tied together only by their newness, this should not be surprising. Mormons, Neopagans, Peoples Temple members, Branch Davidians, and New Agers might all fall into the new religion classification, but this does not point to shared theology, practice, organization, or demographics. Nor does it suggest the size, growth, or decline of the movements. Simply put, some new religions have grown, while others have virtually disappeared since the 1970s. Many groups that gained popular attention in the 1970s, such as the Divine Light Mission, have declined markedly in active membership. On the other hand, the Church of Jesus Christ of Latter-day Saints (Mormons), once a new religion that the nineteenth-century U.S. government sent soldiers to fight against, is now the fourth largest religious body in the United States, with more than 5 million members.[16]

The period since 1978 witnessed several important changes and trends, two of which I will focus on. The first entails the explosion and decline of public and legal battles best described as "cult controversies." The events fomenting this include the tragedies of Jonestown and Waco, the gradual decline of anti-cult movements, and organizational changes occurring within some of the new religions that received negative attention in the 1970s and 1980s, particularly ISKCON and the Unification Church. Second, there has been a shift in the kinds of new religions attracting Americans. Specifically, totalistic, communal, new religions have declined, while more loosely organized, theologically and ritually eclectic movements such as Neopaganism and the wealth of practices placed under the "New Age" umbrella have grown. Why this might be and how it coincides with larger trends in U.S. religion will be the focus of the last section of this chapter.

MAKING AND UN-MAKING THE CULT MENACE

By the mid-1970s, communal new religions such as the Children of God, Unification Church, and ISKCON appeared in mass media reports as dangerous, brainwashing cultists. While the three groups were totalistic in orientation, similarities ended there. As noted above, the Children of God was a new religion formed out of the evangelical Jesus Movement of the late 1960s and early 1970s. The movement veered from being a sect to being a new religion because of the new practices, prophecies, and revelations of its founder, David "Moses" Berg. The Unification Church was a new religion that combined Christianity with the revelations and biblical interpretations of founder Reverend Sun Myung Moon. First formed in Korea in 1954, the movement was known for aggressive proselytizing, regimented communal living, large group weddings, and a new sacred text, the *Divine Principle*. Many members came to believe Moon was the second coming of Christ, a speculation he confirmed by declaring himself the Messiah in 1992.[17] The International Society of Krishna Consciousness, known popularly as Hare Krishnas because of their chanting, was founded in the United States by A.C. Bhaktivedanta Swami Srila Prabhupada in 1966, but holds a theology and lineage stretching back to sixteenth-century Hindu devotionalism to the God Krishna. It must be noted, then, that its roots in Hinduism suggest that it is not a new religion, despite popular conceptions that it is. What was new was its appearance in the United States, where devotees lived communally in ashrams and missionized on city streets and other public places.[18] These three movements, as well as others, gained the negative attention of anti-cult activists, cult "deprogrammers," and popular magazines such as *Reader's Digest* and *McCall's*.[19] But not until the mass suicide of 918 Peoples Temple members in the jungles of Guyana in 1978 did the new religions in general became synonymous with the "cult menace."

The Peoples Temple was founded by James Warren Jones in Indiana in 1956.[20] In 1960 the racially diverse group formally affiliated with the Disciples of Christ, a mainline Protestant denomination. Jones's ministry featured interracial worship, civil rights, faith, healing, and sharp criticism of American capitalism. A white Hoosier whose father was a Klansman, Jones began referring to himself as black, explicitly associating racial minority status with anyone oppressed by the American capitalist system. In the mid-1960s, Jones moved his congregation from Indiana to California, a place which he believed would be safer in the event of nuclear war. By the

1970s, his church had between 5,000 and 7,000 members, and between 1975 and 1977, Jones won two humanitarian awards for his work on social justice and civil rights issues.

During the mid-1970s Jones created a farming commune in the South American jungles of Guyana, a place where Peoples Temple members could practice Jones's religio-political liberation theology, "Divine Socialism." The first members of the church arrived in what would be called "Jonestown" in 1975. Jones moved there in 1977. While many commune members initially seemed happy, Jonestown became the cult menace story that confirmed the media's and anti-cult movement's worst stereotypes. Jones performed fake miracle healings, regularly slept with female members, and had dissidents to the cause of Divine Socialism confined and drugged.[21] Pushed by concerns of some church members' relatives, Congressman Leo Ryan conducted a fact-finding visit to Jonestown. After an apparently positive visit, on the way back to the airport Ryan and his entourage were ambushed and murdered by Peoples Temple assassins. Convinced that the American military would respond by attacking the commune, Jones and his assistants called for a "white night." This was the name given to the commune's recurring "revolutionary suicide" drills, in which members would gather and drink Kool-Aid potentially laced with poison. On the night of November 18, 1978, however, it wasn't a drill. While Jones preached, most members killed themselves by drinking poison. A few shot themselves or their comrades with guns. The children were the first to die, with those too young to drink from a cup injected with syringes.

As the 1980s progressed, numerous controversies involving new religions ensued, including Reverend Moon's 1981 conviction on tax evasion; the mid-1980s controversies surrounding Bhagwan Shree Rajneessh's Rajneeshpuram in Oregon; a steady stream of anti-cult literature, lobbying, and court cases; and late 1980s attention to an underground Satanic, child-sacrificing cult that, by all accounts, didn't even exist.[22] But it wasn't until 1993 that a new religion and its violent demise garnered unprecedented national attention. For fifty-one days, from February 28 to April 19, Americans received television and print media coverage of a standoff between the Branch Davidians and agents from the Bureau of Alcohol, Tobacco, and Firearms (ATF). The incident began when the ATF raided the group's commune outside Waco, Texas, under suspicion that the Davidians were stockpiling illegal guns. The ATF's dramatic armed assault on the large housing compound was met with gunfire. By the end of the first day casualties had been suffered on both sides and a large media contingent surrounded the scene. The standoff ended on April 19, when after multiple hours of an ATF tank gas assault on the commune, the large structure went up in flames with eighty-six men, women, and children dying inside.

To this day, there is no conclusive evidence of how the fire started. The government and anti-cultists suggested that this was another Jonestown-style mass suicide. The few survivors who made it out of the burning commune denied any such action on their part. Indeed, much mystery and ambiguity surrounded the Waco tragedy. The Branch Davidians were a millennialist movement that broke away from the Seventh-Day Adventists in 1929. By the time of the standoff, the movement was led by David Koresh, formerly Vernon Howell, who was seen by many members as a prophet. Specifically, many Davidians thought Koresh possessed a God-given ability allowing him to correctly interpret the Seven Seals referred to in the biblical book of Revelation. While millennialism is a belief held by a number of Christian groups, the Branch Davidians were a new religion that offered a new prophet in Koresh. They also enacted new practices, including polygamist spiritual marriages between Koresh and females in the commune that effectively voided all other marriages among members and included girls as young as fourteen. And Davidian theology, while similar to Seventh-Day Adventist and evangelical premillennialist interest in the end-times, was unique in envisioning the commune as God's chosen people who would prevail against Satan's minions in the battle of Armageddon. In the post-apocalyptic, Christ-triumphant world, the Branch Davidians would repopulate the earth with Koresh's progeny.[23]

Similar to Jonestown, the Branch Davidian/ATF tragedy had the immediate effect of giving anti-cult groups such as the Cult Awareness Network (CAN) and its representatives like Rick Ross public voice through mass media outlets. But by mid-May, only a month later, the Waco incident had virtually disappeared from the airwaves and newsstands. When it returned in a few summer and fall follow-ups, the journalistic frame had changed. Instead of telling the all-too-familiar story of a maniacal cult leader who had brainwashed his followers and led them to death, the new stories suggested government culpability for the standoff's violent ending. Instead of featuring anti-cultists telling readers what "cults" do, magazines such as *Newsweek* turned to religious studies scholars for commentary.[24] At least in terms of media coverage, the Waco incident may be seen as the peak of what was after the gradually declining influence of the anti-cult movement.

Although the tragic demise of the Waco Branch Davidians could not—despite popular misconceptions—be seen as another Jonestown mass suicide, the period since has witnessed a new religion's self-imposed termination within U.S. borders. In the spring of 1997, members of Heaven's Gate saw the appearance of the Hale-Bopp comet as a sign to "exit" their physical bodies through group suicide. On March 28, founder Marshall Applewhite and thirty-eight others—all dressed in black sweat suits and Nike sports shoes—used drugs and plastic bags to leave the material plane of existence with hopes of moving to a spiritual, nonphysical, state of being. The small movement had been around in various forms since the 1970s, mixing elements of Gnostic-style dualism, ufology, science fiction, and Applewhite's revelations and teachings. While the Branch Davidian/ATF standoff was covered by twenty-four-hour news television stations, the medium featured in the Heaven's Gate incident was the Internet. After initial television reports of the mass suicide, thousands of Americans flocked to the group's elaborate Web site. In addition, the movement's source of income came from designing Web sites for businesses.[25]

Jonestown, Waco, and Heaven's Gate represent tragedies that took peoples' lives and offered fodder for anti-cultists who generalized from the negative activities and consequences of a handful of groups to condemn new religious movements in general. The popular image of the "cult menace" has declined in the last decade, however, for at least two primary reasons. First, groups that initially fomented and sustained anti-cult movements in the 1970s and 1980s made changes during the period that made them less controversial to some (but of course, in such a diverse society, not all) outsiders. New religions scholar Laurence Foster has argued that groups which depart significantly from a society's predominant religious, social, and political values are more likely to be labeled dangerously deviant.[26] Conversely, when groups with unusual living arrangements, sexual mores, political views, and religious beliefs change to conform more with their environing culture, negative attention may partly subside. ISKCON, for example, closed their ashram boarding schools in response to the well-documented cases of child abuse occurring within them in the 1970s and 1980s. Additionally, since the mid-1980s, the movement has changed from a communal, totalistic, monastic-style organization to one in which nuclear family structures dominate.[27] The Children of God, renamed the Family, abolished flirty fishing in 1987, as well as making other changes. Likewise, the Unification Church, one-time poster child of the anti-cult movement, has also changed in recent decades, including moves to become a player in right-wing American politics. In the late 1980s the church stepped up interfaith dialogue and activities. They opened their mass weddings to people of any faith who wanted to participate. In addition to these changes, the Moon-owned News World Communications owns several prominent media outlets, including the *Washington Times* and the United Press International News Service. Through these media, Moon and the Unification Church have, like Rupert Murdoch, provided voice to right-of-center political interests. In March 2004, some politicians even unintentionally brought short-lived controversy back to Moon when journalists discovered that some members of Congress had held a coronation ceremony for Moon in a Senate office building.[28]

Perhaps more important to the waning of "cult controversies" than changes implemented by some new religions has been the marked decline in the influence of the American anti-cult movement (ACM). Two specific issues are crucial to this shift. First, the 1980s and 1990s saw the movement's main charge against new religions—brainwashing—fail repeatedly in court cases, giving the ACM little hope of attacking new religions through the legal means. Second, in 1996 the ACM lost its primary organization, the Cult Awareness Network, when it was sued by a Pentecostal who had been forcibly deprogrammed by individuals affiliated with the organization. Jason Scott, an adult member of the Life Tabernacle Church, was legally represented in court by a Church of Scientology attorney. CAN lost the case, was bankrupted by the judgment, and had its assets taken away. At one point, CAN's Web site was even maintained by a group it formerly attacked: Scientologists. The disappearance of CAN left the anti-cult movement without its primary media organ.[29]

THE GROWTH OF NEOPAGANISM
AND NEW AGE SPIRITUALITIES

Concurrent with the peak and subsequent waning of cult controversies in recent years, there has been growing participation in and public prominence of certain new religions and alternative spiritualities. In addition to Mormonism, which has been expanding since its inception, Neopagan and New Age groups, activities, and beliefs have seen increased interest and attention. Different in some significant ways, both Neopaganism and the activities placed under the New Age classification are loosely organized, theologically and ritually eclectic movements that offer a contrast to the communal, totalistic new religions of the 1970s and 1980s and that can be seen as representative of larger trends in contemporary American religion.[30]

Neopaganism is an occult religious movement composed of many loosely connected groups and individuals who look to nature-oriented, often polytheistic religions for inspiration. In breaking this definition down into three components, it must first be noted that Neopaganism is occult in that it concerns itself with matters that are hidden in some way from ordinary, everyday understanding. Neopagans may have secret groups, teachings, and rituals that are kept from the uninitiated. Some practitioners may also believe in occult powers that individuals can tap into through ritual practice and magical training. Second, Neopaganism is not a single, hierarchical organization. There are few churches of Neopaganism, let alone any elaborate national institutional structure. Instead, there are groups and solitary practitioners across the United States who may or may not communicate with other practitioners through the Internet or at local, regional, or national festivals. Third, most Neopagans look to non-Christian, nature-oriented religions for inspiration. Many Neopagans celebrate natural events like moon stages, equinoxes, solstices, and other seasonal events. Many also see the earth and nature as a feminine divine, the Goddess. Some Neopagans also look to ancient Greek, Egyptian, Celtic, Norse, Native American, African, Asian, and other traditions for inspiration.

Although adherent numbers are hard to come by for a new religion that eschews institutions, the 2001 American Religious Identification Survey (ARIS) conducted by Kosmin, Mayer, and Keysar suggests that Neopaganism may be one of the fastest-growing new religions—most likely the fastest—in the United States today. Based on what individuals referred to themselves as, the ARIS reported that Wicca, the largest category of Neopaganism, grew from an estimated 8,000 to 134,000 from 1990 to 2001.[31] Whether this is because of new participants or because individuals are more comfortable identifying themselves as Wiccan, this entails an over 1,500 percent increase.[32] Adding Wicca together with two other categories listed in the ARIS survey ("Druid" 33,000 and "Pagan" 140,000), one can estimate a minimum of 307,000 Neopagans in the United States in 2001, with some in branches of the movement possibly uncounted among the estimated 386,000 in groups listed as "unclassfied."[33] This makes Neopaganism second only to the Latter-day Saints as the largest new religious movement in America at the beginning of the twenty-first century.

But who are the people who make up the growing community of Neo-pagans? Demographically, Neopagans tend to be white, college-educated, middle- and working-class baby boomers, born between 1946 and 1962, and Generation Xers, born between 1962 and 1981. Between 1993 and 1995, sociologist Helen Berger and her colleagues conducted a "Neo-pagan census" of 2,089 individuals. They found that 90.8 percent were white, 64.8 percent female, and 59.8 percent were born between 1946–1965.[34] Also, 75.7 percent had a college degree, had studied at a professional or technical school, held post-graduate degrees, or worked in jobs requiring such training. Regionally, Berger and her colleagues found that the Pacific coast, South Atlantic coast, and Great Lakes region of the Midwest accounted for 54.1 percent of the respondents. Economically, Neopagans were in the middle and working classes, with annual median incomes of $30,000 to $40,000. While this approximated the national median income, Neopagan women on average earned less and Neopagan men more. In addition, 50.9 percent of the respondents listed themselves as "solitary practitioners," meaning they did not regularly engage in Neopagan rituals with others, but rather worshipped by themselves.[35]

Historically, Neopaganism grew in the United States during the 1960s and early 1970s. Unlike many new religions, it is hard to single out one individual as founder. In terms of Wicca, many scholars point to the influence of retired British civil servant Gerald Gardner and later his American student Raymond Buckland. But other individuals, for example Tim Zell who founded the Church of All Worlds in 1961 and Z. Budapest who started the women-only Susan B. Anthony Wiccan coven in 1971, are also important figures in the early years of American Neopaganism.[36] In the 1970s, American Neopaganism developed into a variety of groups and interests. Neopagan Reconstructionist groups that looked to revive certain aspects of ancient Greek, Norse, Celtic, and Egyptian religions appeared. Wicca branched into several varieties, ranging from the highly structured Gardnerians to feminist Dianic covens. Eclectic witches, who combined different traditions together to create new ritual syntheses, would eventually become the largest branch.

The period since the 1980s has seen a major expansion of this new religious movement throughout the United States. Regional and national pan-Pagan festivals, such as ELFest in Indiana, began to dot the land. These events offered practitioners and the curious opportunities to meet and network with others who shared their interests. Neopagan organizations also cropped up, including the Pagan Federation International as well as the SpiralScouts International, a Neopagan version of the Boys and Girls Scouts. An especially interesting and growing organizational affiliation is CUUPS, the Covenant of Unitarian Universalist Pagans. Essentially a new denomination within an established denomination, this Neopagan movement has chapters in more than thirty-five states.

In addition to festivals and organizations, there has been a flourishing of print and Internet Neopagan publications. Originally confined to independent publishers such as Llwellyn Press and small alternative book and magic shops, Neopagan literature, especially Wiccan, now appears on most chain bookstore shelves and large publishing house lists. For many Neopagans, their initial entrance into the nonproselytizing movement was through reading. Practitioner and journalist Margot Adler suggests that Starhawk's *The Spiral Dance*, which sold 50,000 copies from 1979–1985, led to the creation of as many as 1,000 covens.[37] Other works have also proved influential. One of them, Scott Cunningham's *Wicca: A Guide for the Solitary Practitioner*, has consistently remained in the Amazon.com top 1,000 selling books for several years. The Internet has been even more fertile than print media for Neopaganism. Neopagans were among the first religious groups to use the Internet for discussion, networking, and online rituals.[38] Web sites such as *The Witches Voice* (http://www.witchvox.com/) offer information and contacts for practitioners in ways that magazines like *Green Egg* did for Neopagans in previous decades.

Neopagan practices and beliefs vary greatly depending on the specific groups and individuals involved. Most generally, Neopagans place primacy on ritual practices and experience over doctrine. They tend to see the magic they perform in circle casting and other ritual work as efficacious, though whether it works because it taps into real occult powers or because it acts only on a psychological, therapeutic level depends upon each individual practitioner's beliefs. Though nondogmatic in eschewing formal creeds, most Neopagans hold to a code of ethics that suggests you may "do what you want, but harm none," and that any good or ill one performs in the world will return to them three-fold. Many Neopagans—75.2 percent in the Neopagan Census—believe in reincarnation.[39] Among Neopagans, the body, materiality, and the natural world are seen as good. The importance of nature and its identification with the feminine divine in many groups, particularly Wiccan, leads many practitioners to have interests in ecology and stewardship of resources.

Although one can note these broad generalities about Neopagans, a key feature of the movement is its eclecticism. In the same ritual, Neopagans may use the names of Buddhist deities and Celtic goddesses, utilize Egyptian imagery, and engage in Yoruban possession trance drumming. The next ritual event may discard all of these things and instead feature a Lakota sweat lodge ceremony. Practitioners pick and mix, creating a bricolage of rituals, deities, beliefs, and religious material culture. In a personalization, or "subjectivization," of religious faith, Neopagans seek out religious materials, trying and keeping elements that work for them, often ending up with new spiritual combinations.

Another eclectic movement that has come to prominence since the late 1970s is the collection of practices, beliefs, and groups that have become categorized as "New Age." Problems ensue when discussing the New Age movement. Religion scholar Steven Sutcliffe has suggested that the term itself is misleading, as neither "new" nor "movement" really seems to fit much of what is termed "New Age." Sutcliffe argues that New Age is "best understood as a very diffuse milieu of popular practices and beliefs with unstable boundaries, goals, and personnel," suggesting that it is not so much a movement as "a diffuse collectivity: a cluster of seekers affiliated by choice—if at all—to a particular term in a wider culture of alternative spiritual practice."[40] In addition, things dubbed "New Age" are not always new, as they can be seen in nineteenth-century occult movements such as Spiritualism and Theosophy. While the number of people who self-identify their religion as New Age has always been small (28,000 in 1991 and 68,000 in 2001), many of its elements are important to a much larger number of Americans.[41] New Age philosophies and activities can be seen today in alternative medicine, modern psychology, education, business, and even other American religious groups.

Historically, the New Age came out of the same 1960s and 1970s milieu as Neopaganism. The youth counterculture, the growth of Asian religions, and the emergence of transpersonal and humanistic psychologies—in addition to long-standing traditions of occult spirituality in American life—all influenced the New Age movement. The 1980s saw the growth and expansion of New Age activities, publications, and groups. Media reports of the decade focused on some of the more colorful aspects of the New Age, such as crystal healing, past life regression, and channeling. Books such as Shirley MacLaine's 1983 bestseller, *Out on a Limb*, introduced New Age beliefs to the broader public.

The term "New Age" refers to the belief that a new period in human consciousness and development lies on the horizon. In her 1980 book, *The Aquarian Conspiracy*, Marilyn Ferguson predicted a worldwide "knowledge revolution" that would lead to more democratization, holistic learning and medicine, ethical and nonmaterialistic business practices, and human partnership with nature.[42] Called by some the "New Age Bible," Ferguson's book reveals an optimistic view of humankind's ascending an evolutionary ladder that will take it to progressively higher stages of consciousness and development.

Although New Age practices and beliefs, like Neopagan ones, are eclectic and vary greatly, most are focused on personal transformation and healing. One example of a New Age practice is channeling. Channeling is the process of communicating with a nonphysical entity for the purpose of attaining wisdom and knowledge. While channels themselves benefit from the entity's wisdom, they usually act as mediating consultants who impart counseling and knowledge to paying clients. Contemporary New Age channels resemble nineteenth-century Spiritualist mediums with one important difference: Whereas mediums were usually called upon to contact deceased human beings, channels enter into trances and take on the personas of divine and wise beings. The teachings given by channels in possession trances usually contain similar themes: Humans are good, they create their own realities, and they have the divine within them.[43]

Channeling became visible in the 1980s with the appearance of J.Z. Knight, who continues to channel the enlightened being "Ramtha" and has approximately 3,000 client devotees who pay for her services. The interested can participate in seminars and sessions at the Washington-state–based "Ramtha's School of Enlightenment."[44] According to the center's Web site, the "four cornerstones" of Ramtha's teachings are "(1) the statement 'you are God'; (2) the directive to make the unknown known; (3) the concept that consciousness and energy create the nature of reality; and (4) the challenge to conquer yourself."[45] Recently Ramtha and his ideas, channeled by Knight, were the main impetus behind the 2004 Lord of the Wind Films release, *What the Bleep Do We Know?*, starring actress Marlee Matson.

Probably the most well-known channeled teaching to appear in print is *A Course in Miracles*, published in 1976. Channeled by Helen Shucman starting in the 1960s, the divine being who authored the 1,200-page work is the Christian figure Jesus. An estimated 1.5 million copies of the work have been sold, along with a plethora of study guides and supplementary materials.[46] Throughout the 1980s and 1990s, *A Course in Miracles* study groups appeared in living rooms throughout the United States. Interest in the book increased in the mid-1990s when Detroit Unity minister Marianne Williamson appeared on the *Oprah Winfrey Show* for a well-received discussion of the work and her best-selling guide to it, *A Return to Love: Reflections on the Principles of a Course in Miracles* (1993).

Channeling is just one example of a New Age practice that focuses on personal transformation and healing. This concern can also be seen in the work of writers and speakers such as Deepak Chopra. A prolific, best-selling author, Chopra represents the alternative medicine aspect of New Age activities. Chopra is a specialist in internal medicine who became unsatisfied with what he saw as the failures of "Western" medical philosophy. In 1991 he founded the American Association of Ayurvedic Medicine and, in 1995, the Chopra Center for Well-Being. Through his organizations, books, and PBS television specials, Chopra promotes practices such as meditation, yoga, positive thinking, aromatherapy, herbal medicine, and other alternative healing practices.[47]

Even this cursory glance at a few of the items associated with the New Age reveals a diverse and highly variant mix of practices, beliefs, and groups that individuals utilize in their searches for transformative and healing experiences. Religion scholar Sarah Pike correctly suggests that, in addition to spiritual eclecticism, both "New Age and Neopagan beliefs and practices signify a trend in American religion at the end of the twentieth and the beginning of the twenty-first centuries that resists institutionalization and gives value to personal experience."[48]

NEW RELIGIONS AND THE AMERICAN SPIRITUAL MARKETPLACE: ISSUES AND TRENDS

The gradual shift from totalistic, communal new religions to those such as Neopaganism and the New Age, which are more eclectic, loosely bounded, and individually focused, must be put into the context of the tremendous changes taking place in American religion in recent decades. Since 1965, expanding diversity, the decline of denominationalism, increased religious switching, the rise of nonaffiliation, the explosive growth in conservative religions, the stark decline of the theologically moderate mainline, the blurred lines between religion and popular culture, and the increasingly improvisatory and combinative styles of religious practice are just some of the most visible changes.[49] Sociologist of religion Wade Clark Roof has dubbed the contemporary American scene a "spiritual marketplace" in which many individuals seek, pick, and combine beliefs and practices in ways that fit their needs.[50] New religions scholar Lorne Dawson likewise suggests that "religion is increasingly becoming a 'cultural resource' more than a social institution," a comment supported by the growing propensity of many Americans to refer to themselves as "spiritual but not religious."[51] He suggests that there are six features to what he calls "an emerging new religious consciousness." These include an increasing focus on the individual, more attention and authority given to personal religious experience, a pragmatic attitude concerning religious authority and practices, a syncretistic and tolerant approach to other religious perspectives, an increasingly holistic worldview, and a preference for loose and open organizational structures.[52]

While Roof's spiritual marketplace metaphor and Dawson's six features fit Neopaganism and the New Age well, they are not exclusive to either. Indeed, many of the features present in these movements may best be viewed as more pronounced versions of trends occurring in American religion as a whole. Generally, openness to seeking, combining a variety of religious resources, and simultaneously distrusting religious institutions and having confidence in subjective experience are trends that sociologists Roof, Robert Wuthnow, Philip Hammond, and others have found across the religious spectrum.[53] Even specific beliefs popular among Neopagans and New Agers—reincarnation, for example—find support in the larger culture. A 2003 Harris Poll showed that 27 percent of all Americans believed in reincarnation, including 40 percent of all 25–29 year-olds.[54] Scholars argue that religion has increasingly become a resource for "projects of the self," a tool with which individuals actively seek out and experiment with identities and communities.[55] In addition, recent studies suggest that these activities and trends will continue beyond the generations of baby boomers and Generation Xers that they started with.[56]

In suggesting that new religious movements such as Neopaganism are part of larger shifts in American religion and culture that will continue into the near future, one must be careful to not assume the disappearance of strict communal new religions. Concomitant with the expansion of less institutional, individually focused spirituality has been the growth of theologically conservative, tightly bounded, high-demand groups. Pentecostalism and other evangelical varieties of Protestantism, Hasidic Judaism, and a conservative movement within the Roman Catholic Church are all examples of this. To use sociologist Joseph Tamney's term, the "resilience" of conservative religions within the spiritual marketplace suggests that the era of totalistic new religions, if currently muted, is far from over.[57]

Finally, the intensification of religious activity between and beyond group boundaries provides a challenge for scholars who study new, alternative, and other religions today. The current religious milieu highlights the importance of studying "lived religion," examining what people actually do and believe in their everyday religious lives—versus what the creeds and codes of groups they may identify with say they should. Through the careful study of religion as practiced we may begin to unravel the increasingly complex, eclectic, and subjective trends of contemporary American faith.

NOTES

1. For a discussion of Mormonism as a new religious movement, see Jan Shipps, *Mormonism: The Story of a New Religious Tradition* (Urbana: University of Illinois Press, 1985).

2. For Yinger, "cult" was one of six classification types. See J. Milton Yinger, *Religion, Society, and the Individual* (New York: MacMillan, 1957). For a discussion of some problems with the term "cult," see Robert Ellwood and Harry Partin, *Religious and Spiritual Groups in Modern America*, 2nd ed. (Englewood Cliffs, NJ: Prentice-Hall, 1988), 18–29; and James T. Richardson, "Definitions of Cult: From Sociological-Technical to Popular-Negative," *Review of Religious Research* (June 1993): 348–56.

3. See Russell Spittler, *Cults and Isms: Twenty Alternatives to Evangelical Christianity* (Grand Rapids, MI: Baker Book House, 1962), 12. For an evangelical anti-cult bestseller, see Walter Martin, *Kingdom of the Cults* (Grand Rapids: Zondervan, 1965).

4. See Sean McCloud, *Making the American Religious Fringe: Exotics, Subversives, and Journalists, 1955–1993* (Chapel Hill: University of North Carolina Press, 2004).

5. The term "new religious movement," though not negative like "cult," is still an imprecise one that is given different meanings by different scholars. J. Gordon Melton, for example, has noted that "new religions are thus primarily defined not by any characteristic(s) that they share, but by the relationship to the other forms of religious life represented by the dominant churches, the ethnic religions, and the sects." See J. Gordon Melton, "An Introduction to New Religions," in *Oxford Handbook of New Religious Movements*, ed. James R. Lewis (New York: Oxford University Press, 2004), 27.

For an example of a scholar who prefers to use "alternative religion," see Timothy Miller, ed., *America's Alternative Religions* (Albany: State University of New York Press, 1995), 1–10. My strategy in defining "new religious movement" is to focus on the "new" aspect of the movement. While I think this is clearer and less problematic than deciding what is "alternative" to the wide variety of beliefs and practices found in so-called "dominant" religions, it is still ambiguous with regards to (1) just how old a religious movement can be and still be new, and (2) just how dramatically different the movement's beliefs, practices, and texts must be from existing religions to be considered new.

6. See Jon Butler, *Awash in a Sea of Faith: Christianizing the American People* (Cambridge, MA: Harvard University Press, 1990), 225–56.

7. Harmonial religion is a term used by Sydney Ahlstrom, *A Religious History of the American People* (New Haven, CT: Yale University Press, 1972), 1019–36. New Thought refers to a movement that developed out of Christian Science. See Edward Queen II, Stephen Prothero, and Gardiner Shattuck, Jr., eds., *The Encyclopedia of American Religious History* (New York: Facts on File, 1996), 470–71.

8. For a more complete definition and discussion of occult, see Robert Galbreath, "Explaining Modern Occultism," in *The Occult in America*, ed. Howard Kerr and Charles Crow (Urbana: University of Illinois Press, 1983), 11–37.

9. For an historical overview of religion in the period, see Martin E. Marty, *Modern American Religion*, vol. 2: *The Noise of Conflict, 1919–1941* (Chicago: University of Chicago Press, 1991).

10. See www.religioustolerance.org/chr_poll3.htm for a summary chart of polls. For the 1950s religious revival, see James Hudnut-Beumler, *Looking for God in the Suburbs* (New Brunswick, NJ: Rutgers University Press, 1994), 33–38.

11. See David Van Zandt, "The Children of God," in Miller, ed., 127–32.

12. For a fuller description of occult coverage in the period, see McCloud, 103–16.

13. For a history of the anti-cult movement, see Anson Shupe and David Bromley, "The Modern North American Anti-Cult Movement, 1971–1991: A Twenty-Year Retrospective," in *Anti-Cult Movements in Cross-Cultural Perspective,* ed. Anson Shupe and David Bromley (New York: Garland Press, 1994), 3–31.

14. For the term "cult menace," see James Beckford, "The Mass Media and New Religious Movements," in *New Religious Movements: Challenge and Response,* ed. Bryan Wilson and Jamie Cresswell (New York: Routledge, 1999), 103–19. For the *U.S. News* quote, see "The Bizarre Tragedy in Guyana," *U.S. News and World Report* (December 4, 1978), 25.

15. See www.religionwriters.com/public/tips/101104/101104a.shtml.

16. For Divine Light Mission estimates, see www.adherents.com/Na/Na_257. html#1345. For the LDS numbers, see www.adherents.com/rel_USA.html# bodies.

17. An excellent online resource on new religions is the Religious Movements Homepage Project at the University of Virginia. It can be accessed at http:// religiousmovements.lib.virginia.edu/. For discussion of Moon's declaration to be the Messiah, see http://religiousmovements.lib.virginia.edu/nrms/unification2.html.

18. See David Bromley and Larry Shinn, eds., *Krishna Consciousness in the West* (Lewisburg, PA: Bucknell University Press, 1989).

19. For an overview of the period, see "Making the Cult Menace: Brainwashing, Deprogramming, Mass Suicide, and Other Heresies, 1973–1979," in McCloud, 127–59.

20. The narrative appearing here comes from several excellent works on Peoples Temple, namely John Hall, *Gone From the Promised Land: Jonestown in American Cultural History* (New Brunswick, NJ: Transaction, 1987); David Chidester, *Salvation and Suicide: An Interpretation of Jim Jones, the Peoples Temple, and Jonestown* (Bloomington: Indiana University Press, 1988); and Mary McCormick Maaga, *Hearing the Voices of Jonestown: Putting a Human Face on an American Tragedy* (Syracuse: Syracuse University Press, 1998).

21. See Catherine Wessinger, "Foreword," in Maaga, xii.

22. For a volume that discusses these and other "cult controversies," see James Lewis and Jesper Aagaard Peterson, eds., *Controversial New Religions* (New York: Oxford University Press, 2005). For an overview of satanic cult rumors and scares of the late 1980s, see Jeffery Victor, *Satanic Panic: The Creation of a Contemporary Legend* (Chicago: Open Court, 1993).

23. For a study of the Branch Davidians and the Waco incident, see Stuart Wright, ed., *Armageddon in Waco: Critical Perspectives on the Branch Davidian Conflict* (Chicago: University of Chicago Press, 1995).

24. See, for example, "The Book of Koresh," *Newsweek* (October 11, 1993): 27.

25. For one discussion of Heaven's Gate, see Hugh Urban, "The Devil at Heaven's Gate: Rethinking the Study of Religion in the Age of Cyber-Space," *Nova Religio* 3 (2000): 268–302.

26. See Laurence Foster, "Cults in Conflict: New Religious Movements and the Mainstream Religious Tradition in America," in *Uncivil Religion: Interreligious Hostility in America,* ed. Robert Bellah and Frederick Greenspahn (New York: Crossroad, 1987), 185–204.

27. See E. Burke Rochford, Jr., "Family Development and Change in the Hare Krishna Movement," in Lewis and Peterson, eds., 101–17.

28. See John Gorenfeld, "Hail to the Moon King," *Salon.com News* (June 21, 2004).

29. See Anson Shupe, David Bromley, and Susan Darnell, "The North American Anti-Cult Movement: Vicissitudes of Success and Failure," in Lewis, ed., 184–205.

30. For a comparative study of the Neopagan and New Age Movements, see Sarah Pike, *New Age and Neopagan Religions in America* (New York: Columbia University Press, 2004).

31. See Barry Kosmin, Egon Mayer, and Ariela Keysar, *American Religion Identification Survey 2001* (New York: Graduate Center of the City University of New York, 2001), 13.

32. For the percentage, see Cathy Lynn Grossman and Anthony DeBarros, "A Measure of Faith," *USA Today* (December 24, 2001), 4D.

33. See Kosmin, Mayer, and Keysar, 13.

34. See Helen Berger, Evan Leach, and Leigh Shaffer, *Voices from the Pagan Census: A National Survey of Witches and Neopagans in the United States* (Columbia: University of South Carolina Press, 2003), 30, 27.

35. Ibid., 30–32, 12.

36. For a history and overview of Wicca, see Aidan Kelly, "An Update on Neopagan Witchcraft in America," in *Perspectives on the New Age*, ed. James Lewis and J. Gordon Melton (Albany: State University of New York Press, 1992), 136–51. For an older, broader examination of American Neopaganism, see Margot Adler, *Drawing Down the Moon: Witches, Druids, Goddess-Worshippers, and Other Pagans in America Today*, rev. ed. (Boston: Beacon Press, 1986).

37. See Adler, 418–19, 227–28.

38. For one story about Neopagans and the Internet, see Yonat Shimron, "Computerized Faith: Techno-Pagans thrive in the Triangle, worshipping at the altar of the keyboard." *The Raleigh News and Observer*, September 6, 1996, 1E, 4E.

39. See Berger, Leach, and Shaffer, 47.

40. See Steven Sutcliffe, "The Dynamics of Alternative Spirituality: Seekers, Networks, and 'New Age,'" in Lewis, ed., 467. Also see Steven Sutcliffe, *Children of the New Age: A History of Spiritual Practices* (New York: Routledge, 2003).

41. For the 1991 number, see Richard Kyle, *The New Age Movement in American Culture* (Lanham, MD: University Press of America, 1995), 5. For the 2001 number, see Kosmin, Mayer, and Keysar, 13.

42. See Marilyn Ferguson, *The Aquarian Conspiracy: Personal Transformation in the 1980s* (New York: St. Martin's Press, 1980).

43. For a study of New Age channeling, see Michael Brown, *The Channeling Zone: American Spirituality in an Anxious Age* (Cambridge, MA: Harvard University Press, 1997).

44. See "Ramtha's School of Enlightenment: The American Gnostic School" on the University of Virginia Religious Movements Web page, http://religiousmovements. lib.virginia.edu/nrms/Ramtha.html.

45. See http://ramtha.com/html/aboutus/aboutus.stm.

46. For discussions of *A Course in Miracles*, see Arnold Weiss, "A New Religious Movement and Spiritual Healing Psychology Based on *A Course in Miracles*," in *Religion and the Social Order*, ed. Arthur Greil and Thomas Robbins (Greenwich, CT: JAI Press, 1994), 197–215. Also see http://religiousmovements. lib.virginia.edu/nrms/course.html.

47. See http://religiousmovements.lib.virginia.edu/nrms/Chopra.html.

48. See Pike, 26, 171.

49. A number of studies note these changes. See Wade Clark Roof, *A Generation of Seekers: The Spiritual Journeys of the Baby Boom Generation* (San Francisco: HarperSanFrancisco, 1993); Wade Clark Roof and William McKinney, *American Mainline Religion: Its Changing Shape and Future* (New Brunswick, NJ: Rutgers University Press, 1987); Linda Woodhead and Paul Heelas, eds., *Religion in Modern Times: An Interpretive Anthology* (Malden, MA: Blackwell Publishers, 2000); Robert Wuthnow, *The Restructuring of American Religion: Society and Faith Since World War II* (Princeton, NJ: Princeton University Press, 1988); and Robert Wuthnow, *After Heaven: Spirituality in America Since the 1950s* (Berkeley: University of California Press, 1998). For an article that charts denominational shifts and mainline decline, see Richard Ostling, "The Church Search," *Time* (April 5, 1993): 44. See also Kosmin, Mayer, and Keysar, 12–13. For a recent study on similar, yet perhaps more dramatic, trends in the United Kingdom, see Paul Heelas and Linda Woodhead, *The Spiritual Revolution: Why Religion is Giving Way to Spirituality* (Malden, MA: Blackwell Publishers, 2005).

50. See Wade Clark Roof, *Spiritual Marketplace: Baby Boomers and the Remaking of American Religion* (Princeton, NJ: Princeton University Press, 1999).

51. See Lorne Dawson, "The Socio-Cultural Significance of Modern New Religious Movements," in Lewis, ed., 92.

52. See Lorne Dawson, "The Cultural Significance of New Religious Movements: The Case of Soka Gakkai," *Sociology of Religion* 62:3 (2001): 355–56.

53. See Roof, *Spiritual Marketplace*; Wuthnow, *After Heaven*; and Philip Hammond, *Religion and Personal Autonomy: The Third Disestablishment in America* (Columbia: University of South Carolina Press, 1992).

54. Harris Poll, "The Religious and Other Beliefs of Americans 2003," *Harris Interactive* (February 26, 2003), http://www.harrisinteractive.com/harris_poll/index.asp?PID=359.

55. The "project of the self" concept comes from Anthony Giddens, especially *Modernity and Self-Identity: Self and Society in the Late Modern Age* (Stanford, CA: Stanford University Press, 1991). Some scholars have suggested that his theories concerning late modernity and projects of the self may be useful in interpreting the trends in contemporary religion. See Lorne Dawson, "The Socio-Cultural Significance of New Religious Movements," in Lewis, ed., 68–98; and Sean McCloud, "Popular Culture Fandoms, the Boundaries of Religious Studies, and the Project of the Self," *Culture and Religion: An Interdisciplinary Journal* 4:2 (2003): 187–206.

56. See Lynn Schofield Clark, *From Angels to Aliens: Teenagers, the Media, and the Supernatural* (New York: Oxford University Press, 2003); and Christian Smith and Melinda Lundquist Denton, *Soul Searching: The Religious and Spiritual Lives of American Teenagers* (New York: Oxford University Press, 2005).

57. See Joseph Tamney, *The Resilience of Conservative Religion: The Case of Popular, Conservative Protestant Congregations* (New York: Cambridge University Press, 2002).

SUGGESTIONS FOR FURTHER READING

Chidester, David. *Salvation and Suicide: An Interpretation of Jim Jones, the Peoples Temple, and Jonestown*. Bloomington: Indiana University Press, 1988.

Dawson, Lorne L., ed. *Cults and New Religious Movements: A Reader*. Malden, MA: Blackwell, 2003.

Jenkins, Philip. *Mystics and Messiahs: Cults and New Religions in American History*. New York: Oxford University Press, 2000.

Lewis, James R., ed. *Oxford Handbook of New Religious Movements*. New York: Oxford University Press, 2004.

McCloud, Sean. *Making the American Religious Fringe: Exotics, Subversives, and Journalists, 1955–1993*. Chapel Hill: University of North Carolina Press, 2004.

Miller, Timothy, ed. *America's Alternative Religions*. Albany: State University of New York Press, 1995.

Pike, Sarah. *New Age and Neopagan Religions in America*. New York: Columbia University Press, 2004.

Roof, Wade Clark. *Spiritual Marketplace: Baby Boomers and the Remaking of American Religion*. Princeton, NJ: Princeton University Press, 1999.

Index

About the Editor
and Contributors

CHARLES H. LIPPY has been the LeRoy A. Martin Distinguished Professor of Religious Studies at the University of Tennessee since 1994. His interests in American religious life range widely. Among his more recent publications are *Do Real Men Pray? Images of the Christian Man and Male Spirituality in White Protestant America* (2005) and a new edition of the *Encyclopedia of Religion in the South* (2005), co-edited with Samuel. S. Hill.

TORIN D. ALEXANDER, a native of Murfreesboro, TN, holds undergraduate and graduate degrees in physics from Vanderbilt University and the University of California at Berkeley. After receiving an M.Div. from Union Theological Seminary in New York, he moved to Rice University, where he is a doctoral candidate in philosophical theology and African American religion. He is married to Charvonne Boykin Alexander.

STEPHEN C. FINLEY is a Ph.D. candidate in the department of religious studies at Rice University, where he studies African American religion and Islam. He is particularly interested in black religion and the body and also in ways in which religious aesthetics, psychoanalysis, and ritual studies relate to issues of identity, gender, and sexuality.

CHESTER GILLIS is professor and chair of the department of theology at Georgetown University in Washington, DC. He is the author of *Roman Catholicism in America* (1999) and *Catholic Faith in America* (2002) and editor of *The Political Papacy* (2006).

C. KIRK HADAWAY is a sociologist who serves as director of research for the Episcopal Church. He has published eight books, including *Behold*

I Do a New Thing, Rerouting the Protestant Mainstream, and *Church and Denominational Growth.* He is currently president-elect of the Religious Research Association.

SARAH IMHOFF is a Ph.D. candidate in the history of Judaism at the University of Chicago Divinity School. Her research focus is twentieth-century American religious history and culture.

KHYATI Y. JOSHI is an assistant professor in the Sammartino School of Education at Fairleigh Dickinson University. She is the author of *New Roots in America's Sacred Ground: Religion, Race, and Ethnicity* (2006).

PAUL LAKELAND is the Aloysius P. Kelley, S.J. Professor of Catholic Studies at Fairfield University. A specialist in Catholic ecclesiology and postmodern theory, he is author of *Postmodernity: Christian Identity in a Fragmented Age* (1997) and *Liberation of the Laity: In Search of an Accountable Church* (2003), which won the Catholic Press Association's 2004 award for the best book in theology.

PENNY LONG MARLER is a professor of religion at Samford University, Birmingham, AL. She is co-author of *Being There: Culture and Formation in Two Theological Schools* and *Young Catholics at the New Millennium.* She also currently serves as director of the Center for Pastoral Excellence at Samford.

SEAN McCLOUD is assistant professor of religion and modern culture at the University of North Carolina at Charlotte. He is author of *Making the American Religious Fringe: Exotics, Subversives, and Journalists, 1955–1993* (2004).

DAVID G. ROEBUCK received his Ph.D. from Vanderbilt University. He is director of the Dixon Pentecostal Research Center and Archive in Cleveland, TN. Assistant professor of religion at Lee University, he also serves as the executive secretary of the Society for Pentecostal Studies and historian for the Church of God and, since 1996, is a member of the Church of God Historical Commission. He regularly contributes to books and periodicals about the Pentecostal movement.

ROBERTO LINT SAGARENA received his Ph.D. from Princeton University and is assistant professor of religion, American studies, and ethnicity at the University of Southern California. Currently completing a history of the role of religion in the creation of the American Southwest, he has particular interest in Chicano and Latina/o religious history and the history of religion in colonial and post-colonial societies in Mexico and the United States.

SCOTT L. THUMMA received his Ph.D. from Emory University. He is a sociologist of religion at Hartford Institute for Religious Research,

Hartford Seminary. He has studied megachurches since 1988, conducting the first national academic study of megachurches in 1999 and repeating and updating the study in 2005 in conjunction with the Leadership Network.

RANDI JONES WALKER is associate professor of church history at the Pacific School of Religion and serves on the core doctoral faculty of the Graduate Theological Union in Berkeley. She is author of *Protestantism in the Sangre de Cristos, 1850–1920* (1991). *Emma Newman: A Frontier Minister* (2001), and *The Evolution of a U.C.C. Style: Essays in the History, Ecclesiology, and Culture of the United Church of Christ* (2005). Her current research focuses on religion, race, and public policy in the North American West.

ETHAN YORGASON, a cultural/historical geographer, uses Mormonism as his major case study to explore the interconnections among place, region, and identity. He teaches in the department of history and the department of international cultural studies at Brigham Young University–Hawaii and is the author of *Transformation of the Mormon Culture Region*.

About the Advisory Board

PHILIP GOFF is director of the Center for the Study of Religion and American Culture and associate professor of religious studies and American studies at Indiana University-Purdue University Indianapolis, as well as co-editor of *Religion and American Culture: A Journal of Interpretation*. His recent books include *Themes in American Religion and Culture* and the *Columbia Documentary History of Religion in American Since 1945*, edited with Paul Harvey.

R. MARIE GRIFFITH is associate professor of religion at Princeton University. She is author of *God's Daughters: Evangelical Women and the Power of Submission* and *Born Again Bodies: Flesh and Spirit in American Christianity*. She is currently writing a book on links between evangelicalism and sexuality and also co-editing a volume on *Women and Religion in the African Diaspora*.

PAULA KANE is an associate professor at the University of Pittsburgh where she holds the Marus Chair of Catholic Studies. She teaches courses on American religious history, popular religion, religion and film, immigration, and ethnicity. Her scholarly interests include sacred architecture, mystical phenomena, and gender issues in the study of religion. She is presently completing a history of the stigmata in modern Catholicism.

ANTHONY B. PINN is Agnes Cullen Arnold Professor of Humanities and professor of religious studies at Rice University. His research interests include African American religious thought, liberation theologies, religion and popular culture, the aesthetics of black religion, and African American humanism. He is author or editor of sixteen books related to these areas of research.